SUNSHINE AND THE MOON'S DELIGHT
J. M. SYNGE 1871—1909

Still south I went and west and south again,
Through Wicklow from the morning till the night,
And far from cities, and the sites of men,
Lived with the sunshine and the moon's delight.

I knew the stars, the flowers, and the birds,
The grey and wintry sides of many glens,
And did but half remember human words,
In converse with the mountains, moors, and fens.

J. M. Synge, "Prelude", *C.W.*, I, p. 32.

A posthumous portrait of J. M. Synge by Charles Merrill Mount. Reproduced by kind permission of John S. Synge (nephew of the playwright).

SUNSHINE AND THE MOON'S DELIGHT

A Centenary Tribute to
John Millington Synge
1871 — 1909

Edited by
S. B. BUSHRUI

with a foreword by
A. NORMAN JEFFARES

COLIN SMYTHE LIMITED
and
THE AMERICAN UNIVERSITY OF BEIRUT
1972

FOR

MARY BUSHRUI

whose gifts of understanding, compassion and
loyal cooperation can never be repaid
AND

JOHN F. C. SPRINGFORD

whose friendship has meant so much over
the years

REFERENCES AND ABBREVIATIONS

The following abbreviations are used for the more frequently cited works:

Autobiographies: W. B. Yeats, *Autobiographies,* London, Macmillan, 1956.

C.W., I: *J. M. Synge: Collected,Works,* I (Poems), edited by Robin Skelton, London, Oxford University Press, 1962.

C.W., II: *J. M. Synge: Collected Works,* II (Prose), edited by Alan Price, London, Oxford University Press, 1966.

C.W., III: *J. M. Synge: Collected Works,* III (Plays, Book I), edited by Ann Saddlemyer, London, Oxford University Press, 1968.

C.W., IV: *J. M. Synge: Collected Works,* IV (Plays, Book II), edited by Ann Saddlemyer, London, Oxford University Press, 1968.

Essays: W. B. Yeats, *Essays and Introductions,* London, Macmillan, 1961.

Explorations: W. B. Yeats, *Explorations,* selected by Mrs. W. B. Yeats, London, Macmillan, 1962.

Synge: D. H. Greene and E. M. Stephens, *J. M. Synge, 1871-1909,* New York, Macmillan, 1959.

CONTENTS

8 CONTENTS

*

*

*

FOREWORD

A. Norman Jeffares

THIS collection of essays shows the wide attention Synge continues to command. His work is read and performed in many countries throughout the world. The general reasons for his standing as a dramatist are obvious, and the essayists in this volume—who write from diverse viewpoints and from many places—from Canada, France, Germany, Great Britain, Ireland, Japan, Jordan, Syria and the United States—add to our particular understanding of why we respond to Synge's universality as a dramatist, and also show us how his prose and poetry buttress his dramatic art. They also indicate in detail the international interest taken in Synge by scholars and critics and offer us a guide to the ever-increasing information about and criticism of his work: his capacity to create tragedy, his awareness of what a mixture of impulses—exuberant, wayward, comic, ferocious, patient, grasping, despairing, melancholic, poetic—make up the complexity of human life.

Synge's own life was no exception to this complexity: more can still be discovered about it. The late Edward Stephens, his nephew and friend, wrote what is, in effect, a vast social record of the Synge family while collecting materials for a life of the author. In the unpublished typescript—running to many volumes, as yet unedited—there is not only a haunting account of Synge's often lonely youth and early manhood, but also a picture of his evangelical mother: rigorously religious, thoroughly well-meaning, energetic in her triviality, possessive in her sense of family, didactic and utterly uncomprehensive of her son's nature. Those of her letters which are included in the Stephens TS rattle on remorselessly, like the conversation of any typical well-bred lady in Victorian Dublin. She was deeply anxious about finance. The Land War, the tensions of which are so ably recorded in George Moore's *A Drama in Muslin*, threatened the Synge family income—as it had diminished John Butler Yeats's security. There had not been a large income (probably a little over £400 p.a.)—the Act of Union and the Famine and large families had driven many Irish landlords from big houses in the country into the cheaper living provided by the then elegant suburbs of Dublin—but Mrs. Synge would have regarded any suggestion of spending capital as a heresy too ghastly even for contemplation. Hers was the pressing problem of paying for her sons' education, her husband having died in 1872 of smallpox.

Hand in hand with her general financial anxiety marched her worry over matters spiritual. She wrote on J. M.'s seventeenth birthday in 1888:

> I can hardly fancy he is 17. I have been looking back to the time he was born. I was so dreadfully delicate and he poor child was the same. How much mercy has been shown to him in his wonderful restoration to health and Oh! that I could see him showing in his life that he has a due sense of all the mercy vouchsafed to him. I see no sign of spiritual life in my poor Johnnie, there may be some, but it is not visible to my eyes. He is very reserved and shut up on the subject and if I say anything to him he never answers me, so I don't in the least know the state of his mind—it is a trying state, very trying. I long so to be able to see behind that close reserve, but I can only wait and pray and hope.

John Millington Synge had developed a strong interest in natural science in his 'teens. At about the age of fourteen his reading of Darwin's *Origin of Species* began by chance with the words " The similar framework of bones in the hand of a man, wing of a bat, fin of the porpoise, and leg of the horse,—the same number of vertebrae forming the neck of the giraffe and of the elephant,—and innumerable other such facts, at once explain themselves on the theory of descent with slow and slight successive modifications." To John it seemed that the foundations of his mother's religious teaching had been destroyed by the meaning Darwin gave to familiar facts. More than ten years later he remembered the day he first read Darwin:

> I flung the book aside and rushed out into the open air—it was summer and we were in the country, the sky seemed to have lost its blue and the grass its green. I lay down and writhed in an agony of doubt. Till then I had never doubted and had never conceived that a sane and wise man or boy could doubt. I had of course heard of atheists but as vague monsters that I was unable to realise. My memory does not record how I returned home nor how long my misery lasted. I know only that I got the book out of the house as soon as possible and kept it out of my sight till its departure, saying to myself, logically enough, that I was not yet sufficiently advanced in science to weigh his arguments, so I would do better to reserve his work for future study. In a few weeks or days I had regained my composure but this was the beginning.

As E. M. Stephens wisely remarked in his TS it was not just a matter of the family conflict between revealed religion and secular science, but a conflict latent in the religious system his mother had taught Synge. The virtues of faith and an honest searching for truth had been implanted in him. His mother told him Protestantism was free from superstition, depended on "The Open Book" and the use of private judgment. She repeated frequently Matthew (VII: 7): "Seek and ye shall find, knock and it shall be opened unto you." But his research, his reading now opened facts apparently contrary to his faith.

the closely knit system his mother had taught him: the Creation, the Fall and the Redemption by the Atonement. It was virtually impossible for the boy to proclaim his doubts: unbelief would have been received with horror and contempt.

The system of evictions then in force in Ireland posed another problem for him. His mother defended the actions of landlords forcibly: anyone using land not his own without paying rent must incur the strong measures taken by those responsible for enforcing the law. To her query "What would become of us if our tenants in Galway stopped paying their rents?" he had no answer. Everyone around him seemed to agree with his mother. He could not believe they were right. His mother could not comprehend that there was little justice in the law which her son Edward, the land agent, was supporting by evictions. She approved of such actions, brutal as they often were, and thought John should do so too.

The doubts Darwin had begun were further developed by Synge's reading Butler's *Analogy*—rather as John Butler Yeats's faith had been disrupted by reading Butler when he was contemplating a career in the Church of Ireland. But the study of natural science palled. In 1888, when in his own words he "took to the violin and the study of literature with wild enthusiasm", he did, however, retain some of the habits of patience, the methodical processes he had learned from his interest in natural science, for these affected and indeed intensified his desire to be in beautiful surroundings.[1] He was preparing for the entrance examination to Trinity College, Dublin, and, having learned to ride on a penny farthing, advertised for a bicycle. A family friend and bicycle *afficianado*, Robert Miller, gave him a present of an "extraordinary." (This was a bicycle which had its saddle far back, and a front wheel driven by long cranks from the pedals as the rider's feet were not within reach of the front axle. This model was designed to avoid the danger of riding the penny-farthing, which threw its rider forward over the large front wheel if that hit a stone going downhill). Mrs. Synge, deeply worried by the possibility of the family income ceasing to arrive from the Galway tenants because of the Land War, was delighted at the present of the bicycle and wrote to its donor:

> The Lord knows what I need and he will supply me. He has done so hitherto in a wonderful way just according to my needs, as I get poorer my expenses get less and I have just enough to meet them. Sam [J.M.'s brother] is so good and eats up all stale odds and ends and is always satisfied. He keeps the weekly bills down. Johnnie is just the reverse. His delicacy has spoiled him. He is reading very hard now learning Greek, he finds it hard, he has no tutor or grinder [a Dublin name for private teachers who coached pupils], which is a great saving of £2 a month.

The bicycle provided a means of occasional escape into the Dublin or the Wicklow mountains; it carried him further afield into wilder scenery, even though Orwell Park, where the family lived, was then on the edge of farmland and the Dodder, which was nearby, still contained trout and ran through fields. When Synge entered Trinity College, he needed the escape even more. He had all the problems of an undergraduate living at home in intensified form. At first he read what interested him, then suddenly discovered in the first week of 1889 that he had his Junior Freshman examination in less than three weeks' time. His mother disapproved of what might seem normal student life:

> Johnnie was in for his junior freshman exam on last Friday and Saturday—he passed—he is much relieved, as he has been reading furiously for the last fortnight. He would not begin to read in time, so had a great rush to get through, sitting up late—until 4 one night and having a chronic headache the last week. He is determined not to be so foolish again; he has pains in his eyes after it. He has no more now till the Littlego, he has to keep some terms by lectures of course, he has not attended any yet and leads a very solitary life.

She found him increasingly baffling:

> Johnnie is gone in to college on his bicycle through all the rain without a coat or umbrella of course! He is a queer boy. He hates walking in and out of town to lectures, so he goes in his knickerbockers on his bicycle no matter what the weather is, snowing or raining and roads covered with water and mud, he gets well splashed. He does not enjoy the lectures at all and is longing for them to be over, that he may begin his lessons on the fiddle again. His money is all spent in advance. He does not know how to take care of his clothes and won't take advice, he has much to learn poor boy, he is very headstrong. His health is most wonderfully improved, thank God. Oh! that I could say his soul is in health. I hope you pray for him, the only one of all my dear children a stranger to God.

The effect of Mrs. Synge's religious instruction on her son was strong. As Edward Stephens commented perceptively in his TS, she had taught him that to refer to God in any but a strictly religious manner was a sinful taking in vain of the Holy Name, that to use oaths or expletives was a breach of St. James's injunctions (James, V:2), and that to exaggerate was to lie. The sombre restraints—and some of the subtle rhythms—of Synge's prose probably stem from some of this teaching[2]: the plays, however, were enriched by the counter-effect of Irish country speech, especially that of County Wicklow and (perhaps to a lesser degree) that of the Aran Islands.

During his undergraduate days Synge was often irritable. His mother complained to her son Robert in a letter:

> Johnnie's lectures are nearly over and I'm glad of it. I thought they

might shake him out a little, but they have not, he sits up every night studying till one o'clock, or past it, and then he is so sleepy in the mornings he does not get up till just 10 and has a great rush to get to his lectures at 11, and only swallows a mouthful of breakfast! I had to give him his tram fare [probably 2d.], today he was so late he did not go to sleep till 5 he says—he must injure himself I am sure, drinking strong tea and reading so late, and the late morning hours are dreadful. I have to give up trying to persuade him, he will take his own way, and I can only remonstrate sometimes.

Oh how I pray for him, the lost child, far from God. "All things are possible to him that believeth" are our Lord's words so I must trust and not be afraid.

It was increasingly impossible for him to talk to his mother or his brother Sam: they disapproved of the theatre: it seemed to her a profession which led souls to damnation. She could not fathom his view that there was a scope for spiritual life in drama: to her there was only one way, by the acceptance of salvation, to spiritual life. His interest in music deepened and this cut him off more, so that she longed and longed "for the day when he will no longer live to himself." During 1889 he gradually formed his views, until he no longer attended church, arguing with his rigidly minded brother and the local curate. Then came the further turning point, when he decided he would make a living by music. His mother urged his brother Edward to offer him a place in his office "and the prospect of living like a gentleman." One of Edward's friends had a talk with him "advising him very strongly not to think of making it [music] a profession—told him all the men who do so take to drink! And they are not a nice set of men either, but I don't think his advice has had the least effect on Johnnie . . .!"

Though it is possible to understand the reasons for his mother's anxieties it is Synge's own situation which commands our sympathy. The pressures for religious conformity and the equally strong ones for "getting on" were extremely difficult to resist. Yet the Biblical background he derived from his mother's teaching and his own knowledge of English drama mingled with his mother's acceptance of the dispensations of Providence and the fatalism he met with in the Wicklow people. This varied mixture of influences gave extra intensity to his reading of Greek tragedy (notably the *Medea*) in his early undergraduate years, when he paid special attention to the varying rhythm and dialect of Greek dramas. Of modern dramatists he, perhaps, has most nearly captured the same mixed attitudes of detachment and compassion, and the intense emotional relationship he had with the Irish countryside equipped him for abstract yet precise contemplation. He lacked above all else Yeats's great asset of a home where discussion ranged freely and where "getting on" was depreciated by a sympathetic artist father.

When Synge moved to Paris his mother's exacerbating care and possessive, insensitive affection followed him. In 1900 she wrote to his brother Sam that Johnnie's letters were getting shorter and shorter:

> He says nothing. I don't think he likes the advice I give him, to try and earn money by writing what will sell and not that high flown stuff that so few can appreciate.

She was consistent in her failure to understand; her attention had moved from concern about his spiritual welfare to his economic: "He is an extraordinary character and seems to have no ambition to support himself." And in 1902 when his book on Aran had been rejected for the second time she wrote—again resignedly—to Sam that Johnnie had told her of receiving a very sympathetic letter from the publisher

> telling him he read the book with peculiar interest, but there is such a very small part of the public who have an interest in Ireland it would not pay commercially, so he can't publish it. Poor Johnnie! We could all have told him that, but then men like Yeats and the rest get round him and make him think Irish literature and the Celtic language and all these things that they are trying to revive are very important, and, I am sorry to say, Johnnie seems to believe all they tell him.

When Synge first fell in love with Cherry Matheson she rejected him because he had no faith, no settled way of making his living. And she wrote "I remember his saying: 'I am a poor man, but I feel if I live I shall be rich; I feel there is that in me which will be of value to the world.'" He had deserved better of his family and that particular friend, but they were prisoners of their time into whose provincial souls no aesthetic sunlight had shone. The larger world has found the real value of Synge, and treasures it.

Leeds, 1971

NOTES

1. A less pleasant effect of his interest in natural history, particularly his experiments in rabbit breeding, was his feeling of being different because of his youthful ill health—he was a "delicate" child. He wrote in his Black Notebook (probably when he was about twenty-six) that his ill health had led to:

   "... a curious resolution which has explained in some measure all my subsequent evolution. Without knowing, or as far as I can remember hearing, anything about doctrines of heredity, I surmised that unhealthy parents should have unhealthy children—my rabbit breeding may have put the idea into my head—therefore I said I am unhealthy and if I marry I shall have unhealthy children. But I will never create beings to suffer as I am suffering

W. B. Yeats, J. M. Synge and G. W. Russell (AE) fishing on Coole Lake, drawn by H. Oakley. Reproduced by kind permission of Major R. G. Gregory.

Stencil portrait of J. M. Synge by Jack B. Yeats. Reproduced by gracious permission of H. M. the Queen, © *Miss Anne Yeats and Senator Michael B. Yeats.*

so I will never marry. I do not know how old I was when I came to this decision, but I was between thirteen and fourteen, and it caused me horrible misery."

His loneliness was accentuated by a feeling of being isolated by ill health. He sought to avoid intimacy in his misery: obviously his family had affection for him; equally obviously they seemed incapable of understanding him, and he did not make attempts to explain his ideas and his inmost adolescent fears.

2. Stephens remarks in the MS that Synge's resentment at her restrictiveness found expression when, on emerging from an anaesthetic, he shouted, "Damn the bloody Anglo-Saxon language that a man can't swear in without being vulgar."

ACKNOWLEDGMENTS

In the preparation of this volume I have received much valuable help from my students Miss Nadia Hijab, Miss Jihad Shawwaf, Miss Jean Bridgwood, Miss Susan Pratt, Miss Armine Choukassizian and Mr. Riad Nourallah.

I owe a special debt to Professor Neil Bratton, whose warm friendship and advice were indispensable and who helped me greatly in solving many editorial problems.

My gratitude also goes to Miss Hala Sa'id Cochrane for invaluable assistance in compiling the Bibliography, which would never have become what it is without her painstaking efforts, thoroughness and enthusiasm.

My thanks to Captain Hanna Hawa for his assistance.

Finally, I wish to record here my indebtedness to Professor Brigitta Alsleban and Mr. David Nash both of whom have helped me at every stage of the book's progress.

For permission to quote copyright passages grateful acknowledgment is made to the Oxford University Press for material from *The Collected Works of J. M. Synge*.

The extracts from the writings of W. B. Yeats are reproduced by kind permission of Messrs. A. P. Watt & Son on behalf of Michael B. Yeats.

S.B.B.

CENTENNIAL POEM
Marcus Smith

"Isn't it a small thing is foretold
about the ruin of ourselves, Naisi,
when all men have age coming and
great ruin in the end?"

from Synge's *Deirdre, C.W.,* **IV,** p. 211.

John Millington Synge, you've touched me twice before
this time. The standards, *Playboy, Riders,*
the first when I was seventeen, had knocked
my Irish father down, panicked, then talked
and strutted for friends' twopenny praise.

The second five years ago, two days
after getting a cable that my brother
was dead, drowned, leaving our mother
half a world away, torn, leaving me
racing the tide by a murderous sea.

Synge, you've mirrored me twice before.
Tonight, in a lovely land verging war,
I turn your fine Irish pages again,
and with expectant dread, bracketed pride,
knowing all words are just another place to hide,
pray for the enduring strength of Irishmen.

Beirut, October 1969-April 1970

SYNGE'S PLAY OF CHOICE:
THE SHADOW OF THE GLEN

Jean Alexander

EVEN before it first appeared in 1903, *The Shadow of the Glen* was the object of attack on moral grounds, and on the opening night of its performance on a programme with *The King's Threshold* and *Cathleen ni Houlihan*, there were hisses and boos from the audience in spite of the protection afforded by Yeats's plays. The issue was seen as a purely Irish one, calling into question some basic social pieties; Synge's play is still discussed largely in terms of Irish society, even though it presents to an audience some of the very sources of anxiety presented to European audiences by Ibsen's *A Doll's House*. The more inflammatory contemporary implications of the play, and the reaction of Synge's Dublin audience and the newspaper critics, are argumentatively sketched by J. B. Yeats in a letter to *The United Irishman* of 31 October, 1903: "The outcry against Mr. Synge's play seems to be largely dishonest, the real objection not being that it misrepresents Irish women, but that it is a very effective attack on loveless marriages . . ."[1] There is, perhaps, something peculiarly Irish in finding Synge's delineation of women to be an affront to women, but at that time anxiety about social orthodoxy in women was extremely widespread. The feeling was merely intensified by the self-conscious need to bring society under the press of a nationalist orthodoxy.

To some extent *The Shadow of the Glen* was rendered acceptable, at least to literary nationalists, by its source in the Gaelic culture of the west, and W. B. Yeats was the first and most powerful voice to speak for that relationship. In "J. M. Synge and the Ireland of His Time" (1910), Yeats says, "As I read *The Aran Islands* right through . . . I come to understand how much knowledge of the real life of Ireland went to the creation of a world which is yet as fantastic as the Spain of Cervantes. Here is the story of *The Playboy*, of *The Shadow of the Glen;* . . ."[2] From both a nationalist and an anthropological point of view, it was important that the play had sprung authentically from the Gaelic culture. Synge had in part dramatized a primitive story recounted by a folk storyteller, and by doing so had dignified the peasant in finding his imagination worthy of the national stage.

Both approaches continue to have importance in terms of the history of the time, whether literary or sociological, and both are potentially fruitful for a study of plot and theme in Synge's work as a whole. We

find that Synge's sources in folk tales and popular legend are charac-
teristically grosser and more violent than his dramatic versions (this
in spite of the emphasis that readers tend to give to the grotesque and
violent aspects of his drama) and that violence for Synge is philosophi-
cally contained. For example, the effect of the tale which inspired
The Shadow of the Glen, and its justification as a tale, lies in the
satisfaction it offers to man's appetite for destruction:

> Then the dead man got up, and he took one stick, and he gave the other
> to myself. We went in and saw them lying together with her head on
> his arm.
>   The dead man hit him a blow with the stick so that the blood out of
> him leapt up and hit the gallery.
>   That is my story.[3]

Synge's play, in contrast, not only reverses the triumph but also transforms the violence into spiritual violence. On the most basic level,
the physical act of beating with a stick until blood spurted becomes a
verbal attack with images of death; on a moral level, it becomes a
casting out of marital emotion and domestic piety. The transformation
of violence, found in *The Playboy* and *The Tinker's Wedding* in more
spectacular forms, is closely related to the confrontation with nature
which is at the centre of the thematic structure of *The Shadow of the
Glen*.

Similarly, J. B. Yeats's comment deserves to be taken seriously on a
level more dispassionate than that of provocation. Subsequent critics
have agreed, without dissent, that Synge's women, in their vigour and
independence, present an implicit attack on a traditional conception
of womankind. It can certainly be argued also that there is an intentional
attack on marriage, lovelessness aside, for there is no subsequent play
of Synge's which does not mock traditional marriage relationships.
However, these problems seem to be merely aspects of a larger problem;
and one might say that marriage was merely one aspect of the social
rigidity that offended Synge's sense of life.

Although it is illuminating to consider Synge's work in relation to the
two cultures which provided his sources and gave him refractors, the
method of contrast is more useful than the method of comparison.
On the very basic level of plotting, for example, there is a dramatic
contrast between the gross archetypal comic plot and the real action
of the play. The comic plot with which Synge is concerned is not, of
course, purely Irish, and we can find its type in Roman comedy as
well as in medieval farces. As the author's comment on the tale told
by the *shanachie* about the Lady O'Conor indicates, Synge was constantly making a comparatist's connections between the folk literature
of his country and the European tradition:

The incident of the faithful wife takes us beyond Cymbeline to the sunshine on the Arno, and the gay company who went out from Florence to tell narratives of love. It takes us again to the low vineyards of Würzburg on the Main, where the same tale was told in the middle ages, of the 'Two Merchants and the Faithful Wife of Ruprecht von Würzburg'.[4]

In the hardness, the continuity, and the commonality of these elemental folk comedies and tragedies there was something that Synge needed, not only for contrast, of course, but as an element of his synthesis. Yet the function of contrast is the first and most obvious one. The comic plot he is concerned with offers a social view of man and woman in which roles are fixed and clear and in which deviation is sufficiently frequent that a conventional response has been established. In this pattern of right and wrong there is safety; a defence against the wildness of individual feeling and thought and against all the elements of anarchy outside the social structure.

In *The Shadow of the Glen* this safety, and the mechanical conception of human relations implied by the stock comic roles, finds expression not only in the characterization of Dan Burke and Michael Dara, but also in the effect of these two characters on Nora and the Tramp and the play's action while they are active; the tramp trembles before the apparition of the dead man, and Nora counts out the money for Michael. Physical details and details of stage business emphasize the mechanical, especially at the moment of confrontation: "Dan sneezes violently. Michael tries to get to the door, but before he can do so, Dan jumps out of the bed in queer white clothes, with the stick in his hand, and goes over and puts his back against it."[5] Michael, even more than Dan, is characterized entirely in terms of social propriety and economic motivation.

The cottage and the physical action within it belong to the old comedy and to the fixed relations and social control it serves. The objects Synge points to in the cottage are equally elemental: the needle, the libation, the bed, the stick, the coins. The cottage is a protection from the storm, a place of human hospitality within set limits, and a containment of human possibility.

In opposition to the plot and to the presentation by means of objects, the real action of the play, which is the action of imagination, must necessarily be verbal. Synge's preface to *The Playboy of the Western World*, while seeming to celebrate merely the fiery imagination of the primitive people, is clearly celebrating the reality of language as well; "what is superb and wild in reality" is known through language, and speech "as fully flavoured as a nut or apple"[6] depends not on acquaintance with the objects and the forms of physical life but on emotion and intuition, not entirely experienced until the creative act of language has occurred. While it is certainly true that Synge did not perfect his technique, not even his theme, of verbal transformation of reality until he wrote *The Playboy*, he begins the process in *The Shadow of the Glen*.

Finding the reality that Synge intends to find, and the language which is both a part of the reality and its vehicle of expression, requires more than an acquaintance, even an intimacy, with nature. In this respect Synge's conception is much more selective than the Wordsworthian one. In *The Shadow of the Glen*, for example, Dan and Michael are as closely in touch with the nature of the glen, its mountainy ewes, its shadows, as are Nora and the Tramp, but a man may have driven mountain ewes since childhood and never know them well enough to drive them efficiently to market. The sensuous knowledge that is needed for the intuition of a Darcy is perhaps ultimately mysterious, most effectively defined by what it is not. It is not an acquaintance with objects; it is not a tactile, not even essentially a visual knowledge. It is an intuitive recognition of the rhythm of being. At the most primitive level, it is awareness of animals by their breathing and the beating of their hearts. Reality is not known except in the collaboration between what is intangible in man and what is intangible in nature. For this reason Synge conveys the sense of nature most often, in *The Shadow of the Glen*, by wind, mist, bird song, and the sounds of animals.

The reality of imagination depends ultimately upon a vital force in humanity, and to some extent Synge leaves this force ambiguous. The choice of plot, however, even when the plot is discreetly managed, would suggest that Eros provides a key. The approach to the reality of imagination is offered in this play by a man who, in contrast to Dan Burke, is not imaginatively but physically dead; and the memory of this man, Patch Darcy, brings an attitude to nature, to imagination, and to love.

One marriage of nature and man, known to both the Tramp and Darcy, is suggested by the Tramp just before he recounts the death of Darcy:

> . . . crossing the hills when the fog is on them, the time a little stick would seem as big as your arm, and a rabbit as big as a bay horse, and a stack of turf as big as a towering church in the city of Dublin? If myself was easily afeared, I'm telling you, it's long ago I'd have been locked into the Richmond Asylum, or maybe have run up into the back hills with nothing on me but an old shirt, and been eaten with crows the like of Patch Darcy . . .[7]

The glen has wild nights and great storms which result in roaring streams and broken trees with the wind crying through them. It has at all times a movement of dark mist. These are the aspects which are present to Nora throughout the play. Here the exposition of the Tramp makes clear what the implications of the wildness and monstrous deformity in the glen are for the human imagination. Patch Darcy, we are told, ran mad and died in a ditch in the storm, hallucinating. Or to express it more accurately, in terms Dan and Michael would not use, Patch Darcy's imagination has been totally captured by the non-human world, and he has been lost in the fog, the rain, the dark, and the bestial. The Tramp describes the experience in terms of sheep "lying under the ditch and every one of them coughing, and choking, like an old man, with the great rain and the fog . . ."[8]

This madness, or submersion of the human imagination in the natural ambiance, is the danger against which the cottage, and the marriage, and the marketing attitude, defend Nora. Michael Dara, courting, offers the continuation of this protection when he says, ". . . you'll marry me in the chapel of Rathvanna, and I'll bring the sheep up on the bit of a hill you have on the back mountain, and we won't have anything we'd be afeard to let our minds on when the mist is down."[9]

Yet Patch Darcy's sympathy with nature has had its praiseworthy aspect, even in terms of peasant practicality. The Tramp praises both the humanity and the efficiency of Darcy:

> That was a great man, young fellow, a great man I'm telling you. There was never a lamb from his own ewes he wouldn't know before it was marked, and he'd run from this to the city of Dublin, and never catch for his breath.[10]

The vitality of the remembered Darcy is a presence in the play in terms of a semi-mystical unity with the creatures of nature, and in terms of human intimacy in Nora's muted laments for his company. But the sense of the danger of his total irrational sympathy is overriding, in the same way that the destructive aspect of nature dominates the imagination at the beginning of the play.

Until the entrance of Michael Dara, Patch Darcy is the only un-equivocal thematic opposition to the world of Dan Burke, and even in the conversation between Michael and Nora, the tendencies of Nora to allow her thought to roam beyond the forms of domesticity are referred (for the reader) to the dangerous world of Darcy. As she thinks about mortality, Michael is troubled, as he was troubled by the mention of Darcy's name. "I've heard tell it's the like of that talk you do hear from men, and they after being a great while on the back hills."[11] Man outside the fixed structures of society, solitary in the wildness of nature, finds chaos and madness. It is an experience which is terrible yet known to man but, Michael seems to suggest, truly dreadful for a woman. Nora has been close to that experience. The dread of it is in her speech, as she leaves the Tramp to sit with the body of her husband: "isn't a dead man itself more company than to be sitting alone, and hearing the winds crying, and you not knowing on what thing your mind would stay?"[12]

The process of verbal creation then, which is also the process of discovery of reality, begins with an apparently impossible dilemma for Nora, though in terms of traditional comic plotting her problems seem to be solved. Roman comedy would find her in a happy position, for the social aberration of the marriage of a young and lively woman to a dry old man has ceased to exist and Nora can marry a younger, more fruitful man and live happily ever after with the material joy of their mutual holdings. Certainly Synge leads us this way for a little while, both through the expectations of a stock plot and the recoil from the only alternative offered. Nora at first seems to be a practical and stoic peasant very much in the world of Dan Burke, in which objects of nature, or husbands and wives, are comparable to other household goods, to be used in the most expedient way or to be cast out. Nora speaks Dan's language when, in her fourth speech, she states her situation factually: "He's after dying on me, God forgive him, and there I am now with a hundred sheep beyond the hills, and no turf drawn for the winter."[13] From this affective vacuum in the beginning, Nora moves to an intense and tragic awareness of the emotional impossibility of her previous mode of existence:

> I do be thinking in the long nights it was a big fool I was that time, Michael Dara, for what good is a bit of a farm with cows on it, and sheep on the back hills, when you do be sitting, looking out from a door the like of that door, and seeing nothing but the mists rolling down the bog, and the mists again, and they rolling up the bog, and hearing nothing but the wind crying out in the bits of broken trees were left from the great storm, and the streams roaring with the rain?[14]

This transformation of Nora's imagination is the first movement in the verbal action of the play, and it cannot be explained by any of the external action of the play, except as Nora becomes aware of the new action (the courting by Michael) as one that she must resist.

Essentially the transformation depends on the acceptance of the power of nature, undomesticated, and the strain of that nature in herself. The shadow of the glen—so central that it gives the play its title—is the dark side of nature. Most explicitly, the shadow is death. Nora begins to doubt the cottage as a place of safety when her husband is taken by the shadow (at the most literal and superstitious level) as the sun moves towards its setting. From that beginning Nora progresses to a total and rather macabre vision of the dance of death, and of the incapacity of society to hinder it. The choice of life is a choice of the way to die. Men may find wildness or madness, like Darcy, in being too close to the darkness of the glen; or they may be caught suddenly by the shadow, like Dan, within their four walls. For women, we see, there is no safety in the domestic role even before the coming of the shadow, for Nora thinks of Peggy Cavanagh, "who had the lightest hand at milking a cow that wouldn't be easy, or turning a cake, and there she is now walking round on the roads, or sitting in a dirty old house, with no teeth in her mouth, and no sense, and no more hair than you'd see on a bit of a hill and they after burning the furze from it."[15] Here as elsewhere in Synge's work, we are told that death comes for women when sensual beauty and sensual force go; and women know it. That is the slow death of time's erosion. Watching the decay of one's own mind and body may be desolating, but marriage offers a double mortality, for Nora must live with another dying creature. Death in society is a long death, to be confronted every morning in the world:

> Why would I marry you, Mike Dara? You'll be getting old, and I'll be getting old, and in a little while, I'm telling you, you'll be sitting up in your bed—the way himself was sitting—with a shake in your face, and your teeth falling, and the white hair sticking out round you like an old bush where sheep do be leaping a gap.[16]

However, Nora's choice does not merely imply a preference for a quick end. Unspoken but suggested in her ruthless anatomizing of marriage—the same marriage, whether to Dan or to Michael—is the idea that eroticism does not have its abode in the cottage but in the ditch, and that eroticism is the vital principle of life and imagination. In terms of the comic plot with which he began, Synge's play is very discreet in treating sexuality. The original story provides overt physical action to prove the wife's infidelity; *The Shadow of the Glen* gives only the husband's suspicion and Nora's ambiguous statement:

> It's in a lonesome place you do have to be talking with someone, and looking for someone, in the evening of the day, and if it's a power of men I'm after knowing they were fine men . . .[17]

That Nora has not merely talked to men because of the loneliness of the glen has already been indicated by her indifferent comment to the Tramp that her husband was a cold man even before death, yet it seems evident that Synge did not intend to allow his readers or audience to interpret the erotic on the gross level of the folk tale. I think it possible that some strain of prudery may be found in his reticence, but the thematic structure of the play indicates rather that Eros is a generalized nature force, not readily distinguishable from imaginative power. The relationship between nature and the human erotic impulse has been analyzed by Synge himself in his *Autobiography*, for he explicitly links his responses:

> . . . I remember when I was very young, watching a lady in the pew

before me [in Church] and wishing vaguely to stroke her cheek, but I did not know for years that she was considered singularly beautiful. About puberty when the boy begins to look out with an uneasy awakened gaze that lingers because it is not satisfied, I saw in one hour that both nature and women were alive with indescribable radiance— with beauty. Even when the animal feelings were at their height a beautiful woman seemed an always intangible glory.[18]

When the force called Eros is in play in *The Shadow of the Glen*, nature moves and language kindles. When the Tramp affirms his sexual identity in the cautious challenge of the line, "And I was thinking . . . that it's many a lone woman would be afeard of the like of me in the dark night . . . ,"[19] Nora takes up the challenge: ". . . I never knew what way I'd be afeard of beggar or bishop or any man of you at all."[20] After this recognition, the quality of speech becomes emotionally evocative and the images of nature in Nora's dialogue become more violent. The roaring streams, the crying wind, the rolling mists are a source of excitement as well as fear, for they represent a force to her senses s awell as a sign of her solitude. The acceptance of the power of nature nad imagination does not involve disarming nature. Storm, madness, suffering, and death are still in it, but the darkness of nature also contains sensuality. *The Shadow of the Glen* is an exorcism of dread of the dark. At the conclusion of the play, Nora and the Tramp will go out into the condition of nature from which the Tramp fearfully sought shelter in the beginning. They will gladly go out into the rain, and into the night that has such monstrous suggestions for the Tramp's imagination that it evokes for him the madness of Darcy.

Before that is possible in the physical action of the denouement, it must occur in language. The resolution of thematic conflict has really occurred before the crisis of plot (the dead man's rising to avenge himself on the bad wife) in Nora's virtual refusal of Michael Dara; the altered imaginative grasp of nature is of such persuasiveness that even the verbal violence of Dan Burke is coloured by it. Although the discovery of nature is mocked by Dan, and although he offers Nora, in threat, some of the same imagery with which she rejected him, the grotesque prospect of Nora's death merely emphasizes the sensual excitement that has been discovered. Nora, "stretched like a dead sheep with the frost on her, or the big spiders, maybe, and they putting their webs on her, in the butt of a ditch,"[21] provides an image to convey the eroticism, the terror, and the imaginative vitality which the play has revealed in the world outside the cottage.

The full expression of this transformation is given to the Tramp, who now remembers the more aesthetic and sensuously gentle manifestations of nature. In the prose poem of his concluding speech he presents that merging of the intangible beauty of nature and the imagination of man previously discussed, for the Tramp invokes bird song and the songs of men, rather than visual or tactile imagery:

> Come along with me now, lady of the house, and it's not my blather you'll be hearing only, but you'll be hearing the herons crying over the black lakes, and you'll be hearing the grouse, and the owls with them, and the larks and the big thrushes when the days are warm . . . it's fine songs you'll be hearing when the sun goes up, and there'll be no old fellow wheezing the like of a sick sheep, close to your ear.[22]

Although the Tramp is given the poetry of transformation, he is neither the active principle of the play nor is he Synge's voice in the play. He is by no means a dramatic version of the Wicklow tramp described with such admiration by Synge:

> . . . Though now alone . . . he has been married several times and reared children of whom he knows no more than a swallow knows of broods that have flown to the south. Like most tramps he has the humour of talk and ideas of a certain distinction . . . and this old marauder who has lived twice as long and perhaps ten times more fully than the men around him [is] aware of his distinction . . . If you do not follow his sometimes mumbled phrases he will call a blight from heaven on your head, though your silver is only warming in his pouch.[23]

The Tramp of *The Shadow of the Glen* is more timid than this, and lacks the pride, the fierceness, and perhaps the hardness. These qualities are possessed by Nora, and they make possible the imaginative play of the Tramp.

Unquestionably Synge's women are strong; but there is no other woman in the plays comparable to Nora except Deirdre. The arrogance of Deirdre with her aging suitor has its parallel in Nora's proud claims that she fears no man, and that she has always been a hard woman to please; the impropriety of Deirdre the would-be queen scrambling for nuts and twigs in the woods has a parallel in Nora's whistling for Michael in the dark: "Did ever you hear another woman could whistle the like of that with two fingers in her mouth?"[24] But essentially the quality that distinguishes these two women from Synge's other women, who are even more sensuously vigorous, is the power of intelligence and will. The choice of lives made in *The Shadow of the Glen* and *Deirdre of the Sorrows* is a choice that must be deliberate and intelligent if it is to be valid. It cannot be a yielding to illusion; it cannot depend as, for example, the Tramp's fancy tends to do, on an elision of the dark or bitter elements of reality.

Nora, more than any other character, is in the position to make the choice most dramatically and most effectively. Occupying the world of realism, she does not have Deirdre's protection of romance, immortality, and ecstasy. She ranges the middle-ground between the strictures of society and the anarchy of nature, and between the fool and the madman. When she leaves the middle-ground, she does so in full knowledge, without illusion. The proposition of *The Shadow of the Glen* is that the tragic recognition of the nature of mortality leads to a choice of total, if brief, experience in which the fruition of life is in exposure and sensuous vulnerability.

The corollary, suggested by the concluding lines of the play, with Dan and Michael sitting down to drink together, is that society, which is built for safety, attempts to purge its more vital elements, for they are not conducive to "a long life and a quiet life, and good health with it."[25] The mockery of society even in its most primitive forms (the family, the village) that we find in all of Synge's plays is perhaps to be traced to its source in this idea; and in his observations of tramps in his notebooks, Synge states explicitly that the tramp is the outlaw of peasant society because of his superior vitality and intelligence.

In *The Shadow of the Glen*, the strong sense of life and the will to pursue it are given to Nora, rather than to the Tramp, partly because the woman's choice is the one of maximum risk; and the play is basically concerned with the acceptance of risk for the sake of vital existence. Moreover, this heightened awareness and will, completed by the poetic transformation of the Tramp, clearly dramatize the basic choice of Synge himself. It is the choice which gives the body of his dramatic work the clarity and unity it possesses, and its astonishingly complete integration of the sophisticated and the naive: the boldness of an existentialist with the innocence of a herd from the hills.

NOTES

1. Quoted by Greene and Stephens, *Synge, p.* 149.
2. *Essays*, p. 326.
3. *C.W.*, II, p. 72.
4. *Ibid.*, p. 65.
5. *C.W.*, III, p. 53.
6. *C.W.*, IV, p. 54.
7. *C.W.*, III, p. 37.
8. *Ibid.*, p. 39.
9. *Ibid.*, p. 51.
10. *Ibid.*, p. 47.
11. *Ibid.*, p. 49.
12. *Ibid.*, p. 41
13. *Ibid.*, p. 33.
14. *Ibid.*, p. 49.
15. *Ibid.*, p. 51.

16. *Ibid.*
17. *Ibid.*, p. 49.
18. *C.W.*, II, pp. 12-13.
19. *C.W.*, III, p. 37.
20. *Ibid.*
21. *Ibid.*, p. 55
22. *Ibid.*, p. 57.
23. *C.W.*, II, p. 195.
24. *C.W.*, III, pp.41-43.
25. *Ibid.*, p. 59.

RIDERS TO THE SEA: A NOTE
T. R. Henn

I

I DO NOT think that we realize the full ambiguity of the title of the play at our first reading; perhaps not even when we have known it through many readings and performances. On the surface it is clearly the play of the two Riders, the living man on the Red Mare, and the phantasm of the dead on the Grey Pony. One might see them as Jack Yeats did in his illustration for *The Aran Islands;* the half-wild horses, ridden by the islanders without saddle, bit or bridle, but with a halter that might be quickly knotted up out of the new rope that is hanging on the cottage wall. Behind, in depth, we may be aware of the horse as a fear-image; the chariots and horses; power and destruction; even the mysterious horses of the Bible. There are the white, red, black and pale horses— the horse of death—in Revelation (VI:2); the horses of Zechariah (I:8 and VI:2); perhaps even the text from the prophet (Zechariah, x:5): "the riders on horses shall be confounded." We should not forget Synge's extensive reading in the Bible.

Move a little into the background, and the Riders are the fishermen of the Islands, as in Norse and Homeric imagery. They are the riders who use the frail curraghs of that coast; the long high prowed boats, built of lath and tarred canvas (once of skins) that can live where no other type of boat can be launched. Over the long Atlantic rollers one does indeed have something of the sensation of riding; and, till one is accustomed to them, the fear of the sea that one encounters in them is profound. As Synge has pointed out in *The Aran Islands,* most of the fishermen of his time met (sooner or later) their death in them: usually when drunk on "the grey poteen" that was one of the few comforts of their lives. But there are other things that Synge does not mention. If one fell out of one of them the crew might refuse to rescue him, might even smash his fingers as he clung to the gunwhale; for it is ill-luck to take back anything that the Sea has tried to claim. Nor did the men of the islands learn to swim—many of that western coast refuse to do so still—believing that this skill would merely prolong the inevitable drowning. The riders of the horses and of the curraghs in which men go down to the sea are linked in the title. Odysseus, shipwrecked, rides a plank "like a horse."[1]

So too there is, in our background consciousness, the traditional lore of the drowned man: Clarence's dream, the famous lyric of *The*

Tempest, the even more famous passage from "Lycidas":

> Ay me! Whilst thee the shores, and sounding Seas
> Wash far away, where ere thy bones are hurld,
> Whether beyond the stormy *Hebrides*,
> Where thou perhaps under the whelming tide
> Visit'st the bottom of the monstrous world . . .[2]

Behind this and the following passages from the play is the common thought of the drowned sailor of Horace[3] and the three handfuls of dust that are the needed ritual if the grave is not to be unquiet:

> How would it be washed up, and we after looking each day for nine days, and a strong wind blowing a while back from the west and south?[4]

> *　　　*　　　*

> Ah, Nora, isn't it a bitter thing to think of him floating that way to the far north, and no one to keen him but the black hags that do be flying on the sea?[5]

> *　　　*　　　*

> There does be a power of young men floating round in the sea, and what way would they know if it was Michael they had, or another man like him, for when a man is nine days in the sea, and the wind blowing it's hard set his own mother would be to say what man was in it.[6]

II

It is perhaps desirable to enlarge a little on the background of the play at the time of Synge's visits to the Islands. The "desolate stony place,"[7] the last outposts of man's husbandry in the Atlantic, were then the setting for the most primitive peasantry in Europe. It is not easy for the casual tourist of today to imagine the life of seventy years ago, though the mysterious forts of Dun Aengus still guard the offshore cliffs—from what invader? The horses had to be sent to the mainland, to winter on pasture that was better than the little stony fields; or to be sold at Galway Fairs. Like the Burren, that strange area of limestone outcrop in North Clare that lies to the southwest, there was, as in Cromwell's description of that county "not enough timber to hang a man, water to drown him, or earth to bury him."[8] The graves in the shallow patches of soil were, like Donne's, constantly re-used "Some second guest to entertain."[9] Synge gives a macabre description of an island funeral in *The Aran Islands:* the measuring of the coffin-space by a bramble torn from the hedge, the throwing up of the bones from the old grave, the old woman who recognized her husband's skull, and withdrew to a corner of the churchyard to lament over it. These things I have seen; and without some understanding of them we do not realize the emotional significance of the "fine white boards" for a coffin, Maurya's profound satisfaction that Michael has found a "clean grave" in the Far North.[10] Throughout the play there runs the bitter sense of loss, the importance of ritual burial, that pre-historic man laboured so greatly to achieve by dolmen and passage grave.

There are other depth-images that we do well to note. The "cake" that is turned out of the oven is the flat home-made soda bread, baked in iron pans on the hearth; a hunk of it is commonly the sole food for a journey for the fishermen in their curraghs. Its ritual significance is clear; but Maurya's failure to give it to her son has in it something of the negation of a sacrament. The meeting place is by the spring well; we may remember, perhaps, the image from the Psalms (Lxxxiv:6): "Who passing through the vale of misery use it for a well." The new rope—like all such things it comes from the mainland, and is a thing of price—will serve for a halter for the horses or for lowering a coffin into a grave. Each cottage will have a tiny lamp, on or near the dresser with some crude holy picture beside it; and close to it, the basin of holy water which now is almost exhausted—from repeated use in tribulation and blessing. The knot in the string that holds the bundle of clothes is "perished with the salt water";[11] Synge noted in *The Aran Islands* the perpetual dampness of the salt-sodden clothes, the rheumatism that was only to be countered by the poteen, as in East Anglia the fen-dwellers fought the dread ague with opium. And may there not be some symbolism in the cutting of the knot by a knife bought from a stranger?[12] remembering the Three Fates and the "abhorréd shears" of "Lycidas."[13] Something, but not a great deal, may be brought out in production; the table has been used for mixing the bread-dough, and one of the girls wipes it down hastily as Bartley's body is brought in at the doorway. It is, I think, a mistake to fill the cottage with properties not mentioned in the text, fishing-nets and so forth; or to play it against a background of the noise of waves. It is best to cultivate simplicity, and, above all to let the rhythms and cadences speak for themselves. Unless the Irish accent and its intonations are familiar, it is best not to attempt them; the stride of the speech carries the subtly-shifting advance and retreat of the action, the finely-differentiated character of the four protagonists.

III

Against some such background, of which the symbols are in the main archetypal and rooted both in tradition and in the simplicities of living, we may see the miniature tragedy. Perhaps it is the only complete one-act tragedy in any literature, for it requires no space to develop its characteristic momentum. Its conflict is the perennial one of man, driven by adventure or necessity against the Sea; itself the source of life and of death. The end comes inexorably, and this again is traditional. Dunbar's "Lament for the Makaris" may stand to embrace them all:

> Since for the Death remeid is none,
> Best is that we for Death dispone
> After our death that live may we:—
> *Timor mortis conturbat me.*[14]

So Maurya

> No man at all can be living for ever, and we must be satisfied.[15]

—set against Dante's

> In la sua voluntade è nostra pace.[16]

For death and the Sea take all; but the Sea takes the young before their time, so that it acquires a new and hostile dimension, an auxiliary of Death. In it there are the constant ironic reversals. Maurya takes Michael's stick, lest she should "slip on the big stones":

> In the big world the old people do be leaving things after them for their sons and children, but in this place it is the young men do be leaving things behind them for them that do be old.[17]

Synge's anti-clerical irony is subtle and pervading; I believe that its cumulative effect gave rise to the general uneasiness of the Dublin audiences that led to the riots of 1907 over *The Playboy of the Western World*. I wonder whether there may not be an oblique reference (for the "big stones" recur twice) to the familiar text in the Psalms (XCI. 12):[18]

> [Angels] shall bear thee up...lest thou dash thy foot against a stone...

And a culminating point of irony is in the references—that seem to be emphasized, twice, intentionally—to the *young* priest:

> NORA: Didn't the young priest say the Almighty God won't leave her destitute with no son living?
> MAURYA: It's little the like of him knows of the sea . . .[19]

and we hear the intonation of scorn in the mother's voice; that changes at the last to a pathetic bewilderment:

> . . . It isn't that I haven't prayed for you, Bartley, to the Almighty God. It isn't that I haven't said prayers in the dark night till you wouldn't know what I'd be saying . . .[20]

The end, in misery and even starvation in a house of three women that has lost all the breadwinners, is a benediction; thankfulness for the clean burial in the far north (clean, for a body of nine days battered by those remorseless tides is best hidden in the kindness of earth),

and the white boards that will make Bartley's coffin. In her elegiac
blessing of the living and the dead Maurya attains the stature of a
priestess; so that the production in terms of plainsong was wholly
appropriate (as in Vaughan Williams' opera):

> May the Almighty God have mercy on Bartley's soul,
> and on Michael's soul,
> and on the souls of Sheamus and Patch,
> and Stephen and Shawn [*bending her head*] . . .
> and may He have mercy on my soul, Nora,
> and on the soul of everyone is left living in the world.[21]

With those last words the death-stricken cottage on the island becomes
as it were a microcosm of the world. *Who* is left alive? Let the mother,
that had those hard births,[22] bless those that are living.

IV

It is a characteristic of the world's greatest literature—the Bible,
Homer, Horace, Dante, Shakespeare—that one never opens the book,
even in old age, without finding something that one had not seen before.
So with *Riders*. It is sixty years since I first read it, and I have written
of it since. I know the fishermen of those islands and that coast; I have
used their craft, and maybe won even a little of their skills in them.
I know, from seaward, the mercilessness of the great surf on those
rocks. I have seen great actresses interpret Maurya: the greatest,
perhaps, Sybil Thorndike. I thought that I had perceived the inward-
ness of the classic tragedy.[23]

But one thing I believe I have missed till I began to think about
this little essay. Why cannot Maurya bless Bartley, give him the
sacramental bread, as he passes by the spring well? For it is not the
shock of seeing Michael's phantasm on the grey pony; "something
choked the words in my throat"[24] *before* she looks up, crying, to see
that vision. Michael has fine clothes on him, and new shoes on his
feet; we are aware, faintly, of a resurrection image.

But what was Maurya's relation to her son Michael, and why did
her blessing for Bartley stick (like Macbeth's *Amen*) in her throat?
We know that Macbeth could not assent to the blessing because he was
not in a state of Grace. Synge sometimes hints at a mystery of the
shadows, like Patch Darcy in *The Shadow of the Glen*. It is true that
there are dark words before Bartley goes off on the horses, and these
may be broken by the blessing at the well. One of her complaints
against his going is that there will be "no man in it to make the coffin"[25]
if Michael's body is found. The white boards (paid for at a big price,
and this is admirably perceptive of peasant psychology), the deep

grave, seem to relate to a specially-beloved son. Michael's clothes are spread out on the table[26] beside his brother's corpse. Is Michael the beloved son, and is it for that reason that Bartley's death is received with a terrible resignation?

> She's quiet now and easy; but the day Michael was drowned you could hear her crying out from this to the spring well. It's fonder she was of Michael, and would any one have thought that?[27]

Are "sorrow's springs" exhausted; did the death of Michael numb Maurya's capacity to lament? Or does the vision of the figure on the grey pony, with fine clothes and new shoes on his feet, achieve a kind of divine resonance, as of Michael and all the angels?

V

We may praise the overwhelming power of this tiny play; its economy and reticence of statement; its images that are vécu, rooted in the reality of daily living. It has the laconic brevity of a Greek play, of which the basic myth is known to all the audience. It needs no exposition to unfold the characters. Its momentum is that of the Atlantic waves that gather their rhythms and their destructive forces out of the limitless ocean of necessity. Repeated reading, listening, seeing productions with many emphases (but with only one culmination in the high tradition, the *lusis* of lyric tragedy) may combine with some knowledge of that intricate and difficult subject, the rhythms, cadences and intonations of Anglo-Irish prose, to illuminate our understanding. That understanding embraces (but cannot exhaust) the mystery of death and loss; the women who are left to weep; and the benediction of death which must, as ever, lie between Christian resignation; and the bitter lamentation that runs through recorded literature.

NOTES

1. *Odyssey*, XIII.
2. *Poetical Works of Milton*, II (Oxford, Clarendon Press, 1955), p. 169, ll. 154-158.
3. *Odes*, I, xxviii.
4. *C.W.*, III, p. 9.
5. *Ibid.*, p. 17.
6. *Ibid.*, pp. 25-27.
7. W. B. Yeats, "In Memory of Major Robert Gregory", *Collected Poems* (London, Macmillan, 1958), p. 149.
8. This remark is usually attributed to Oliver Cromwell while on one of his punitive expeditions in the West. There are various versions.

9. "The Relique", *The Poems of John Donne*, (London, Oxford University Press, 1953), p. 62.
10. *C.W.*, III, pp. 25, 27.
11. *Ibid.*, p. 15.
12. Steel, which is a strong protection against evil—see *The Shadow of the Glen* (*C.W.*, III, p. 41)—loses its virtue or becomes actively unlucky unless it is paid for; hence the slight inflexion of Cathleen's words in *Riders to the Sea* (*C.W.*, III, p. 15): "—the man *sold* us that knife."
13. *Poetical Works of Milton*, II, p. 16, l. 75.
14. *The Poems of William Dunbar*, edited by W. Mackay (Edinburgh, Porpoise Press, 1932), p. 23.
15. *C.W.*, III. p. 27.
16. *Divine Comedy*, Paradiso III, l. 84.
17. *C.W.*, III, p. 13.
18. Perhaps this is far-fetched. See Synge's poem "The Mergency Man", *C.W.*, I, p. 58.
19. *C.W.*, III, p. 21.
20. *Ibid.*, p. 25.
21. *Ibid.*, p. 27.
22. Cf. Euripides' *Medea* (*Collected Plays of Euripides*, trans. Gilbert Murray, London, Allen and Unwin, 1954, p. 16, ll. 250-252):
". . . sooner would I stand
Three times to face their battles, shield in hand,
Than bear one child."
23. See the Preface to my edition of *The Plays and Poems of J. M. Synge* (London, Methuen, 1963); and to the chapter in my *Harvest of Tragedy* (London, Macmillan, 1956).
24. *C.W.*, III, p. 19.
25. *Ibid.*, p. 9.
26. We may note, but need not stress, another sacramental suggestion. Before the coffin is made, the single work-table is the natural place for a corpse to be stretched. See also *The Shadow of the Glen* (*C.W.*, III, p. 33).
27. *C.W.*, III, p. 25.

SYNGE'S "PERPETUAL 'LAST DAY' ": REMARKS ON *RIDERS TO THE SEA*

David R. Clark

LEAVING George Bernard Shaw aside as peripheral to the Irish dramatic movement, one thinks of John Synge as the first of its dramatists, antedating Sean O'Casey, outshining Lady Gregory, and being pure dramatist, not poet turned dramatist as was Yeats. The essential dramatic quality which distinguished Synge from Yeats, the Irish lyric poet, and from James Joyce, the Irish prose artist, may be defined in terms of a famous passage of Joyce's *A Portrait of the Artist as a Young Man:*

> The dramatic form is reached when the vitality which has flowed and eddied round each person fills every person with such vital force that he or she assumes a proper and intangible aesthetic life. The personality of the artist, at first [in the lyric] a cry or a cadence or a mood and then [in epic] a fluid and lambent narrative, finally [in drama] refines itself out of existence, impersonalises itself, so to speak. The aesthetic image in the dramatic form is life purified in and reprojected from the human imagination. The mystery of aesthetic like that of material creation is accomplished. The artist, like the God of creation, remains within or behind or beyond or above his handiwork, invisible, refined out of existence, indifferent, paring his fingernails.[1]

I doubt that Joyce had John Millington Synge in mind in this description of the dramatist. But the passage (whether or not it is the last word on the differences among the lyric, epic and dramatic forms) is quite close to W. B. Yeats's picture of Synge. There was in Synge's work a "furious impartiality, an indifferent turbulent sorrow"[2] wrote Yeats after Synge's death. And it was through turning to drama and particularly drama of the life of the Irish country people, drama in dialect, that Synge was able to "refine himself out of existence," to purify the life he saw and experienced and to re-project it from his imagination.

At the time of his historic meeting with Yeats, in Paris in 1896, Synge was an unknown, unpublished poet, translator, and critic. Yeats wrote an account of the meeting in a 1905 essay:

> He had learned Irish years ago, but had begun to forget it, for the only language that interested him was that conventional language of modern poetry which has begun to make us all weary . . . I said: 'Give up Paris . . . Go to the Aran Islands. Live there as if you were one of the

people themselves; express a life that has never found expression.'
I had just come from Aran, and my imagination was full of those grey
islands where men must reap with knives because of the stones.

    He went to Aran and became a part of its life, living upon salt fish
and eggs, talking Irish for the most part, but listening also to the
beautiful English which has grown up in Irish-speaking districts, and
takes its vocabulary from the time of Malory and of the translators
of the Bible, but its idiom and its vivid metaphor from Irish.[3]

Yeats writes that in 1898 having "settled for a while in an Aran
cottage" Synge "became happy, having escaped at last, as he wrote,
'from the squalor of the poor and the nullity of the rich.' "[4] Synge made
five visits to Aran in the summers of 1898 through 1902. In all, he
stayed more than four months on the islands.

    During this same period the Irish dramatic movement was born.
In 1899 the Irish Literary Theatre was started by Yeats, Lady Gregory,
Edward Martyn, and George Moore. This was followed in 1903 by
the Irish National Theatre Society, based on a company of Irish actors
led by Frank and W. G. Fay. The latter was to play leading roles in
most first performances of Synge's plays.

    Synge had finished his book *The Aran Islands* by November 1901,
although it was not published until 1907. In the summer of 1902 he
had written *The Shadow of the Glen* and *Riders to the Sea* and the
first draft of *The Tinker's Wedding*. *Riders to the Sea* was first published
in *Samhain*, an occasional review edited by W. B. Yeats, in September
1903. *The Shadow of the Glen* was staged by the Irish National
Theatre Society in Molesworth Hall, Dublin, in October 1903, and
raised considerable opposition because of its ironically realistic picture
of Irish life, and *Riders to the Sea* was staged on 25 February, 1904, in
the same place, but with much less excitement resulting. When, as a
result of a gift by Miss Annie E. Horniman, the Abbey Theatre opened
its doors on 27 December, 1904, Synge, along with Yeats and Lady
Gregory, was one of the three directors.

    Thus Synge became a dramatist. An artist of Synge's type had to
"take the first plunge into the world beyond himself, the first plunge
away from himself that is always pure technique, the delight in doing,
not because one would or should, but merely because one can do."[5]
What Synge could do was to express the life of Aran in unique dramatic
actions and dramatic speech. Synge became "consciously objective",
Yeats says, through stepping out of himself into the Aran characters and
the Aran speech. "Whenever he tried to write drama without dialect he
wrote badly, . . . because only through dialect could he escape self-
expression, see all that he did from without, allow his intellect to judge
the images of his mind as if they had been created by some other mind."[6]

    In Joyce's figure the artist, like the God of Creation, has made a new world. Yeats, on the other hand, thinking of the dramatic artist as one whose piercing vision sees and recreates society, uses the figure of the Last Judgment, the Second Coming and the making of a new heaven and new earth. Rejecting "abstractions and images created not for their own sake but for the sake of party" the imaginative writer can "make pictures for the mind's eye and sounds that delight the ear, or discover thoughts that tighten the muscles, or quiver and tingle in the flesh, and so stand like Saint Michael with the trumpet that calls the body to resurrection . . ."[7] So Yeats wrote in "J. M. Synge and the Ireland of His Time."

This quality of impartial and inexorable judgment appears in the style and technique of *Riders to the Sea*, with its simplicity, objectivity, bareness, and concentration. But it is also interesting that the very apocalyptic imagery which Yeats uses to describe Synge's work appears as a major image pattern in this play. Among the powerful Biblical allusions in *Riders to the Sea* are several from the book of Revelation or the Apocalypse. For example, in Revelation (XXI: 4-5) we read: "And God shall wipe away all tears from their eyes; and there shall be no more death, neither sorrow, nor crying, neither shall there be any more pain: for the former things are passed away. And he that sat upon the throne said 'Behold, I make all things new.'" One of the disconcerting peculiarities of the life pictured in the play is that many of the objects that relate to the dead are brand new, whereas the living must be content with old things. Saved from the pig with the black feet—an image more terrible than Yeats's boar without bristles that roots the sun out of the sky—the new rope is wanted by Maurya to lower Michael's coffin into the ground if his body should be found, but is used by Bartley as a halter for the red mare which he will ride to his death. Bartley takes off his own shirt, heavy with salt, and puts on a newer one, the shirt of the dead Michael. The most impressive emblem of newness is in the wide white boards meant for Michael's coffin but used for Bartley's. The spectre of Michael on the grey pony when Maurya sees it has "fine clothes on him, and new shoes on his feet."[8]

The red mare which Bartley rides and the grey pony on which Michael appears also echo Revelation (VI: 8), the description of the four horsemen of the Apocalypse. The grey horse is particularly relevant: "And I looked, and behold, a pale horse: and his name that sat on him was Death, and Hell followed with him."

But there is more to it than this. Given these hints one may find an extraordinary dimension added to the figure of Michael. See how Michael broods over the play from first to last! Maurya has been mourning him for days and the girls have, too. He possesses their minds. Maurya is always going down by the sea to look for his body. The action

of the bundle of clothes takes up much of the play. Michael's clothes
hang in the corner. Maurya takes his stick to help her walk over the
stones. Moreover, the grief for Michael is part of the chain of events
that causes Bartley's death. Bartley insists on going to Galway in bad
weather because now—Michael being dead—all the weight of responsibility for supporting the family rests on him, and this causes his own
death. Maurya, possessed by the bitterness of Michael's death, refuses
to return Bartley's blessing when he leaves against her will. (It is
unlucky to make such a refusal to anyone who goes on a journey.)
When, remorseful, she goes to the spring well to give Bartley the bread
and return his blessing, the apparition of Michael on the grey pony
frightens her so that she does neither. Finally, it is this pale horse with
its pale rider that knocks Bartley into the sea. Michael is dead, and yet
he's *there*. He becomes a supernatural presence overshadowing all the
other characters and their actions.

The significance of this presence expands overwhelmingly when
we consider the suggestions inherent in the names of the characters.
Maurya, Mary of the seven times wounded heart: what other name
could Maurya have? Bartley's is an ordinary name, the name of a
mortal. He is the living son. But Michael is the name of an Archangel,
the Prince of the Archangels, he who is like God. In Daniel (xii: 1)
we are told, "And at that time [that is, the end of the world] shall
Michael stand up, the great prince, who standeth for the children of
thy people . . ."; and in Revelations (xii: 7) we read, "And there was
war in heaven! Michael and his angels fought against the dragon . . ."
It is Michael who drives Satan out both in the original fall of the rebel
angels and at the end of the world. Among the offices of St. Michael
are these: (1) to fight against Satan (2) to rescue the souls of the faithful
from the power of the devil especially at the hour of death (3) to call
away from earth and bring men's souls to judgement. In Normandy
in Mont-Saint Michel (which Synge of course knew) St. Michael is
the patron of Mariners.[9] Some of these allusions are ironic enough,
but they are all relevant to the power of this image of Michael in the
play, a figure whom we the audience never know but as a dead, yet
somehow living, and therefore supernatural, presence. The effect is
to underline the suggestions of classical fate with suggestions of
Christian apocalypse—the terrible more than the pious aspects of it—
and it helps give this play the quality to which Yeats referred in Synge
when he said of him: "He was one of those unmoved souls in whom
there is a perpetual 'Last Day,' a perpetual trumpeting and coming
up for judgment."[10]

Yeats's general estimate of *Riders to the Sea* was very high. When
it was first published he wrote that it "seems to me the finest piece of
tragic work done in Ireland of late years. One finds in it, from first to

last, the presence of the sea, and a sorrow that has majesty as in the work of some ancient poet."[11] In the preface to Synge's *Poems and Translations* he praises the play's universality: "The old woman in the *Riders to the Sea*, in mourning for her six fine sons, mourns for the passing of all beauty and strength . . ."[12] But Yeats does have a specific negative criticism of the play. In "J. M. Synge and the Ireland of his Time" he wrote, "I remember saying once to Synge that . . . I liked *The Shadow of the Glen* better than *Riders to the Sea*, that seemed for all the nobility of its end, its mood of Greek tragedy, too passive in suffering, and had quoted from Matthew Arnold's introduction to *Empedocles on Etna* to prove my point."[13]

Empedocles on Etna is a tragic poem which Arnold withdrew because in it and in other works like it

> . . . the suffering finds no vent in action . . . a continuous state of mental distress is prolonged, unrelieved by incident, hope, or resistance; . . . there is everything to be endured, nothing to be done. In such situations there is inevitably something morbid, in the description of them something monotonous. When they occur in actual life they are painful, not tragic; the representation of them in poetry is painful also.[14]

Arnold had said earlier that

> . . . It is not enough that the Poet should add to the knowledge of men, it is required of him also that he should add to their happiness. "All Art," says Schiller, "is dedicated to Joy, and there is no higher and no more serious problem than how to make men happy. The right Art is that alone, which creates the highest enjoyment— . . . In presence of the most tragic circumstances, represented in a work of Art, the feeling of enjoyment, as is well known, may still subsist; the representation of the most utter calamity, of the liveliest anguish, is not sufficient to destroy it: the more tragic the situation, the deeper becomes the enjoyment; and the situation is more tragic in proportion as it becomes more terrible."[15]

Is the play too passive in suffering? The action of *Riders to the Sea* might be paraphrased: To persevere, against overwhelming odds, in the face of constant and ultimate defeat, in the attempt to protect and preserve and foster the family. This is the action that Maurya has been engaged in for years and that Bartley, with his new responsibility, is just starting to be engaged in. I think that any of the little actions will fall into this pattern. Cathleen's spinning is the attempt to clothe the family—to provide yarn out of which to make socks which will come back half torn off from the beaten bodies of her brothers. Even the dropped stitches on the socks hint of the ultimate futility of human effort. Yet Cathleen returns to her spinning after having examined the bundle of Michael's clothes. She bakes a loaf for Bartley, forgets to give it to him; Maurya goes down to the spring well to take him the bread and to give him her blessing, but fails to do either. At the end of the play Cathleen is offering the loaf to the men who will make Bartley's coffin. They are to eat it there in the house while they work. Even the white boards represent a continual and futile attempt. Bought for Michael, kept for Maurya, they are finally all ready to be fashioned into a coffin for Bartley—but there are no nails to finish the job. Someone will have to find some nails.

The new rope is bought to lower Michael's coffin, yet preserved with difficulty from the pig with the black feet; then it makes a halter for Bartley's red mare, which he rides to his death.

The girls try to spare Maurya's feelings by keeping the sight of the bundle of Michael's clothes from her. Yet when she has seen the ghost of Michael himself, Cathleen thinks it better to show her the clothes to prove that Michael has had a clean burial. But then the body of Bartley is brought in. Like the attempt to let Maurya have some sleep, the first thing that happens in the play, these efforts to protect Maurya are futile.

The action of Maurya in trying to keep Bartley at home and Bartley's action in insisting on going may equally be described as to persevere, against overwhelming odds, and in the face of constant and ultimate defeat, in the attempt to protect and preserve and foster the family. All the members of the family stick it out to the end. The plot line is very simple. Not what is included, but what is left out, is remarkable. For example, there is no young man around who has an interest in twenty-year old Cathleen. That would be an interest in another family, another hearthfire; and the action here is to attempt to preserve this hearthfire.

The quality of Synge's achievement is shown by the way in which critics are concerned to demonstrate that this little play is not as tragic as Shakespeare or Sophocles. Thus Ronald Peacock says:

> As a tragedy *Riders to the Sea* is without doubt remarkable in the way it presents unpretentious heroism opposing Sea and Tempest that hang like Fate over men's lives. But it has nothing whatever of the complexity of the tragic processes in human life that we find handled and mastered by the greatest writers. *Riders to the Sea* is a fine piece of tragic art precisely because it does *not* compare with *Oedipus Rex* or the tragedies of Shakespeare. It is elemental but also bare and excessively simple.[16]

Let us look at this simplicity: plays are often described as having a three-part movement—the exposition, the complication, and the unravelling. Kenneth Burke, as Francis Fergusson interprets him, conceives a tragic rhythm of action from purpose through passion to perception.[17] Denis Donoghue explains this rhythm: ". . . The hero (or, if you prefer, the soul) moves from 'purpose' (the taking of a step, an attitude) through action or passion (the pain arising from action) to final perception, a new awareness."[18] But Donoghue does not think that *Riders to the Sea* follows this pattern: ". . . At any stage, the taking by Maurya of a positive course of action is impossible because the scales are too heavily weighted against her (a human conflict is one thing, but conflict between an old woman and the Sea is another). For this reason, action is frustrated, purpose cannot even be formulated. The play ends in Maurya's Acceptance, rather than in any positive perception."[19]

I feel, however, that the play does have the tragic rhythm. And certainly the scales are no more heavily weighted against Maurya than they are against Oedipus. Surely unalterable destiny is an even stronger opponent than the sea. In the first part of the play the characters do take various steps, various attitudes. Maurya is always either in her room seeking rest or on the seashore seeking the body of Michael or in the kitchen seeking to prevent Bartley from going to Galway— Bartley, her youngest son, over whom she can still seek to have some influence. At the same time, the exposition tells us that Bartley has determined to go. Meanwhile Cathleen and Nora take the step of hoping to identify the clothes in the bundle as Michael's and to keep the identification from Maurya. The complication or the passionate stage of the rhythm sets in when Bartley's and Maurya's reasoned purposes clash— Bartley goes off against his mother's will and Maurya refuses him her blessing. The two girls are impatient with the mother and in their impatience forget Bartley's bread. The attempt to improve the situation by sending Maurya to the spring well with Bartley's bread only worsens it. Maurya again withholds her blessing and also sees Michael's ghost, which throws her into terror. The girls' attempt to keep Maurya from knowing of Michael's death is foiled by Maurya's vision, which not only establishes Michael's death in her mind but also presages Bartley's.

This is the low point of the play. Maurya is sunk in despair. Of the optimistic young priest she says, "It's little the like of him knows of the sea . . . Bartley will be lost now, and let you call in Eamon and make me a good coffin out of the white boards, for I won't live after them."[20]

Maurya's attitude here is clearly too self-concerned to be tragic. What Donoghue says about the play as a whole is true about this passage. He quotes a modern description of the tragic experience by F. R. Leavis: "The sense of heightened life that goes with the tragic experience is conditioned by a transcending of the ego—an escape from all attitudes of self-assertion . . . the experience is constructive or creative, and involves recognizing positive value as in some way defined and vindicated by death . . . Significance lies, clearly and inescapably, in the willing adhesion of the individual self to something other than itself."[21] Here Leavis is getting at something like what Yeats and also Arnold had in mind about joy in the tragic close.

". . . On this basis," Donoghue believes, " 'Riders to the Sea' does not constitute the tragic experience, for at least three reasons: firstly, because Maurya's acceptance which ends the play has in it nothing of the positive 'willing adhesion of the individual self to something other than itself'; secondly, because there is in the play no significant equivalent of 'the valued', and thirdly, because in the final analysis the play does not give 'the sense of heightened life.' We may even add a fourth reason, that Maurya's sufferings are determined by forces which do not include her will or her character."[22]

Let us examine the final passage of the play. The cry is heard in the distance by Cathleen and Nora. The third stage of the play, the unravelling, the moment of perception, is beginning. As Maurya tells how Patch's body was brought to the door at some point in the past, Bartley's body is brought to the door in the present.

At first Maurya is lost in a half dream, still in the daze which began with her vision of Michael's ghost. She confuses the deaths of Patch and Michael and Bartley. But immediately she recovers and deals with the matter in hand. When Cathleen says that Michael has been found in the far north, Maurya has one of the most realistic speeches in the play. The old woman still has a strong grasp of reality: "There does be a power of young men floating round in the sea, and what way would they know if it was Michael they had, or another man like him, for when a man is nine days in the sea, and the wind blowing, it's hard set his own mother would be to say what man was in it."[23]

This bitter speech is spoken still from the hell of Maurya's despair—the desperate state of a mother who has lived in perpetual uncertainty about the fate of her children. But the uncertainty ends at this point. The clothes are Michael's. The body is Bartley's. Maurya's struggle is over. "They're all gone now, and there isn't anything more the sea can do to me . . ."[24] Maurya's stature as a tragic heroine must be measured by the power of her opponent the sea and by the length of her struggle against it. In this she is contrasted with Bartley, who, I think, must be played as very young, and who is so easily killed in one of his very first encounters with the sea. Maurya also stands at the opposite pole from the young priest with his easy piety. We are reminded of the end of *King Lear*: "The oldest hath borne most: we that are young/Shall never see so much, nor live so long." All the actions which were started earlier in the play are ended here. The bundle which was concealed from Maurya is now opened and Michael's clothes spread by Maurya over Bartley's feet. The body that Maurya has sought for nine days by the sea shore is found—but it is ironically Bartley's body, not Michael's. The sleep that Maurya was seeking in the opening lines will now come to her. "It's a great rest I'll have now, and great sleeping in the long nights after Samhain . . ."[25]

She sprinkles the Holy Water, but she is only half-risen out of her hell of misery and self-pity and self-concern. Consider the cruelty and callousness of such lines as ". . . and I won't care what way the sea is when the other women will be keening."[26] But "*She kneels down again, crossing herself, and saying prayers under her breath.*"[27]

Cathleen fills the pause by returning to the subject of the white boards. A page back Maurya has asked Cathleen to call in Eamon to make her a coffin. Now Cathleen speaks to an old man of his and Eamon's making a coffin for Bartley. The "fine white boards" of which she speaks in an almost Homeric epithet and the "new cake" they are to eat while building the coffin paradoxically fill the room with suggestions of the scene of potential life, the lively scene that will go on tomorrow while the coffin is being built. The sound of building should be a cheerful sound, a sound connoting new life. The newness that this building process will herald is the newness of Maurya's exhausted peace.

But there is another reason for calling attention to the white boards at this time. Mentioning them points up the fact that Maurya is no longer talking about her own death. She has risen out of the self-concern and self-pity which broke her for a moment, and now she stands up to deliver lines which have a very positive degree of that self-transcendence which Leavis and Donoghue require. It also appeals to a positive value— the peace of God which passes understanding. It is no longer just sleep which she has acquired. It is peace.

They're all together this time, and the end is come. May the Almighty God have mercy on Bartley's soul, and on Michael's soul, and on the souls of Sheamus and Patch, and Stephen and Shawn [*bending her head*] . . . and may He have mercy on my soul, Nora, and on the soul of everyone is left living in the world.[28]

In these words another of the lines of action has its completion. Earlier Maurya, resisting Bartley's going, has refused to return him her blessing. Later she tries to give it, and the words choke in her throat, and she looks up and sees Michael's ghost. But now in the words "God have mercy on Bartley's soul" she frees him for his journey and frees herself from the tensions that went with her earlier refusal. The family is, in some ironic sense that is beyond bitterness, truly together now. The conflicts are over.

It has not been noted, I think, that the conflict between Bartley and Maurya continues in the play to this point and disappears when she now returns the blessing which she earlier refused.

But if that speech appealed to Almighty God, the final speech returns to earth and speaks with almost Homeric epithets again of "a clean burial," "a fine coffin," "a deep grave," and ends with a great commonplace about mortality. The simplicity of it, coming out of the intensity of her experience of bereavement is most impressive and I find in these last two speeches the sense of heightened life which Donoghue seeks for in vain:

> Michael has a clean burial in the far north, by the grace of the Almighty God. Bartley will have a fine coffin out of the white boards, and a deep grave surely . . . What more can we want than that ? . . . No man at all can be living for ever, and we must be satisfied.[29]

It is a heightened life which can endure so much.

Synge in the execution of this plot has succeeded in imitating the action he intended to imitate, and that action is a serious, complete and great one. It seems to me that the character of Maurya and the strength of her struggle must be measured by the length of time she held out against her great opponent. If there is too much passive suffering, not enough positive will in Maurya and her play—that is because Synge chose an action which is suffering, the action of enduring. The fault, then, if any, is in the aim and not the execution.

But if we judge by effect alone, I think we still have to call this little play one of the great modern tragedies because it has that effect of tragic catharsis which Aristotle described as the specific effect of tragedy: to rouse pity and fear in order to transcend them in a consciousness and concern which is no longer self-centred. The change of tone, in the last speeches of the play, from the pronoun "I" to "we" ("we must be satisfied"), from self-concern to universal concern signify the achieved effect of tragedy which Yeats described in another of Synge's plays as "a reverie of passion that mounts and mounts till grief itself has carried [one] beyond grief into pure contemplation . . . that tragic ecstasy which is the best that art—perhaps that life—can give . . ."[30] "The persons upon the stage . . . greaten till they are humanity itself. We feel our minds expand convulsively or spread out slowly like some moon-brightened image-crowded sea."[31] We are "carried beyond time and persons to where passion, living through its thousand purgatorial years, as in the wink of an eye, becomes wisdom . . ."[32]

NOTES

1. *The Portable James Joyce*, with an introduction and notes by Harry Levin (New York, Viking Press, 1947), pp. 481-482.
2. *Autobiographies*, p. 520.
3. *Essays*, pp. 298-299.
4. *Autobiographies*, p. 344.
5. *Ibid.*

6. *Ibid.*, p. 345.
7. *Essays*, p. 316.
8. *C.W.*, III, p. 19.
9. *The Catholic Encyclopoedie* (1911) X, pp. 275-276.
10. *Autobiographies*, p. 511.
11. *Explorations*, p. 106.
12. *Essays*, p. 309, Cf. p. 300.
13. *Ibid.*, p. 336.
14. Matthew Arnold, "Preface to the First Collected Poems," *The Strayed Traveller, Empedocles on Etna, and Other Poems,* with an introduction by William Sharp (London, Walter Scott [1896]), p. 291.
15. *Ibid.*
16. *The Poet in the Theatre* (London, Routledge, 1946), p. 92.
17. K. Burke, *A Grammar of Motives* (New York, Prentice-Hall, 1945), pp. 38-40; F. Fergusson, *The Idea of a Theater* (Princeton University Press, 1949), p. 18.
18. "*Riders to the Sea:* A Study," *University Review*, I, 5, Summer 1955, p. 56.
19. *Ibid.*, p. 57.
20. *C.W.*, III, p. 21.
21. "*Riders to the Sea:* A Study," *loc. cit.*, p. 57. Donoghue cites F. R. Leavis, "Tragedy and the 'Medium'," *The Common Pursuit* (London, Chatto and Windus, 1952), pp. 131-132.
22. *Ibid.*
23. *C.W.* III, p. 23.
24. *Ibid.*
25. *Ibid.*, p. 25.
26. *Ibid.*
27. *Ibid.*
28. *Ibid.*, pp. 25-27.
29. *Ibid.*
30. *Essays*, p. 239.
31. *Ibid.*, p. 245.
32. *Ibid.*, p. 239.

Arthur Sinclair as The Blind Man in The Well of the Saints.
Reproduced by kind permission of Gabriel Fallon and the Abbey Theatre Design Department.

Scenes from the Arabic production of Synge's The Well of the Saints (*Nabn al-Haqiqah*) translated by the Lebanese poet Nusi al-Haj and produced by Munir Abu Dibbs at the Baalbeck International Festival 1969.

THE WELL OF THE SAINTS
AND THE LIGHT OF THIS WORLD

M. J. Sidnell

IT IS A quality of the plays of Synge that though they are most accessible
to the common understanding, they have proved to be extraordinarily
insoluble in the critical crucible. Since the early days when adverse
criticism of his plays was based on a vulgar code of morality and the
defence on his humour, poetry and realism, commentary on the plays
has taken two main approaches. First, there has been a sophisticated
continuation of moral criticism, beginning from the assumption that
there is a "moral" to be found in some form, usually transmuted,
inverted or cancelled by a reductive multiple irony. In recent years,
one of the most favoured transmuted forms of moral content presented
to our view has been that of the aesthetic analogue whereby, for example,
Martin Doul, the blind beggar, becomes a figure for the artist forsaking
reality to live in an Ivory Tower and Christy Mahon a poet in essence;
The Well of the Saints and *The Playboy of the Western World* are described as works based on the contraries of dream and actuality—or
some such opposition—with the poetic imagination as the mediator.[1]
The other main critical approach has been archetypal, the presentation
of mythical, particularly Christian, analogues to elicit the typicality of
the actions of Synge's plays.[2] Here, I propose to take another tack, to
examine in *The Well of the Saints* what I take to be Synge's insistence
in this play (as in others) on the translation *back* from metaphor to
nature, from the typical to the particular and from morality to the
concreteness of experience.

Death is a necessary prerequisite for canonization but in this play we
have a living saint. The People's sense of reality is expressed by their
idiomatic usage. They anticipate the formalities of canon law by ex-
tending adjectival saintliness to its nominal form. A "Saint" in the
dramatis personae alone would make the play historical; in the People's
mouths the designation has, necessarily, an ironical colouring, one
which deepens in those speeches in which the Saint sounds like an
imperious parish priest: "Let you take that man and drive him down
upon the road."[3] Irony is not, however, primarily directed at the
authenticity of the Saint; there is no doubt that his miracles are real
and his appearance proves the asceticism of his life, the rigour with
which he upholds traditional Christian values. In question is the
adequacy of those values and of the experience on which they are

founded. The chief effect of the uncanonical designation is of a collapse of a usual temporal sequence. We are not given the usual historical view of the (completed) life of a recognized saint; instead the People in the play act in conjunction with an only slightly doubtful one. Unlike the Women of Canterbury for whom the actual world is transfigured by their recognition of its intersection with eternity, the People (from whom the Douls are distinct) exist in a world in which actuality is in a comfortable accommodation with a conception of the eternal represented by the Saint. Necessarily Christ-like and perhaps reminiscent of St. Kevin (the historical saint of the place),[4] the Saint is not a veiled form of either but rather an embodiment of a principle. Like a stream round a stone the life of the community flows round him.

The ordinary life of the community is represented as work, gossip, wooing and wedding, a pattern temporarily disrupted by Martin Doul's obstinate refusal to take his assigned place. The setting for these activities is the cycle of the seasons—or rather part of the cycle, for the first act takes place in late autumn and the second and third in winter and spring. There is no summer in the play and the missing season indicates the incompleteness of the Douls' experience. The Saint's experience is incomplete, too, for he is absent from the winter world of the second act.

The second act has work and sexuality for its themes and the Saint's earlier advice to the People is especially pertinent to it:

> . . . you'd do well to be thinking on the way sin has brought blindness to the world, and to be saying a prayer for your own sakes against false prophets and heathens, and the words of women and smiths, and all knowledge that would soil the soul or the body of a man.[5]

'The words of women and smiths" not only echoes St. Patrick but also points to the two characters from whose way Martin turns in his final choice of blindness. The scene for Act Two is the roadside before "a forge, with broken wheels etc., lying about. A well near centre . . ." Martin Doul's task is to sit in the "black wintery air,"[6] cutting freezing sticks. Timmy the Smith has stripped Martin of his coat and will soon set him to "roasting" before the fire in the forge. The world Martin has found himself in is uncommonly like hell as traditionally described. When Timmy complains that Martin has done "the devil's work" with his "talk of fine looks"[7] we recall that Timmy did that work for the Douls. Moreover the work Martin is now performing for Timmy may be thought of under the same category, especially if one recalls, as Synge did, that "In Irish folklore, smiths were thought to be . . . more or less in league with the powers of darkness."[8] But however tempting it may be to slide from suggestion to metaphor and from ocular vision to the metaphysical kind, Act Two is not overall a vision of hell but, on the contrary, a view of the world which stimulates in Martin the vision of hell with which the act ends:

> . . . may God blight them this day, and my own soul the same hour with them, the way I'll see them after, Molly Byrne and Timmy the Smith, the two of them on a high bed, and they screeching in hell . . . It'll be a grand thing that time to look on the two of them; and they twisting and roaring out, and twisting and roaring again, one day and the next day, and each day always and ever.[9]

Together, Molly and Timmy are responsible in Martin's eyes for the misery of his condition as a sighted man. Molly is piqued in the first act that the Saint would "walk by the finest woman in Ireland . . . and not trouble to raise his two eyes to look upon her face,"[10] but in kindling Martin's lust, enjoying the tribute of his words, denying, ridiculing and exposing him, part of her womanly nature is fulfilled at Martin's expense. Martin, however, does not merely suffer, he and his wife have also contributed to the general discontent:

> But it's a queer thing the way yourself and Mary Doul are after setting every person in this place, and up to Rathvanna, talking of nothing, and thinking of nothing, but the way they do be looking in the face.[11]

Having ignored it initially, the Saint later mentions "the image of the Lord is thrown upon men,"[12] but he has no spiritual light to shed on this phenomenon and Martin has to make do with the light of this world, by which he finds only Molly Byrne pleasing to his sight:

> It's a power of dirty days, and dark mornings, and shabby-looking fellows . . . we do have to be looking on when we've our sight, God help us, but there's one fine thing we have, to be looking on a grand, white, handsome girl the like of you . . . and every time I set my eyes on you, I do be blessing the saints, and the holy water, and the power of the Lord Almighty in the heavens above.[18]

That Molly Byrne or her like should be the perspective through which Martin is brought to praise God is apparently outside the Saint's understanding of the relationship between God and man.

Tiresias, Oedipus and Gloucester (pagans all, be it noted) are precedents enough to suggest that eye-sight is not to be equated with the apprehension of reality. Nor in *The Well of the Saints* is the Christian metaphor of light and darkness assumed, even in an inverted form. On the contrary that simple metaphorical antithesis is destroyed by the complex actuality of the play. When, at the second coming of the Saint, Martin Doul chooses to remain in darkness, the choice is made on the grounds of experience and knowledge—both quite obviously partial—and the issue is not between reality and delusion (or actuality and imagination) but between various ways of understanding the world.

There is reality and delusion in both sight and blindness. As we see in the last act, the ways of understanding the world are based upon experience of it, and these ways are distinguished, detached from the customary muddle of life, at the climax of the dramatic action—Martin's choice of blindness. Before turning to the moment of choice, however, there is something to be said about the condition which makes the choice possible, the miraculous cure of the first act.

The cure takes place in the context of two kinds of misunderstanding. The first arises from the Douls' preoccupation—made intense by deprivation—with the delights of the eye and from the false reports of Timmy and others who have fed the flame. The disillusionment that comes with sight is twofold: of lesser importance is the inevitable discovery by each of the ugliness of the other; and the worse shock is the self-image that each sees in the mirror of the other's words. In the latter case, as elsewhere in the play, the tongue that reports, not the eye that sees, is the immediate cause of misery. (Mary's function, incidentally, becomes a passive one after the Douls' reciprocal viewing of the first act; a weakness in the play, perhaps). For the audience, of course, the initial contrast between the report and the view depends upon the ironic conjunction of the words of the Douls and their appearance in the stage presentation. When the audience is confronted with the contrast for the second time, through the eyes of the Douls themselves, they see the difference feelingly. The audience, like the People, is seeing now in a new way, as the recently blind see. There is a sense in which the Douls, the People and the audience are all the subjects of that first part of the action of the play to which Synge pointed in his discarded title, *When the Blind See*.

The second misunderstanding associated with the cure is the Saint's assessment of the Douls and his ignorance of the delusion they enjoy. In his eyes they are the representatives of the wretchedness of the world for whom God's mercy is as appropriate as the praise they should return for it. Having no cause for personal vanity, the Douls, as the Saint sees them, should be the more ready to free themselves of it; moreover the proper use of the gift of sight, he advises, is not to be "minding the faces of men" but to observe "the splendour of the Spirit of God . . . shining out through the big hills."[14] His advice presents two difficulties: first, the timing of the cure is unfortunate in that it is followed by bleak winter days in which the splendour he speaks of is scarcely apparent; more seriously he does not acknowledge any discrepancy between spiritual and bodily beauty in the human form such as appears revealed to Martin in the shape of Molly.

Whatever else it may be, it is not surprising to us that Martin should find the appearance of the world a frustration and a cheat. Molly Byrne is real enough in one way but though Martin's sight urges on his other senses she might as well be for them an optical illusion. Even if he could have her he would soon find her no more than a trick of the eyes. As Mat Simon shrewdly observes to Molly herself:

> ... it's more joy dark Martin got from the lies we told of that hag is kneeling by the path, than your own man will get from you, day or night, and he living at your side.[15]

Part of the experience on which Martin has to base his choice is the sight of Molly who, for all her beauty, belongs in hell, and the sight of the Saint who, for all his godliness, disgusts the eye:

> ... for if you're a fine saint itself, it's more sense is in a blind man and more power maybe than you're thinking at all. Let you walk on now with your worn feet, and your welted knees, and your fasting, holy ways have left a big head on you and a thin pitiful arm.[16]

In opposing the Saint, Martin becomes in one way like him, for as the Saint sees by a spiritual light God's splendour so Martin in his mind sees "a grand sky, and . . . lakes, and broadening rivers, and hills are waiting for the spade and the plough."[17] But though both find ordinary sight insufficient or worse, their understandings of the world are quite different, as the name Doul (an approximation to an Irish form for Devil) suggests.[18] The opposition of the Saint and Doul is Blakean, the two views held in tension by their incompleteness, for though Martin has "never set eyes on the summer,"[19] and it might make a difference if he had, yet neither has the Saint looked on Molly Byrne's face nor come to terms with the vanity and lust of Martin's human kind.

All Synge's plays end with death or departure and in *The Well of the Saints*, the Douls set off southwards at the end of the play. In some ways their proposed journey recalls Christian's progress through the Valley of the Shadow:

> ... we'd have a right to be gone, if it's a long way itself, where you do have to be walking with the slough of wet on the one side and a slough of wet on the other, and you going a stony path with the north wind blowing behind.[20]

However, the Douls' actual journey will be unlike Christian's allegorical one in that Christian has the light from God's candle, which the Douls have denied themselves, to guide him through the worst part. If the Douls should escape the ditch "into which the blind have led the blind in all ages" there will be other hazards to beset their dark way. Timmy the Smith prophesies:

> There's a power of deep rivers with floods in them where you do have to be lepping the stones and you going to the south, so I'm thinking the two of them will be drowned together in a short while, surely.[21]

The words of smiths are suspect and, here, Timmy sounds like the neighbours who attempt to restrain Christian. So the allegory of *The Pilgrim's Progress*, though apparently quite consciously echoed by Synge,[22] is one that may be applied in quite contrary ways to the play, which is to say that it had best not be *applied* at all. The echo does, however, force upon us an examination of the given experience of the play in an attempt to discover, as from life itself, the unassigned meaning.

The understanding of the Saint and the different understanding of the People are presented with simplicity and clarity by Synge as the setting of the complex experience of Martin Doul. The spiritual insight of the Saint is valued but not shared by the People who, nevertheless, are brought into a kind of alliance with him when he marries the couple at the end of the play. In Martin's understanding, the Saint's view is inadequate and the accommodation in the world achieved by Timmy and Molly leads, he hopes, to hell. After he has seen, Martin, finding no place in that ill-founded alliance of Saint and People, chooses a different way entirely. Synge has displayed the experiential basis of Martin's choice in rigorously physical terms: the *voice* of a "fine, soft, rounded woman"[23] contrasted with the "wicked grin"[24] of Molly when she is "making game with a man";[25] sunshine and cloud alternately seen and felt; the blind couple attempting to hide from the People. In such images and actions the metaphor of light and darkness is exploded and the actuality put in its place. What we make of Martin's choice is the way out of the play's action into reflection; the reconstruction, if we want it, of metaphor and metaphysic from an unaccommodated man's fragments of reality.

NOTES

1. See for example Alan Price, *Synge and Anglo-Irish Drama* (London, Methuen, 1961), especially pp. 161 and 176.
2. See for example Northrop Frye, *Anatomy of Criticism* (Princeton University Press, 1957), pp. 38 *et. seq.*
3. *C.W.*, III, p. 145. I wish to express here my great indebtedness to Professor Saddlemyer's edition with its invaluable textual and other notes.
4. The "lonely mountainous district on the east of Ireland" is near Ballinaclash in South Wicklow. See *C.W.*, III, p. 70, note 4.
5. *C.W.*, III, p. 91.
6. *Ibid.*, p. 103.
7. *Ibid.*, p. 111.
8. *Ibid.*, p. 90, note 5.
9. *Ibid.*, p. 123.
10. *Ibid.*, p. 89.

11. *Ibid.*, p. 111.
12. *Ibid.*, p. 139.
13. *Ibid.*, p. 111.
14. *Ibid.*, p. 101.
15. *Ibid.*, p. 93.
16. *Ibid.*, p. 149.
17. *Ibid.*, p. 141.
18. Cp. W. B. Yeats, "The Book of the Great Dhoul and Hanrahan the Red," *The Secret Rose* (London, Lawrence and Bullen, 1897).
19. *C.W.*, III, p. 141.
20. *Ibid.*, pp. 149-151.
21. *Ibid.*, p. 151.
22. *Ibid.*, p. 150, note 1: "To Meyerfield Synge explains 'a slough of wet' as 'a wet quagmire or bog. Do you remember the "Slough of Despond" in *Pilgrim's Progress* of Bunyan? The word is used in the same sense in Ireland now'."
23. *Ibid.*, p. 73.
24. *Ibid.*, p. 143.
25. *Ibid.*

靈驗

坪内博士戯曲案

The cover of the Reigen by Dr. Shoyo Tsubouchi (1859–1935) published by Kinkido
in 1914, showing a priest and two blind beggars. The photographs of this and the two
illustrations on the following page were kindly supplied by Dr. Oshima.

Frontispiece for Act II of the Reigen, *before the blacksmith's shop.*

Frontispiece for Act I of the Reigen, *a village road before an old temple.*

CHRISTY MAHON AND THE
APOTHEOSIS OF LONELINESS
Augustine Martin

I

"It'll be a poor thing for the household man where you go sniffing for a female wife".   (Michael James)
The Playboy of the Western World, C.W., IV, p. 153.

AGREEMENT is general among critics that *The Playboy of the Western World* is a masterpiece. But there is still a curious diversity of opinion about the precise nature of its excellence. Those among its first audience who were not infuriated by the play were puzzled by it. Those who did not condemn it in sociological terms as a libel or a travesty of Irish life wondered what else it might be. Synge himself hastily called it an "extravaganza"[1] and swiftly withdrew the label. Yeats, arguing with a judge in court, preferred to call it an "exaggeration."[2] Even when critics took the debate beyond the cockpit of affronted patriotism they could not reach agreement either on its dominating theme or on the allied problem of its dramatic category.

Una Ellis-Fermor called it a "tragi-comedy" which took for its main theme "the growth of fantasy in a mind or a group of minds."[3] Ann Saddlemyer expands this insight when she suggests that "in *The Playboy* we see the power of the myth to create a reality out of the dream or illusion itself."[4] Professor Henn in his Introduction to the Methuen edition of the *Plays and Poems* outlines seven possible readings of the play. He suggests that it might be seen as a "semi-tragedy"; as a "free comedy", in which moral issues are reversed, transcended or ignored in the desire for "energy"; as a "Dionysiac comedy"; as a "satire" in which Christy becomes a "comic Oedipus"; as "mock-heroic" in which Christy becomes a "comic Odysseus"; as "a tragi-comic piece with the Widow Quin as Nausicaa"; and finally, a reading he seems to favour, as a tragedy with Pegeen as the "heroine-victim",[5] Norman Podhoretz in a persuasive essay suggests that the play has "the myth of rebellion against the father as its basis."[6] P. L. Henry sees Christy as the "Playboy-Hero" and finds parallels to him in *Beowulf* and the heroic Irish sagas.[7] Stanley Sultan finds in Christy's person "a pervasive, sincere and full-fledged analogue to Christ."[8] Alan Price sees it primarily as a play in which "Christy's imagination transforms the dream into actuality."[9] Ann Saddlemyer believes that "*The Playboy of the Western World* deals with the actual creation of myth."[10] Synge himself has remarked that "there are, it may be hinted, many sides to *The Playboy*";[11] the critics continue to bear him out. Clearly the play is capable of yielding a wide diversity of valid readings, depending what "side" one approaches it from. But where is its centre? What basic myth or fable does it enact? What theme is embodied in that fable? What kind of play is it? These are still questions worth asking.

II

More than one critic has complained that the end of *The Shadow of the Glen* is unconvincing. The reconciliation between Daniel Burke and Michael Dara—who after all had been planning to supplant him as Nora's husband—has been seen as too sudden, too much of a *volte-face*. "I was thinking to strike you, Michael Dara," Burke says, "but you're a quiet man, God help you, and I don't mind you at all."[12] The point of course is that they are two of a kind; they are settled men, householders. They want a world in which they can have their drinks in peace. Michael Dara is no longer a threat once Nora and the Tramp, the people of passion and poetry, have been expelled. With their expulsion society has righted itself and can get on with its quotidian business. The pattern is central to Synge's comedies. As the curtain falls on *The Well of the Saints* the free-booters, Martin and Mary Doul, have departed, and the Saint leads in the settled man, Timmy the Smith, and his bride to be married. In *The Tinker's Wedding* the Priest is left "master of the situation"[13] while the tinkers retreat into their vagrant irresponsibility. The end of *The Playboy* gives a richer, more complex, version of the same basic pattern. Michael James remarks with relief that "we'll have peace now for our drinks,"[14] while a disconsolate Pegeen laments, too late, the loss of her only playboy. She realizes that Christy's visitation had presented her with a vivid possibility of passion and poetry, and that she has failed to grasp it. With the exit of Christy, launched on his "romping lifetime", the spirit of Dionysus has departed. She is back where we had found her at the first curtain, in the world of Sean Keogh and the papal dispensation and the trousseau that must be ordered from Castlebar.

The two life-views offered by the play may usefully be called Dionysiac and Apollonian. Dionysiac is the more easily acceptable: Daniel Corkery was perhaps the first to apply it when he rejected the term "extravaganza"—"Dionysiac would have served him better, meaning by that word the serving of the irresponsible spirit of natural man."[15] Northrop Frye, on the other hand, describes Apollonian comedy as "the story of how a hero becomes accepted by a society of gods."[16] If we take the definition at its "low mimetic"[17] level we can see that *The Playboy*, for a good deal of its action, shapes like this kind of comedy, only to swerve into Dionysiac triumph in its final resolution.

It is clear from the early drafts[18] of the play that Synge considered and rejected many different kinds of ending: he contemplated a possible marriage between Christy and the Widow Quin, a *menage a trois* involving the two Mahons and the Widow Quin, even a wedding between Christy and Pegeen. But it became increasingly clear to him that his material demanded that Christy refuse membership of the settled community, and also that the discovery of his own nature involved the discovery and recognition of his real father and the rejection of the pseudo-Dionysian Michael James. For despite his recklessness at the wake, despite his willingness—at least while he is drunk—to have Christy as a son-in-law, Michael James ends up with a pathetic anxiety to protect our "little cabins from the treachery of law."[19] On the other hand Old Mahon's final "Is it me?" and "I'm crazy again"[20] betoken his delighted recognition that Christy is really his son, instinct with the same savagery, energy and *braggadocio*.[21]

Indeed one can discern three groups of characters in the play, and distinguish them in terms of the Dionysiac and Appollonian postures. Old Mahon from the beginning and Christy towards the end embody the Dionysiac freedom, energy and excess. Shawn Keogh and the offstage but influential Father Reilly, at their low mimetic level, represent a version of the Apollonian—the rational, the settled, the well-ordered existence. The latter attitude finds expression not only in character and social pattern but in a sort of ritual invocation of "the Holy Father and the Cardinals of Rome,"[22] of "St. Joseph and St. Patrick and St. Brigid and St. James."[23] In between is a group—one might call them the "pseudo-Dionysians"—who waver between the two positions. Michael James, Philly and Jimmy rejoice in the Bacchantic excess of Kate Cassidy's wake, but when their security is threatened they opt for the domestic pieties. They salute the Dionysiac vigour and daring; in the person of Christy they try to accommodate it, even to use it. But their ambivalence is patent, and it provides a good deal of the play's comic incongruity, as with Jimmy's remark before leaving for the wake: "Now, by the grace of God, herself will be safe this night, with a man killed his father holding danger from the door."[24]

Pegeen is torn between the two attitudes. Her intended marriage to Shawn clearly implies no acquiescence to his values. When he asserts that "we're as good this place as another, maybe, and as good these times as we were forever," she replies with scorn:

As good, is it? Where now will you meet the like of Daneen Sullivan knocked the eye from a peeler, or Marcus Quin, God rest him, got six months for maiming the ewes, and he a great warrant to tell stories of holy Ireland till he'd have the old women shedding down tears about their feet. Where will you find the like of them, I'm saying?[25]

The irony of her situation is, of course, that when she does encounter the likes of them in Christy she proves unequal to the challenge thus presented. She recognises in Christy a kinsman of the poets—"fine fiery fellows with great rages when their temper's roused"[24]—and approves. But she tries to domesticate him, to tame his fire. When she is presented in the final scenes with the full reality of his fiery nature she fails. As Norman Podhoretz puts it, she "can perceive greatness but cannot rise to it."[27] She is the tragic figure of the play. But that is not to agree with Professor Henn that the play is a tragedy, her tragedy.

The play is Christy's. It is about his escape to freedom between the Scylla and Charybdis of loneliness on the one hand and domination on the other. It is about his collision with settled society and his victorious rejection of it in favour of a new triumphalist attitude to the world. If the collision with society had resulted in his destruction the play would have been a tragedy. As it celebrates the victory of the aggressive individual will over the immoveable forces of society it must be deemed a Dionysiac comedy—the only great one of its kind that I know.

The core of this comedy is Christy's loneliness. Synge went to great pains to enunciate this theme, to build it up gradually till it achieves full expression half-way through the play. In the early drafts[28] Christy's loneliness is dwelt on at length in his conversation with Pegeen in the first act; but much of the material is later struck out with the marginal note—"Reserve this lonesome motif for II."[15] Eventually it is towards the middle of Act II that the theme gets its full orchestration. There, when Pegeen threatens to send him away Christy replies with bleak realism, "I was lonesome all times and born lonesome, I'm thinking, as the moon of dawn."[30] This is the crux of his condition. How is he to heal the wound of his lonesomeness? Can he do so without exchanging one kind of domination for another? Because it seems at this point that he can only have Pegeen on her own overbearing terms. At this point he is willing to accept those terms; as yet he knows no better, he has not fully discovered himself. When she relents ("Lay down that switch and throw some sods on the fire. You're pot-boy in this place, and I'll not have you mitch off from us now"[31]) his relief is painful:

CHRISTY [*astonished, slowly*]. It's making game of me you were [*following her with fearful joy*], and I can stay so, working at your side, and I not lonesome from this mortal day.[32]

It will be helpful to trace Christy's development to this point of the drama.

III

Christy comes in out of the darkness: he has been "groaning wicked like a maddening dog"[33] in the furzy ditch—"a dark lonesome place."[34] As he tells his story there is a touching contrast between the delight he is getting from such unexpected and appreciative company and the loneliness out of which he has emerged. He describes himself as "a poor orphaned traveller, has a prison behind him, and hanging before, and hell's gap gaping below."[35] His home is "a distant place . . . a windy corner of high, distant hills."[36] Since Tuesday was a week he has been "walking forward facing hog, dog or divil on the highway of the road."[37] When Pegeen probes him about the girls he might have beguiled in his travels another, and important, aspect of his lonesomeness is revealed in his reply:

> I've said it [his story] nowhere till this night, I'm telling you, for I've seen none the like of you the eleven days I am walking the world, looking over a low ditch or a high ditch on my north or south, into stony scattered fields, or scribes of bog, where you'd see young limber girls, and fine prancing women making laughter with the men.[38]

In the same sentence the deprivation of his past and his emerging sexual confidence are suggested.

The story of his domination by his father unfolds alongside the theme of his lonesomeness. In his description of Old Mahon in the horrors of drink the full Dionysiac chord is struck:

> It's that you'd say surely if you seen him and he after drinking for weeks, rising up in the red dawn, or before it maybe, and going out into the yard as naked as an ash tree in the moon of May, and shying clods against the visage of the stars till he'd put the fear of death into the banbhs and the screeching sows.[39]

The presence of Old Mahon in Christy's life had in itself been ferocious and formidable. It became unbearable, we are told in the second act, when he tried to force Christy into marriage with the woman who had suckled him as a child. It is this that rouses his spirits to "a deed of blood." When Norman Podhoretz suggests that the play's underlying myth is "rebellion against the father"[40] he gives us, I believe, precisely half the story. The other half is the recognition and acceptance of the father, and this is enacted in the reversal at the end, after the second and deliberate "killing." In the meantime Christy must discover and reject an alternative and different father in Michael James, a different form of female domination in Pegeen Mike. It is significant that Pegeen is the first person to offer him violence when first he enters the Flaherty cabin, and that she behaves towards him with the most surly possessiveness (*seizing his arm* and *shaking him*) when the Widow Quin makes her play for him towards the end of Act I. Before she leaves, the Widow Quinn warns him that "there's right torment will await you here if you go romancing with her like."[41] Therefore, though Christy may be ingenuously happy with his "great luck and company",[42] the audience watching the first curtain fall has its own well founded reservations.

At the opening of Act II we find Christy transformed with the prospects of companionship which his new life seems to hold for him. He can henceforth spend his days "talking out with swearing Christians in place of my old dogs and cat."[43] Immediately he has an audience of young girls to whom he retells the story which has now grown to heroic proportions.[44] He is praised for his eloquence as well as for his daring. The toast proposed to him and the Widow Quin by Sara Tansey compares them—both killers, and loners—to the "outlandish lovers in the sailor's song"[45] and goes on to invoke the extravagant Dionysiac values to which Christy now aspires in his imagination, but which he has yet to embody and realize in life and action:

> Drink a health to the wonders of the western world, the pirates, preachers, poteen-makers, with the jobbing jockies, parching peelers, and the juries fill their stomachs selling judgments of the English law.[46]

It is at this moment that Pegeen returns, drives them from the house, and turns on Christy with quite gratuitous cruelty. Here we see some of the "torment" that the Widow Quin had predicted for him. And it is here that the theme of loneliness is given its full expression. Christy is forced to choose between an obedient security with Pegeen on the one hand and the lonesome roads on the other. One could argue that this is Christy's first failure: he hasn't grown sufficiently into his new self to make the choice appropriate to his nature. As Synge seems to have worked harder on this than on almost any other scene in the play it is worth examining at length:

> CHRISTY [loudly]. What joy would they [the neighbour girls] have to bring hanging to the likes of me?
> PEGEEN. It'd queer joys they have, and who knows the thing they'd do, if it'd make the green stones cry itself to think of you swaying and swiggling at the butt end of a rope, and you with a fine, stout neck, God bless you! the way you'd be a half an hour, in great anguish, getting your death.
> CHRISTY [getting his boots and putting them on]. If there's that terror of them, it'd be best, maybe, I went on wandering like Esau or Cain and Abel on the sides of Neifin or the Erris Plain.
> PEGEEN [beginning to play with him]. It would, may be, for I've heard the Circuit Judges this place is a heartless crew.
> CHRISTY [bitterly]. It's more than judges this place is a heartless crew. [Looking up at her.] And isn't it a poor thing to be starting again and I a lonesome fellow will be looking out on women and girls the way the needy fallen spirits do be looking on the Lord?
> PEGEEN. What call have you to be lonesome when there's poor girls walking Mayo in their thousands now?

CHRISTY [*grimly*]. It's well you know what call I have. It's well you know it's a lonesome thing to be passing small towns with the lights shining sideways when the night is down, or going in strange places with a dog nosing[47] before you and a dog nosing behind, or drawn to the cities where you'd hear a voice kissing and talking deep love in every shadow of the ditch, and you passing on with an empty hungry stomach failing from your heart.

PEGEEN. I'm thinking you're an odd man, Christy Mahon. The oddest walking fellow I ever set my eyes on to this hour to-day.

CHRISTY. What would any be but odd men and they living lonesome in the world?[48]

Two points are worth making here. Christy talks in the language and imagery of an outsider. It is the moving imagery of a traveller looking in at the settled world, wondering what it is like, certain that it alone holds the answer to his deprivation. Furthermore the warmth of this settled world is continuously seen in terms of sexual love. The one implies the other; his choice is between Pegeen Mike and exterior darkness. They slowly work towards a reconciliation, almost a declaration of love. But Pegeen's final remark before the entry of Shawn Keogh establishes her dominance in the relationship:

I'm thinking you'll be a loyal young lad to have working around, and if you vexed me a while since with your leaguing with the girls, I wouldn't give a thraneen for a lad hadn't a mighty spirit in him and a gamey heart.[49]

His "wildness" is approved, so long as it dances to her tune.

Meanwhile the forces of society are working for his expulsion. Shawn Keogh, ambiguously abetted by the Widow Quin, tries to bribe him with a suit of clothes and a ticket for America. He fails, and the plot seems set fair for a romantic resolution, when Old Mahon appears. There is savage dramatic irony in the scene where Christy cowers behind the door and listens to his past being rehearsed for the Widow Quin in his father's contemptuous vision:

MAHON [*with a shout of derision*]. Running wild, is it? If he seen a red petticoat coming swinging over the hill, he'd be off to hide in the sticks, and you'd see him shooting out his sheep's eyes between the little twigs and leaves, and his two ears rising like a hare looking through a gap. Girls indeed!

WIDOW QUIN. It was drink maybe?

MAHON. And he a poor fellow would get drunk on the smell of a pint . . . ![50]

It is now evident that Christy must defeat or outwit his father if he is to realize his expectations. For the first time we find a genuine, if impotent, anger rising in him; and this anger is embodied in rhetoric that becomes more vivid and fearless as the play proceeds:

> CHRISTY [*breaking out*]. His one son, is it? May I meet him with one tooth and it aching, and one eye to be seeing seven and seventy divils in the twists of the road, and one old timber leg on him to limp into the scalding grave. [*Looking out.*] There he is now crossing the strands, and that the Lord God would send a high wave to wash him from the world.[51]

The second act ends therefore with Christy poised between a past that holds only humiliation, impotence and loneliness, and a future that seems to offer him the vivid things—love, companionship, admiration and, more problematically, freedom.

When Old Mahon reappears at the opening of Act III the resemblances between him and Christy are deftly emphasised. He too has been walking the roads "and winning clean beds and the fill of my belly four times in the day, and I doing nothing but telling stories of that naked truth."[52] He is as vainglorious about the resilience of his skull as Christy was about his "one single blow." He has Christy's eloquence if not his lyricism. He exults in the wildness of his excess: at one time he had seen "ten scarlet divils letting on they'd cork my spirit in a gallon can; and one time I seen rats as big as badgers sucking the life blood from the butt of my lug . . ."; the authorities in the Union know him as a "terrible and fearful case, the way that there I was one time screeching in a straitened waistcoat with seven doctors writing out my sayings in a printed book . . ."[53]

Furthermore, like his son, he is constantly described in the language and imagery—whether his own or Christy's—as an outsider, a wanderer. Though he owns a farm he never appears as a householder; he is consistently evoked in terms of the open air, the roads, the taverns, the prisons and asylums. We recall how Christy had described him to Pegeen in Act I as "a man never gave peace to any saving when he'd get two months . . . for battering peelers or assaulting men",[54] and we recall that Pegeen had admired a certain Daneen Sullivan and another Marcus Quin who not only boasted similar feats but who had the eloquence to make them into a "gallous" story. It is also notable that Old Mahon's descriptions of Christy present him in terms of the hills, the fields and the road—never of the house. These clear indications of an elemental kinship between them tend subtly to offset their mutual antagonism throughout and help to prepare us not only for their reversal of roles, but also their reconciliation in the recognition scene at the end. This recognition is hinted at when Old Mahon, watching the races on the strand, sees his own son carrying all before him. But he is not ready yet for the real recognition—that Christy is truly his son, an even greater "playboy" than himself. This insight can only be reached when Christy recognises Mahon as his real father, thereby rejecting the men of Mayo and their law-fearing timidity, and by transcending his infatuation for Pegeen.

But first, in that remarkable love scene with Pegeen in Act III, we are permitted to see Christy in full possession of his powers of eloquence, passion and tenderness playing for "the crowning prize"[55] and winning. Here Christy carries Pegeen triumphantly into his out-door world: the language in which he wooes her is redolent of move-ment, of the outdoors, of "Neifin in the dews of night."[56] She baulks coyly for a moment at his "poacher's love,"[57] but cannot help yielding to it: "If I was your wife, I'd be along with you those nights, Christy Mahon, the way you'd see I was a great hand at coaxing bailiffs, or coining funny nicknames for the stars of night."[58] Christy for the first time seems to be winning on his own terms. The play seems to be moving towards the resolution of traditional romantic comedy, with a wedding between Christy and Pegeen, and a possible second between Old Mahon and the Widow Quin—a victory for Apollo. But Pegeen is not Nora Burke; and the play turns swiftly towards a different and altogether more satisfactory conclusion.

Christy is now "mounted on the spring-tide of the stars of luck";[59] Pegeen swears to wed him "and not renege";[60] Michael James—not without fumbling reservations—gives them his drunken blessing. It seems the moment of extreme felicity: Christy has found status, love, a new father. But it is a false felicity, because his real father is still alive. The sudden appearance of Old Mahon changes everything. Immediately Pegeen reneges. Her reason is the social one: she thinks it bad "the world should see me raging for a Munster liar and the fool of men."[61] Christy now goes through a series of traumatic insights. First he tries to deny Old Mahon. He then appeals vainly for help to the two women. Then a vision of his past loneliness drives him to desperation:

> CHRISTY. And I must go back into my torment is it, or run off like a vagabond straying through the Unions with the dusts of August making mudstains in the gullet of my throat, or the winds of March blowing on me till I'd make an oath I felt them making whistles of my ribs within.[62]

The language and reference are strongly reminiscent of his father's. Now Old Mahon threatens him; the crowd jeers him; he begins to see the truth of his situation, the folly of his desire to be one of them:

> CHRISTY [in low and intense voice]. Shut your yelling, for if you're after making a mighty man of me this day by the power of a lie, you're setting me now to think if it's a poor thing to be lonesome, it's worse maybe go mixing with the fools of earth.[63]

His second insight comes after he has "killed" Old Mahon the second time. He thinks that Pegeen will take him back now, will "be giving me praises the same as in the hours gone by."[64] But he must transcend this vanity. She rejects him more emphatically: for her there is "a great gap between a gallous story and a dirty deed."[65] Again invoking the social ethic she urges the Mayo men to take him to the peelers "or the lot of us will likely be put on trial for his deed to-day."[66] As she prepares a lighted sod to "scorch his leg", he realizes the foolishness of his love for her. Now he is utterly alone, and it is significant that now his terror disappears. His true nature emerges in all its fierceness. His language rises to a fine reckless crescendo:

> CHRISTY. You're blowing for to torture me? [*His voice rising and growing stronger.*] That's your kind, is it? Then let the lot of you be wary, for if I've to face the gallows I'll have a gay march down, I tell you, and shed the blood of some of you before I die.
> SHAWN [*in terror*]. Keep a good hold, Philly. Be wary for the love of God, for I'm thinking he would liefest wreak his pains on me.
> CHRISTY [*almost gaily*]. If I do lay my hands on you, it's the way you'll be at the fall of night hanging as a scarecrow for the fowls of hell. Ah, you'll have a gallous jaunt I'm saying, coaching out through Limbo with my father's ghost.
> SHAWN [*to* PEGEEN]. Make haste, will you? Oh, isn't he a holy terror, and isn't it true for Father Reilly that all drink's a curse that has the lot of you so shaky and uncertain now.
> CHRISTY. If I can wring a neck among you, I'll have a royal judgment looking on the trembling jury in the courts of law. And won't there be crying out in Mayo the day I'm stretched up on the rope with ladies in their silks and satins snivelling in their lacy kerchiefs, and they rhyming songs and ballads on the terror of my fate? [*He squirms round on the floor and bites* SHAWN'S *leg.*]
> SHAWN [*shrieking*]. My leg's bit on me! He's the like of a mad dog, I'm thinking, the way that I will surely die.
> CHRISTY [*delighted with himself*]. You will then, the way you can shake out hell's flags of welcome for my coming in two weeks or three, for I'm thinking Satan hasn't many have killed their da in Kerry and in Mayo too.[67]

It is now that Old Mahon comes in again, "to be killed a third time",[68] and the two father figures, representing two different life-views, confront each other. Michael, sobered and diminished, pleads "apologetically" for the safety of his little cabin and his daughter's security while Old Mahon rejoices in a future of bravado and adventure in which his son and he will "have great times from this out telling stories of the villainy of Mayo and the fools is here."[69] It is here that Christy has his final insight and his ultimate victory. He now knows that he not only has mastered himself but subdued his father as well. He will go, but the roles will be reversed; he will be "master of all fights from now."[70] He has at last discovered his true Dionysiac nature, and in discovering it he has shaken off all domination and transfigured his lonesomeness into a posture of gay, predatory adventure. In the parting speech the wildness of the father is elevated and transformed in the poetry and passion of the son:

> CHRISTY. Ten thousand blessings upon all that's here, for you've turned me a likely gaffer in the end of all, the way I'll go romancing through a romping lifetime from this hour to the dawning of the judgment day . . . [71]

So the freebooters take to their proper element, the road, and the timid people of Mayo take to their drinks, their hopes, their lamentations. The astringent light of comedy has clarified each role, defined each relation.

NOTES

1. Quoted by Green and Stephens, *Synge*, p. 240.
2. *Freeman's Journal*, 31 January 1907, p.8. The passage occurs in the prosecution of Patrick Columb (sic) for creating a disturbance at a performance of *The Playboy of the Western World*. Yeats is being cross-examined by Mr. Lidwell, for the defendant, before Mr Mahony:
   "Mr Lidwell: Did you read the play? Yes, and passed it.
   Mr Lidwell: Is it a caricature of the Irish people? It is no more a caricature of Ireland than *Macbeth* is a caricature of the people of Scotland or *Falstaff* a caricature of the gentlemen of England. The play is AN EXAMPLE OF THE EXAGGERATION OF ART. I have not the slightest doubt but that we shall have more of these disturbances.
   Mr Lidwell: Is the play typical of the Irish people? No! It is an exaggeration.
   Then you admit it is a caricature? An exaggeration."
3. *The Irish Dramatic Movement* (London, Methuen, 1954), p. 175.
4. *J. M. Synge and Modern Comedy* (Dublin, Dolmen Press, 1967), p. 23.
5. *The Plays and Poems of J. M. Synge* (London, Methuen, 1963), pp. 57-58.
6. "Synge's *Playboy*: Morality and the Hero," *Essays in Criticism*, III, 3, July 1953, p. 337.
7. "The Playboy of the Western World," *Philologic Pragensia*, Rocnik VII, Číslo 2-3, 1965.
8. "A Joycean Look at the *Playboy of the Western World*," *The Celtic Master*, ed. Maurice Harmon (Dublin, Dolmen Press, 1969), p. 51.
9. *Synge and Anglo-Irish Drama* (London, Methuen, 1961), p. 162.

10. *Op. cit.*, p. 21.
11. *Synge*, p. 244.
12. *C.W.*, III, p. 59.
13. *C.W.*, IV, p. 49.
14. *Ibid.*, p. 173.
15. *Synge and Anglo-Irish Literature* (Cork University Press, 1931), p. 185.
16. *Anatomy of Criticism* (Princeton University Press, 1957), p. 43.
17. *Ibid.*, p. 366. Low mimetic; a mode of literature in which the characters exhibit a power of action which is roughly on our own level, as in most comedy and realistic fiction.
18. *C.W.*, IV, p. 295 *et. seq.*
19. *Ibid.*, p. 173.
20. *Ibid.*
21. *Ibid.*
22. *Ibid.*, p. 63.
23. *Ibid.*, p. 65.
24. *Ibid.*, p. 77.
25. *Ibid.*, p. 59.
26. *Ibid.*, p. 81.
27. "Synge's *Playboy*: Morality and the Hero," *loc. cit.*, p. 344.
28. *C.W.*, IV, p. 82, notes 1-7.
29. *Ibid.*, note 1.
30. *Ibid.*, p. 111.
31. *Ibid.*
32. *Ibid.*, p. 113.
33. *Ibid.*, p. 61.
34. *Ibid.*
35. *Ibid.*, p. 71.
36. *Ibid.*, p. 75.
37. *Ibid.*
38. *Ibid.*, p. 81.
39. *Ibid.*, pp. 83-85.
40. "Synge's *Playboy*: Morality and the Hero," *loc. cit.*, p. 337.
41. *C.W.*, IV, p. 91.
42. *Ibid.*, p. 93.
43. *Ibid.*, p. 95.
44. The heroic motif in this play is treated thoroughly and perceptively by P. L. Henry, "The Playboy of the Western World," *loc. cit.*
45. *C.W.*, IV, p. 105.
46. *Ibid.*
47. In the Methuen (Henn, *op. cit.*) and in all other previous editions I have consulted the word is "noising". Professor Saddlemyer changes it to "nosing" but provides no textual note on the emendation.
48. *C.W.*, IV, pp. 109-111.
49. *Ibid.*, p. 113.
50. *Ibid.*, p. 123.

51. *Ibid.*, p. 125.
52. *Ibid.*, p. 135.
53. *Ibid.*, pp. 143-145.
54. *Ibid.*, p. 85
55. *Ibid.*, p. 147.
56. *Ibid.*
57. *Ibid.*
58. *Ibid.*, p. 149.
59. *Ibid.*, p. 157.
60. *Ibid.*
61. *Ibid.*, p. 161.
62. *Ibid.*, p. 163.
63. *Ibid.*, p. 165.
64. *Ibid.*
65. *Ibid.*, p. 169.
66. *Ibid.*
67. *Ibid.*, pp. 169-171.
68. *Ibid.*, p. 171.
69. *Ibid.*, p. 173.
70. *Ibid.*
71. *Ibid.*

THE TINKER'S WEDDING

Vivian Mercier

PEACHUM [*to* POLLY]. Married! . . . Do you think your mother
and I should have lived comfortably so long together if ever we had
been married? Baggage!

MRS. PEACHUM. I knew she was always a proud slut, and now the
wench hath played the fool and married, because, forsooth, she would
do like the gentry!

John Gay, *The Beggar's Opera*, I, 8.

I

WE need not speculate about whether Synge knew *The Beggar's Opera*
or not—he died long before its famous revival in the 1920's—for
we know that he found the essentials of *The Tinker's Wedding* in County
Wicklow. In his brief essay or *reportage*, "At a Wicklow Fair," the
following passage occurs:

> Then a woman came up and spoke to the tinker, and they went down
> the road together into the village. "That man is a great villain," said
> the herd [shepherd], when he was out of hearing. "One time he and
> his woman went up to a priest in the hills and asked him would he wed
> them for half a sovereign, I think it was. The priest said it was a poor
> price, but he'd wed them surely if they'd make him a tin can along with
> it. 'I will, faith,' said the tinker, 'and I'll come back when it's done.'
> They went off then and in three weeks they came back, and they asked
> the priest a second time would he wed them. 'Have you the tin can?'
> said the priest. 'We have not,' said the tinker; 'we had it made at the
> fall of night, but the ass gave it a kick this morning the way it isn't fit for
> you at all.' 'Go on now,' says the priest. 'It's a pair of rogues and
> schemers you are, and I won't wed you at all.' They went off then,
> and they were never married to this day."[1]

As a clue to Synge's characterization of the Priest in *The Tinker's
Wedding*, it is worth asking who first told the story of the priest and the
tinker—assuming it is a true story and not a piece of folklore. As told
by the herd to Synge, it seems to illustrate the incorrigibility of tinkers
rather than the avarice of priests. Very likely the priest himself would
tell the story in just this way, laughing half-contemptuously at the
effrontery of the tinkers. A similar construction can be put on the
behaviour of the priest in the final version of *The Tinker's Wedding*: he
is a generous enough man according to his lights, although by no means
a saint, but he resents being "played for a sucker," as most of us do.

Although Synge worked on *The Tinker's Wedding* again after he had perfected his special mode of comedy in *The Well of the Saints* and *The Playboy of the Western World*, it was first written, as he notes at the end of his preface to the published play, "about the time I was working at 'Riders to the Sea,' and 'In the Shadow of the Glen.' "[2] One might be tempted to think that the weakness of the finished play stems mainly from the minimal nature of the anecdote on which it was based, but Synge had no more to work with initially in *The Well of the Saints* or *The Playboy*. Ann Saddlemyer allows us to watch Synge extracting, step by step, most of the possibilities from the fundamental situation in the latter play. The various outlines for *The Playboy* as a whole and for the individual acts[3] show us Synge's constructive genius in a nutshell. It is a pity that Professor Saddlemyer does not allow us to watch the growth of *The Well of the Saints* in similar detail.

About the growth of *The Tinker's Wedding*, Professor Saddlemyer reveals to us rather more and rather less than we really need to know. Was it necessary to print *both* the first manuscript draft *and* the first typescript,[4] when they are basically so similar, being the only two extant one-act versions of the play? Both correspond roughly to Act II of the final version. The tinker couple are getting ready for the wedding when a woman from a neighbouring cottage goes to the well and, as she returns, finds that her can is leaking. On the spur of the moment, the male tinker sells her the new can he has just made for the priest; when the latter appears impatiently at the door of the church, the tinkers tell him that they have already left the can with his housekeeper. The priest, knowing that his housekeeper is away, becomes indignant at their ruse and refuses to marry them. He sees the police approaching along the road and threatens to denounce the tinkers to them, alleging their thefts of an ass and hay as in the final version. The tinkers flee without tying the priest up or suffering his Latin malediction.

The typescript is somewhat longer and richer in detail than the manuscript, but neither of these brief one-acts allows any scope for the development of character. The priest is a conventional authority-figure, fat and very short-tempered. The young tinker woman (here called Nora, rather than Sarah, Casey) has none of the capriciousness that she shows in the finished play. All she wants is not to be called bad names any more when selling cans at the fair. Her intended husband does not show the reluctance to marry of his counterpart in the finished play and need not be spurred on by jealousy. Mary Byrne is already a little more firmly drawn than the other tinkers, but she is neither bawdy nor alcoholic. Part of one speech of hers, however, survives almost unchanged from the first typescript to the final version; indeed, it is present in the original manuscript, though very differently worded there:

> MARY [*to the priest*] . . . It's a long time we are now going round on
> the roads, father and son and his son after him or maybe mother
> and daughter and her daughter again, and what is it we wanted any
> time with going up into the church, and swearing—I'm told there's
> swearing in it—a word no man would believe? Or what is it we
> wanted with putting dirty rings on our fingers would be cutting our
> skin maybe in the cold nights when we'ld be taking the ass from
> the shafts, and pulling the straps the time they'ld be slippy with
> going round under the heavens in the rain falling?[5]

It is no accident that Synge retained this speech so tenaciously, for in
a sense it is the "moral" of the whole play. The tinkers and "the
establishment" are too much at odds for any compromise to be possible.
If they move one step from their pagan—possibly even prelapsarian—
world, they might as well travel the whole way and give up their nomadic
life altogether. This Synge would not want them to do, for reasons
that may be guessed, but that I shall try to make explicit later.

The priest is not tied up in a sack when Mary delivers this speech
in the two earliest drafts. In the typescript version he answers her
sharply: "What is it I care if the like of you are married or not? It's
herself is after talking me round with the long tongue she has."[6]
This gives Mary the opportunity for a reply that occurs later and in
truncated form in the final version:

> MARY. Herself is young, God help her, and the young don't be know-
> ing any time the thing they want. But I've had one man and another
> man, and a power of children, and it's little need we had of your
> swearing, or your rings with it, to get us our bit to eat, and our bit
> to drink, and our time of love when we were young men or women,
> and were fine to look at.[7]

In these speeches Mary is saying very much what Peachum says in the
quotation from *The Beggar's Opera* given above.

Professor Saddlemyer dates the original MS. draft from Summer
1902 and the first typescript from Autumn 1903. In Spring 1904 comes
the first two-act version, Typescript "B". I wish that Professor Saddlemyer had printed more of this version than merely the passages,
afterwards omitted, showing the tinker children and the village children.
Obviously, once Synge had decided to write the play in two acts, the
interview in which Sarah persuades the Priest to marry her and Michael
became an indispensable part of Act I. I believe that the weakest point
of the play as we have it lies in the ambiguous treatment of the Priest.
Mary Byrne's character is already implicit in the speeches quoted from
Typescript "A," and she only needs to be expanded into a sort of female
Falstaff. Sarah's and Michael's characters, as developed, largely

embody archetypal male and female attitudes toward marriage. But the
Priest of Act I is viewed more sympathetically by the author and the
tinkers than the Priest of Act II and his counterpart in the one-act
drafts. Did Synge mean us to understand that the Priest is drunk in
Act I and sober in Act II? If so, he might have dared to be more explicit
in drafts than in the published version. The latter, indeed, is explicit
enough up to a point:

> MICHAEL. Whisht. I hear some one coming the road.
> SARAH [*looking out right*]. It's some one coming forward from the
> doctor's door.
> MICHAEL. It's often his reverence does be in there playing cards,
> or drinking a sup, or singing songs, until the dawn of day.
> SARAH. It's a big boast of a man with a long step on him and a
> trumpeting voice. It's his reverence surely; and if you have the ring
> done, it's a great bargain we'll make now and he after drinking his
> glass.[8]

The references to drinking, together with the Priest's willingness to
sit and drink some of Mary's porter, suggest that he "has a sup taken,"
but Synge drops no hint of it in the stage directions of the published
version.

The Priest is at first rather brusque with Sarah in Act I and finds it
hard to grasp the idea that she wants to get married. Then he is astonished at her suggestion that he marry her without payment. But
eventually he agrees to marry her "for a pound only, and that's making
it a sight cheaper than I'd make it for one of my own pairs is living here
in the place."[9] When she pretends to weep, insisting that the price is
still too high, he tries to comfort her and reduces his fee to fifteen
shillings and the gallon can.

When Mary Byrne comes in and presses him to drink, he finally
consents "*with resignation.*" Then he relaxes completely and becomes
very human:

> PRIEST. If it's starving you are itself, I'm thinking it's well for the like
> of you that do be drinking when there's drouth on you, and lying
> down to sleep when your legs are stiff. [*He sighs gloomily.*] What
> would you do if it was the like of myself you were, saying Mass with
> your mouth dry, and running east and west for a sick call maybe,
> and hearing the rural people again and they saying their sins?
> MARY [*with compassion*]. It's destroyed you must be hearing the sins
> of the rural people on a fine spring.
> PRIEST [*with despondency*]. It's a hard life I'm telling you, a hard
> life, Mary Byrne; and there's the bishop coming in the morning,
> and he an old man, would have you destroyed if he seen a thing at
> all.[10]

The Priest may sound rather foolish and indiscreet, but he has won some of our sympathy, and he wins more when, appalled by Mary Byrne's ignorance of and irreverence toward prayer, he reduces his fee by a further five shillings; as he says to Sarah, "I wouldn't be easy in my soul if I left you growing into an old, wicked heathen the like of her."[11]

Admittedly, from the point of view of the average Irish Catholic 65 years ago, to treat a priest as a comic character at all was in the worst of taste. Yet the basic kindliness of Synge's Priest in Act I could lessen the sense of shock at his presentation as a figure of fun. At his first appearance in Act II the Priest is somewhat impatient but still entirely human:

PRIEST [*crying out*]. Come along now. Is it the whole day you'd keep me here saying my prayers, and I getting my death with not a bit in my stomach, and my breakfast in ruins, and the Lord Bishop maybe driving on the road to-day?[12]

When he finds the empty bottles in the bundle where the can should be, he is deeply hurt:

PRIEST. Did ever any man see the like of that? To think you'd be putting deceit on me, and telling lies to me, and I going to marry you for a little sum wouldn't marry a child.[13]

When Sarah threatens to kill Mary for the trick she has played in stealing and selling the can, the Priest is still more sorry than angry: ". . . wasn't I a big fool to have to do with you when it's nothing but distraction and torment I get from the kindness of my heart?"[14]

It is not until Sarah begins to threaten him with personal violence that he in return threatens the tinkers with the police. Sarah then promises that the tinkers will smash all his windows and steal all his hens in revenge. Not till then does Synge insert the stage direction "*losing his temper finally.*" The tinkers' response to the Priest's rage is instant and violent: they bind and gag him and make him swear not to tell the police if they free him. He keeps his word, for, as he says in his last speech, "I've sworn not to call the hand of man upon your crimes to-day; but I haven't sworn I wouldn't call the fire of heaven from the hand of the Almighty God."[15]

As we review the Priest's behaviour in Act II, it perhaps does not seem very inconsistent with that in Act I. What really shocks us is the rough treatment he receives from the tinkers. We have come to sympathize with him, and he simply does not deserve either the brutality actually practised upon him or the threat to drown him. Even more than Pegeen's burning of the Playboy's shin with a lighted sod, this violence seems forced, melodramatic, and aesthetically out of place in a comedy. Aesthetic considerations aside, it was bound to offend pious members of the audience. Furthermore, it lacks credibility. No tinker not out of his mind with drink would have dared to assault a priest in Synge's lifetime. And if Michael refuses to believe that "the Lord would blight [his] members"[16] for laying hands on a priest, why should he be afraid a few moments later of the Priest's Latin malediction?

Synge first used the ending with the Priest tied in sacking in Typescript "D," which Professor Saddlemyer dates from Spring 1906. If her dating is correct, this twist of the plot was not added defiantly by Synge after the hostile reception of *The Playboy* in 1907. He may have felt that he had not established a strong enough contrast between the attitudes of the Priest and the tinkers earlier in the play; when the Priest laments the hardness of his lot in Act I, he seems to be coming round to the view of life held by the tinkers, and this is precisely where the subtlest humour of the play is to be found. Suddenly, at the end of Act II, Synge changes key and brings the whole situation to the verge of tragedy. There is no element of slapstick about the tying up of the Priest—it is done in deadly earnest. *The Tinker's Wedding* would have been a better play if the Priest and the tinkers had preserved their wary mutual respect and envy, a sort of sportsmanlike antagonism, throughout both acts.

Certainly violence is an essential part of the Irish folk stereotype of the tinker, along with lying, wheedling, thieving, drunkenness and lechery. But the violence is usually thought of as directed against fellow tinkers, male and female, rather than against established society. Stealing, begging, and fortune-telling are far safer ways of overcoming that enemy than outright violence, which is always countered by the violence of the police. Sarah threatens Mary with violence for stealing the can, but never puts her threat into practice. It would have been better if the violence against the Priest had been left as a mere threat also. By putting it into execution, the tinkers forfeit our sympathy, and at the same time we are temporarily forced to view the Priest as a martyr, a role quite out of keeping with our idea of his character.

II

I have more than once put forward the view elsewhere that Syngean comedy is essentially "mock-pastoral" in form, to use William Empson's term for describing works like *The Beggar's Opera*. (As a matter of fact, John Gay himself described an earlier work of his, *The Shepherd's Week* 1714, as a mock-pastoral.) *The Tinker's Wedding* is a fair sample of the genre, but all Synge's four comedies fit into it, and none better than *The Well of the Saints*. Synge himself described *The Shadow of the Glen* and *The Well of the Saints* each as "a play" in the published versions, whereas *The Tinker's Wedding* and *The Playboy of the Western*

World each went forth as "a comedy," but no definition of comedy that will fit the second pair can exclude the former two.

In all these four plays, the values of an "anti-society" of tramps, blind beggars, tinkers, and criminals are contrasted with those of established society—and shown to be equally valid. Peachum, the informer and receiver of stolen goods in *The Beggar's Opera* (I, 1), sets forth the equation as follows:

> A lawyer is an honest employment, so is mine. Like me too, he acts in a double capacity, both against rogues, and for 'em; for 'tis but fitting that we should protect and encourage cheats, since we live by them.

In each of Synge's mock-pastoral plays the comic hero (or heroine) is an anti-hero, owing no allegiance to any but the anti-society. He and/or she is banished from the stage before the final curtain, and established society in effect says "Good riddance," but our hearts go with the Tramp and Nora, with Martin and Mary Doul, with Christy Mahon, and we have nothing but mocking laughter for the solid folk who remain behind. Pegeen's last wild cry tells us that her heart too has gone with "the only playboy of the western world."[17]

Do our hearts go with the tinkers at the end of *The Tinker's Wedding*, when, as the stage direction tells us, "*They rush out, leaving the* PRIEST *master of the situation*"?[18] That is precisely the question I have been trying to answer in the first part of this essay. For the reasons stated, my own subjective answer is negative. The tinkers have forfeited my sympathy, yet I am not sure that Synge intended them to do so. It would be illogical to claim, however, that the end of this comedy *must* repeat the "formula" of the other three, since the formula is only arrived at by induction from those three plays and was never given conscious shape by Synge himself.

What we can say with certainty is that *The Tinker's Wedding* defines the anti-society and claims for it an equality with established society. Mary's last speech to the Priest, which has already been quoted in draft form, affirms the validity of the tinker way of life: ". . . it's little need we ever had of the like of you to get us our bit to eat, and our bit to drink, and our time of love when we were young men and women, and were fine to look at."[19] She says nothing about the satisfying of other than material needs, but then the Priest as presented by Synge has little to say about spiritual satisfactions. Perhaps this is where the real weakness in his characterization lies. He envies the tinkers because they can eat and drink and sleep whenever they want to. His spiritual duties are presented merely as physical burdens: ". . . saying Mass with your mouth dry, and running east and west for a sick call maybe, and hearing the rural people again and they saying their sins[.]"[20] Finally, he envies the tinkers their freedom from obedience to authority, while he lives constantly in fear of his bishop.

It is true that the Priest is horrified by Mary Byrne's heathenism and asks God to have mercy on her soul, but he offers no positive spiritual values, only the possibility of escape from damnation. As the tinkers do not believe in an after-life, they are not impressed. They run in fear from the Priest at the end of the play only because he is threatening to bring down immediate fire from heaven and end their lives at once. Sarah's one clearly stated motive for wanting to be married is worldly: ". . . from this day there will no one have a right to call me a dirty name . . ."[21] Mary Byrne points out that a wedding ring will not keep Sarah from growing old and losing her beauty, and goes on to suggest that it may increase the pains of childbirth: ". . . it's the grand ladies do be married in silk dresses, with rings of gold, that do pass any woman with their share of torment in the hour of birth . . ."[22] This possibility almost puts Sarah off marriage altogether until she decides that Mary doesn't know anything about "the fine ladies."

I have said earlier that the tinkers' world possibly antedates the Fall of Man. As we know from God's curse on Eve, the pains of childbirth did not exist before the Fall, and in this respect at least the tinker women are closer to the Garden of Eden than their bourgeois counterparts. On the other hand, the tinkers are not exempt from the curses of death and work. But they seem never to have eaten of the Tree of Knowledge, for they have no sense of sin. A wholly paradisal anti-society is to be found only in *The Well of the Saints*. In Act I of that play we do not realize that the blind beggars Martin and Mary Doul are Adam and Eve in Eden, for they seem old and ugly and weak and poor. But in Act II, after they have regained their sight, we may suddenly realize that the curse of Adam has belatedly fallen upon Martin. In the first place, now that he can see, he must work: "In the sweat of thy face shalt thou eat bread." In the second place, his newly opened eyes lead him to sin through his desire for Molly Byrne. In the third place, though he has always been subject to death, he never became aware of it until he could see "the old women rotting for the grave."[23] No wonder he is happy to lose his sight again in Act III and resents it when the Saint tries to drag him from his private Eden by curing his blindness once more.

The other comedies cannot offer quite such an Edenic life in the anti-society, but the Tramp's last two speeches in *The Shadow of the Glen* suggest that the world of nature will at least be kinder to Nora than the world of men. Here is the second of these speeches:

> TRAMP [*at the door*]. Come along with me now, lady of the house, and it's not my blather you'll be hearing only, but you'll be hearing the herons crying out over the black lakes, and you'll be hearing the grouse, and the owls with them, and the larks and the big thrushes

when the days are warm, and it's not from the like of them you'll be hearing a talk of getting old like Peggy Cavanagh, and losing the hair off you, and the light of your eyes, but it's fine songs you'll be hearing when the sun goes up, and there'll be no old fellow wheezing the like of a sick sheep close to your ear.[24]

More paradisal still are Christy's visions of his married life with Pegeen in Act III of *The Playboy*:

Let you wait to hear me talking till we're astray in Erris when Good Friday's by, drinking a sup from a well, and making mighty kisses with our wetted mouths, or gaming in a gap of sunshine with yourself stretched back unto your necklace in the flowers of the earth.[25]

Christy even thinks he'd "feel a kind of pity for the Lord God is all ages sitting lonesome in his golden chair."[26]

But unless one is happily blind like Martin and Mary Doul, such harmony with nature is only for the young. Mary Byrne's final speech in Act I of *The Tinker's Wedding* foreshadows the terror of old age and the slow, certain approach of death that haunts every page of *Deirdre of the Sorrows* and makes Deirdre eager to die while she is still young and unwithered:

Maybe the two of them [Michael and Sarah] have a good right to be walking out the little short while they'd be young; but if they have itself, they'll not keep Mary Byrne from her full pint when the night's fine, and there's a dry moon in the sky . . . Jemmy Neill's a decent lad; and he'll give me a good drop for the can; and maybe if I keep near the peelers to-morrow for the first bit of the fair, herself won't strike me at all; and if she does itself, what's a little stroke on your head beside sitting lonesome on a fine night, hearing the dogs barking, and the bats squeaking, and you saying over, it's a short while only till you die.[27]

If Synge had presented Sarah as believing that marriage in church would guarantee her eternal life, thus freeing her from Mary's anguish, the struggle between established society and the anti-society in *The Tinker's Wedding* would be far more intense than it is, more on a level with that in *The Well of the Saints*. As it is, neither the world of the tinkers nor the world of the Priest seems to have much to offer an old woman like Mary Byrne.

III

It is natural to think of the works produced by the Irish Literary Revival as what Empson would call "versions of pastoral." Idealization of the Irish peasant was widespread during the early stages of the movement, while most of the writers were still much higher than the peasant in the social scale and thus neither saw him clearly nor felt him as a personal threat—except, of course, when he began a rent strike.

Perhaps the most interesting Irish pastoral manifestation was linguistic. As Empson writes,

> The essential trick of the old pastoral, which was felt to imply a beautiful relation between rich and poor, was to make simple people express strong feelings . . . in learned and fashionable language . . .[28]

But the new Irish pastoral, written by members of the middle and upper classes, sought "to make simple people express strong feelings" in a stylized version of the language of the simple people themselves. In Synge's *Deirdre of the Sorrows*, for instance, high and low speak the same language—a dialect almost identical with that spoken by the tinkers in *The Tinker's Wedding* or the fisherfolk in *Riders to the Sea*. Similarly, Lady Gregory retells the Old Irish sagas in "Kiltartanese," a stylization of the dialect spoken by her own tenants. The Gaelic League sought to revive Modern Irish, native speakers of which were among the poorest of the poor. Many of the most enthusiastic Leaguers were members of the middle and upper classes, yet they chose as their linguistic norm not the Classical Modern Irish of the bardic poets but current colloquial Irish, *cainnt na ndaoine* ("the speech of the people").

In the end, though, an astonishing amount of the pastoral writing turned out to be mock-pastoral. Not only Synge's plays but Yeats's are full of mock-pastoral figures. Consider the following list of characters from Yeats (the plays are listed in the order of *Collected Plays*):

The Old Woman in *Cathleen Ni Houlihan;*
The Tramp in *The Pot of Broth;*
The Blind Man and the Fool in *On Baile's Strand;*
The Fool in *The Hour-Glass;*
The Beggars in *The Unicorn from the Stars;*
The Players in *The Player Queen;*
The Lame Man and the Blind Man in *The Cat and the Moon;*
The Stroller in *The King of the Great Clock Tower;*
The Fool in *The Herne's Egg;*
The Old Man and the Boy in *Purgatory;*
The Blind Man in *The Death of Cuchulain.*

All of these are members of the anti-society and almost all must make their way by begging and/or stealing; the Players and the Stroller may earn their living, but established society regards them as pariahs: perhaps all the musicians in the plays should be included along with them. *The Pot of Broth*, first performed in October 1902, antedates all of Synge's plays: it was the first comedy of the Literary Revival in which a mock-pastoral character outwitted settled folk—in this case a small farmer and his wife—and got off scot-free. In at least two other early plays by Yeats, *The Land of Heart's Desire* and *Cathleen Ni*

Houlihan, the values of Irish peasant life had been implicitly rejected. In other words, the mock-pastoral figure, be he tramp or tinker, stands opposed to peasant society in the same way that the artist was believed to stand opposed to bourgeois society. Synge makes this equation of tramp with artist absolutely explicit in "The Vagrants of Wicklow":

> In the middle classes the gifted son of a family is always the poorest—usually a writer or artist with no sense for speculation—and in a family of peasants, where the average comfort is just over penury, the gifted son sinks also, and is soon a tramp on the roadside.[29]

It is unimportant to our examination of *The Tinker's Wedding* whether this observation of Synge's be sociologically sound or a piece of arrant mythmaking: Synge believed it and based his sympathy for the tinker way of life upon it.

But the professional and land-owning classes were not destined to control the Irish theatre for ever. Protestant (Yeats, Synge, Lady Gregory, Lennox Robinson, Lord Dunsany) or Catholic (George Moore, Edward Martyn), they eventually gave way to the lower-middle and working classes. It happened that O'Casey, the first working-class Irish dramatist, showed great sympathy for mock-pastoral characters like "Captain" Boyle and "Joxer" Daly in *Juno and the Paycock*, though in his Communist Party days he ought to have condemned them as members of the *lumpenproletariat*. But if we turn to George Shiels, who, as Robert Hogan so rightly says, "wrote the typical Abbey play of the 1930's and 1940's,"[30] we find the true antidote to mock-pastoral comedy. Shiels mainly writes about and presumably came from the small shopkeeper class in a small town—Ballymoney, Co. Antrim. In his two most successful plays, *The Rugged Path* and *The Summit*, however, he focuses on a law-abiding family of farmers, the Tanseys, and their struggle against the lawless Dolis family. Peter Dolis murders an old man for a small sum of money; although Michael Tansey does not want to earn the hated title of informer, he finally decides to give evidence against Peter, who is acquitted, however, and returns from his trial to terrorize the Tanseys. Here *The Rugged Path* ends. It was the first Abbey play ever to achieve fifty consecutive performances, and there is no doubt that the audience sided with the Tanseys. In the sequel, *The Summit*, the Tanseys' neighbours, who had at first supported the Dolis family, undergo a change of heart; this "ensures the banishment of Peter Dolis and a speedy end to the reign of his lawless tribe."[31] In spite of the use of the word "tribe" here, the Dolis family were not tinkers but mountain farmers; still, if they had been tinkers, Shiels might have dealt even more sternly with them. A whole body of legislation designed to encourage the "itinerants" to settle down and become law-abiding citizens is now on the statute books of the Republic of Ireland.

Priests on the Irish stage were few in number after Synge until Paul Vincent Carroll introduced a whole spectrum of them in *Shadow and Substance* (1937) and *The White Steed* (1938). He showed that priests could be fastidious or philistine, tolerant or bigoted. In *The Wayward Saint* (1955), Carroll put on the stage a priest who is unequivocally comic, a sort of holy fool with a measure of unholy slyness.[32] One feels that Carroll knows the Catholic clergy from the inside, whereas Synge could only know them from the outside.

The last paragraph of Synge's preface to *The Tinker's Wedding* offers a generalization that no Irishman could quarrel with:

> In the greater part of Ireland, however, the whole people, from the tinkers to the clergy, have still a life, and view of life, that are rich and genial and humorous.

But he continues thus:

> I do not think that these country people, who have so much humour themselves, will mind being laughed at without malice, as the people in every country have been laughed at in their own comedies.[33]

Here lies the crux: in what sense were the early Abbey Theatre plays "their own" for the Irish country people? Lady Gregory arranged a performance or two in Loughrea and Foynes in 1903, but otherwise all professional performances took place in Dublin, or London. Yeats admits that "In some country village an audience of farmers once received [*The Pot of Broth*] in stony silence . . ."[34] He thought it was because they had never seen a play, but the real reason was surely that the farmers saw a tramp getting the better of one of themselves and didn't think it a laughing matter. Furthermore, Synge might believe that he laughed at the country people "without malice," but they would naturally feel that Protestant playwrights of English stock and high social position could hardly be free from malice or, at best, condescension.

To see the Irish people laughing at themsleves without any sense that alien eyes are watching, one has to learn Gaelic. As I have shown in *The Irish Comic Tradition*, the Gaelic upper classes often laughed maliciously at their social inferiors. A close analogue to *The Tinker's Wedding* in Gaelic must have been known to Synge, however, for Douglas Hyde published a Gaelic text and English translation of *An Siota 's a Mháthair* ("The Lout and His Mother") in 1906.[35] Hyde first came across the poem in oral tradition, then obtained two MS versions, and also used a printed version published in the *Gaelic Journal* "six years ago"; Synge could therefore have come across the poem independently, or Hyde might have shown it to him before publication or he might have seen it during the prior serial publication of *The Religious Songs of Connacht* in *The New Ireland Review*. In any case,

by the end of 1906, Synge could hardly *not* have known "The Lout and
His Mother."

This anonymous poem, dated 1815 in one MS, mainly consists of an
argument between an old beggarwoman and her illegitimate son. He
reproaches her for her poverty and says that her piety has done her more
harm than good. When she promises him better things in a future life,
he makes fun of both heaven and hell. He also attacks the Roman
Catholic clergy for their love of money:

> As for marriage it is too dear a business,
> Three gold guineas and a crown to the clerk . . .
> And sure what everyone says after all the business
> Is, that it is the mamram pego[36] which makes the marriage.[37]

A little farther along in the poem the lout says to his mother:

> Silly, you hag, and foolish are your sayings;
> Sure if you were dead to-morrow morning
> And I were to bring you to a priest tied up in a bag
> He would not read a Mass for you without hand-money,
> And as for charity, the name of it is bitter to him.[38]

I have often wondered whether the notion of the old hag's being brought
to the priest tied up in a bag did not suggest to Synge that he should
have his priest tied up similarly: indeed, Hyde's phrasing, "to a priest
tied up in a bag," is ambiguous at best. Professor Saddlemyer's date
of Spring 1906 for the addition of this detail to the play makes my
speculation all the more tempting.

After all his blasphemy and anti-clerical satire, the lout ends the
squabble very piously with a prayer that the Christ-Child will not allow
anyone to be damned; then he announces that he is going to be married
the next day. The poet himself concludes his poem with the wish:

> If there is folly in it—Christ make it right!
> Mercy from God on us, and let each one ask it.[39]

This is entirely in the spirit of a medieval "retraction."

Synge himself offered something very close to a retraction in the
typescript draft of his preface to *The Tinker's Wedding* dated 20
November 1907:

> I do not think these country clergy, who have so much humour—and
> so much heroism that everyone who has seen them facing typhus or
> dangerous seas for the comfort of their people on the coasts of the
> west must acknowledge—will mind being laughed at for half an hour
> without malice, as the clergy in every Roman Catholic country were
> laughed at through the ages that had real religion.[40]

The ending to the preface as it now stands is less apologetic, but it looks the more sincere because of that. I don't suppose any Irishman today would accuse Synge of malice. At most he can be blamed for lack of empathy or lack of tact.

Ultimately, Synge can be shown to be truer to Irish tradition, and particularly to Gaelic tradition, in all four comedies, than the critics who denounced him as unIrish. But the fact remains that *The Shadow of the Glen* and *The Tinker's Wedding* are far less satisfying than the other two comedies. *The Shadow of the Glen* ends sentimentally, unlike the folktale on which it is based.[41] *The Tinker's Wedding*, on the other hand, ends too savagely. Christy Mahon's savagery is pardonable because wreaked on a bully (his father) and a coward (Shawn Keogh), but the tinkers' savagery is inexcusable because wreaked on one who is essentially kindly and muddleheaded, for all the awesome power that stands behind his priestly office.

NOTES

1. *C.W.*, II, pp. 228-229.
2. *C.W.*, IV, p. 4.
3. *Ibid.*, pp. 294-304.
4. *Ibid.*, pp. 272-284.
5. *Ibid.*, p. 284.
6. *Ibid.*
7. *Ibid.*
8. *Ibid.*, pp. 11, 13.
9. *Ibid.*, p. 15.
10. *Ibid.*, p. 19.
11. *Ibid.*, p. 23.
12. *Ibid.*, p. 39.
13. *Ibid.*, p. 41.
14. *Ibid.*, p. 43.
15. *Ibid.*, p. 49.
16. *Ibid.*, p. 45.
17. *Ibid.*, p. 173.
18. *Ibid.*, p. 49.
19. *Ibid.*
20. *Ibid.*, p. 19.
21. *Ibid.*, p. 35.
22. *Ibid.*, p. 37.
23. *C.W.*, III, p. 117.
24. *Ibid.*, p. 57.
25. *C.W.*, IV, p. 149.
26. *Ibid.*, p. 147.
27. *Ibid.*, p. 27.
28. William Empson, *Some Versions of Pastoral* (London, Chatto and Windus, 1935), p. 11.
29. *C.W.*, II, p. 202.

30. Robert Hogan, *After the Irish Renaissance* (Minneapolis, University of Minnesota Press, 1967), p. 33.

31. Mathew O'Mahony, *Progress Guide to Anglo-Irish Plays* (Dublin, Progress House, 1960), p. 83. See also Hogan, pp. 33-39. I saw both plays in 1940-1941.

32. See Hogan, pp. 52-63, for an account of Carroll that focuses on his changing treatment of the Catholic Church and her clergy.

33. *C.W.*, IV, p. 3.

34. W. B. Yeats, *Plays in Prose and Verse* (New York, Macmillan, 1930), p. 429.

35. Published in *Abhráin Diadha Chúige Connacht*, or *The Religious Songs of Connacht*, II (Dublin and London, M. H. Gill & Son, and T. Fisher Unwin, n.d. [1906]), pp. 294-315.

36. Hyde is puzzled by *mamram pego* in the Gaelic, but "pego" is English slang for "penis"; *mamram* or *meamram* (Latin *membrana*) usually means "parchment"; could it stand for Latin *membrum* here?

37. "The Lout and His Mother", *loc. cit.*, p. 309.

38. *Ibid.*, p. 311.

39. *Ibid.*, p. 315.

40. *C.W.*, IV, pp. 3-4, Note.

41. For this, see *C.W.*, II, pp. 70-72.

SYNGE'S *DEIRDRE* AND THE SORROWS
OF MORTALITY

John Rees Moore

I

After three extended visits to the Aran Islands, Synge was convinced that he had discovered a way of life "still at the patriarchal stage, ... the people are nearly as far from the romantic moods of love as they are from the impulsive life of the savage."[1] In other words, they were not subject to the ills of the literary imagination but neither were they mere primitives incapable of civilized reflection. But to a literary man escaping the decadence of sophisticated Paris their unromantic simplicity *did* have a kind of romance. Far from the madding crowd and equally far from a Bohemian élite, their life was reflected in their language, and both had a "wholeness" lost to the up-to-date European.

They became in Synge's mind a model for a kind of art that would show a reality neither modern nor unmodern, but as unchanging as the rocks and tides their life depended on. By comparison with the Aran Islanders, the mainland Irish were already corrupt, being more priest-ridden and more inhibited by social custom. Yet there was still hope for them, at least for the ones courageous enough to reject the law which would impoverish life in the name of dull piety. The conflict in Synge's plays comes from the struggle of the natural man to free himself from the constrictions imposed by custom. Loyalty to the ways of the tribe is a protection against the utter loneliness of independence, but to submit to convention is spiritual death. Nature, though it offers no escape from death, can give solace to those capable of responding to its constant variety and its dependable rhythms.

Riders to the Sea, the only play of Synge's with an Aran setting, is also atypical in its distance from "the big world." Narrow, constricted, intense, this play has no space for satire or humour any more than it does for lyrical appreciation of the beauties of nature. Maurya's life is a struggle as long as she has any family to worry about. Relieved of the struggle, she attains a kind of tragic freedom. Here death is the opponent, and society hardly matters; no one is rebelling against the tyranny of convention. Maurya's loneliness results from no will nor act of her own; in fact, as the action progresses our sense that her calamity was pre-destined increases. The only solace seems to be having reached bottom: there isn't anything more the sea can do to her. And yet even here Maurya's poise, ironically misinterpreted by her daughters as mere

senile collapse, is a subtle assertion of independence from the expectations of society. The calm dignity of Maurya's closing speech is in
marked contrast to her earlier querulous whining. She has achieved a
stoical, if hardly joyful, acceptance of nature.

In *The Playboy of the Western World* the shape of the action is indeed
different. Christy turns the tables on a world that would raise him on
its shoulders and then beat him to his knees. And the delicious irony is
that the frustrated romanticism of this world provides the ladder for a
puny boy to climb to independent manhood. In a sense, Christy has as
little to do with achieving his comic freedom as Maurya does in achieving her tragic freedom. He has to wait till almost the end of the play to
discover with delighted surprise, when the terror of torture hangs over
him, that he is now the master instead of the victim of fear. He doesn't
need the reappearance of his father to be saved; it only prevents his
being hanged. But the comic reunion of father and son ironically
underlines not only Christy's transformation but the great divide that
separates these two playboys who defy all communal shackles from those
who bow their imaginations to the laws of convention. Denied the fulfilment of a romance based on illusion, Christy fares forth immunized
to the cruel vacillations of worldly credulity, shifting the tragedy intended for him into the heart of a now truly disillusioned Pegeen.
Neither love nor death is ultimately serious, as they must be in tragedy.

It was not until his last, unfinished play, *Deirdre of the Sorrows*, that
Synge attempted to combine the breadth of comedy with the intensity
of tragedy. He turned to something he had not tried before, a mythical
story already hallowed by many retellings. He had been seriously
attracted by the story as early as 1901, and he translated a version of it
from the modern Irish. He also had the advantage of Lady Gregory's
experiments in putting the old saga material into a more or less contemporary dialect. What Synge did *not* want to do was follow the
example of Yeats in emphasizing the distance of the ancient heroes and
heroines from contemporary life; he wished instead to show them
as "natural" human beings expressing their passions as though their
story were just now occurring for the first time. Yet he could not, of
course, disregard the tradition, nor did he want to. Unlike Gide or
Cocteau or Sartre, who have used Greek myths to dramatize sophisticated modern views of the world, Synge wanted to evoke a life as far
removed as possible from argument and ideology. It is certainly too
crude to say he wanted to make kings and queens into peasants, and
incredible as well, but he did want to show the elemental simplicity of
certain permanent human emotions, a simplicity that undercuts
differences in rank, in culture, even in nationality. But this universality
had to be rooted in the local. To a man of Synge's wide experience of
the "common people," the literary tradition he cared for was of value

because it demonstrated how little the basic idiom of life changes in a place where men know little of progress or fashion and much of the collective wisdom of their forebears.

Though Synge wanted to deal with "the entire reality of life,"[2] he is firmly in the pastoral tradition. Basically contemplative, pastoral depends on the contrast between the active world where men busy themselves with "getting on" and a stiller world where the pleasures of merely existing have pride of place. In *Deirdre of the Sorrows* the love of hero and heroine is, in spite of the furious activity to which it leads, a state of suspended animation. Since this condition is peculiarly recalcitrant to dramatic treatment, Synge must render it through lyric remembrance. For instance, Deirdre remembers

> . . . or the time I've been stretched in the sunshine when I've heard Ainnle and Ardan stepping lightly, and they saying, "Was there ever the like of Deirdre for a happy and sleepy queen?"[3]

A "happy and sleepy queen"! This is a state of innocence in which before and after do not matter, for the fullness of the moment is all. It is as though the world were created merely for the delectation of these aboriginal lovers. But they have stolen their paradise and must pay for it. In one sense, the entire world of the play is pastoral, including Conchubar; in another, the pastoral is the missing centre, first anticipated and then longingly recalled. The romance of the play is youth lovingly nested in a beneficent nature; the reality is comfortless old age so jealous of the love it lacks that it will put the whole world to flame in pursuit of its obsession.

If we took seriously the reality Synge gives us, we would find the world unbearable. But the language softens and distances reality, no less in the "harsh" passages than in the more sweetly lyrical. If the woes of reality are incurable, they are also, paradoxically, unreal. For we know that the story is a fairy tale, and Synge is careful to emphasize in the first act how miraculous a tale he is unfolding. When Deidre appears in her queenly regalia we should be as impressed at the transformation as Naisi and Lavarcham are. The young queen announces, "I am Deirdre of the Sorrows."[4] The moment of assumption has arrived: the scene makes manifest the irreversible conjunction of Deirdre and her predestined role. The occasion is a triumphant one, for intolerable reality will be left behind when these ideally matched lovers embark on their love-journey for what is, in effect, the land of Tir-nan-Oge. And though, being mortal, their return to earthly reality is inescapable, *that* part of their story lies on the other side of their blissful vacation in exile from the rude passions of loveless men.

In the universe of Synge's drama you either extricate yourself from the *dharma*[5] of everyday life or you are crushed by the heavy weight of mass prejudice. Conventional wisdom, the feelings and values of those who protect themselves from their own individuality by unthinking obedience to the dogmas of religion or the rules of society, is a fraud. And in the Ireland that Synge wrote of, this conventional wisdom was dominated by the institution of Catholicism. It is not surprising that Catholic audiences took offence. Nor was the wisdom Synge would put in its place any help in promoting Irish nationalism. For Synge—as a dramatist—implies no more faith in political action than in religious consolation. It would be misleading to say he "advocates" anything, but the "stoicism, asceticism, ecstasy"[6] which he thought an ideal art should celebrate seem in his work to have (to put it mildly) little connection with Christianity. They come, rather, from a pagan sense of gods indwelling in nature and in man (when he conceives of himself as a part of nature). Perhaps one might say that the stance he admires is a tough wonder, a sensitivity to moral and physical beauty combined with the courage to resist compromise with one's ideal values. Since these values are inseparable from the humours of the earth, and really not subject to amendment by reform, they depend on a kind of rugged individualism. To be ascetic is to inure oneself to the pain of life, to be stoical is to armour oneself against specious illusion, and to attain ecstasy is to experience the liberation that comes when, no longer hemmed in by fear, the soul is at one with itself. Christy Mahon, ready to "go romancing through a romping lifetime from this hour to the dawning of the judgment day,"[7] knows something of this joy, but Deirdre alone among Synge's characters gives full resonance to the mingled sweetness and sorrow of true ecstasy.

II

After his experience on the Aran islands Synge is confirmed in his preference for an archaic way of life as opposed to the thinner existence of civilization, though he has no illusions about the desperation that is never far from the surface of that primitive life. In *Deirdre* he idealizes a pastoral type of existence by never letting us forget the intimate connection between heroic passion and its natural scene. Conchubar has, so to speak, isolated himself from nature in his prison-like fortress, whereas Naisi and Deirdre realize the fullness of their love in the sympathetic forests of Scotland. In the third act Deirdre remembers:

> I see the trees naked and bare, and the moon shining. Little moon, little moon of Alban, it's lonesome you'll be this night, and tomorrow night, and long nights after, and you pacing the woods beyond Glen Laid, looking every place for Deirdre and Naisi, the two lovers who slept so sweetly with each other.[8]

The moon is a tutelary deity who took a proprietary pleasure in these two children of Nature. It is neither a pale disc in the sky nor the Muselike figure invoked so often in conventional love poetry. In fact Deirdre can afford to take a rather familiar, if tender, tone in addressing it ("Little moon, little moon") because the lovers were in perfect harmony with their surroundings. Nature inspired neither awe nor fear, but a companionable affection. The lover's absence is imagined as leaving a gap in Nature. And in addressing the moon Deirdre is really talking to herself. She is, if you will, preparing herself for a return to Mother Nature since Father Time has blocked her way.

Synge wants to face the full brutality of human existence and yet insist on the possibilities of transcendence. The tale of Deirdre as narrative is dramatic enough, but it is not rich in the kind of dramatic circumstance appropriate to the theatre. The heroine must fulfil the destiny foretold her, yet the legend is very cavalier about motives. Quite properly, it dwells on marvels and mystery, the piteous fatality of events and the simple and (typically) violent reactions of the characters to circumstance. To examine the motives of behaviour too closely, let alone to worry about realistic plausibility, would weaken the effect of divine inscrutability that gives the old tale much of its power and charm. Whatever is may not be right, but the very arbitrariness of fate somehow makes it comforting, assures us that anything so strange and powerful must be authentic and free from doubt. But the more the majestic figures of myth are reduced to human proportions, the more we expect (perhaps oddly) that they should be makers of their own fate, even though they may often misunderstand what they are doing and why they are doing it. In drama (well, pre-Beckettian drama anyway) the chain of cause and effect is essential to unity of action, and Synge, for all his interest in being "rich and copious in his words,"[9] is thoroughly traditional in his concern with structure. In fact, his plays are "classical" in form if not in feeling. So in *Deirdre* he must wrestle with the problem of why his characters act as they do (and *must* do). There is time for Deirdre to commune with nature, but not at the expense of advancing the action. Ideally, each moment should have a life of its own as it passes yet justify its relations to the moments before and after.

Synge succeeds in the first act in making us feel Deirdre's attachment to the woods and glens around her. By isolating her, Conchubar has, ironically, already set in motion the fate he hoped to evade. He has confirmed *nature* in Deirdre, made her realize fully how unnatural a life with Conchubar would be. The urgency of escaping Conchubar's net is convincing, but Naisi's willingness to run away with Deirdre seems too easy, though a sufficiently beautiful Deirdre could undoubtedly make this defect into a virtue in a good performance. In Thomas Kinsella's version of *The Sons of Usnech* there is no doubt at all why

Naisi goes. Deirdre searches him out and "cunningly quickened her steps and made to pass him as if she did not know him." Naisi begins their conversation:

—That is a fine heifer going by.
—The heifers grow sleek where there are no bulls.
—You have the bull of this country: the king of Ulster.
—Of the two I would pick a game young bull like you.
—Little fear. There is a prophecy.
—Do you reject me?
—I do.
　　Without thought she rushed and clutched his ears and spoke in his face:
—Here are shame and mockery on your head if you do not take me with you.
—Leave off, woman. Leave off.
—You will do it, she said, binding him in honour.
He uttered a terrible cry. And at that cry Ulster filled and leaped with fear and men trembled and lifted up their swords, each staring.[10]

The unwilling Naisi is trapped by the code of honour, drawn into a doom nothing less than the threat of disgrace could have made him accept. By comparison with this Deirdre, Synge's heroine does seem to fit Yeats's otherwise odd description of her as one "who might be some mild modern housewife but for her prophetic wisdom."[11] At any rate, the story from the Book of Leinster (in Kinsella's version) would appear to have some advantages.

But Synge's real difficulties occur in the second act. Naisi and Deirdre *know* they should not return to Ireland if they value their lives. Synge has to use Fergus and his promise of safe conduct as a motive for the return of the lovers, but it runs counter to his real theme, which is that those who have discovered the inner meaning of ideal love and tasted the sweets of youthful paradise should choose suicide as the obvious alternative to growing old. But Fergus's lure assumes that security is the chief issue, that once the lovers can be persuaded of Conchubar's good faith in granting them sanctuary—in other words, the chance to grow old in peace—the whole problem will be solved. Deirdre knows—or should know—very well that the dilemma so poignantly revealed when she overhears the "man talk" of Fergus and Naisi cannot be resolved by returning to Ireland. The sorrows of mortality are incurable. If we want to be too clever by half, we can say that the return of the lovers represents a death wish, but this seems morbid in a way that goes against the grain of the old story *and* against Synge's intent as well. If the play is to be a tragedy, the acceptance of death must be a cruel and difficult thing, not a luxurious indulgence. And we know that Synge wanted a "healthy" art. The best that Synge can do is to suggest that since the halcyon days (and nights) of love are over, it would be nice to see home once more before dying. In the Red Branch saga, where love lacks sentimental encumbrances, Naisi makes the decisions, curtly brushing aside Deirdre's womanish fears. He counts on the code of honour to guarantee his safety and is primarily concerned with the military situation. Love, however pleasant, is the enemy of honour, and for a warrior honour must come first.

In the saga inevitable doom stalks Deirdre and the three brothers. Despite the well-nigh incredible efforts of the betrayed heroes, efforts that can only be defeated by the spells of Cathbad the Druid, each step towards death proceeds with ritualistic punctilio in what still remains surprisingly close to an ancient rite of sacrifice. The pattern behind such tales—called Elopements—is seasonal, essentially the conflict of winter and summer. The stories of Diarmuid and Grania, Tristan and Iseult, Lancelot and Guinever are famous examples of the type, which undoubtedly evolved from religious rituals celebrating the transcendent power of love. May Day was traditionally a time of sexual license when boys and girls spent a night in the forest and often returned knowing each other in a new way. On a more elevated level, the cults of the Great Mother and the Dying God, represented, for example, by the love of Aphrodite and Adonis, also lie behind the later stories. The typical situation is a triangle in which the Old Man loses his young wife to a youthful lover whom she chases and binds to herself by putting him in a dilemma where he is damned if he does and damned if he don't. Reluctantly, he elopes with the young lady whom he would never have thought of choosing and thereby guarantees that he will be the victim of the Old Man's revenge. (Winter must give way to summer—and summer to winter.) Though the lovers act in deliberate defiance of the moral law, the Young Man has our complete sympathy. His innocence is carefully established by the impossible conditions imposed upon him. Symbolically, they prove that this love transcends the contingencies of ordinary existence and is a law unto itself.[12]

In Synge's play, as in other dramatic versions of the story, the complexities of Naisi get short shrift because he is the passive character, the one to whom "things happen," while Deirdre's energy continually forces the issue. Yet by tradition he is a great warrior, "and the head and shoulders of Naoise are above all the other men in Ireland"[13] as Lady Gregory describes him in her retelling. But he is also the kind of man who, though not in the least effeminate, has the feminine qualities of charm and beauty, a musical voice and a gentle protectiveness. In describing Lancelot, Heinrich Zimmer gives us the archetype:

> He represented something very different from the heroic medieval ideals of his companions, something much less timely, more profoundly human and enduring. Sir Lancelot is an incarnation of the ideal of

manhood that exists, not in the world of masculine social action, but in the hopes and fancies of the feminine imagination.[14]

Synge is able to give us something of this—notably if obliquely in the quarrel scene before Naisi goes out to face death. But, to put it rudely, Naisi for the most part seems an infatuated and not too bright young fellow hopelessly (if nobly) lost in the swirl of passion and intrigue relentlessly carrying him toward death. He owes what stature he has to Deirdre: her devotion to him implies his unique qualities as a lover.

III

By trying to "domesticate" the saga material, to give it a degree of peasant realism, Synge deliberately foregoes "archaic" advantages. What really moves him in the story of Deirdre is the pity of it, and the elegiac evocations of youth and nature do become steadily more moving. The necessities of dramatic exposition and the deeper values of the poetic theme never properly coalesce. No wonder he struggled so hard and long with the play!

And yet, for all its inadequacies, we would not want to be without it. It is unique not only in the work of Synge but in the whole of modern drama. A heroical-lyrical-pastoral-mythical-realistic play! If it fails from trying to do too much (and in my opinion Synge could not have mended its inner contradictions even if he had lived to revise it), it also succeeds to some extent in all its compartments. In a good production it would be continually interesting, and most important, its power is cumulative. Yeats has given a sufficient tribute to the effectiveness of Deirdre's speeches after the death of Naisi. After (mis)quoting Deirdre's remark to Naisi in the quarrel scene—"Is it not a hard thing that we should miss the safety of the grave and we trampling its edge"[15]— Yeats continues,

> That is Deirdre's cry at the outset of a reverie of passion that mounts and mounts till grief itself has carried her beyond grief into pure contemplation. Up to this the play has been a Master's unfinished work, monotonous and melancholy, ill-arranged, little more than a sketch of what it would have grown to, but now I listened breathless to sentences that may never pass away, and as they filled or dwindled in their civility of sorrow, the player, whose art had seemed clumsy and incomplete, like the writing itself, ascended into that tragic ecstasy which is the best that art—perhaps that life—can give.[16]

Yeats's own *Deirdre* (produced at the Abbey in 1906) was an attempt to achieve tragic ecstasy, but unlike Synge he deliberately set his story at a "mythical" distance from the everyday world at the start of the play. One might say that the musicians regulate the "flow" of the action back towards its ancient source. Though his play begins at the same point in the narrative as Synge's third act does, Yeats has far more plot in his small space than Synge uses in his last act. For Yeats must show the whole relationship between Deirdre and Naisi as well as lead his heroine gradually up the ascent towards acceptance of her divinity. At last prepared to be a bride in a marriage on the other side of death, she will be happy and triumphant at having circumvented Conchubar and escaped the "cage" he had so cunningly prepared for the lovers. Her whole effort is bent toward achieving the ritual poise that will make her worthy of her story, and she succeeds. Synge's Deirdre is much more conventionally tragic—and more natural. Her threnody has the impact of unpremeditated grief. Though she insists that what she is about to do will make her story one of joy and triumph in times to come, the stronger feeling that comes through is of an admirable and pitiful courage facing the cold, dark night ahead. It is little good her fame will do *her*. But for a brief moment the blaze of her passion does indeed hold the world's dark cruelty at bay.

Yeats did not find pity a congenial emotion. At least he rejected it as a proper theme for literature. The true aristocrat (that is, or includes, the genuine hero) was superior to such condescension. Synge, lacking the "supernatural" resources Yeats felt he had recovered for himself, had the compensation of responding to the beauty and sadness of the natural world more keenly than Yeats did. The stoical quality Synge considered so important was for him a necessary protection against the tears in things. And only a stern (but also humorous) sense of reality preserved Synge from sentimentality. As the *Playboy* proved, Synge was inescapably aware of the ironical ambiguities of imagination. Christy Mahon becomes the playboy of the western world (I wonder how much of its fame the play owes to its marvellous title?) by an act of collective fantasy, and in the end one is hard put to say whether the playboy is a feigning poet or a new man.[17] But the bad things men do to each other are as much the responsibility of imagination as are the triumphs that raise man above the brutes. Death, however, resists metamorphosis. A death may be falsely reported—and there is nothing funnier than a corpse that refuses to remain corpsed—but the odour of death permeates Synge's work, even when he is playing games with it. And since in *Deirdre* humour is not available as a safety valve, the grimness of death becomes oppressive. Naisi and Deirdre need all the vitality they can summon to keep on approaching the devouring time that hungrily awaits them. In the first act they are escaping to an as yet unachieved love; from then on we see them looking back with longing on a precarious love that is already slipping away. We never get to see them enjoying themselves.

Comedy depends on timing, but tragedy depends on time. And the foreseen end of tragedy makes of time a powerful magnet. We wait in fascination for the inevitable horror to unfold. When the characters *also* regard what is to come with however bitter an acquiescence we may well feel an uncomfortable morbidity has entered the proceedings. Yeats (it seems to me) avoids this in his *Deirdre* by making the reactions of his characters to their assigned roles the true subject of the play. Because Synge wants his characters to be more "human", however, they mourn their lot but keep on hoping (until almost the end) that somehow it can be avoided. Knowing that they cannot escape the ravages of time whatever they do, they nevertheless decide to rejoin the familiar world of men (which means to re-enter history). Because they *fear* the end of love their choice is really no choice. Once having lost confidence in themselves (and each other), they are right to feel that their decline is irreversible. So, as Synge is at pains to make clear, they do not go because Fergus convinces them that Conchubar has had a change of heart; they go because *they* have to. It is a typical Syngean irony that the catastrophe draws closer essentially because it has already occurred before Fergus arrives in Scotland.

The heroic resolve to settle for all or nothing, for an ideal love or an absolute death, is in the grand tradition of romantic tragedy. But the way Synge allows enlightenment to occur somewhat diminishes the heroic effect. Deirdre learns, from overhearing Naisi admit to Fergus that he hopes to keep any failing of his love from showing in his eyes, that her lover is prepared to practice deceit. It dawns on her that well-meaning treachery from within is a greater threat to the ideal than malicious treachery from without. Deirdre has gambled on love as the only secure absolute in a slippery world; now love has become as slippery as everything else. When she changes her mind about going home, the bewildered Naisi resists her arguments because, manlike, he confuses loyalty with love. At last, "heartbroken," he is forced to yield to her inexorable logic; he is a defeated man. So Conchubar, for all his menace, becomes essentially a *symbolic* dragon.

Nevertheless, Synge still plays with suspense in the last act. Naisi and Conchubar are about to shake hands in a new-found friendship when the embattled Ainnle cries for help. The false hope flickers out. The die is cast and war to the death has commenced. This moment of near reconciliation underlines the helplessness of good will confronted by the momentum of destiny. Conchubar, of course, is as much the victim of illusion as the two lovers are. Thinking that power and cunning would enable him to recapture the pleasures of youth, he learned that lovers could be killed but love could not. Being old, he cannot understand that the secret of Deirdre's irresistible beauty is the purity of her youthful integrity. Ironically, Conchubar would not want to bargain for less. No compromise is possible: the familiar tragic impasse.

Synge's Conchubar is allowed his own tragic pathos. Lavarcham, Deirdre's loyal protector, turns her maternal attention to Conchubar when he is left a broken man. "I have a little hut where you can rest Conchubar, there is a great dew falling." To which he replies "[*with the voice of an old man*] Take me with you, I'm hard set to see the way before me."[18] In contrast, Yeats's Conchubar ends with proud defiance, proclaiming that in spite of all, his course of action was right. For Synge, man's consciousness of his own mortality is at the heart of tragedy. Yeats has less respect for death; he thinks of it as a barrier to be hurdled by the hero with a tall enough imagination. In passing we remark that the kind of intellectual passion exemplified by Oedipus is foreign to both conceptions.

IV

It is obvious that Synge's *reality* is equally far removed from the "joyless and pallid"[19] life of the modern city and from the kind of bucolic misery reflected in Patrick Kavanagh's *The Great Hunger*. However surprising the news might be to those who thought Synge the quintessence of degradation, his reality is moral. He thought art should reflect a mood in harmony with nature because such a mood "is healthy and worthy of a place in the temple of the things that we admire." He continues (in one of his notebooks):

> The thin and sickly artist fears nature. A life spent in the making of paste jewels seems wasted among the flowers of the country; and the poor player of dances is distressed by the music of the spheres . . . The art we call decadent, or at least the more unholy portion of the art we call decadent, is not the fruit of disordered minds but rather the life of a people far from the real fount of all artistic inspiration.[20]

Living according to Nature is indeed one of the ancient Stoic principles, though Synge's stoicism is more of the heart and less of the head. He exalted the virtues of manliness and decency and continually mocked mean-spirited hypocrisy and the cruelty it leads to. As a moral realist he upholds health and sanity against sickness and decadence. He might well have said, "Wordsworth, thou should'st be living at this hour."

Times change, and to many Synge may now well appear as a useless conservative. He wanted to re-establish a lost connection between Art and Nature. And in order to be near "the real fount of all artistic inspiration," the artist should immerse himself in the life of a people whose minds are still unviolated by ideas of the kind that, say, Oscar Wilde made his stock in trade. But the features of life and art that so unsettled Synge have surely become more pronounced today. On the return from one of his trips to the Aran islands Synge wrote:

I have come out of an hotel full of tourists and commercial travellers, to stroll along the edge of Galway bay, and look out in the direction of the islands. The sort of yearning I feel towards those lonely rocks is indescribably acute. This town, that is usually so full of wild human interest, seems in my present mood a tawdry medley of all that is crudest in modern life. The nullity of the rich and the squalor of the poor give me the same pang of wondering disgust; yet the islands are fading already and I can hardly realise that the smell of the seaweed and the drone of the Atlantic are still moving round them.[21]

Granted, Galway may not be the best that modern civilization has to offer, any more now than it was then, but the disadvantages Synge observed would be a thousand times worse in any great civilized metropolis. And Synge feels acutely how quickly the impressions of that other, stiller world of nature are drowned out by the imperious "noisiness" of a city.

All too modestly, Synge claimed to find in the folk imagination what was wild in reality; he conceived of himself as a kind of mediator between his illiterate and literate countrymen, bringing the good news from the country to the theatregoer in the city. Actually, his plays are a stylization of life from which he excluded the more demeaning aspects of reality—he wrote in a letter to Stephen MacKenna that if he told, "which Heaven forbid, all the sex horrors I have seen I could a tale unfold that would wither up your blood."[22] One wishes he had tried, just once! But it was quite enough for him to bring *Irish* sex on to the stage at all. One shudders to think what he would have said of the kind of reality brought to the stage by a Tennessee Williams on the one hand or a Beckett on the other. Surely they would have seemed to represent a giving in to the enemy rather than a sane and healthy resistance. Synge displays benighted people, stupid people, timid people on the stage, but he shies away from real wickedness, real sickness, real despair. He has no language for those things.

What he does have a language for is the reaching out of lonely people toward some cosmic energy. If only enough imagination were brought to bear, a miracle might happen; but Synge is suspicious of the supernatural. Yet he needs it, if only to play with it. And for realism too, of course. Because it *is* real to most of his characters. It offers the promise or threat of validating their deepest hopes or fears. Nora Burke in *The Shadow of the Glen* is typically obsessed with the grim imagery of old age and death, but when faced with the present reality of wandering the roads, homeless and exposed to the elements, the "miracle" comes to pass that saves her from the fate of being fastened to a dying animal, for that is essentially how she sees *any* husband. The Tramp promises to make Nature a home for her (temporarily at least) in a way that a human household never could be. Nature itself becomes the supernatural principle, the *deus ex machina*. But perhaps it is in *The Well of the Saints* that Synge makes clearest his ironical view of miracles. The brutality of deception and undeception is exhibited in people with the terrible innocence of childish cruelty. The most unrelenting irony, however, comes from the saintly saint. The good man has restored the sight of two "pitiful sinners"[23] so that they can see the Spirit of God in the splendours of nature with no thought at all of the consequences of his act. He can recommend only that this poor couple learn to live like saints. He leaves them to feast their eyes on the "poor, starving people of Ireland"[24] while he goes about his business of restoring missing faculties to the deaf, the dumb, the blind, and the crazy with which the country is, one gathers, plentifully supplied. He may be a good man, but apparently he serves a country impervious to divine benevolence— certainly he himself has had (quite unintentionally) a baneful effect on the morals and manners of God's sheep.

Curiously enough, there is less brutality, less harshness, in Synge's tragedies than in his comedies, or rather it is distanced by the melancholy lyricism in which it is embedded. The full-throated and unhurried cadences, on which T. R. Henn has some interesting and valuable technical comment,[25] often give the effect of holding the present at bay while the imagination plays with memory or anticipation. Even when Naisi is "frantic" he has time to respond to Deirdre's coldness a moment before he goes out to his death with what we might call poetic enlargement:

> They'll not get a death that's cruel and they with men alone. It's women that have loved are cruel only, and if I went on living from this day I'd be putting a curse on the lot of them I'd meet walking in the east or west, putting a curse on the sun that gave them beauty, and on the madder and the stone-crop put red upon their cloaks.[26]

This is at a fair distance from "reality". From "if I went on living" to the end, Naisi is projecting into a future he himself regards as hypothetical emotions he will have no time or need for a few minutes hence. And that is the heart of the matter: caught in the world of action, the thinking and suffering being rebels against the indignity of being reduced to a mortal body. He creates his own past and future to brace himself against the onrush of annihilating time. What is "wild" in Synge's reality is the straining *away* from the dirty facts of life toward that mastery of circumstance that only poetic contemplation can authenticate. Poised between the inescapable dust that claims her and her passionate conviction that something within her is not dust, Deirdre vibrates in tragic tension.

NOTES

1. *C.W.*, II, p. 144.
2. Letter to Stephen MacKenna, 28 January 1904, quoted by Greene and Stephens, *Synge*, p. 158.
3. *C.W.*, IV, p. 219.
4. *Ibid.*, p. 207.
5. I use this term because it seems peculiarly appropriate to suggest the close connection between character, custom, and the moral order, though it does not, of course, have the "Holy" association here that it has in Indian philosophy. See Heinrich Zimmer, *Philosophies of India*, ed. Joseph Campbell (Princeton University Press, 1951), especially p. 163.
6. Synge's words quoted by Yeats, *Aut.*, p. 509.
7. *C.W.*, IV, p. 173.
8. *Ibid.*, p. 267.
9. *Ibid.*, p. 53.
10. Thomas Kinsella, *The Sons of Usnech* (Dublin, Dolmen Press, 1954), p. 9. Kinsella translates from the Book of Leinster.
11. *Explorations*, p. 11.
12. For a convenient summary of these background matters, see Alwyn Rees and Brinley Rees, *Celtic Heritage* (London, Thames and Hudson, 1961), pp. 279-296.
13. Lady Gregory, *Cuchulain of Muirthemne* (Gerrards Cross, Colin Smythe, 1970), p. 95. First published in 1902 by John Murray.
14. Quoted in *Celtic Heritage*, p. 293.
15. Cf. these lines quoted by Yeats (*Essays*, p. 239) with Synge's (*C.W.*, IV, p. 255).
16. *Essays*, p. 239.
17. Augustus John tells us in *Chiaroscuro* (London, Jonathan Cape, 1952, pp. 198-199) an amusing anecdote, illustrating the diversity of opinion regarding *The Playboy of the Western World*:
    "Irishmen are incalculable. Once when I was in the Café Royal with John Quinn and George Moore, the subject of Synge's *Playboy of the Western World* cropped up. I was shocked to discover that Quinn and Moore, otherwise at opposite poles, agreed in missing the whole point of the play. Against all my protestations, these two insisted that Christie Mahon, the Playboy, was a fine, tall, devil-may-care type of fellow, when in fact as Synge made it clear he was a timid little 'stump' of a chap (while an embryonic poet), who, under the blandishments of two female admirers (played to perfection by my friends, Sally and Molly Allgood), convinced himself that he *had* really killed his 'Da', and was accordingly made a hero of, and *was* a hero till, overtaken by the victim, who, with head bloody still, but far from bowed, drove his son home, like a beaten cur. Little Willie Fay, the very counterpart of Christie Mahon, filled the role as no one will again."
    Certainly John has remembered an ending nothing like any of the

published texts, but it is easy to see why a theatregoer might remember Christy (quite correctly) in both of these opposite ways.

18. *C.W.*, IV, p. 269.
19. *Ibid.*, p. 53.
20. Quoted by Ann Saddlemyer, " 'A Share in the Dignity of the World': J. M. Synge's Aesthetic Theory", *The World of W. B. Yeats*, ed. Robin Skelton and Ann Saddlemyer (Dublin, Dolmen Press, 1965), p. 243.
21. *C.W.*, II, pp. 102-103.
22. *Synge*, p. 157.
23. *C.W.*, III, p. 101.
24. *Ibid.*
25. *The Plays and Poems of J. M. Synge*, ed. T. R. Henn (London, Methuen, 1963), pp. 17-19.
26. *C.W.*, IV, p. 257.

ART, NATURE, AND
"THE PREPARED PERSONALITY"

A Reading of *The Aran Islands* and Related Writings

Ann Saddlemyer

In my plays and topographical books I have tried to give humanity and this mysterious external world.

> Synge's Notebook, 1907.

I wished to be at once Shakespeare, Beethoven and Darwin.

> "Autobiography", *C.W.*, II, p. 12.

"He was a drifting silent man full of hidden passion, and loved wild islands, because there, set out in the light of day, he saw what lay hidden in himself."[1] It has become almost commonplace to illustrate the miracle of transformation from notebook to art by comparing *The Aran Islands* and Synge's Kerry and Wicklow articles with his plays. Using Yeats's perceptive comment above as a guide, I would like to suggest that a closer reading of Synge's prose works might provide not only a further insight into careful craftsmanship but also a deeper understanding of the man himself.

A study of Synge's travel sketches reveals not merely a topographical survey, a sociologist's notebook, and a folklorist's goldmine,[2] but a personal record of the moods, atmosphere and colouring of the Irish countryside and people as they are reflected in a sensitive observer. "I have given a direct account of my life on the islands, and of what I met among them," Synge wrote in his introduction to *The Aran Islands*, "inventing nothing, and changing nothing that is essential."[3] Throughout he remains the passive but understanding witness, reacting to each subtle alteration in weather and temperament, sharing briefly in the emotional climate of the life he was privileged to penetrate, recording accurately and sharply the daily life of the islanders in their relationship with the natural world. We as readers see clearly because he felt intensely, and it is this strange but complete involvement as much as actual deeds and events which provided him with the material for his plays. But the adventures he records also reflect the contours, emotions and temperament of the author's personality, for this journey to the western world was also an exploration and revaluation of his own consciousness.[4] Like the deliberately and carefully sustained tension of his mature drama, *The Aran Islands* poises delicately and surely between objective, amoral, deliberate description of the hardships of the islander's daily life and the luxurious evocation of Synge's own mystical reactions to the inner life as he sensed its reflection in the primitive world about him.

Examined with this tension in mind, the pattern of details becomes not an apparently chronological ordering of daily happenings, but a systematic arrangement designed to expose through the externals of life the unconsciousness of a people, the background of a race, and the inner life of the poet. This selection is implied in his Introduction: he has altered "nothing that is essential," but at the same time he admits that on these primitive islands "many changes are being made, that it was not worth while to deal with in the text."[5] Factual descriptions of industry and manufacture are followed by tales of the fairies, giving way to reminiscences of the priest; the impersonal keen at the burial of an old woman is matched later with the intense grief at the death of a young man; a returned American who is said to be dying walks with feverish excitement as a foreigner on the rocks where he was born, and Synge leaves him for the thrill of a dangerous crossing to Inisheer, the sharp sense of the sea's urgency and power making way a few pages later for a nightmare of frenzied self-absorbing dance. With each cycle of events he reports, the exhilaration reaches a higher peak, the author's reserve before the forces of nature is further dissipated, the barrier between the islander and the natural and supernatural forces about him loosens. While circling outward to encompass more of the islands Synge probes inward to the soul of the people and through them to himself, much as the cormorants and crows, temporarily released from the fog's confinement, swoop and swirl on the cliffs about his head communicating and performing in a wild outburst of exultation.[6] And finally, copying the technique of the story-tellers he uses so effectively as controls and checks within each chapter, he adapts the framework of the *seancha* itself ("That is my story.") to his tale of the folk: "I am in Aranmore" circles till it meets the final coda, "The next day I left with the steamer."[7] Nothing is invented, nothing is changed, but all is carefully selected and arranged to reveal further encompassing patterns.

The rest of Synge's prose, though incomplete and unpolished, indicates the same intentional patterning and engrossing ambition; it is even hinted at in some of the occasional reviews and newspaper articles laboriously churned out for cash. For although only *The Aran Islands* was completed to the author's satisfaction, a creased scrap of paper found among his papers after his death suggested that he was contemplating a further volume or two from his Wicklow articles and "what is permanent" among the *Manchester Guardian* and Kerry articles.[8] Recently the late Dr. Alan Price has sensitively combed the papers Synge left behind to discover "Various Notes about Literature" and significant autobiographical sketches; an examination of his note books reveals further notes of artistic intention.[9] With these assorted comments of aesthetic theory and private confessions as additional evidence and Synge's *Aran Islands* as a guide, it is possible to establish with some confidence the *leitmotivs* essential to his view of the world as they are reflected in the patterning of his prose.

Not surprisingly, considering his studious approach to literature and language, one discovers that Synge, like Yeats, Wilde and Shaw, was not only aware of but apparently influenced by the aesthetic doctrines of those great nineteenth century synthesizers, Pater, Ruskin, and Morris. Like his older colleagues, he took from that inherited aesthetic what he wished, distilling, adapting and altering it to suit his own temperament, literary ambition, and vision of life. He too was concerned with style, that "portrait of one's own personality, of the colour of one's own thought."[10] Gradually, consciously, independently, although not necessarily systematically, he too sought and conceived of his ideal pose. Also not surprisingly, given his early training at the Royal Irish Academy of Music and later on the continent, the key to his theory lies in a concept of universal harmony, the supreme example of which of course is music. But Synge would enlarge on Pater's prescription that "All art constantly aspires towards the condition of music." Similarly, he would seek Pater's "hard gemlike flame" in an identification with the natural world rather than by perfecting the artificial, as Wilde did to shield himself from "the sordid perils of actual existence."[11] For Synge, as he discovered in his own life, music is not the end but a means—perhaps the most successful means—of achieving unity with the universe. "There are even natures who have no firm consciousness of an intellectual movement unless registered by some definite sound or melody, and for them the memory of voyages is but a medley of musical suggestion,"[12] he commented in an early notebook of his travels on the continent. In his autobiography (written about 1896 while he was in Paris) he recalls the ecstasy of playing in an orchestra in the spring, with the aura of lilacs and a woman's sensual beauty wreathing through the music: "the suave balm that draws out intricate characteristics from places not open to the world [helped me] to realize that all emotions depend upon and answer the abstractions of ideal form and that humanity as God is but the first step toward a full comprehension of this art."[13] A year or so later the hero of his first completed play relates the divine harmony of music to the Romantic concept of the divinity of Nature (rather improbably during the course of a marriage proposal): "The world is an orchestra where every living thing plays one entry and then gives his place to another. We must be careful to play all the notes. It is for that we are created . . . Every life is a symphony. It is this cosmic element in the person which gives all personal art, and all sincere life, and all passionate love a share in the dignity of the world."[14]

That Synge was both nature-mystic and dramatist, and that each aspect is revealed in terms of the other, was pointed out by Una Ellis-Fermor in her brief chapter on his plays.[15] But although his experiences on Aran crystallized and heightened his artistic and philosophic sensibilities so that they achieved artistic form in his plays, his early autobiographical writings indicate clearly the direction he was to take. Throughout the notebooks of 1895-98 while he was studying in Paris or walking the hills of Wicklow, and later during his first visit to Aran in the early summer of 1898, Synge developed his concept of the harmonic progression of existence, the cycle of experience in man which reflects the cycle of experience in nature, the responsibility of the artist to contrive a hierarchy of all his moods and passions, and in so doing to recognize that the joys and sorrows of passion and ecstasy, the bitterness of disease and death, the perfection of art and the wildness of evil, the crude barbarous instincts of both child and savage, are all necessary to the wholesomeness of art and the sanity of man.[16] "All emotions have neither end nor beginning, they are a part of a long sequence of impulse and effect. The only relative unity in art is that of a whole man's lifetime."[17] Just as the complete expression of a personality "will reveal evolution from before history to beyond the science of our epoque,"[18] so the eternal problem in all the greater arts is to find "a universal expression for the particular emotions and ideas of the personality of the artist himself."[19] Harmony in art can be achieved only when man has established harmony within himself; and the greatest harmony in man is discoverable during those moments when is he at one with the natural world. "A human being finds a resting place only where he is in harmony with his surroundings," he writes after his first visit to Aran, "and is reminded that his soul and the soul of nature are of the same organization."[20] But the artist must be aware of this process of harmonization. Often, he tells us in his autobiography, "I worked myself into a sort of mystical ecstasy with music and the works of Carlyle and Wordsworth . . . I began to write verses and compose. I wished to be at once Shakespeare, Beethoven and Darwin."[21] As deliberately as Yeats had, he set about to experience and fashion a style of life and prose which would exemplify the values of this holy trinity and at the same time allow the prepared personality freedom for further growth.

Looking back he recognized the early development of a nature-mystique and the hypersensitivity which encourages a lonely temperament. As a child he had rejected the "man-made" in favour of the "natural"[22] and "untouched";[23] as a schoolboy-naturalist he had become acquainted with the "passionate and receptive" moods of night;[24] as a young man his sexual awakening was sublimated in an ecstatic pilgrimage to the sun.[25] Psychic adventures he was to describe on Aran were familiar occurrences in the fogs and rainy autumn evenings of Wicklow,[26] when the strange splendour of Ireland mingles with an air of strained regret. And just as he would identify the fog's "grey obsession twining and wreathing itself among the narrow fields" with the Aran Islander's isolation and desolation in a world of mist, so he identifies his sense of separateness and painful sensitivity with the vagrants of Wicklow[27] and in so doing establishes the part he himself wished to play: "Man is naturally a nomad . . . and all wanderers have finer intellectual and physical perceptions than men who are condemned to local habitations. The cycle, automobile and conducted tours are half-conscious efforts to replace the charm of the stage coach and of pilgrimages like Chaucer's. But the vagrant, I think, along with perhaps the sailor, has preserved the dignity of motion with its whole sensation of strange colours in the clouds and of strange passages with voices that whisper in the dark and still stranger inns and lodgings, affections and lonely songs that rest for a whole lifetime with the perfume of spring evenings or the first autumnal smoulder of the leaves."[28] "It need hardly be said that in all tramp life plaintive and tragic elements are common, even on the surface. Some are peculiar to Wicklow. In these hills the summer passes in a few weeks from a late spring, full of odour and colour, to an autumn that is premature and filled with the desolate splendour of decay; and it often happens that, in moments when one is most aware of this ceaseless fading of beauty, some incident of tramp life gives a local human intensity to the shadow of one's mood."[29] For Synge the artist *must* be a tramp: "The hunter, poacher and painter are the only men who know nature. The poet too often lets his intellect draw the curtain of connected thought between him and the glory that is round him."[30] In turn the tramp's innate harmony illuminates the the natural world: "Beautiful as these Wicklow [glens] are in all seasons, when one has learned to know the people one does not love them as Wordsworth did for the sake of their home, but one feels a new glory given to the sunsets by the ragged figures they give light to."[31] Later he would give the most poetic speeches in his plays to a tramp and a poacher, and in his poetry reject the ecstasy of Angus, Maeve and Fand to celebrate instead the realities of Red Dan Sally's ditch; finally he would add a further role to this cycle of experience and sign his love letters to Molly Allgood, "Your old Tramp."

"Is not style . . . born out of the shock of new material?" Synge once remarked to Yeats.[32] On Aran Synge discovered much that, like the *poitín* of Inishmaan, brought "a shock of joy to the blood."[33] Ideas, perceptions and emotions required only the savage simplicity of a life freed from the complexity and mediocrity of the civilized world to discover the harmony which completes the person and provides great art. Aran became that resting place which could remind Synge most forcibly that "his soul and the soul of nature are of the same organization."[34] "I cannot say it too often," he comments in his notebook, "the supreme interest of the islands lies in the strange concord that exists between the people and the impersonal limited but powerful impulses of the nature that is round them."[35] Here was the spiritual treasure denied to modern man who dwelt in cities and constructed artificial barriers between himself and the natural world; in these islanders could be found that divine simplicity of passion where all the notes in the symphony might for a short time longer still be played. "Their minds have been coloured by endless suggestions from the sea and sky, and seem to form a unity in which all kinds of emotion match one another like the leaves or petals of a flower. When this atmosphere of humanity is felt in the place where it has been evolved, one's whole being seems to be surrounded by a scheme of exquisitely arranged sensations that have no analogue except in some services of religion or in certain projects of art we owe to Wagner and Mallarmé."[36]

In Inishmaan where the men seem to be moved "by strange archaic sympathies with the world,"[37] one "is forced" to believe in a "sympathy between man and nature";[38] the sea not only provides "judgment of death"[39] but educates;[40] the immense solitude after nightfall creates distinction.[41] Similarly, on these islands the natural and the supernatural are but states on the same spectrum of existence: "The wonder is a rare expected event, like the thunderstorm or the rainbow, except that it is a little rarer and a little more wonderful";[42] the aged storytellers break up his final party through nervousness about the fairies;[43] and old Pat Dirane describes the system of fairy tithing.[44] One aspect of nature reflects another while interpreting the moods and hidden passions of the islanders.[45] Here too reactions to the external world mingle with man's sensual nature; "the strange beauty of the women" seems not only to provide "a possible link between the wild mythology" of the fairy world[46] but to reflect "the whole external symphony of the sky and seas", with the "wildness and humour and passion kept in continual subjection by the reverence for life and the sea that is inevitable in this place."[47] Through the women also the "strangely reticent temperament of the islanders" gives way at odd moments in "magnificent words and gestures" or, less pleasantly, in harsh jeers and shrieks, to the passion which he senses is "the real spirit of the island."[48] Observing the burial ceremony of an old woman, he comments, "This grief of the keen is no personal complaint . . . but seems to contain the whole passionate rage that lurks somewhere in every native of the island. In this cry of pain the inner consciousness of the people seems to lay itself bare for an instant, and to reveal the mood of beings who feel their isolation in the face of a universe that wars with winds and seas."[49] Finally, lest we should overlook the relationship between the exultation of joy and the dark impulse to violence, his eye lights with delight on the one touch of brightness in this world of mist and cloud: "What has guided the women of grey-brown western Ireland to clothe them in red ? The island without this simple red relief would be a nightmare fit to drive one to murder in order to gloat a while on the fresh red flow of blood."[50]

Occasionally this search for the primitive bears traces of William Morris and even Rousseau: "much of the intelligence and charm" he finds in the people might be attributed to "the absence of any division of labour" and varied skills necessary to such a hard life;[51] every article, being hand-crafted, provides "something of the artistic beauty of medieval life";[52] the "general simplicity of their lives" gives them the "physical perfection" of natural aristocrats;[53] on Inishmaan, the child-like charm which the people "share with the birds and flowers" is un-touched by the modern eagerness for gain that he sees reflected on the larger more civilized island.[54] During an eviction he is struck by the unattractive "mechanical police" who "represented aptly enough the civilization for which the homes of the island were to be desecrated" and compares them distastefully as they lay "sweating and gasping" in the heat with the islandmen, "who walked up and down as cool and fresh-looking as the sea-gulls."[55] In this patriarchal life, "perhaps the most primitive that is left in Europe,"[56] the family and the hearth rule supreme,[57] and the application of the machinery of modern justice is absurd and artificial to "a man who will not do wrong unless he is under the influence of a passion which is as irresponsible as a storm on the sea."[58] Here "the entrancing newness of the old,"[59] where even the stones he rests on and the stories he records are evidence of an ancient world,[60] brings both a thrill of delight and inconceivable distress.[61] He confides more recklessly to his notebook, "With this limestone Inishmaan however I am in love, and hear with galling jealousy of the various priests and scholars who have lived here before me. They have grown to me as the former lover of one's mistress, horrible existences haunting with dreamed kisses the lips she presses to your own. The thought that this island will gradually yield to the ruthless-ness of 'progress' is as the certainty that decaying age is moving always nearer the cheeks it is your ecstasy to kiss. How much of Ireland was formerly like this and how much of Ireland is today Anglicized and civilized and brutalized . . . Am I not leaving in Inishmaan spiritual treasure unexplored whose presence is as a great magnet to my soul ? In this ocean alone is [there] not every symbol of the cosmos ?"[62]

But just as awareness of the sharpness of life and "the supreme beauty of the world"[63] erupts, like the inner consciousness of the people of Inishmaan, only at rare moments of danger or breathless excitement,[64] intense joy brings with it the distressing realization that man's span is brief, that death too is part of the universal cycle.[65] The islander's dangerous, primitive life, caught between nature's misery and splendour, might correspond to the sensitive varying moods of the artist,[66] but at the same time it alienates. Standing between this primitive world and the artificial, civilized life which has trained him, Synge can sympathize with and sometimes share, but he can never belong to Aran:

> In some ways these men and women seem strangely far away from me. They have the same emotions that I have, and the animals have, yet I cannot talk to them when there is much to say, more than to the dog that whines beside me in a mountain fog. There is hardly an hour I am with them that I do not feel the shock of some inconceivable idea, and then again the shock of some vague emotion that is familiar to them and to me. On some days I feel this island as a perfect home and resting place; on other days I feel that I am a waif among the people. I can feel more with them than they can feel with me, and while I wander among them, they like me sometimes, and laugh at me sometimes, yet never know what I am doing.[67]

The *duine uasal*[68]—especially the artist—is privileged to observe and for a short time enter the peace and dignity of "this little corner on the face of the world," but he can never possess it.[69] It will remain as tantalizing and luring as the oriental landscape he evokes in comparison;[70] and, like the wild, ragged jesters of Inishere, he must hide his loneliness and desolation in laughter.[71]

But, according to Synge's notebook suggestions, it is just these singular qualities that the artist must develop and recognize in himself that allow him the privilege of grasping the full significance of the primitive life while prohibiting complete involvement in it. At times perhaps this incomplete understanding, like the purity with which old Mourteen recited Irish poetry, can even heighten awareness.[72] "Real art is always a suggestion; an intangible emotion lurks behind the things that we produce as life lurks within the body."[73] The artist who stands squarely in the midst of mankind and the beauties of nature while responding to "the inner and essential mood of the things [he] treats of" is more likely to capture what is profound and unique in this world and direct us more surely to what is permanent in the other world.[74] ". . . what is highest in poetry is always reached where the dreamer is leaning out to reality, or where the man of real life is lifted out of it, and in all the poets the greatest have both these elements, that is they are supremely engrossed with life, and yet with the wildness of their fancy they are always passing out of what is simple and plain."[75] Artists such as Pierre Loti, despite his admirable sensibility to the wonder of the world, and the erudite Huysmans, because they live "far from the real fount of all artistic inspiration" can never produce this wholesome, harmonious mood; neither can dogmatic or historical works, no matter how beautiful.[76] "All Utopian work is unsatisfying, first because it [is] weak and therefore vague and therefore wanting in uniqueness, and also because it is only the catastrophes of life that give substance and power to the tragedy and humour which are the two poles of art. The religious art is a thing of the past only—a vain and foolish regret—and its place has been taken by our quite modern feeling for the beauty and mystery [of] nature, an emotion that has gradually risen up as religion in the dogmatic sense has gradually died. Our pilgrimages are not to Canterbury or Jerusalem, but to Killarney and Cumberland and the Alps . . ." Looking back on his work and travels in 1907, he concluded this note with the admission, "In my plays and topographical books I have tried to give humanity and this mysterious external world."[77]

The Aran Islands was not his first attempt to order and number his own passions. *Vita Vecchia*, suspiciously similar in pattern and design to Dante's *Vita Nuova* and begun during his travels in Italy, was followed by "a series of dreams to my later life" as told in the study *Étude Morbide*.[78] But he was not yet at ease with himself, nor could he see his own place in the cosmic design; the result was the kind of unhealthy morbidity he was to deplore in the decadents, and he later dismissed his hateful "morbid thing about a mad fiddler in Paris."[79] When the time came for him to record and recreate the mysterious external world he sensed reflected in Aran, he once again chose a technique which would reveal the outer life and simultaneously expose the mysteries of the artist's inner life. But now, thanks to the sense of direction provided by Yeats and the Irish literary movement, he could feel secure both in himself and his purpose in the literary pattern of the universe. Significantly, he omitted from his published volume the following self-conscious re-examination of his past in the light of the present; self-pity and sentimental posturing have no place in a world of joy and hardness:

I have talked with no one through another day of rain and tempest, and now in the evening have drifted away among memories I still hold and cherish from my years of roving in the world. Sometimes I sit upon a couch that stands at the end of a balcony grown over with wild vines where birds are singing in the acacias and the Rhine is running within a stone's throw but I only look at a girl who sits with her work a little way from my feet and hear her quaint and childish complaining of the small things that [happened] during the months I spent in another part of Germany. Again I [picture] a river, the Arno, at the same season of a later year. I am kneeling [on] the floor of an attic listening to an Italian that is singing love songs in the street. Beside me a girl is kneeling also and talking Italian with only seldom a turn that shows her Polish origin. A sod of turf falls in the grate and another frantic burst of the hurricane shakes the island underneath me. I turn on the other side in my chair and dream of things still further off. I am in a cathedral

far down the nave in the obscure tranquillity of the unlit evening
ceremonials far before us voices are intoning a litany, and a form
kneeling at my side is sending prayers to Heaven that have hampered
my career. Then the raging winds chant a cadence to my inner powers
and I am playing with my whole adolescent excitement in an orchestra
of men and women. On the desk before me is spread out the *Eroica*
score of Beethoven but I know it almost entirely by heart and my eyes
are turning without ceasing to a desk near the front of the platform
where a Jewish woman is playing also with the rarest talent and
precision. A cry from the baby, and I wake to a winter's night upon
this bare rock in the Atlantic. Have I not reason to join my wailing
with the winds, who have behind me the summer where I lived and
had no flowers and the autumn with the red leaves of the forest and
never gathered my store for the winter that is freezing at my feet? I
have wandered only some few thousand miles yet I am already beyond
the dwelling place of man.[80]

Synge completed *The Aran Islands* early in 1903, and for the next
few years spent most of his time learning the art of the theatre. But
although he never returned to Aran, the "spirit of the west of Ireland,
with its strange wildness and reserve," "the half-savage temperament
of Connaught"[81] still lured him. In August 1903, he made his first
visit to County Kerry, and continued to make his pilgrimage each year
until ill health conquered in 1907. But some things were different.
The *Manchester Guardian* commission in 1905 forcibly brought to his
attention the unhappiness and distress that accompanies the colour
and attractiveness of life in the west of Ireland[82]; his experience in the
theatre further sharpened his sensitivity to the social man within
nature's hierarchy; perhaps most important of all, his love affair with
Molly Allgood gave him a sense of emotional self-fulfilment. The
essays on West Kerry convey again the worship of nature's mystery and
"indescribable grandeur" that rouses admiration and grief, loneliness
and excitement.[83] A voyage in a curagh brings again exultation and
"indescribable enjoyment," and the women continue to charm.[84] The
islanders of the Blaskets particularly, with their "kindliness and merry-
making," their life "full of riot and severity and daring" have "a
quality and attractiveness" more in keeping with a ballad than the
reality of town life[85]; and the sight of these wild islands and the sea that
surrounds them, "alive with the singularly severe glory that is in the
character of this place," is as clear and cold and brilliant as a poet's
fancy.[86]

But the very brilliance of West Kerry invokes a difference both in the
life Synge portrays and the mood with which he presents it. He had been
a familiar stranger on Aran; on the Blaskets and the Dingle peninsula,
although a welcomed guest, he is even further removed. Two passages
deleted from his published articles reveal the heightened awareness of

the wanderer:

> I missed to an extraordinary degree the faces that have been round me
> for these few weeks that seem so long. I do not feel the distress I felt
> sometimes when I left Aran but I have a despondency which is not
> preferable . . . Yet I know even while I was there I was an interloper
> only, a refugee in a garden between four seas. It is curious I have a
> jealousy for that island—the whole island and its people—like the
> jealousy of men in love. The last days I was there a stranger—a middle-
> aged and simple-minded man from an inland district—[was staying
> there too] and all the time I was making arrangements to come [away]
> I was urging him, I hardly know why, to come away also. At last I was
> successful and he came away in the canoe beside me, but without any
> particular plans. He made his own way to this village where he meant
> to stay a few days in the same inn, and I saw him in the afternoon.
> Then he disappeared. I made enquiries and I heard he had been seen
> late in the evening riding quickly towards Dunquin where one leaves
> for the Island. An inexplicable but fearful jealousy came over me;
> who was he that he should enjoy that life and quiet when I had left it ?
> Who was he that he should sit in my place by the chimney and tell
> stories to the old men and boys ? I was walking about my room in
> extravagant rage when I heard his step on the stairs, and he told me
> he had been out for a ride only. What mystery of attraction is in
> that simple life ?[87]

Later, as he lay on the edge of a cliff watching the girls and men
gathering moss in the sea below him, and revelled in the morning's
"singularly brilliant liveliness" he finally removes himself completely
from the role of dispassionately involved observer:

> The scene last night of story-telling had an old-fashioned dignity and
> this outside pageant of curiously moving magnificence made me shudder
> to think of the seedy town life most of us are condemned to. I think
> especially of the commercial theatre with its stultifying vulgar charac-
> ter quite without one gleam of the light of the world.[88]

The prepared personality had developed further on the scale of
experience; as both artist and man now, that world was not for him.

But the impulse of the young aspirer who had scribbled ten years
before his definition of organic morality, "life held to level of most
inspired moments,"[89] still directs all experience towards harmonic
progression. When we come to Synge's final aesthetic statements, the
prefaces to his plays and poetry, we find distilled there the same
underlying theme of cosmic harmony and passionate counterpoint,
the same plea for wholesomeness in life and art, the same delight in the
bitter as well as the sweet, laughter and grief, reality and joy, the same
acceptance of the brutality of the human and the exaltation of the
beautiful. To Synge all art was indeed a collaboration; the artist in tune

with life and nature, standing alone and aware at the heart of the universe, sympathizes both with humanity and with "this mysterious external world." And in so doing, he comes to know himself.

NOTES

1. See W. B. Yeats's prose elegy, "J. M. Synge and the Ireland of his Time," *Essays*, p. 330; see also pp. 326-327.
2. See Grattan Freyer, "The Little World of J. M. Synge," *Politics and Letters*, IV, 1948, p. 5; Richard Bauman, "John Millington Synge and Irish Folklore," *Southern Folklore Quarterly*, XVII, December 1963, pp. 267-279; Edward J. O'Brien, Introduction to *The Aran Islands* (Boston, Luce, 1911), pp. xii-xiv.
3. *C.W.*, II, p. 47.
4. See Alan Price, "Synge's Prose Writings: A First View of the Whole", *Modern Drama*, XI, 3, December 1968, p. 225.
5. *C.W.*, II, p. 47.
6. *Ibid.*, pp. 73-74.
7. *Ibid.*, p. 49, 184.
8. Because the executors insisted on publishing all of the essays, Yeats withdrew his introduction to the 1910 *Collected Works;* see *C.W.*, II, pp. xiii-xiv.
9. All notebooks and manuscript material referred to in this article are in the possession of Trinity College, Dublin, with whose permission they are here quoted.
10. Quoted by Ann Saddlemyer in " 'A Share in the Dignity of the World': J. M. Synge's Aesthetic Theory," *The World of W. B. Yeats*, ed. Robin Skelton and Ann Saddlemyer (Dublin, Dolmen Press, 1965), p. 245.
11. The influence of Pater's general conclusions in *The Renaissance* was so pervasive that it is difficult to attribute any doctrine with certainty. I feel that Yeats and Synge would both have agreed with Gilbert's synthesis in Wilde's significant essay "The Critic as Artist" (*Complete Works of Oscar Wilde*, with an introduction by Vyvyan Holland, London and Glasgow, 1966, p. 1020): "For there is no art where there is no style and no style where there is no unity, and unity is of the individual."
12. Unpublished manuscript, Trinity College, Dublin.
13. *C.W.*, II, pp. 14-15.
14. *C.W.*, III, p. 176; see also *C.W.*, II, p. 3 and *The World of W. B. Yeats*, p. 248.
15. *The Irish Dramatic Movement* (London, Methuen, 1954), p. 154.
16. See especially "Various Notes about Literature" (c), (d) and (j) in *C.W.*, II, pp. 348-351.
17. *The World of W. B. Yeats*, p. 243.
18. *C.W.*, II, p. 3.
19. *C.W.*, III, p. xxviii.

20. *The World of W. B. Yeats*, p. 245; see also the hero of "Etude Morbide," *C.W.*, II, p. 35.
21. *C.W.*, II, p. 12.
22. *Ibid.*, p. 5.
23. *Ibid.*, p. 12.
24. *Ibid.*, pp. 9-10.
25. *Ibid.*, pp. 12-14.
26. *Ibid.*, pp. 199-200, 213-219, 234-235.
27. *Ibid.*, pp. 202, 208.
28. *Ibid.*, pp. 195-196.
29. *Ibid.*, p. 204.
30. *Ibid.*, p. 10.
31. *Ibid.*, p. 228 note; pp. 196, 236.
32. Reported by Yeats, *Autobiographies*, p. 531
33. *C.W.*, II, p. 73.
34. *The World of W. B. Yeats*, p. 245.
35. *C.W.*, II, p. 75, note 1.
36. *Ibid.*, p. 102, note 1.
37. *Ibid.*, p. 142.
38. *Ibid.*, p. 75.
39. *Ibid.*, p. 162.
40. *Ibid.*, p. 135.
41. *Ibid.*, pp. 129-130.
42. *Ibid.*, pp. 128-129.
43. *Ibid.*, p. 184.
44. *Ibid.*, p. 82.
45. *Ibid.*, pp. 82, 102, note 1.
46. *Ibid.*, p. 54, note 1.
47. *Ibid.*, p. 143, note 1; pp. 113-114.
48. *Ibid.*, pp. 92, 74.
49. *Ibid.*, p. 75.
50. *Ibid.*, p. 54, note 1.
51. *Ibid.*, p. 132.
52. *Ibid.*, p. 59.
53. *Ibid.*, p. 66.
54. *Ibid.*, pp. 116, 106.
55. *Ibid.*, pp. 89-91.
56. *Ibid.*, pp. 53, 57.
57. *Ibid.*, pp. 89, 144.
58. *Ibid.*, pp. 95-96.
59. *Ibid.*, p. 394.
60. *Ibid.*, pp. 65, 69.
61. *Ibid.*, pp. 117, 121, 126-127.
62. *Ibid.*, p. 103, note 1.
63. *Ibid.*, p. 240.
64. *Ibid.*, pp. 97, 118-120.
65. *Ibid.*, pp. 139, 240.
66. *Ibid.*, pp. 74, 132-33.

67. *Ibid.*, p. 113.
68. "Noble person," as Synge was addressed by the Aran Islanders.
69. *C.W.*, II, pp. 143, 162.
70. *Ibid.*, pp. 77, 89.
71. *Ibid.*, pp. 140-142.
72. *Ibid.*, pp. 56, 112.
73. *The World of W. B. Yeats*, p. 241.
74. "Various Notes about Literature," *C.W.*, II, p. 349; see also *The World of W. B. Yeats*, pp. 248-250.
75. *C.W.*, II, p. 347.
76. *Ibid.*, pp. 350, 395; *The World of W. B. Yeats*, pp. 243, 250.
77. *C.W.*, II, pp. 350-351.
78. *Ibid.*, p. 16.
79. "Vita Vecchia" and "Etude Morbide" were written between 1895 and 1897 while he was living in Paris; in the autumn of 1895 he studied Italian, and the following spring spent four months in Italy.
80. *C.W.*, II, p. 110.
81. *Ibid.*, pp. 124, 122.
82. *Ibid.*, pp. 286, 339-343.
83. *Ibid.*, pp. 245-246, 253, 268, 280.
84. *Ibid.*, p. 256.
85. *Ibid.*, pp. 247, 237, 238, 252-253.
86. *Ibid.*, p. 248.
87. *Ibid.*, pp. 258-259.
88. *Ibid.*, pp. 263-264.
89. Notebook 17, written about 1896-1899, Trinity College, Dublin.

THE AUTOBIOGRAPHY OF J. M. SYNGE

Lanto M. Synge

When I was about fourteen I obtained a book of Darwin's. It opened in my hands at a passage where he asks how can we explain the similarity between a man's hand and a bird's or bat's wing except by evolution. I flung the book aside and rushed out into the open air—it was summer and we were in the country—the sky seemed to have lost its blue and the grass its green. I lay down and writhed in an agony of doubt.

"Autobiography," *C.W.*, II, p. 10.

. . . the expression of a personality will reveal evolution from before history to beyond the science of our epoque . . .

"Autobiography," *C.W.*, II, p. 3.

I

The *Autobiography* of John Millington Synge has now been published twice: first in 1965 by the Dolmen and Oxford University Presses; and secondly in the following year in the latter press's *J. M. Synge: Collected Works*. Edited on both occasions by Dr. Alan Price this short work was constructed from a number of different and disjointed MSS.

It is evident that Synge had always intended to write an autobiography; the earliest MS is in a notebook[1] written between 1896 and 1898 while additional passages and revisions were made up to 1907. Dr. Price assembled the *Autobiography* from three sources.[2]

Two other autobiographical essays are included in the *Collected Works: Vita Vecchia* consists of a number of poems linked together by a prose narrative, while *Etude Morbide* is in diary form. These were also written in the late 1890s and were revised in 1907; they continue in a veiled form the story of Synge's life while he was studying music and literature on the continent.

In this essay I shall attempt to show the importance of Synge's *Autobiography* as literature (yet so unlike the plays), as a document of social history and as a biographical essay of first-rate importance to readers of Synge's works and of the works of some of his contemporaries.[3]

The embryonic character of the early part of Synge's short life is fascinating, especially as it contained very varied fields of thought, the endless broodings of a sensitive young artist. His apparently sudden blossoming out in a completely unpredicted career is in fact largely explained oy the *Autobiography*, which concerns only his youth[4] but at the same time carefully explains the process of his significant beliefs.

With reference to the other autobiographical material, especially *Etude Morbide*, we can follow in the *Autobiography* the birth and development of the revolutionary convictions of Synge's mind. These were often held in spite of the beliefs of close relations and loved friends. For a long time, disagreeing with his family, Synge had nobody to share his convictions with:

> Till I was twenty-three I never met or at least knew a man or woman who shared my opinions.[5]

Frequently such convictions came between him and his girl-friends and indeed they prevented his marriage to Cherry Matheson.[6]

These original and controversial views were mostly connected with religion but they also arose from his love of nature, which began at a very early age. The poet was also an active and keen musician and his approach to the art is interestingly outlined in the *Autobiography*. As nature, religion and music are the main topics of this work, I have made them the subjects of the central sections (III, IV, V) of this essay.

II

Speaking of biography and autobiography, André Maurois[7] (Clark Lectures 1928) stressed that it was of paramount importance that such writings should have artistic merits as well as offering factual accounts of men's lives. "Natural history" without literary qualities makes dull reading and is not beautiful. What is important is that truth is maintained in conjunction with an artistic creation that makes pleasant reading. A picture of oneself is rarely pleasing and so good autobiography is an art which is seldom mastered. Many writers have found it so difficult that they have decided to include autobiographical truth in the frame of a novel.[8]

Synge's *Autobiography* is both personal and artistic; he succeeded admirably in combining the documentary with the aesthetic, partly by keeping the work brief and partly by describing a short period of time; he succeeded by writing about the development of his mind and spent little time and space giving us factual details and dates.[9] The result is that the work is a whole and describes the sequence of events in a way that is comparable with the narration of a journey. With proportions that are grand and noble, the teller displays a poet's genius in being able to show us through doorways into vast halls of thought. The next three chapters deal with these individually but I must stress that the success of the work lies in the achievement of the writer in showing these subjects to be joined by a growth that makes themone.

Up to the time when Synge went to the Aran Islands, W. B. Yeats says, he was guilty of "morbid melancholy."[10] Synge certainly was unusually quiet and pensive as a young man but the apparent brooding, though no doubt sometimes morbid, was merely the slightly introspective musings of a young artist. Many artists go through such a phase which is not necessarily unhealthy. In the stage of being "a conscious artist" Synge was not unduly introspective though he was obviously a sensitive and meditative man. Yeats referred to him as "that enquiring man, John Synge"[11] and again as

> And here's John Synge himself, that rooted man,
> "Forgetting human words," a grave deep face.[12]

The autobiography records particularly vividly the changing beliefs of Synge's youth, due to the unusual circumstance of his writing at the early age of twenty-six or twenty-seven. The account is in no way morbid; it is on the contrary humorous in places.

In the opening of the work Synge mentions the difficulty of combining biographical writing with art:

> I do not think biography—even autobiography—can give this revelation. [i.e. the "almost cosmic element in the person which gives great art"]. . . [13]

but he goes on to say how such works can fulfil the purpose of art by showing us the timelessness of what he calls "the sequence of existence":

> If by the study of an adult who is before his time we can preconstruct the tendency of life and if—as I believe—we find in childhood perfect traces of the savage, the expression of a personality will reveal evolution from before history to beyond the science of our epoque.[14]

Already wildly excited by the theories of evolution Synge's artistic leanings urged him to record his youth and the growth of his mind. Unfortunately he never completed the *Autobiography* but the work was drafted sufficiently often to make it well worth publishing.

III

From about the age of seven Synge says he was fascinated by nature, much more so than most children: "Even at this time I was a worshipper of nature."[15]

He tells us much about this aspect of his childhood in the *Autobiography*—which is important as it led him into difficulties concerning his religious beliefs (as I shall explain later), into having a definite scientific awareness and chiefly into his development as an artist, one of whose aims was to record the "colour of locality."

At this early age Synge and his brother Samuel[16] shared a disgust for objects which were "made" rather than natural, and the poet tells us how he "would not allow [his] nurses to sit down on the seats by the [River] Dodder because they were [man-]made." Then the poet continues:

> I had a very strong feeling for the colour of locality which I expressed in syllables of no meaning, but my elders checked me for talking gibberish when I was heard practising them.[17]

Considerably later this "colour of locality" was to be expressed in the delightful language which is really a mixture of Elizabethan English and Irish syntax. We may recall how this too was at first greeted as gibberish.

As a child Synge's two great nature companions were his brother and his cousin, Florence Ross. It was with Samuel that he "invented" folklore and adventures for a legendary character which they called "Squirelly". Synge attributes these games to a dreamy, fanciful imagination, "a legendary instinct." He says,

> I was a sort of poet with the frank imagination by which folklore is created.[18]

Again, soon after this, Synge describes how his poetical imagination of an ideal place and companion is suddenly shattered:

> Although I had the usual affection for my near relations I began while still very young to live in my imagination in enchanted premises that had high walls with glass upon the top where I sat and drank ginger-beer in a sort of perpetual summer with one companion, usually some small school-fellow I hardly knew. One day the course of my class put me for a moment beside my temporary god, and before I could find a fit term of adulation he whispered an obscene banality which shattered my illusions.[19]

But "real affections and imagination acted together" in his friendship with Florence Ross, who was his first cousin and was like a sister to him. From the age of ten Synge was devoted to Florence and he records in the *Autobiography* their free and happy relationship. They shared an interest in a number of pets which they bred from, and together they collected observations of natural history which they recorded assiduously in a notebook. Both were superstitious and could have "evolved a pantheistic scheme" but though they talked frankly on all other subjects, religion did not interest them. At this period they were more interested in "definite life"; they studied ornithology, read books on the subject and clubbed their resources for a ten-shilling telescope. "This period," Synge says, "was probably the happiest of my life. It was admirable in every way." Curiously adult, their friendship seemed perfect and complete:

> In the day-time we played tennis or watched the birds . . . and we wandered arm in arm about among the odours of the old fashioned garden till it was quite dark watching the bats and moths. I loved her with a curious affection that I cannot pretend to analyse and I told her with more virile authority than I since possess that she was to be my wife.[20]

Shortly after this however the relationship of the two children suffered and changed as the result of a visit by Traill relations from South America.[21] Florence Ross temporarily deserted her boy friend for a Traill boy and this hurt Synge terribly:

> I was stunned with horror. I complained to no one, but I fretted myself ill in lonely corners whistling 'Down in Alabama' the only love-song I knew . . . Thus I learned very young the weakness of the false gods we are obliged to worship.[22]

For a year, until the Traills went home again, Synge's affection was not fully accepted but he continued, alongside his studies of Euclid, to watch birds and in the spring collected eggs. He tells us he kept careful notes of all he thought interesting with the intention of writing a book on birds when old enough. He was fortunate in his collection of eggs but regretted that he did not have Florence's full assistance. Yet he says:

> I remember telling—or intending to tell her—that each egg I found gave three distinct moments of rapture: the finding of the nest, the insertion of [the] egg successfully blown in my collection, and, lastly, the greatest, exhibiting it to her.[23]

After the Traills' departure Florence's love for Synge was renewed but they began a different relationship. It was now a case of "being in love." They no longer walked arm in arm or even shook hands. Coyness made their love private and individual.

> I used to kiss the chair she had sat on and kiss the little notes she sometimes sent me till I blotted the ink.[24]

Now wearing long trousers and reading Scott, Synge had grown into a period of secret self-consciousness.

On account of ill health Synge missed much time at school, but staying at home for long periods he had leisure to continue his natural history studies and, having given up school altogether, "began to collect moths and butterflies and other insects, a pursuit which kept me engrossed for several years."[25] Synge joined the Dublin Naturalists Field Club when it was founded by eminent botanists in 1886. He was an active member for two years and was the proud possessor of an extensive collection of butterflies and moths. The collection was mostly built up by himself alone; for Florence was now away frequently and their "childish intimacy" was no longer possible. Making this collection introduced Synge to a more solitary life, going off searching for himself while others were at school or for other reasons were away from home.

> It gave me a great fondness for the eerie and night and encouraged a lonely temperament which was beginning to take possession of me.[26]

Encouraged by his love of wandering over field and mountain and also by his unusual religious convictions which his family could not understand, it is this "lonely temperament" aspect of his character which has been most clearly remembered by his friends. Mr. Barton of Glendalough House, Annamoe, remembers how while the Synges were staying at Tomriland House, the young poet would wander around his family grounds. Lady Gregory in a letter to my grandfather also recalls Synge's solitary wanderings, at Coole Park:

> When staying here he loved to go for a lonely ramble in the woods, and seemed to take such an interest in any detail of natural history or country life.[27]

In his sixteenth year "everything changed"; he took up the violin, began a serious study of literature and at the same time

> began taking very long walks among the Dublin mountains, of which I soon knew every turn and crevice.[28]

However, a change in his appreciation of nature had come upon him similar to that which Wordsworth experienced. Synge recalls:

> I . . . lost almost completely my interest in natural science although the beauty of nature influenced me more than ever.[29]

There are many similarities between Synge and the greatest of all nature poets, Wordsworth—always one of Synge's favourite poets. Wordsworth is referred to several times in the *Autobiography* and in *Etude Morbide*.

There are certainly Wordsworthian echoes in Synge's early poetry, and their philosophies were also closely allied. The "pantheistic scheme" which Synge contemplated was much stronger in the Romantic poet but both experienced a love of nature which was at first, as children, a matter of "dizzy raptures"[30] but later an "innate feeling for the profound mysteries of life." Like Wordsworth also, Synge shows how, as a child, he was incapable of being frightened by death. Wordsworth allowed the little girl to go on emphasising "we are seven" even though two were dead,[31] but Synge's mother felt it her duty to force her son to weep by telling him the unpleasant details of an aunt's death. As both grew up the two poets sensed changes; they began to fear death and lost that early enchantment which "haunted [them] like a passion."[32]

> In my childhood the presence of furze bushes and rocks and flooded streams and strange mountain fogs and sunshine gave me a strange sense of enchantment and delight.[33]

Both Wordsworth and Synge recognised more important qualities in their natural surroundings as they grew older but citing Wordsworth's "Ode", Synge considered Wordsworth had failed to recognise in nature the complete expression of divinity. He saw Wordsworth had experienced a most important change—

> For I have learned
> To look on nature not as in the hour
> Of thoughtless youth—[34]

but that change was different from his own:

> The feeling of primitive people is still everywhere the feeling of the child; an adoration that has never learned or wished to admire its divinity. This feeling everyone will recognize in Wordsworth's *Ode*, though he does not seem perhaps to give it its truest interpretation.[35]

Synge grew up to see the beauty of nature as "an expression of divine ecstasy rather than a mere decoration of the world" while Wordsworth was

> well pleased to recognize
> In nature and the language of the sense
> The anchor of my purest thoughts, the nurse,
> The guide, the guardian of my heart, and soul
> Of all my moral being.[36]

Out of the excited untempered beatings of his heart developed a contemplative, solitary and often lonely man who felt the depth and greatness of the tragedy that is inherent in life. Wordsworth called it "the still, sad music of humanity."[37] It was nature that thus introduced Synge to art and this is acknowledged in the opening paragraph of the *Autobiography*; it is the combination of the "cosmic element in the person" (the emotions) with the "dignity of nature" which produces great art. In *Etude Morbide* Synge says that in this way art must transcend nature:

> ... unless we are able to produce a myth more beautiful than nature— holding in itself a spiritual grace beyond and through the earthly— it is better to be silent.[38]

Synge was much indebted to nature's beauty as the raw material and

inspiration of his art. One of the chief tasks of the *Autobiography* was
to acknowledge this very clearly:

> Natural history did [much] for me . . . To wander as I did for years
> through the dawn of night with every nerve stiff and strained with
> expectation gives one a singular acquaintance with the essences of the
> world. The obscure noises of the owls and rabbits, the heavy scent of
> the hemlock and the flowers of the elder, the silent flight of the moths
> I was in search of gave me a passionate and receptive mood like that
> of early [man] . . . The forces which rid me of theological mysticism
> reinforced my innate feeling for the profound mysteries of life.[39]

IV

The Synge family has always had an ecclesiastical tradition and in
the eighteenth century produced four bishops and an Archbishop of
Tuam in successive generations. More recently a member of the family was among the founders of the Plymouth Brethren.

Later the family became strongly Evangelical and it was this aspect
of his mother's beliefs that the young J. M. Synge could not accept.
His dissatisfaction with the narrowness of puritanical Christianity not
only came between him and his mother but also prevented Cherry
Matheson's acceptance of his offer of marriage. His renunciation of
Christianity caused misery for both of them and for Mrs. Synge, who
wrote in a letter to Robert (her eldest son):

> Cherry came in this morning and is quite decided that she could not
> be joined to one of his opinions, and she says she is awfully sorry,
> . . . I suffer more than she does . . . He looks in misery . . . Johnnie
> has spoken quite openly to Cherry, and she is quite shocked . . .[40]

Synge was greatly distressed but he felt he must have the courage of his
convictions and continued to remain steadfast. Mrs. Synge and
Samuel,[41] who were the two members of the family most concerned
with Synge's unorthodoxy, apparently did not understand this and
eventually had to cease pretending that it was his ill health that kept
him away from church.[42] Synge was not an atheist;[43] he was certainly
aware of the supreme power though not in the shape of the Christianity
of the period.

In the *Autobiography* Synge describes how his different views
developed and how they caused him loneliness. As a timid child he was
terrified of Hell; he thought one night that he was "irretrievably
damned" and cried so much that his mother was sent for. He recalls
humorously:

> She comforted me with the assurance that the Holy Ghost was con-
> victing me of sin and thus preparing me for ultimate salvation. This

was a new idea, and I rather approved. Later in the day while I was playing in the drawing-room I overheard my mother telling my aunt about my experience. While I gave no sign of attention I was inwardly flattered that I had caused this excitement and that the Holy Ghost should single me out so distinctively.[44]

More seriously Synge goes on to say:

> ... the ... cruelty of introducing the idea of Hell into the imagination of the nervous child has probably caused more misery than many customs that the same people send missionaries to eradicate.[45]

Unconsciously barbaric, Mrs. Synge also felt it her duty to make her young son fear death. However, such attempts failed and Synge recounts how his aunt's death only made the woods more lovely:

> I had never been so happy. It is a feeling like this makes all primitive people inclined to merry making at a funeral.[46]

Irish funerals are often celebrated with a sumptuous wake and Synge gives an excellent account of one in *The Aran Islands*.[47]

"Religion remained a difficulty and occasioned terror to me for many years" but Synge was loath to offend his mother and relatives more than he could help and he took pains not to. At home he refused to discuss religious matters although it is evident that Mrs. Synge was worried about him:

> Oh! that I could say his soul is in health. I hope you pray for him, the only one of all my dear children a stranger to God.[48]

She continued to try and restore him to her faith and sometimes begged Samuel to assist in a joint effort. But for all they did they could not change his convictions. There was a little relief when

> he allowed last night to Sam, that Christianity is good for depraved humanity such as cannibals and the heathen in general.[49]

Synge's study of natural history gave him a "scientific attitude" towards theories of existence. With Florence Ross he discussed all subjects but not religion though they were "both well-versed in Christianity":

> The monotheistic doctrines seem foreign to the real genius of childhood in spite of the rather maudlin appeal Christianity makes to little children.[50]

Growing older, Synge and his cousin were more interested in "definite life" and Synge took a scientific approach in collecting butterflies, moths and other insects while the range of his academic studies was ever widening.

When he was fourteen he read a book by Darwin and he describes the profound effect the theory of evolution had on him. At first he was extremely shocked and disgusted by it and wished he had never seen the book. He had it removed from the house as soon as possible but it had made an indelible impact upon him and he found himself considering Darwin's theories more and more:

> My studies showed me the force of what I read, [and] the more I put it from me the more it rushed back with new instances and power.[51]

The result of this was misery; he felt himself the "playfellow of Judas." Soon he regained composure and read books "of Christian evidence"; but these pleased him less and less and eventually, at the age of sixteen or seventeen he "renounced Christianity after a good deal of wobbling":

> My study of insects had given me a scientific attitude—probably a crude one—which did not and could not interpret life and nature as I heard it interpreted from the pulpit.[52]

This caused him a sense of "shame" at the thought of being an infidel. Reading Carlyle, Leslie Stephen and Matthew Arnold, he made for himself as he tells us:

> . . . a sort of incredulous belief that illuminated nature and lent an object to life without hampering the intellect.[53]

This belief found expression in the second stanza of an untitled poem written in the 1890s:

> For my own soul I would a world create,
> A Christless creed, incredulous, divine,
> With Earth's young majesty would yearning mate,
> The arms of God around my breast intwine.[54]

Synge says in the *Autobiography* that the opposite to "the narrow churchman or reformer who knows no ecstasy" is the truly religious man who "feels most exquisitely the joy of contact with what is perfect in art and nature." This man "hides the greatest number of Satanic or barbarous sympathies" but he is also in touch with the fundamentals of religion. The point is clearly put in *Etude Morbide*:

> All living things demand their share of joy, and I see no permanent joy apart from the creation or touching of beautiful forms or ideas. This is the immortal fragment of religion.[55]

But these personal and unorthodox views caused the young poet much loneliness[56] and made a chasm between himself and his relations and friends. It was a "terrible experience" for it wasn't for six or seven years that he discovered somebody who shared his opinions. Yeats paid tribute to his courage in "J. M. Synge and the Ireland of his Time":

To speak of one's emotions without fear or moral ambition, to come out from under the shadow of other men's minds, to forget their needs, to be utterly oneself, that is all the Muses care for.[57]

Synge felt horribly presumptuous in disagreeing with the Fellows of Trinity College (Dublin) but he was convinced that in fact the views he had arrived at represented "the real opinion of the world." Rid of "theological mysticism" he was now aware of the "profound mysteries of life." In *Vita Vecchia* he wrote:

We do wrong to seek a foundation for ecstasy in philosophy or the hidden things of the spirit—if there is a spirit—for when life is at its simplest, with nothing beyond or before it, the mystery is greater than we can endure. Every leaf and flower [and] insect is full of deeper wonder than any sign the cabbalists have invented.[58]

This shows well the strength of Synge's devotion to beauty, what he called at one time "intangible glory," at another "divine ecstasy" and what other men vaguely label as God.

V

Except for the isolated member who is alleged to have been renamed "Synge" by Henry VIII as a reward for his singing voice,[59] the family has not had a musical tradition. J. M. Synge's great interest in music and his near adoption of the art as a profession was another of those unexpected characteristics which at first surprised and later worried his anxious mother.[60]

Though in the end Synge realised he was not fit for a musical profession, the art was for many years his chief interest. This aspect of the poet's career has not been duly recognised by his biographers and critics. It is important not only because he devoted eight of his best years (probably 1886-1894) to music, but also because it played a major part in the development of his artistic talents.

Music for Synge was "the finest art"; a religious ecstasy "as multiform as the varieties of liquid." A life with it could only be compared with a saint's life:

Even in the preparatory discipline there is much that is similar in the saint's life and in the artist's. We have the same joy of progress, the same joy in infinitely exact manipulation, (the saint with his daily actions, the artist with his materials) the same joy of creation . . .[61]

In the *Autobiography* he tells how he worked himself into "a sort of mystical ecstasy" with a combination of music, Carlyle, and Wordsworth. He exclaims with joyful recollection:

I found the mysterious mansion I had dreamed, [and] I played with morbid assiduity.[62]

Being for him the height of all art, "this extraordinary instinct of music which leads to such ecstasy" was almost too much for him but in the wonderfully strong, bold conclusion of the *Autobiography* he says:

> For the hypersensitive organization the musical excitement is perhaps too powerful, too nearly a physical intoxication, but it is not surprising that when I found in the orchestra the world of magical beauty I dreamed of, I threw aside all reasonable counsel and declared myself a professional musician.[63]

This passage is one of the most interesting in the whole work. It explains why Synge failed as a professional musician. The "extraordinary instinct" was indeed too much for him; like so many artists, especially young ones, he was too involved in his work to be able to take "reasonable counsel." Synge's affinity to music was so great that he was not fully in control of his musical ideals. This was, I believe, the cause of his nervousness and was why he eventually decided to abandon a musical career.

One of his earliest musical memories has particular charm and shows remarkably objective and sympathetic views. About the age of seven he remembers going to St. Patrick's Cathedral, Dublin, every Sunday and after being "strained almost to torture by the music" seeing in contrast, after the services, hordes of poor children playing outside the cathedral. Observing the "wild" and "barbarian" fighting and the segregation of boys and girls, from a shadowy place, he compared two aspects of tragedy:

> . . . I remember there was something appalling—a proximity of emotions as conflicting as the perversions of the Black Mass—in coming out suddenly from the white harmonies of the Passion according to St. Matthew among this blasphemy of childhood.[64]

The sight of these slums made him aware of "the ecstasy of pity and with it the thin relish of delightful sympathy with the wildness of evil which we all feel but few acknowledge even to themselves."[65]

Synge was sixteen when he took up the violin; this and his study of literature began to eclipse his interest in natural science. He was a keen music pupil and two years later he enrolled as a student at the Royal Irish Academy of Music. The violin was put down temporarily when he had to make a special effort to pass the entrance examinations for Trinity College, Dublin. He passed "with a squeak" as his mother described it, and became an undergraduate in 1888.[66] However, the poet's connections with Trinity were limited as he spent as little time as possible in the university and did the minimum amount of reading. Although he won Hebrew and Irish prizes he was content with a "gentleman's" pass degree which he received in December 1892.

He made few friends at Trinity; and although his tutor was Anthony

Traill,[67] a cousin, he seldom visited him. Throughout his career there Synge was more interested in his violin and continued to play music and to study its history and theory. Even for light entertainment he was devoted to the fiddle and loved playing amongst country people.[68] He also loved listening to fiddlers in the country and we may recall an ecstatic experience which he recounts in *The Aran Islands*. From Inishmaan he writes:

> Last night, after walking in a dream among buildings with strangely intense light on them, I heard a faint rhythm of music beginning far away on some stringed instrument.
>
> It came closer to me, gradually increasing in quickness and volume with an irresistibly definite progression. When it was quite near the sound began to move in my nerves and blood, and to urge me to dance with them.
>
> I knew that if I yielded I would be carried away to some moment of terrible agony, so I struggled to remain quiet, holding my knees together with my hands.
>
> The music increased continually, sounding like the strings of harps tuned to a forgotten scale, and having a resonance as searching as the strings of the 'cello.
>
> Then the luring excitement became more powerful than my will, and my limbs moved in spite of me.
>
> In a moment I was swept away in a whirlwind of notes. My breath and my thoughts and every impulse of my body, became a form of the dance, till I could not distinguish between the instruments and the rhythm and my own person or consciousness.
>
> For a while it seemed an excitement that was filled with joy, then it grew into an ecstasy where all existence was lost in a vortex of movement. I could not think there had ever been a life beyond the whirling of the dance.[69]

Then he describes how he woke up with a shock. All the experiences of this dream are closely related to those Synge had in connection with concert music but the last paragraph especially may be compared with this description of playing in an orchestra, from the *Autobiography*:

> No other emotion that I have received was quite so puissant or complete. A slight and altogether subconscious avidity of sex wound and wreathed itself in the extraordinary beauty of the movement, not unlike the sexual element that exists in all really fervent ecstasies of faith.[70]

As a serious student of the violin Synge was warned by his teacher that nervousness would mar a professional career:

> . . . he had thought of taking up music as a profession, but his master in Dublin told him he could never make a success of it on account of his extreme nervousness.[71]

There are hints in the *Autobiography* suggesting Synge was very nervous, but it is in *Vita Vecchia* that he describes how he breaks down with nervousness when small boys come in and listen to him playing. In *Etude Morbide* he relates how before a concert his "nervousness is appalling." "Bent double with pain" the result was again a breakdown. Synge was desolate for this proved that a musical profession was impossible. He saw it coming. Before the concert he wrote:

> I have given up everything for music, and tomorrow I am going to fail utterly.[72]

Playing in orchestras Synge was wholly successful and felt complete satisfaction:

> The collective passion produced by a band working together with one will and one ideal is unlike any other exaltation.[73]

With the Academy orchestra he performed in two notable concerts; in 1891 his first was held in the Ancient Concert Rooms where the first offerings of the Irish Literary Revival were later to be produced. His second, in 1892, was in the Molesworth Hall where two of his own plays were produced some years later. Soon after this second concert he distinguished himself further by winning a scholarship in counterpoint.

As well as being a performer Synge was indeed an ambitious and active composer though unfortunately only a few fragments of his musical works have survived. In the *Autobiography* he tells of the vaulting ambitions he had just before he qualified for Trinity and says:

> I would go down on my knees at times with my music paper on a chair before me and cry to God for a melody.[74]

As a child his little compositions were noted by members of the family, especially by his mother, who wrote in one of her letters:

> [Johnnie] is always composing little airs and making out accompaniments for them on the piano, which I have to play.[75]

A few years later she mentions her son's musical compositions again:

> Sam heard him playing the piano at Greystones . . . He told Sam afterwards that he had composed the little piece he played . . . He has never played for me, though I asked him. He seems shy of doing so.[76]

But Synge took his composing seriously and recorded carefully in his notebook when he finished his pieces. In May 1893 he recorded that he had "started words and music for an opera on Eileen Aruine."[77] He obviously enjoyed composing and found it the easiest form of expression but he realised that even as a composer his abilities were limited:

Music is the finest art, for it alone can express directly what is not utterable, but I am not fitted to be a composer.[78]

As either performer or composer Synge gradually realised that there was little hope for the future. Though he was fully determined and in his early years declared himself professional, in the later autobiographical essays concerning his life on the continent he shows what a strain such a life would have been.

Rather bitter in *Etude Morbide*, ("I love music, it is barred from me; I was ambitious, I am thrust aside . . ."), he finally announced his decision in 1894 to give up music as a serious study. In a happier mood he turned his attention to literature and learning foreign languages and bade farewell to music in verse:

> For thee I would have led my life,
> Have braved a breadless, barren strife.
> I was not destined for the glee
> True musicians find in thee.[79]

However, when Synge revised his *Autobiography* only two years before he died, he preserved his happy musical memories and this is not surprising as he owed so much to what he learned through music.

Even the construction of the *Autobiography* is in a musical form in which various contrasting themes are harmoniously resolved. The opening melody has Mozartian freshness and depth:

> Every life is a symphony, and the translation of this life into music, and from music back to literature or sculpture or painting is the real effort of the artist.[80]

This simple process was carried out in such a way that, quite apart from his attempt to make a profession of music, we must acknowledge that it was important in the development of Synge's mind and as the medium between life and literature, the second art he chose for his expression.

VI

Despite its brevity Synge's *Autobiography* is among his most interesting works. It is in no way what one would expect of an autobiography for it is unusually frank and there is a singular lack of factual details "for the records."

Its chief interest lies in giving us flash-like glimpses of the poet's growing mind and of the times in which he lived. Its intrinsic beauty is of a quality which one would not expect of an autobiography.

The work is obviously from the pen of a poet and the prosody of every sentence has been carefully thought out. One of the most perceptive passages concerns the young man's endless ambitions:

When I was fiddling I mourned over the books I wished to read; when I was reading I yearned for all manner of adventures. Vulgar sensuality did not attract me but I was haunted by dreams of the verdant liberty that seemed to reign in pagan forests of the south.[81]

Another favourite passage is his description of playing in a symphony orchestra and being aware of participation in the much larger universe:

I remember particularly the long blue days of a June that I spent looking out over the four strings of my violin into the filling leaves and white erect florescence of a chestnut and a wilderness of plants beneath it that crushed and strangled each other in a green and silent frenzy of expression . . . One is lost in a blind tempest [of music] that wails round one with always beautiful passion, the identity is merged in a . . . symmetrical joy, cathedrals build themselves about one with the waves of purple storm, yet one remains sane and a man.[82]

The sheer beauty of these passages is evidence of a most satisfying communion with the grandeur of the world. They are the acknowledgment of real happiness and a kind of worship.

That is one quality of the *Autobiography*. The second is its depiction, as a social document, of behaviour of the late nineteenth century. It shows clearly one man's struggle out of a series of social conventions into new beliefs which, though revolutionary at that time, became much more widespread soon after.

Closely allied to this is the third quality, the value of the work as a biographical document of especial use to literary historians and critics of Synge's plays and poetry.

In his youth he had "boundless" ambitions: "I wished to be at once Shakespeare, Beethoven and Darwin." Synge never managed to be all three at one time but—in the reverse order—he was in turn a scientist, a musician and a poet. Each occupation developed partly from the former.

At first a simple nature-lover and then an entomologist Synge became dissatisfied with the narrow Evangelical religion he had been brought up in. With his discovery of Darwin's theory of evolution he sought a wider philosophy which he linked with the universal language of music. Then the course of his life turned him back to a *particular* field in which he felt qualified as the result of his wider experience. The general language of music prepared him for his poetical career in a unique way.

It is fortunate that Synge told us how his ideas developed. He was keen to do so from an early age[83] as he realised his mental progress was particularly exciting. In *Etude Morbide* he said:

I try to persuade myself that my personality is also my universe, and that the difficulties in my system only enhance its perfection by the joy I gain as I surmount them.[84]

This was indeed true and the difficulties he had to surmount were great. His personality was worthy of translation into art:

> . . . as the laws of the world are in harmony it is this almost cosmic element in the person which gives great art.[85]

NOTES

Specific references are given only for the longer quotations from Synge's prose.

1. Notebook 15 in the Synge Estate.
2. Notebook 15 and items 21 and 52 in the Synge Estate.
3. As the poet's great nephew I feel qualified to deal with this work which is in many ways very personal and is closely connected with the family. However, I trust I have limited personal sympathies sufficiently to allow an objective critical approach. I am indebted to members of my family and to Dr. T. R. Henn for much information and helpful advice.
4. The work was originally entitled *My Youth.*
5. *C.W.,* II, p. 11.
6. Yeats, and also Synge's biographers, have remarked on how Synge was at his best in female company and confided more in women than in men.
7. *Aspects of Biography,* trans. S. C. Roberts (Cambridge University Press, 1929).
8. Cf., for example, James Joyce's two attempts in *Stephen Hero* and *A Portrait of the Artist as a Young Man.*
9. We may remember André Maurois' comment in *Aspects of Biography* (p. 151): "If we now proceed to posthumous autobiographies we note at once that the only perfect examples are those in which the author has described only the development of a mind."
10. *Essays,* p. 321.
11. "In memory of Major Robert Gregory," *Collected Poems,* p. 149.
12. "The Municipal Gallery Revisited," *Ibid.,* p. 369.
13. *C.W.,* II, p. 3.
14. *Ibid.*
15. *Ibid.,* p. 5. Cf. Wordsworth's "Lines Composed Above Tintern Abbey," *The Poetical Works of William Wordsworth,* II, ed. E. De Selincourt (Oxford, Clarendon Press, 1944), p. 263:
    > ". . . wilt though then forget
    > That on the banks of this delightful stream
    > We stood together, and that I, so long
    > A *worshipper of Nature,* hither came
    > Unwearied in that service."
16. Four years older, Samuel was the poet's closest brother.
17. *C.W.,* II, p. 5.
18. *Ibid.*

19. *Ibid.,* p. 6.
20. *Ibid.,* p. 8.
21. Synge's mother was a Traill. The Traills were living in South America, not India, as stated in the *Autobiography.*
22. *C.W.,* II, p. 8.
23. *Ibid.*
24. *Ibid.,* p. 9.
25. *Ibid.* I feel there is more than coincidence in the fact that at least three successive generations of our family have produced entomologists.
26. *C.W.,* II, p. 9.
27. Unpublished letter to Samuel Synge, 27 February 1928.
28. *C.W.,* II, p. 9. The same could be said of the Wicklow Mountains. Cf. *The Shadow of the Glen* and *The Tinker's Wedding.*
29. *C.W.,* II, p. 9.
30. "Lines Composed Above Tintern Abbey," *loc. cit.,* p. 261.
31. See "We Are Seven," *The Poetical Works of William Wordsworth,* I, pp. 236-238.
32. "Lines Composed Above Tintern Abbey," *loc. cit.,* p. 261.
33. *C.W.,* II, p. 12.
34. "Lines Composed Above Tintern Abbey," *loc. cit.,* p. 261.
35. *C.W.,* II, p. 13.
36. "Lines Composed Above Tintern Abbey," *loc. cit.,* p. 262.
37. *Ibid.,* p. 261.
38. *C.W.,* II, p. 35.
39. *Ibid.,* pp. 9-10.
40. Quoted by Greene and Stephens, *Synge,* p. 55. Cherry Matheson tried in vain to convert Synge. In "Etude Morbide" he relates how the Chouska tried to involve him in mysticism and largely succeeded. Glibly, she sees their love as a religious experience (*C.W.,* II, p. 35): "Mon ami, we have walked with God . . . Mon ami, our love is religion."
41. Samuel was himself too much of a scientist and scholar to try and alter his brother's beliefs. They did not discuss religious matters and remained on the best of terms. There is no significance in the poet's reputed demonstration in refusing to be present at Samuel's first sermon.
42. Cf. Synge's remark to Cherry Matheson (quoted by Greene and Stephens, *Synge,* pp. 51-52): "It is very amusing to me coming back to Ireland to find myself looked upon as a Pariah, because I don't go to church and am not orthodox, while in Paris amongst the students I am looked upon as a saint simply because I don't do the things they do . . ."
43. Synge writes (*C.W.,* II, p. 11): "I had of course heard of atheists but as vague monsters that I was unable to realize."
44. *C.W.,* II, p. 4.
45. *Ibid.,* pp. 4-5.
46. *Ibid.,* p. 7.

47. See "The Aran Islands, I," *Ibid.*, pp. 74-76.
48. Mrs. Synge's letter to her son Robert quoted by Greene and Stephens, *Synge*, p. 19.
49. Mrs. Synge's letter to her son Robert quoted by Greene and Stephens, *Synge*, p. 43.
50. *C.W.*, II, p. 7.
51. *Ibid.*, p. 10.
52. *Ibid.*, p. 11.
53. *Ibid.*
54. *C.W.*, I, p. 6. Skelton entitles the poem "The Creed." There is another version of the poem not included in *C.W.*, I. I quote the two stanzas of this version; the first stanza shows Synge's appreciation of childhood, which is a dominant theme in the *Autobiography*, and the second is significantly different from the version quoted above:

> "The joy of childhood, nature-blessed at peace,
> Would I rewin, there blending blades of hope,
> Nor mid sad cities, dowered domes, would cease
> For man, truth, woman, pureness, love to cope.
>
> For mine own soul I would a world create,
> A curious creed, not credulous, divine;
> My soul with lonely loveliness would mate
> Till gleams of glory were to name as mine."

55. *C.W.*, II, pp. 31-32.
56. In an unusual mood described in "Etude Morbide" (*C.W.*, II, p. 30) Synge remarks: "I feel a lack in my scepticism which leaves no name for malediction, and envy Job, who had his choice to curse God and die."
57. *Essays*, p. 339. Yeats himself frequently hid behind masks and perhaps this is why he was so impressed with that quality in Synge which he described as "Passionate and simple like his heart")"In Memory of Major Robert Gregory," *loc. cit.*).
58. *C.W.*, II, p. 24.
59. See [Mrs] L. M. Synge, *The Family of Synge or Sing* (Chester, privately published, 1937).
60. Mrs. Synge wrote in a letter to Robert (quoted by Greene and Stephens, *Synge*, p. 21): "Johnnie is so bewitched with music that I fear he will not give it up. I never knew till lately that he was thinking of making his living by it seriously; he spares no pains or trouble and practises from morning till night, if he can. Harry [Stephens] had a talk with him the other day, advising him very strongly not to think of making it a profession. Harry told him all the men who do take to drink! And they are not a nice set of men either, but I don't think his advice has had the least effect on Johnnie . . . The sound of the fiddle makes me quite sad now. I used to think it was only a harmless amusement and it kept him out of mischiefs, but it seems now likely to lead him to mischief."

61. *C.W.*, II, p. 31.
62. *Ibid.*
63. *Ibid.*, p. 15.
64. *Ibid.*, p. 6.
65. *Ibid.*
66. *Synge*, p. 14.
67. Anthony Traill, later Provost of Trinity.
68. Professor Walter Starkie, himself an expert violinist described this aspect of Synge's friendship with the Irish peasantry in a meeting I had with him last year.
69. *C.W.*, II, pp. 99-100.
70. *Ibid.*, p. 14.
71. Cherry Matheson quoted by Greene and Stephens, *Synge*, p. 144.
72. *C.W.*, II, p. 27.
73. *Ibid.*, p. 14.
74. *Ibid.*, p. 12.
75. Quoted by Green and Stephens, *Synge*, p. 20.
76. *Ibid.*, p. 43. He was even nervous before his mother.
77. *Ibid.*, p. 36.
78. *C.W.*, II, p. 35.
79. Quoted by Greene and Stephens, *Synge*, p. 20.
80. *C.W.*, II, p. 3.
81. *Ibid.*, p. 12.
82. *Ibid.*, p. 14.
83. The first MS. is dated 1896-1898.
84. *C.W.*, II, p. 32.
85. *Ibid.*, p. 3.

A NOTE ON THE POEMS OF J. M. SYNGE

Francis Warner

SYNGE's editors differ widely in their estimation of his poems. At one in appreciating the achievement of his plays, their verdicts are not so unanimous when his non-dramatic poetry is under consideration. Indeed, one could scarcely find two more opposite evaluations, by well-disposed editors, of one slight body of poetry. Robin Skelton, editor of the *Poems* volume in the Oxford University Press edition of the *Collected Works* of J. M. Synge, states his considered judgement in the opening paragraph of his Introduction:

> The verses which were published in 1909 and 1910 are not only admirable, but also important from an historical point of view, in that they had a considerable influence upon W. B. Yeats, and also upon much English and Irish poetry of the twentieth century. It is high time that as complete a collection of Synge's poems as is reasonable should be published in order both to document his 'poetic progress' and to bring into the light many good poems which have not previously been available for consideration.

The verses published in 1909 and 1910 include all those that Synge wished published. The proofs were corrected by him, and the book was published by the Cuala Press just fifteen days after his death. There were sixteen poems and eleven translations, together with a brief Preface by Synge of five paragraphs. It is on this corpus that Synge wished to be judged as a poet, and on an augmented edition of which T. R. Henn, in *The Plays and Poems of J. M. Synge*, bases his critical appreciation:

> It is just to say that at nearly every point the breakdown is caused by sheer failure of technique; a lack of desire to shape and re-shape until a poem becomes a unity . . .
> The achievement of the Poems, then, is slight ... They are valuable for the light they throw on Synge's personality, and on the plays; as well as for some rough vigorous balladry.

In such a case as this, where critical opinions diverge so sharply, it may be as well for a fresh investigator to avoid any generalizations at this stage, and confine himself to a reading of one poem that may not be dismissed as wholly incompetent. One, moreover, that is not "rough vigorous balladry", and perhaps—to alter the traditional angle of vision—one that has remained unpublished until Mr. Skelton's publication of it in 1962. Mr. Skelton has given it the title "The Masque of May", and it consists of two verses of six lines each. There is no punctuation. The first verse reads:

> The chiffchaff and the celandine
> The blackbird and the bee
> The chestnut branches topped with green
> Have met my love and me
> And we have played the masque of May
> So sweet and commonplace and gay.[3]

The emotion is clear, nature has come to meet the poet and his love in the garb of May; there are two birds, a flower, a bee and the first shoots of leaves on a chestnut tree. Whether the "we" refers merely to "my love and me", or includes the personified manifestations of nature is not clear, though the general feeling, thanks to the three adjectives of the last line, is. There are two rhymes, no contortions of syntax such as we find on other occasions, usually for the sake of rhyme; and the placing of the longer word, whose meaning is in direct contrast to its individuality in this stanza, "commonplace", is effective, coming as it does to separate the adjectives "sweet" and "gay". The atmosphere is not allowed to become too serious, and a touch of self-mockery reins back a tendency to sentimentality, to hold it in the realm of the charming.

Verse two, using the same technique, is not so successful:

> The sea's first miracle of blue
> Bare trees that glitter near the sky
> Grow with a love and longing new
> Where went my love and I
> And there we played the masque of May
> So old and infinite and gay.[4]

The syntax is less clear—we are not sure where they went, if not under the trees beside the sea—and the emotion generated by the lovers is projected on to the sea and bare trees in a pair of poetic exaggerations that do not seem earned by the quality of the poetic emotion involved in creating them. The sea's first "miracle" of blue may be the first light of morning or a dozen other visual experiences, and the trees glittering "near the sky" only serve to reveal the inadequate vision of the spectators beneath. Indeed, this may be true of the poem as a whole. Synge is so close to his subject that he can no more detach the poem from its emotional source in a delivered birth than he can see that though the trees are high, to say that they glitter near the sky is to ask for too willing a suspension of disbelief.

The last line relies on our recollection of the rhythmic pattern of the last line of stanza one. To achieve the effect at which he is aiming, his penultimate adjective must be more than we are anticipating, and so delight by surprising expectation. It does not. Indeed, it is so clearly the geometric opposite of the word in the same place in stanza one, and so vague, containing neither music, shape, colour nor concept, that we fail to be either sensually or metaphysically pleased. In stanza two the charm of the first stanza has been lost owing to inadequacy of invention and a failure of common technique.

Something may be learned from this. The subject matter is that of many of the poems—love in a natural, usually Irish, context. Relaxed pressure of imagination and modesty of technical achievement, content as it is to remain within the realm of the easily attainable, is common to the greater number. He may be meditating on age:

> I've thirty months, and that's my pride,
> Before my age's a double score,
> Though many lively men have died
> At twenty-nine or little more.
>
> I've left a long and famous set
> Behind some seven years or three,
> But there are millions I'd forget
> Will have their laugh at passing me.[5]

but the quality of thought remains the same. In view of the fact that this was a poem he chose for his volume, it is hard to understand why he permitted the obvious awkwardness of the sixth line to remain unrevised. Or he may turn to a given moment in a love experience, real or imagined:

> In a nook
> That opened south,
> You and I
> Lay mouth to mouth.
>
> A snowy gull
> And sooty daw
> Came and looked
> With many a caw;
>
> 'Such,' I said,
> 'Are I and you,
> When you've kissed me
> Black and blue!'[6]

Whether the image of two lovers, having completed their embraces, looking the one like a white gull and the other a sooty daw (or each a mixture of both) is worth an entire poem depends on the treatment. The irregular word order of the second line of the last stanza may be defended as being the opposite of the same line in stanza one; but as it is also—and more importantly—there to gain a rhyme for "blue", the reader is uneasy. Does it matter, save for the rhyme's sake, that the nook opened south?

On the other hand, when his emotion is less lyrical, we may expect something with a harder edge. Such is promised on first reading "A Wish":

> May seven tears in every week
> Touch the hollow of your cheek,
> That I—signed with such a dew—
> For a lion's share may sue
> Of the roses ever curled
> Round the May-pole of the world.
>
> Heavy riddles lie in this,
> Sorrow's sauce for every kiss.[7]

The style is familiar. May-poles range from Herrick to Yeats's Yggdrasil, riddles are most familiar to us perhaps in Campion and his colleagues and Anglo-Saxon poetry, and tears, cheeks, dew, lions, roses and global imagery are all over-familiar from poets such as A.E. What is lacking here in the reader's mind is a conviction that the virtuosity of the technique compels curiosity enough to disentangle the riddle. The familiar connotations of "lion's share" militate against an over-serious acceptance of the problem posed, and the concept of Synge suing for a lion's share of all the roses that ever curled round the May-pole of the world is not immediately arresting.

Synge can do better than this, as in "The Curse: To a sister of an enemy of the author's who disapproved of 'The Playboy' ":

> Lord, confound this surly sister,
> Blight her brow with blotch and blister,
> Cramp her larynx, lung, and liver,
> In her guts a galling give her.
> Let her live to earn her dinners
> In Mountjoy with seedy sinners:
> Lord, this judgment quickly bring,
> And, I'm Your servant, J. M. Synge.[8]

Humour redeems the insincerity of the exuberance, as it does in "On An Island", which ends

> You've cooped the pullets, wound the clock,
> And rinsed the young men's drinking crock;
> And now we'll dance to jigs and reels,
> Nailed boots chasing girls' naked heels.
> Until your father'll start to snore,
> And Jude, now you're married, will stretch on the floor.[9]

and fails to in "To the Oaks of Glencree":

> My arms are round you, and I lean
> Against you, while the lark
> Sings over us, and golden lights, and green
> Shadows are on your bark.
>
> There'll come a season when you'll stretch
> Black boards to cover me:
> Then in Mount Jerome I will lie, poor wretch,
> With worms eternally.[10]

It would be tempting to quote from Synge's Preface for justification,

> In these days poetry is usually a flower of evil or good; but it is the timber of poetry that wears most surely, and there is no timber that has not strong roots among the clay and worms.[11]

were it not that Synge wrote just two paragraphs later in that same Preface a partial disclaimer:

> The poems which follow were written at different times during the last sixteen or seventeen years, most of them before the views just stated, with which they have little to do, had come into my head.[12]

Even the clay and worms of Mount Jerome fail to save this crude juxtapositioning of warm human embracing a tree and talking to it of birdsong and shadows, and the same man thinking ahead to the time when the tree will become boards for his decomposing corpse.

All the same, juxtapositioning of a more effective kind lies behind the success of "Dread". The contrast drawn between the ceremonial formalities of the Church's ritualization of human love, and the warm immediacy of two lovers under a window out of sight is startling and effective.

> Beside a chapel I'd a room looked down,
> Where all the women from the farms and town,
> On Holy-days and Sundays used to pass
> To marriages, and christenings, and to Mass.
>
> Then I sat lonely watching score and score,
> Till I turned jealous of the Lord next door . . .
> Now by this window, where there's none can see,
> The Lord God's jealous of yourself and me.[13]

Whereas the contrast in "To the Oaks of Glencree" is trite, and we leave the poem no wiser than we came, "Dread" creates an atmosphere of farm and townswomen coming on Sundays and Holy-days to Catholic services and observes it from a vantage-point above them; by inference, Synge implies his own warm woman in his arms is preferable to the chaste piety of the religious people below, even if his is unsanctified: indeed the Lord God Himself is jealous of Synge's present-tense predicament.

So the main themes of Synge's poetry can be seen, together with their stronger and weaker forms of expression. Most deal with the contrast between love and death, some with death alone—whether his own or that of such as "Danny". A few with drinking, such as the "Epitaph: After reading Ronsard's lines from Rabelais", or dancing and conviviality such as "Beg-Innish". A third group create the feeling of aloneness, in "Winter: With little money in a great city", and a fourth are pastoral of memory or song after the manner of Wordsworth, "In Glencullen", "Epitaph", "Prelude" and—not so Wordsworthian—"On A Birthday".

Throughout, the diction is simple, the rhyme-schemes are elementary. Those that deal with death are violent unless they involve his own decease, when they tend to become morose; in comparison with the objective violence of

> But seven tripped him up behind,
> And seven kicked before,
> And seven squeezed around his throat
> Till Danny kicked no more.
>
> Then some destroyed him with their heels,
> Some tramped him in the mud,
> Some stole his purse and timber pipe,
> And some washed off his blood.[14]

The odds were twenty-nine to one, and the cause of Danny's death the fact that

> 'He's left two pairs of female twins
> Beyond in Killacreest,
> And twice in Crossmolina fair
> He's struck the parish priest.'[15]

The "rough, vigorous balladry" of which Henn speaks is well illustrated by this poem. Not so successful, perhaps, is "Patch-Shaneen", a poem on a subject that had also been treated by Coventry Patmore with great success, that of a husband waking to find his wife dead beside him. Synge's

> Till on one windy Samhain night,
> When there's stir among the dead,
> He found her perished, stiff and stark,
> Beside him in the bed. . .
>
> And when the grey cocks crow and flap
> And winds are in the sky,
> 'Oh, Maurya, Maurya, are you dead?'
> You'll hear Patch-Shaneen cry.[16]

seems no more than a pale imitation of the Scottish ballad "Sweet William's Ghost":

> Then up and crew the red, red cock,
> And up then crew the gray:
> 'Tis time, 'tis time, my dear Margret,
> That you were going away.'[17]

and set beside Patmore's hesitant strength in "The Azalea", Synge's poem is seen to be no more than unremarkable verse.

When Synge's own death is the subject the tone is either whimsical:

> And so when all my little work is done
> They'll say I came in Eighteen-seventy-one,
> And died in Dublin . . . What year will they write
> For my poor passage to the stall of Night?[18]

where the half-memory of Ovid's cry from his mistress' arms strengthens the final line in a way that is not typical of the rest of Synge's poetry; or, much more frequently, it is contrasted with his living love, as in "A Question":

> I asked if I got sick and died, would you
> With my black funeral go walking too,
> If you'd stand close to hear them talk or pray
> While I'm let down in that steep bank of clay.
>
> And, No, you said, for if you saw a crew
> Of living idiots pressing round that new
> Oak coffin,—they alive, I dead beneath
> That board—you'd rave and rend them with your teeth.[19]

The emotion is clear, the final image of a distraught woman gnawing the idiots perhaps rather overdrawn. It is emotion as Synge would like it to be rather than as it is, and as a result self-indulgent. Preferable, in spite of the grossness of its rhymes, is the "healthy violence" of "The 'Mergency Man":

> 'We'll wash our hands of your bloody job.'
> 'Wash and welcome,' says he, 'begob.'
>
> He made two leps with a run and dash,
> Then the peelers heard a yell and splash.
>
> And the 'Mergency man in two days and a bit
> Was found in the ebb tide stuck in a net.[20]

The love poems use traditional devices of hyperbole and contrast— Synge's mistress is "the Queen/Of all are living, or have been". All those he names—

> Judith of Scripture, and Gloriana,
> Queens who wasted the East by proxy,
> Or drove the ass-cart, a tinker's doxy.
> Yet these are rotten—I ask their pardon—
> And we've the sun on rock and garden;[21]

and "In Kerry" he takes the emotion to a deeper level, recording

> What change you'd wrought in graveyard, rock and sea,
> This new wild paradise to wake for me . . .[22]

and then remembering that just such sexual excitement had brought the previous generations to birth, now buried:

> Yet know no more than knew those merry sins
> Had built this stack of thigh-bones, jaws and shins.[23]

This emotion is also created with gentle effect in the beautiful two-verse poem "In Glencullen", where for once the subject is exactly appropriate to Synge's unambitious technique:

> Thrush, linnet, stare, and wren,
> Brown lark beside the sun,
> Take thought of kestrel, sparrow-hawk,
> Birdlime and roving gun.
>
> You great-great-grand-children
> Of birds I've listened to,
> I think I robbed your ancestors
> When I was young as you.[24]

Again, as in the first verse of "The Masque of May", the humour places the emotion for us and prevents it becoming over-rich.

So, too, with the drinking poems. Dr. Henn's detailed analysis of the translations, and especially of the: "Epitaph: After reading Ronsard's lines from Rabelais": should be studied, and needs no recapitulation here. But the cheerful mockery of "Beg-Innish", another drinking song, may be seen to have affinities with the macaronic poems of the Scots poet Dunbar:

> We'll have no priest or peeler in
> To dance in Beg-Innish;
> But we'll have drink from M'riarty Jim
> Rowed round while gannets fish . . .[25]
>
> (Synge's "*Beg-Innish*")
>
> I will na preistis for me sing,
>   Dies illa, dies ire;
> Na yit na bellis for me ring,
>   Sicut semper solet fieri;
> Bot a bag pipe to play a spryng,
>   Et unum ail wosp (inn sign) ante me.[26]
>
> (Dunbar's "Testament of Mr. Andro Kennedy")

In each, a robust affirmation of the pleasures of life, set against the restraints of religion as represented by its ministers, is achieved, though in this example it is Dunbar who brings in the theme of death, not Synge. The contrast, however, between the thinness of abstract "poetic" beauty, and the robustness of earthy life spiced with a hint of the illegal, is amply illustrated—rather as Wordsworth had done in a milder way in "The Tables Turned" without the masculine bravado—

> Books! 'tis a dull and endless strife:
> Come, hear the woodland Linnet,
> How sweet his music! on my life,
> There's more of wisdom in it.[27]

Synge, in his turn, breaks with the poetry of the Celtic twilight to recapture a hint of the tone of a poet he admired a great deal, and indeed translated, Francois Villon:

> Adieu, sweet Angus, Maeve, and Fand,
> Ye plumed yet skinny Shee,
> That poets played with hand in hand
> To learn their ecstasy.
>
> We'll stretch in Red Dan Sally's ditch,
> And drink in Tubber fair,
> Or poach with Red Dan Philly's bitch
> The badger and the hare.[28]

The eight-line "Epitaph" draws on Wordsworth, emphasising rather the solitariness of the "silent sinner" against a backcloth of nature and the seasons:

> A silent sinner, nights and days,
> No human heart to him drew nigh,
> Alone he wound his wonted ways,
> Alone and little loved did die.
>
> And autumn Death for him did choose,
> A season dank with mists and rain,
> And took him, while the evening dews
> Were settling o'er the fields again.[29]

and the theme of "aloneness" forms the central emotion of two other poems, one urban, "Winter: With little money in a great city", ending

> For I go walking night and noon
> To spare my sack of coals.[30]

and the other rural ("*Prelude*"):

> I knew the stars, the flowers, and the birds,
> The grey and wintry sides of many glens,
> And did but half remember human words,
> In converse with the mountains, moors, and fens.[31]

"On A Birthday" takes the lark of springtime as his emblem, to welcome in Lady-day, and to serve as the pretext for a roll-call of proper nouns that recall in different ways Marlowe, Herrick and Flecker:

> Friend of Ronsard, Nashe, and Beaumont,
> Lark of Ulster, Meath, and Thomond,
> Heard from Smyrna and Sahara
> To the surf of Connemara,
> Lark of April, June, and May,
> Sing loudly this my Lady-day.[32]

We remember Jaques' instructions to Amiens, "Sing it: 'tis no matter how it be in tune, so it make noise enough",[33] forgiving the ornithological inaccuracy and the patently manufactured rhyme (and hence the third line) for "Connemara".

Mr. Skelton's edition of the *Poems* unearths some thirty-five or so unpublished poems, most of which Synge wisely decided to omit from his own selection. They fall into the same categories as those so far mentioned, and one or two deserve a second reading. "In Spring", for instance, combines the loneliness of the solitary with the season of love:

> Buds are opening their lips to the South
> Sparrows are pluming their mates on the sill
> Lovers are laying red mouth to mouth
> Maidens are marging their smocks with a frill
>
> Yet I lie alone with my depth of desire
> No daughter of men would I choose for my mate
> I have learned loving and lived to require
> A woman the Lord had not strength to create[34]

It is a strange poem. The four centre-rhyme present participles of stanza one create a curiously languid air which is built on in stanza two when we find that this is not a love poem in the ordinary sense of the word at all, but an account of an erotic urge without an object. In "The Meeting" Synge has an object for his emotion, and celebrates it in such extreme terms that the poem's final line breaks off in our hands, both metrically and in view of its metaphysical weight:

> Then in the hush of plots with shining trees
> We lay like gods disguised in shabby dress,
> Making with birches, bracken, stars and seas,
> Green courts of pleasure for each long caress;
> Till there I found in you and you in me
> The crowns of Christ and Eros—all divinity.[35]

Nothing has prepared us for this Crashaw-like merging of Eros and Christ. Indeed, if the art of the love poem is to make appreciable and freshly imaginative what is intimate, then in very few cases can Synge be said to be a fine love poet. The disproportion at the heart of his own articulation of his feelings topples poem after poem into sentiment or banality. Some simply remain intimate and no more, such as "The Omission":

> Today you have tutored and healed my head
> Have taught me to see you and love you apart
> But you have not forgiven the words I said
> You have not renewed me the life of my heart.[36]

There is scarcely enough here to claim our attention, and technical achievement is minimal. So it is with so many of the tiny poems that it is with a measure of relief that we watch him—albeit in Job-like and literary stance—curse:

> I curse my bearing, childhood, youth
> I curse the sea, sun, mountains, moon,
> I curse my learning, search for truth,
> I curse the dawning, night, and noon.
>
> Cold, joyless I will live, though clean,
> Nor, by my marriage, mould to earth
> Young lives to see what I have seen,
> To curse—as I have cursed—their birth.[37]

Though we scarcely believe him, we admire the tension between energy and, for once, poetic control in the second stanza, and also the overall shape of the poem.

Synge was a fine dramatist who was not a good poet. The translations from Petrarch and Villon are better than his own original verses, and it is significant that these translations are into English prose. The mannered prose of the plays, coming as it does in a realm somewhere between prose and verse, a kind of liturgical mandarin, employing both Gaelic and Elizabethan syntax and homely, down-to-earth imagery of a striking and dramatically effective kind, this prose was Synge's great stylistic achievement. The poems add nothing to it, and may be regarded as the occasional memorials of private romances; verses written when ear, mind and imagination were not fused into bright focus as they were when he created *Riders To The Sea* and *The Playboy*, but rather one or other working independently. The verses are not vehicles for deep thought so much as occasional fancy. We read them as an act of homage to the man, but turn to the plays to appreciate his genius.

NOTES

1. *C.W.*, I, p. xi.
2. *The Plays and Poems of J. M. Synge*, ed. T. R. Henn (London, Methuen,

1963), pp. 274-275, 278

3. *C.W.*, I, p. 54.
4. *Ibid.*
5. *Ibid.*, p. 59.
6. *Ibid.*, p. 53.
7. *Ibid.*, p. 51.
8. *Ibid.*, p. 49.
9. *Ibid.*, p. 35.
10. *Ibid.*, p. 47.
11. *Ibid.*, p. xxxvi.
12. *Ibid.*
13. *C.W.*, I, p. 40.
14. *Ibid.*, p. 57.
15. *Ibid.*, p. 56.
16. *Ibid.*, p. 36.
17. *English & Scottish Popular Ballads*, ed. H. C. Sargent and G. C. Kittredge, (Cambridge, Mass. 1904), p.165.
18. *C.W.*, I, p. 33.
19. *Ibid.*, p. 64.
20. *Ibid.*, p. 58.
21. *Ibid.*, p. 34.
22. *Ibid.*, p. 55.
23. *Ibid.*
24. *Ibid.*, p. 48.
25. *Ibid.*, p. 37.
26. *The Poems of William Dunbar*, ed. by W. Mackay MacKenzie (Edinburgh, The Porpoise Press, 1932), p. 74.
27. *The Poetical Works of William Wordsworth*, IV, ed. by E. De Selincourt and Helen Darbishire (Oxford, Clarendon Press 1947), p. 57.
28. *C.W.*, I., p. 38.
29. *Ibid.*, p. 31.
30. *Ibid.*, p. 63.
31. *Ibid.*, p. 32.
32. *Ibid.*, p. 60.
33. *As You Like It*, iv, 2, 9.
34. *C.W.*, I p. 27.
35. *Ibid.*, p. 43.
36. *Ibid.*, p. 25.
37. *Ibid.*, p. 14.

SYNGE AND LADY GREGORY

Elizabeth Coxhead

I

WHEN W. B. Yeats made his fruitful suggestions to his new friends, J. M. Synge and Lady Gregory, that they should visit the Aran Islands in search of folk tales and inspiration, they took his advice. Their visits coincided in May of 1898, and each, having expected to be the only stranger on the islands, was disconcerted to see the other in the distance. They did not speak.

But when Lady Gregory got back to her Galway home, Coole Park, Yeats came to stay with her, and told her of this protégé, who seemed to him full of talent, so far aimless and undirected. She immediately wrote to Synge, still in Aran, and invited him to come to Coole on his way home.

This was the first of five visits, none of them of any long duration. The scenery of Coole, with its lush woods and swan-dappled lake, made less appeal to him than the stark rocky outline of Aran, and as his letters show, he was irritated by the atmosphere of adulation surrounding Yeats.

But the visit marked the beginning of a steady friendship with Lady Gregory. She found him a wonderful listener; "one never has to re-arrange one's mind to talk to him",[1] she said. He found in her stimulus and encouragement to write his book on the islands, and to think about becoming a dramatist, and contributing to the Irish theatre movement they had in mind. And both of them were deeply interested in folklore and the folk speech,[2] and had taken the trouble to learn Irish in order to study it—something Yeats never did.

Lady Gregory had also pointed to the way in which this peasant speech, much of it a mental translation by people who were used to thinking in Irish, could be used as literature. She was working on her translations of the ancient Irish epics into the dialect of the Coole district, which her friends named "Kiltartan" after the hamlet nearest to her house. When the first volume, *Cuchulain of Muirthemne*,[3] came out, Synge told Yeats that he found in it the dialect he had been trying to master;[4] he reviewed it enthusiastically in *The Speaker* (7 June 1902), and he wrote to Lady Gregory herself: "Your *Cuchulain* is part of my daily bread."[5] Later, her three-act plays on Irish history, *Kincora* and *The White Cockade*, showed him that dialect need not be confined to peasant plays, but could be put into the mouths of kings and queens. She records with pride that "J. M. Synge had said my method had made the writing of historical drama again possible."[6]

But there, I think, the influence of one dramatist on the other ends. In temperament and outlook they were miles apart; they drew water from the same well, but used it in very different brews. Lady Gregory owed most to the French classic drama (she translated many of Moliere's plays into "Kiltartan"); Synge was a Romantic through and through. Lady Gregory admired single-mindedness and the heroic gesture; Synge's view of human nature was altogether more sardonic. She stuck faithfully to her Galway peasant speech, achieving a remarkable variety of effects with it; but he ranged widely, incorporating phrases from English-speaking Kerry and Wicklow into his dramatic language, which became one of far greater poetic richness than hers.

To compare them, therefore, as has sometimes been done, and to treat Lady Gregory as though she were a pale copy of Synge, is quite beside the point. She is, on the contrary, his ideal complement, a fact which the Abbey Theatre is now recognising by putting on an occasional double-bill of their plays. To ignore her work, as was done for many years after her death, is to rob Synge of a dimension, just as (granted the difference in scale of genius) we cannot get the full measure of Shakespeare if we know nothing of Marlowe, Ben Jonson or Webster.

In any case there was, as I have tried to show elsewhere,[7] much less collaboration between the Abbey dramatists than has generally been supposed. The picture of a writing team at Coole, constantly interfering in each other's work, bears no relation to fact. Lady Gregory supplied Yeats and Douglas Hyde with plots she had found in her folklore collecting, and would doubtless have done the same for Synge had he required it, but he did not. She was obliged to collaborate with Yeats when, as frequently happened, he appealed for her help. The result, except in the political playlet of *Cathleen ni Houlihan*, was never very happy, as her dramatic temperament was no more akin to Yeats's than to Synge's. In a play like *The Unicorn from the Stars*, it is all too easy to see where he leaves off and she begins.

II

The real collaboration between Synge and Lady Gregory was over the management of the Abbey Theatre, of which he became one of the three directors when it was formed into a limited liability company in 1905. Here, they were very much in agreement, both being determined to keep the essential Irishness of the company's work. They resisted

Yeats's plan to introduce an English producer and leading lady over the head of Willie Fay, but were over-ruled, with deplorable results.

The real service rendered by Lady Gregory to Synge was her long fight, both in his lifetime and after his death, to get a hearing for his plays.

When he brought her the manuscripts of *The Shadow of the Glen* and *Riders to the Sea*, she at once recognised their quality, and read them aloud at a literary party in her London flat in January of 1903.[8] Both were then staged by Willie and Frank Fay and their group of Dublin amateurs (who were to develop into the Abbey company) at the Molesworth Hall, the first in October of that year, the second in the following February. Willie Fay produced, but Lady Gregory worked hard to get the staging accurate and to import properties from Aran. "*Riders*," she noted in her diary, "will probably be a stock piece for a long time and ought to be well staged."[9]

With *The Shadow of the Glen* began the trouble that was to haunt the work of Synge. The fervent Nationalists felt that he was weakening the cause of Irish independence by showing the Irish character in an unfavourable light, and two of the leaders, Arthur Griffith and Maud Gonne, walked out of the first performance. *The Well of the Saints* was disliked; *The Tinker's Wedding*, which would have aroused the hostility of the Catholic Church, could not be put on at all; and by the time that *The Playboy of the Western World* was given its first performance in January 1907, it was plain that the Nationalists were "gunning" for Synge and that the week could not be expected to pass off quietly.

Nevertheless, Yeats went off to keep a lecture engagement in Scotland; Synge was already too ill and dispirited to fight his own battle; and it was upon Lady Gregory that the burden fell of keeping the play going (it could not be said to be heard) during the nights of uproar. Her nephew Hugh Lane and his friends from Trinity College tried to help her quell the riots, but she would not have the police used; they were regarded as servants of the British authority, and that would have played straight into the Nationalists' hands. It was not until the play was given in Oxford and London, later that year, that it could be appreciated for the masterpiece it is. And when after Synge's death she took the company to America, the rows started all over again, and even included threats on her life. She met them with the same sturdy determination.[10]

Her courage was the more admirable in that she did not really like *The Playboy of the Western World* herself: a sad but explicable fact. She was a Victorian, and of her time; Synge an Edwardian, and ahead of his. Christy, the Playboy, looks forward to the beatniks and hippies of today. Lady Gregory was very much on the side of youth, and rebellious youth at that; she had, in her quiet way, rebelled against parental conservatism herself. But she wanted the rebellion to be in favour of some fine cause, the liberation of Ireland, or the fighting of a famine, or simply (as in her noble little play *MacDonough's Wife*) the assertion of the artist as a king among men.

She could feel scant sympathy for Christy's rebellion, with its undertone of ruthlessness, nor for the programme he finally announces: "I'll go romancing through a romping lifetime from this hour to the dawning of the judgment day."[11]

More to her taste was the play for which she had to render Synge a melancholy posthumous service. *Deirdre of the Sorrows* is commonly spoken of as "unfinished"; in fact it existed in several drafts, this being the method by which Synge always worked.[12]

Lady Gregory and Yeats, with the help of Molly Allgood, Synge's fiancée, had to bring the versions together and evolve a final text. In *Our Irish Theatre*, her history of the Abbey, Lady Gregory records how they toiled anxiously over this production, "through snowy days and into winter nights, until rheumatism seized me with a grip I have never shaken off."[13] When acted, *Deirdre of the Sorrows* was not a success, probably because Molly was still too dazed by the shock of Synge's death to do justice to the chief part, and it has seldom been given since. This, in my view, is an utterly unjustifiable neglect. Uneven it may be, but it is a very great play, with passages of poignancy and of sheer verbal beauty unequalled elsewhere in Synge.

III

Was Synge grateful to Lady Gregory for all she did to promote his name and fame? The answer, alas, would seem to be "No"; he took it calmly for granted. But then, so did the other dramatists whom she helped, Yeats most of all. It was left to her last great protégé, Sean O'Casey, to come to her defence, and point out how shamelessly she had always been used by other people at the Abbey, how continually distracted from her own work. "In the theatre", he wrote in his *Autobiography*, "among the poets and playwrights, herself a better playwright than most of them, she acted the part of a charwoman, but one with a star on her breast."[14]

In defence of Synge, it must be remembered that his best work was done under the shadow of death; whether consciously or unconsciously, he knew that his time was short. He went his way with desperate concentration, scarcely glancing at his colleagues' plays. Lady Gregory was to write to Yeats afterwards that neither of them ever had a compliment from him (not quite true in her own case, as I have shown), and that she doubted whether he felt a moment's gratitude for all they had gone through fighting his battles. But she said it in no spirit of bitterness. She made allowances, and she felt his death deeply, believing, as so many of us have done since, that he had much more to give the world.

Another cause of Synge's withdrawing more into his shell in those last years was his engagement to Molly Allgood, sister of Sara Allgood, and herself an actress under the stage name of Maire O'Neill. It was regarded by Lady Gregory as a disaster, and had Synge lived and the marriage come about, there seems little doubt that it would have been. Molly was nineteen years old, to Synge's thirty-four; she was a Roman Catholic; she was uneducated; apart from the theatre she had scarcely a taste in common with him. And although a brilliant little actress she was a naughty and troublesome girl, a fermenter of indiscipline in the Company, an increaser of the burdens already harassing Lady Gregory and Willie Fay. Lady Gregory made no secret of her hope that one of the many men with whom Molly flirted, thereby causing Synge much heartache, would carry her off and leave him undeceived and free.

What Lady Gregory could not know was that the excitement and stimulus derived by Synge from this last and greatest love affair of his life were to tingle through *The Playboy* and *Deirdre*. That Molly made him unhappy does not signify; happiness is a by-product, with which genius can seldom afford to be concerned.

In the end, perhaps, Lady Gregory came to appreciate this. There is a note of true understanding in the letter which she wrote to Molly after Synge's death:

> I have just been sent a letter written to me by Mr. Synge just before his operation last year. He tells me of his having hoped to marry at Easter, and asks me in case of his death to do what I could for you. I know you will be touched by this proof of his thought for you, as I am touched by his having written as it were a farewell to me. It was so strange getting it now, when I thought I should never hear a word from him again.

And she concludes on a typically Gregory heroic note:

> I hope you are keeping well and keeping your courage, as he would have wished you to do.[15]

She never forgot Synge, and she watched with increasing satisfaction his fame "going round the world". She would have been deeply grateful to learn that he is appreciated in the Arab World. She could claim with modest pride:

> . . . We have done our best for Synge's work since we lost him, as we did while he was with us here.[16]

It had been a fine and generous literary friendship, and that is its best epitaph.

NOTES

1. Lady Gregory, *Our Irish Theatre* (New York and London, G. P. Putnam's Sons, 1914), p. 121.
2. Lady Gregory's Irish was in fact much better than Synge's, who could read texts but hardly make himself understood in conversation, so I was told by an Aran Islander who remembered him.
3. Published in 1902 (London, John Murray).
4. Lady Gregory, *Our Irish Theatre*, p. 124.
5. *Ibid.*
6. Lady Gregory, *Selected Plays*, chosen and introduced by Elizabeth Coxhead (London, Putnam, 1962), p. 173 Notes.
7. In my *Lady Gregory, A Literary Portrait* (London, Macmillan, 1961).
8. Lady Gregory, *Our Irish Theatre*, p. 125.
9. Lady Gregory, unpublished diary (February, 1904) in the Berg Collection.
10. For the full story of *The Playboy* riots in England and America see Lady Gregory, *Our Irish Theatre*, pp. 109-118, 130-134, 169-252.
11. *C.W.*, IV, p. 173.
12. He must have been the first genius to compose directly on to the typewriter, a historic little machine in a wooden case which is still in the possession of his family.
13. Lady Gregory, *Our Irish Theatre*, p. 138.
14. Sean O'Casey, *Autobiographies*, II (London, Macmillan, 1963), p. 122.
15. Unpublished letter dated 22 May 1909, from Lady Gregory to Molly Allgood; now in Elizabeth Coxhead's possession.
16. Lady Gregory, *Our Irish Theatre*, p. 139.

YEATS'S CONCEPTION OF SYNGE

Robert O'Driscoll

I

"I DID NOT SEE, until Synge began to write, that we must renounce the deliberate creation of a kind of Holy City in the imagination, and express the individual."[1] This is W. B. Yeats writing in 1909. Critics of Yeats have traced the change in his thought and style to various influences: his disillusionment with the emergence of middle-class Ireland, the influence of Ezra Pound and the imagist poets, the influence of the metaphysical poets and the influence of the theatre. But Yeats himself is explicit as to the nature of the change in his aesthetic theories in the essays he wrote between 1902 and 1910, and it is to these essays we must turn to explore the force which he says was responsible for that change, the life and work of John Millington Synge.[2]

Let us look briefly at Yeats's work during the eighteen-nineties when he was indeed consumed with a kind of "Holy City" in the imagination, with a world of intellectual essences, of impossible purities. In *The Wind Among the Reeds* the spirit, symbolized by the wind, stirs the human heart, symbolized by a reed, with longing for an ideal spiritual world. What awakens man's thirst for spiritual perfection, however, also awakens his consciousness of the imperfection of the material world. The heart, forgetting that mortality is a condition of immortality, is caught in uneasy tension between what it desires and what is not possible as long as it retains its humanity. It is led finally to the impossible purity of the spiritual ideal to which it has awakened and it cries out for the destruction of the material forms which, paradoxically, embody the spiritual essence it craves:

> I would that the Boar without bristles had come from the West
> And had rooted the sun and moon and stars out of the sky
> And lay in the darkness, grunting, and turning to his rest.[3]

In *The Wind Among the Reeds* Yeats is led to the point where the destruction of the material world is desired. His faith in the existence of the ideal and his realization of the impossibility of attaining it as long as man is endowed with a broken bewildering body leads him to believe that the ideal can be achieved only when the light of the manifest world has been snuffed out. Rationally he is led into the irrational, into the unknown, into the darkness he wishes to descend upon the world, and the poems seem to indicate that this surrender to the unknown is necessary before man can be freed from dependence on the material world. *The Wind Among the Reeds* takes a prophetic leap into the dark; the rest, for Yeats at least, is an act of faith and surrender.

But the position is an impossible one. Without an imperfect material world there can be no thirst for spiritual perfection, no opportunity for the agony of the human heart to be expressed. In *The Wind Among the Reeds*, therefore, Yeats is led beyond the symbolic approach, for the true symbolist must convey man's sense of frailty as well as his thirst for perfection, his vulnerability as well as his vision. The true symbolist must preserve the precarious balance between form and spirit, one of which is as significant as the other.

Despite the impossibility of the position into which he had worked himself in *The Wind Among the Reeds*, however, Yeats continued to explore the apocalyptic concepts on which the volume is based, and in 1902, with the help of Douglas Hyde and Lady Gregory, wrote *Where There is Nothing*, a play in which the central character, Paul Ruttledge, explores ways of destroying the material world, first through open defiance of the law, then through meditation, preaching, mortification of the flesh, and finally with armies. *Where There is Nothing* is a crude irregular play, but when Yeats was writing it he made certain discoveries: that it is impossible to destroy the world by direct physical action, that the battle between the material and the spiritual, between sense and spirit, is not cosmic but individual, not external but internal, not immediately or ultimately resolved but endless: it is fought within each individual mind and can be won or lost in a moment: "we cannot destroy the world with armies," Paul cries at the end of the play, "it is inside our minds that it must be destroyed, it must be consumed in a moment inside our minds."[4]

II

With the violent and dramatic emergence of John Millington Synge on the Irish literary scene Yeats no longer had to look to ancient legend or beyond the manifest world for his apocalyptic symbols. For there in his own country and in his own theatre was the living embodiment of all he was struggling to create. In the personality of John Synge and in his emotional plays and poems Yeats saw a symbol which embodied the aesthetic and apocalyptic qualities he himself had been emphasizing: strength, self-sufficiency, laughter, the union of contraries, of joy and sorrow, "asceticism, stoicism, ecstasy,"[5] the "perfection of personality" and the "perfection of its surrender,"[6] all the qualities he later embodied in his great apocalyptic symbol, the "shape with lion body and the head of a man" in "The Second Coming,"[7] the uncompromising combination of instinct and intellect, of overflowing turbulent energy and brooding intellectual silence. *Where There is Nothing* had emphasized the reckless raging violence of the apocalyptic agent, but with the example of Synge before him Yeats emphasizes joy, exaltation, ecstasy, the expression and realization of personality, the energies of the body as well as the ideals of the mind.

When Yeats said to Synge, "Go to the Aran Islands. Live there as if you were one of the people themselves; express a life that has never found expression",[8] he was not merely giving sound advice to a friend. He was making possible the means by which a part of his own nature could find dramatic expression, for Yeats saw his contemporaries and the figures of myth and history as a projection of his own personality. Goethe had said, "We do the people of history the honour of naming after them the creations of our minds",[9] and Yeats was fond of quoting the remark. When he presented mythical, historical, or contemporary figures in his work he was not interested in expressing some external or historical truth but in finding in these figures the means by which his own complex moods could find expression. In these personalities, he posits, a writer may discover "precisely that symbol he may require for the expression of himself."[10] Synge is a symbol in Yeats's mind, and J. B. Yeats's compliment to his son, "We have given a tongue to the sea cliffs,"[11] was in a way truer of this projection of the poet's personality than it was of the poet himself.

As well as being a symbol in Yeats's mind, a personality which mirrored his own moods, Yeats saw Synge as a perfect symbolist. Earlier, during the eighteen-nineties, he had differentiated between symbolism, materialism, and transcendentalism. The transcendentalist, he argued, sees matter as essentially evil, as something that separates man from the freedom and truth he desires. The materialist, on the other hand, regards matter as the sole reality, and admits only the existence of a material world which we perceive with our senses and corroborate by analytic science. The symbolist, however, posits the existence of two worlds, the material and the spiritual, the one manifest and visible, the other hidden and invisible, but the visible material world is seen as the way in which an invisible spiritual essence becomes manifest. The symbolist recognizes the uniqueness and sacredness of all living forms, but to him the external world is not the truth but an expression or embodiment of the truth, is the shadow not the substance, the mirror of reality not the reality itself. But although, the symbolist would argue, the external world has no independent reality, it is not dispensable because it provides man with the means by which the elements in his own mind find expression, as Yeats says in his book on Blake, the "symbols or correspondence whereby the intellectual nature realizes or grows conscious of itself in detail."[12] The material world, therefore, serves as a concrete means whereby the poet can express subjective moods. As Yeats puts it in a late poem "Coole Park and Ballylee, 1931":

> For Nature's pulled her tragic buskin on
> And all the rant's a mirror of my mood . . .[13]

But during the latter part of the eighteen-nineties Yeats, as we have seen, came to regard the material world as the enemy of the ideal, and it was his reluctance to recognize this implicit absurdity in the human condition, that matter is as essential as spirit, is indeed the means through which spiritual essences express themselves, that led him to the impossible position he articulated in *The Wind Among the Reeds*.

Synge was to provide him with a way of escape from this dilemma, for Synge found in the material world, and particularly in the life and language of the west of Ireland, the "metaphors and examples"[14] by which he could express his own emotion and thought. Before Aran Synge's work, Yeats contends, was brooding and morbid because he was attempting to express his emotions directly in the poems he was writing. He had not yet found an "objective correlative", a concrete way of making his emotions objective. In the Aran Islands, however, in the harsh grey stones and the "hardship of the life there",[15] in the seasonal changes and the nuances of light and shade, he found a concrete correspondence for the emotions that permeated his own soul: he was, Yeats writes, "a drifting silent man full of hidden passion, and loved wild islands, because there, set out in the light of day, he saw what lay hidden in himself".[16] The Aran Islands, according to Yeats, satisfied "some necessity" in Synge's nature[17] and when he observed the life of the islanders or collected their sayings and stories he was discovering in these stories and sayings the means by which the subjective elements in his own mind could find objective expression. Art, Yeats argues, must use the external world as a symbol "to express subjective moods",[18] and in Synge he found a perfect example of the type of synchronization possible between an artist's mood and the external experiences he presents in his work.

III

Synge went to the Aran Islands in 1898 and by the summer of 1902 he had completed his first two plays, *The Shadow of the Glen* and *Riders to the Sea*. With these plays before him, and also the works of Nietzsche, to which he had also been introduced at the time, Yeats could see his own work during the eighteen-nineties and that of his contemporaries in clearer perspective. As a consequence his style and interests underwent a dramatic change, and it is the aesthetic basis for this change which he articulates in *Samhain*, the organ of the Irish Dramatic Movement, and in the essays he later collected in *The Cutting of an Agate* (now included in *Essays and Introductions*).

The scientific movement, Yeats argues in these essays, had pushed literature into one of two directions: into subservience to an external reality or a concern with rarefied essences. One type was concerned with the spiritual element which the other literature denied, but denied the interest in common life with which the other literature was overly concerned. Yeats, as we have seen, was concerned with rarefied essences during the eighteen-nineties; during the first part of the twentieth century, however, Synge restored for him the balance between art and life, the spiritual and the common, and he created out of the acceptance and juxtaposition of the two a truly tragic emotion.

Synge, as we know, turned from the habitual humanitarian, topical, and political interests of contemporary literature to a living folk tradition, a tradition untouched by the scientific investigations resulting from the restless Renaissance, and where the artist could excite in one visionary but vulnerable moment the radical mystery and innocence before man fell a slave to the external world, before the stage was desecrated with naturalism, mimicry, and a mechanical sequence of ideas. By expressing in his work a life which had never been expressed in literature, Synge, Yeats claims, helped establish the foundation of a new art and a new style, a new mood of the soul. For unlike contemporary dramatists, he did not write for ulterior social or humanitarian reasons; he had no desire to impress a real or imaginary audience, and in his work there is neither judgment nor moral indignation: he had, Yeats writes, "no wish to change anything, to reform anything; all these people pass by as before an open window, murmuring strange, exciting words".[19] In his plays it is not the motive, "that excitement of the will in the presence of attainable advantages",[20] that matters, but the articulation in subtle rhythms and words of the struggle within himself, the indifferent revelation of his own personality. He had the self-sufficiency and strength to reject from his thought all that would be detrimental to this articulation of passionate activity, and the life he loved and lived is reflected in his work "as in the still water of a pool".[21]

By personality, the concept with which he becomes increasingly preoccupied after 1902, Yeats means something similar to what he had meant by symbolism during the eighteen-nineties. The concept of symbolism had been built on a belief in the uniqueness and sacredness of all living forms, and a symbol, we have seen, he regarded as the physical manifestation of a thought or mood. By the end of the eighteen-nineties, however, symbolism had become associated in his mind with an unreal spiritual art, and he supplants it with the term "personality".

Personality Yeats suggests is the expression without regard to blame or acclaim, circumstance or accruing advantage, of the energy which is unique to an individual engaged in active life. It is concerned with the energy of the body as well as the energy of the mind. It is the overflow of passionate activity, a "conflagration of all the energies of active life",[22] the releasing of an energy that comes from the whole man, the spontaneous expression of a moment of intense life, "an eddy of life purified from everything but itself".[23] Personality is the living personal element in life and literature, "the breath of men's mouths",[24] what is vital for each individual: "I have always come to this certainty," Yeats writes in 1906, "what moves natural men in the arts is what moves them in life, and that is, intensity of personal life, intonations that show them, in a book or a play, the strength, the essential moment of a man who would be exciting in the market or at the dispensary door".[25] What is important in the literature produced from personality is not the external world, not revolution or reformation, logic or observation, not the "communicable and forecastable and discoverable",[26] but the expression of the emotion in the soul of a man involved in active life, and this expression is, Yeats contends, as unpredictable and as irregular as the lightning.

Personality is therefore the overflow of passionate energy and style is the energy that remains in a work after the dictates of logic and necessity have been satisfied.[27] When personality is expressed in drama, however, when an artist makes visible to the senses of the audience something he has felt in the depths of his own soul, some dramatic device must be used to temper the outflow of expression, to preserve dignity of dramatic movement and thus exclude from the drama "the animation of common life".[28] Great schools of drama, Yeats argues, are distinguished by the device they have chosen to check the rapidity of dialogue and expression. The Greeks discovered it by excluding action from the stage and by the constant presence of the Chorus before whom characters had to "keep up appearances" while expressing the most vehement of passions. Shakespeare achieved this check on expression by the "slow, elaborate structure" of his blank verse and by his use of the psychological soliloquy.[29] But most modern dramatists, Yeats contends, by picturing an external reality on the stage, had made expression of the deeper reality in the mind impossible or at most indirect. Synge, however, was able to give direct expression to his personality and yet retain dignity of dramatic movement in two ways: first, by his use of the actual physical life and geographical features of the west of Ireland because there, "set out in the light of day, he saw what lay hidden in himself",[30] and second, by the language he placed in the mouths of his characters, the concrete meditative cadences of Kerry and Aran, which lacking "definition" and "clear edges", and being "full of traditional wisdom and extravagant pictures",[31] was a perfect medium for the "drifting emotion, the dreaminess, the vague yet measureless desire"[32] characteristic of both the author and island people:

> ... without dialect he wrote badly, and he made several attempts, because only through dialect could he escape self-expression, see all that he did from without, allow his intellect to judge the images of his mind as if they had been created by some other mind. His objectivity was, however, technical only, for in those images paraded all the desires of his heart.[33]

Synge's emphasis on language was significant, for language, Yeats argues, is the "chief garment of life",[34] and holds the same relationship to artistic beauty as the flesh to human beauty: "What the ever-moving, delicately moulded flesh is to human beauty, vivid musical words are to passion".[35]

With this language, too, Synge was able to unite the contraries which for Yeats are at the core of all great art: "It gave him imaginative richness and yet left to him the sting and tang of reality".[36] In the microcosm of a phrase or word, therefore, Synge could capture the joy of life and art and yet communicate the naked realities of material existence, all "that stings into life the sense of tragedy".[37] Yeats recognizes in Synge's life and work the acceptance of the material world which the spiritual artist rejects, and out of Synge's juxtaposition of reality and imagination, Yeats could not only see, for perhaps the first time, how a truly tragic emotion can be created, but he could see also before his very eyes the living embodiment of the emotion.

All noble things, Yeats writes, "are the result of warfare; great nations and classes, of warfare in the visible world, great poetry and philosophy, of invisible warfare, the division of a mind within itself, a victory, the sacrifice of a man to himself".[38] The struggles in the external world mirror the struggles in the soul, and what is important in Synge's work is not the victory which the military man or politician seeks, but the articulation of the struggle within the soul of the artist. Out of the warfare between an impossible spiritual dream and the indignities of material life, tragic ecstasy, the moment when joy and sorrow are one, is produced. Joy, Yeats argues in 1907, is born in the "making and mastering" of the material world, of all that is below the soul, and the possibility for joy resides "in the hands and in the tongue of the artist."[39] Sorrow, on the other hand, is born in the recognition and submission to all that is greater than man, the things of eternity; it is born in man's soul "by the unlikeness to himself of all that comes before him" in vision or contemplation.[40] The great moment in the arts, and Yeats could see as great a moment in a Synge phrase as in a Synge play, the moment of ecstasy, happens when man experiences joy for all that he is, can apprehend and articulate, and at the same time sorrows for all that he is not. The great characters of literature, Yeats writes:

... speak out of an ecstasy that is one-half the self-surrender of sorrow and one-half the last playing and mockery of the victorious sword before the defeated world . . . the nobleness of the arts is in the mingling of contraries, the extremity of sorrow, the extremity of joy, perfection of personality, the perfection of its surrender, overflowing turbulent energy, and marmorean stillness; and its red rose opens at the meeting of the two beams of the cross, and at the trysting-place of mortal and immortal, time and eternity.[41]

For Yeats the moment of artistic creation duplicates not the moment of creation, as Coleridge would have it, but the moment of death, when the accidental world slips away from the artist and the artist is consumed into the beauty he has created or believes to exist. But until the supreme act is possible, until the body is cast off in the grave, the artist must return after his moment of vision to the material world to which he has become indifferent. Life, therefore, becomes an endless oscillation between the material and spiritual, and death the supreme consummation of the ecstatic process. The artist labours through "many lives and many deaths",[42] for in his mind there is an endless battle, a perpetual Last Judgment. This is what Yeats means when he writes of Synge:

He was one of those unmoved souls in whom there is a perpetual "Last Day", a perpetual trumpeting and coming up for judgment . . . We pity the living and not such dead as he. He has gone upward out of his ailing body into the heroical fountains. We are parched by time . . . He had the knowledge of his coming death and was cheerful to the end, even joking a little when that end had all but come. He had no need of our sympathies. It was as though we and the things about us died away from him and not he from us.[43]

The tragic ecstasy that Yeats saw in Synge's life and work is closely linked in Yeats's mind with his concept of the mask, the idea that although a work of art is created from life it is in its permanence and perfection the opposite of all that man is in daily life. Yeats's theory of the mask develops about the figure of Synge:

I am certain that my friend's noble art, so full of passion and heroic beauty, is the victory of a man who in poverty and sickness created from the delight of expression, and in the contemplation that is born of the minute and delicate arrangement of images, happiness and health of mind.[44]

When Synge had physical strength and health he delighted in presenting on the stage "ugly surprising things", the grotesque, the "harsh facts" of material life, but when death called him he was consumed with beauty, and beauty only.[45] The characters in the plays, Yeats contends, are driven by a dream of an impossible life and Synge, acutely conscious of the gulf between what the imagination creates and the realities of material life, brings that dream before his audience by presenting on the stage its contrary: he "sets before us ugly, deformed or sinful people, but his people, moved by no practical ambition, are driven by a dream of that impossible life".[46]

And yet Yeats's theory of the mask works on a deeper level as far as Synge is concerned. In Synge Yeats could see the mask of the Ireland of his time, an embodiment of the opposite of what his country demanded or expected. "When a country produces a man of genius", Yeats writes, "he never is what it wants or believes it wants; he is always unlike its idea of itself . . . Synge was the rushing up of the buried fire, an explosion of all that had been denied or refused, a furious impartiality, an indifferent turbulent sorrow."[47] In failing to understand plays which embodied their own folk traditions, by taking in "gloomy earnest" what had been created in a spirit of fantasy, by refusing to recognize that the same streak of "satiric fantasy" was in themselves, the new middle class, Yeats argues, revealed their separation from the deep life of their country.[48] Yeats himself welcomed the attacks on Synge's work, for they corroborated in his mind the birth of something original, of a new movement in the arts, of "values not yet understood, of a coinage not yet mastered".[49] Synge was attacked, he contends, because of his style, his individual way of seeing the world, his presentation of unique characters in his work. He was a subjective man in an objective age, his individuality and self-sufficient solitude being resented by an audience who could only find strength in numbers. In the controversy over Synge's work Yeats could see the beginning of the successful overturning of the doctrines that had dominated his country since the days of Young Ireland, the substitution of a "self-consistent vision" for external historical truths.[50]

IV

In summary we may say that Yeats's concept of the mask and his theory of tragic ecstasy developed about the figure of Synge. He conceived of Synge as an apocalyptic agent, as possessing the self-sufficiency and indifference of the pure artist. Synge was a symbol in his mind, a projection of his own personality, and contrariwise, he saw Synge as a perfect symbolist, an artist who used the external world to express subjective moods. But most important Synge restored for Yeats the proper relation between art and life, and as a consequence of his work Yeats turned from the literature of intellectual essences to the literature of personality, the literature of the whole man, of "blood, imagination, intellect, running together",[51] a literature which celebrates the energies of the body as well as the energies of the mind, which captures the intensity of personal life that moves a man who is free from fear and dependence on external circumstance. Yeats puts the transition in his work succinctly when he writes in 1903: "The close of the past century was full of a strange desire to get out of form, to get to some kind of disembodied beauty and now it seems to me the contrary impulse has come. I feel about me and in me an impulse to create form, to carry the realization of beauty as far as possible".[52] Art, Yeats realizes now, must shrink "from all that is of the brain only, from all that is not a fountain jetting from the entire hopes, memories, and sensations of the body".[53] True art, Yeats realizes in 1906, is sensuous and rises out of the body "as the blade out of the spear-shaft, a song out of the mood, the fountain from its pool";[54] it bids us "touch and taste and hear and see the world" and would not move us if "our thought did not rush out to the edges of our flesh".[55] The artist, therefore, must put his "ordinary self" into his writing and in singing his own life he discovers the sweetness and rhythmic movement "in those who have become the joy that is themselves":[56]

> I entered into myself and pictured myself and not some essence when I was not seeking beauty at all, but merely to lighten the mind of some burden of love or bitterness thrown upon it by the events of life.[57]

In 1898 Yeats had written an essay called "The Autumn of the Body" but in 1906 he writes one called "The Thinking of the Body". In 1906, also, he writes about a girl playing a guitar where voice, facial expression, and movements of the body combined to produce a single unified image, "that is not of the fingers and the mind only but of the whole being".[58] Yeats admits that he could not have been as interested in the guitar player during the eighteen-nineties as he was in 1906.

There are, therefore, two ways ever before literature:

> . . . upward into ever-growing subtlety, with Verhaeren, with Mallarmé, with Maeterlinck, until at last, it may be, a new agreement among refined and studious men gives birth to a new passion, and what seems literature becomes religion; or downward, taking the soul with us until all is simplified and solidified again. That is the choice of choices—the way of the bird until common eyes have lost us, or to the market carts . . .[59]

The artist must, Yeats realized as a consequence of Synge's work, exercise firm control over the characters he creates; otherwise he can be drawn off into an "impersonal land of sound and colour".[60] Spiritual art must be made truly symbolic and concrete; emotion must be related to emotion by a system of concrete ordered images; the ideal world must be made solid and "consistent enough for the soul's habitation".[61] The artist must not be drawn off into rarefied essences nor on the other hand should he remain in the market place, but he should ascend "out of common interests, the thoughts of the newspapers, of the market-place, of men of science, but only so far as we can carry the normal, passionate, reasoning self, the personality as a whole".[62]

True art, Yeats realizes now, must neither be too abstracted from the world or too much a part of it. The journalist concerns himself with the impermanent, with contemporary experiences and contemporary interests, with what "never recurs".[63] The saint, on the other hand, cuts himself off from the world, "the great passions that trouble all and have but a brief recurring life of flower and seed in any man", and seeks instead "not an eternal art, but his own eternity".[64] The artist stands between journalist and saint: unlike the journalist, he frees himself from all that is impermanent in the world, and unlike the saint he does not seek what is "still and fixed", but makes his home "in the serpent's mouth".[65]

The agony of the artist is that he must always remain himself and while he cannot remain in the market place he cannot be tempted from the expression of passionate activity by the vision of eternity that constantly allures him. Poets of intellectual essences or the eaters of Indian hemp can abstract themselves from the world and thereby achieve that impartiality, that freedom from judgment and condemnation, which is not possible for those who remain in the world. In their abstraction from life, however, they are spared the agony but denied the ecstasy that is the fate of man in his human sphere. Out of the acceptance of the whole man, his indignities as well as his exaltations, the artist creates an eternal and, although Yeats would have abhorred the word, a relevant art. "We, who are believers", Yeats writes, "cannot see reality anywhere but in the soul itself, and seeing it there we cannot do other than rejoice in every energy, whether of gesture, or of action, or of speech, coming out of personality, the soul's image."[66]

Synge was the major influence in Yeats's career at this period. There were, other influences, chiefly Nietzsche, which I have not explored in this paper. Indeed, Professor Lorna Reynolds claims in a recent paper that in Synge Yeats found the embodiment of the philosophical principles he was discovering in Nietzsche, but the development of that point I leave for another occasion and another scholar.

NOTES

1. *Autobiographies*, pp. 493-494.
2. For earlier explorations of the influence of Synge on Yeats see S. B. Bushrui, *Yeats's Verse-Plays: The Revisions, 1900-1910* (Oxford, Clarendon Press, 1965), pp. 209-226; Alan Price, *Synge and Anglo-Irish Drama* (London, Methuen, 1961), pp. 51-58.
3. W. B. Yeats, *Collected Poems* (London, Macmillan, 1958), p. 68.
4. *The Variorum Edition of the Plays of W. B. Yeats*, ed. R. K. Alspach (New York, Macmillan, 1966), p. 1158.

5. *Essays*, p. 308.
6. *Ibid.*, p. 255.
7. W. B. Yeats, *Collected Poems*, p. 211.
8. *Essays*, p. 299.
9. *Explorations*, p. 144.
10. *Ibid.*, p. 148.
11. *Autobiographies*, p. 23.
12. *The Works of William Blake*, (London, Bernard Quaritch, 1893) I, p. 237.
13. Yeats, *Collected Poems*, p. 275.
14. *Essays*, p. 277.
15. *Ibid.*, p. 331.
16. *Ibid.*, p. 330.
17. *Ibid.*, p. 325.
18. *The Letters of W. B. Yeats*, ed. A. Wade (London, Rupert Hart-Davis, 1954), p. 607.
19. *Essays*, p. 300.
20. *Ibid.*, p. 304.
21. *Ibid.*, p. 328.
22. *Ibid.*, p. 277.
23. *Explorations*, p. 154.
24. *Ibid.*, p. 95.
25. *Essays*, p. 265.
26. *Ibid.*, p. 279.
27. See Yeats's essay, "Poetry and Tradition," *Essays*, pp. 253 ff.
28. *Essays*, p. 333.
29. *Ibid.*
30. *Ibid.*, p. 330.
31. *Ibid.*, p. 334.
32. *Ibid.*, p. 299.
33. *Autobiographies*, p. 345.
34. *Explorations*, p. 108.
35. *Ibid.*, p. 167.
36. *Essays*, p. 336.
37. *Ibid.*, p. 327.
38. *Ibid.*, p. 321.
39. *Ibid.*, p. 254.
40. *Ibid.*, p. 255.
41. *Ibid.*, pp. 254-255.
42. *Ibid.*, p. 137.
43. *Autobiographies*, p. 511.
44. *Essays*, p. 321.
45. *Ibid.*, p. 308.
46. *Ibid.*, p. 304.
47. *Autobiographies*, p. 520.
48. *Essays*, p. 338.
49. *Explorations*, p. 186.
50. *Ibid.*, p. 230.

51. *Essays*, p. 266.
52. *The Letters of W. B. Yeats*, p. 402.
53. *Essays*, pp. 292-293.
54. *Ibid.*, p. 295.
55. *Ibid.*, p. 292.
56. *Ibid.*, p. 271.
57. *Ibid.*, pp. 271-272.
58. *Ibid.*, p. 269.
59. *Ibid.*, pp. 266-267.
60. *Ibid.*, p. 268.
61. *Ibid.*, p. 294.
62. *Ibid.*, p. 272.
63. *Ibid.*, p. 286.
64. *Ibid.*
65. *Ibid.*, pp. 287, 288.
66. *Explorations*, p. 170.

THE *PLAYBOY* RIOTS
Richard M. Kain

"SYNGE is invaluable to us because he has that kind of intense narrow personality which necessarily raises the whole issue",[1] W. B. Yeats wrote to John Quinn on 15 February 1905. The issue, as he explained earlier in the same letter, was that "We will have a hard fight in Ireland before we get the right for every man to see the world in his own way admitted".[2] Indeed, "Irish national literature, though it has produced many fine ballads and many novels written in the objective spirit of a ballad, has never produced an artistic personality in the modern sense of the word", not even Clarence Mangan, who "differed merely . . . in being miserable", and "had not thought out or felt out a way of looking at the world peculiar to himself."[3]

Yeats anticipated Synge's next play like a war-horse sensing battle:

He will start next time with many enemies but with many admirers. It will be a fight like that over the first realistic plays of Ibsen.[4]

That next play was to be *The Playboy of the Western World*. Yeats had predicted accurately, for the fight turned out to be one of the landmarks in Irish theatre history.

Pressures had been mounting since the first public performance staged by the Irish Literary Theatre in May 1899. Irish public opinion had long been torn by religious and political differences, and the wound caused by the rejection of Parnell had not healed. Even among nationalists there were divisions regarding the revival of Irish, the degree of militancy, and the role of the Catholic Church. Some felt that ancient Irish legend was pagan, others thought it irrelevant, still others considered it too sacred for adaptation to the modern stage. A full analysis of the mingled strands of public opinion has yet to be made. Such a study would require extended research into many periodicals which flourished at the turn of the century. David H. Greene and Edward M. Stephens, in their biography of Synge, indicate the positions of the leading newspapers. *The Irish Times* represented the Ascendancy, largely Protestant, with an interest in the arts. *The Irish Independent* remained somewhat Parnellite in its freedom from clerical interference, but was not extremely nationalist. *The Freeman's Journal* supported Parliamentary nationalism, with deference to the hierarchy. *The Daily Express*, once somewhat liberal, had changed hands, becoming more conservative, but showing an interest in the literary movement. Finally, the most dogmatic was Arthur Griffith's nationalistic weekly, *The United Irishman*. The picture is further complicated when one considers the journal of the Gaelic League, *An Claidheamh Soluis* ("Sword of Light"), the publications of the Irish Literary Theatre, *Beltaine*, *Samhain*, and *The Arrow*, as well as other periodicals such as *The New Ireland Review*, *The Leader*, and the *All-Ireland Review*.

It is only to be expected that the Irish should be extremely sensitive to any seemingly unfavourable depictions of their character. For centuries they had been termed "the wild Irish" or "the mere Irish", and had been held as subject for laughter and amusement. The "stage Irishman" was a type, both on and off stage, despised by those who cherished an ideal national image. Susan Mitchell, a minor poet who, for her topical verses, might almost deserve the title of comic laureate of the day, gave utterance to Irish resentment in one of her humorous poems. Though herself a member of the Protestant Ascendancy, she knew native Ireland well enough to write an impassioned conclusion to her "Ballad of Dermody and Hynes":

> We are a pleasant people, the laugh upon our lip
> Gives answer back to your laugh in gay good fellowship;
> We dance unto your piping, we weep when you want tears;
> Wear a clown's dress to please you, and to your friendly jeers
> Turn up a broad fool's face and wave a flag of green—
> But the naked heart of Ireland, who, who has ever seen?[5]

It is the story of subject races everywhere, oppressed and underprivileged.

Even Synge's close friend, the journalist and student of philosophy Stephen MacKenna, betrayed anxiety regarding the role of a cultural movement in an emerging nation. From Berlin he wrote to Synge in early 1904 or late 1903, contrasting the freedom of the artist with the responsibility of a national theatre:

> You should be free as artist, *penseur*. Whether you should be played I do not know. I think art has many mansions . . . I mean vaguely that I like the phillistine [*sic*] idea of a purely fantastic unmodern—forgive me if I borrow "unIbsenified"—ideal, breezy-spring-dayish Cuchulainoid, *etc.*, national theater.[6]

There was, MacKenna felt, fundamental soundness in what the philistine says, the nonsense being "more in the way it is said". As for Ireland, he continued:

> I confess I believe in the ripeness and unripeness of nations and class Ireland blessedly unripe. Modern problems even in peasant robes I do not like to see made public property in Ireland yet. Give us our own literary nationhood first, then let us rise to our frieze-clad Ibsens.[7]

Things being as they are, he would prefer such themes (*The Shadow of the Glen* was the play under discussion) not on the stage but in book form. By way of apology he concludes: "I fear I am a philistine. Do forgive me."[8]

Greene and Stephens print a rough draft of Synge's reply, stronger in wording than the letter he actually sent. Excusing himself for his "volley", he denied that the Irish people were any more innocent than the Norwegians or Germans, with their Ibsen and Sudermann and Hauptmann. He disclaims advocacy of "morbid, sex-obsessed drama in Ireland", simply because "it is bad as drama", rather than on the grounds of the Irish having "any peculiar sanctity, which I utterly deny".[9] As for the purely idealistic drama, *The Shadowy Waters* "was the most *distressing* failure the mind can imagine—a half-empty room, with growling men and tittering females".[10] Of course some plays of that type might be more successful, "but no drama can grow out of anything other than the fundamental realities of life which are never fantastic, are neither modern nor unmodern and, as I see them, rarely spring-dayish, or breezy or Cuchulainoid."[11] What Ireland needs is more, rather than less frankness:

> I think squeamishness is a disease, and that Ireland will gain if Irish writers deal manfully, directly and decently with the entire reality of life.[12]

Synge makes a plea for a cultural dynamism which resembles Yeats's concept of the anti-self:

> . . . I think the law-maker and the law-breaker are both needful in society —as the lively and volcanic forces are needed to make earth's crust habitable—and I think the law-maker is tending to reduce Ireland, or parts of Ireland, to a dismal, morbid hypocrisy that is not a blessed unripeness.[13]

Yeats's best expression of the idea that the artist is a Prometheus, a god-destroyer or god-defier, can be found in a passage from "The Death of Synge" in the *Autobiographies*.[14] As a diary entry in the summer of 1909, about four months after his friend's death, he described his response to one who argued that Home Rule was delayed because England felt Ireland was cruel, and that hence no Irish writer "should write a sentence to make them go on thinking that." Yeats replied, "When a country produces a man of genius he never is what it wants or believes it wants; he is always unlike its idea of itself." Giving as one example the emergence of Burns in a Scotland which "believed itself religious, moral and gloomy", Yeats went on to the case of Ireland, and its need for someone of Synge's flinty temper:

> Ireland, since the Young Irelanders, has given itself to apologetics. Every impression of life or impulse of imagination has been examined to see if it

helped or hurt the glory of Ireland or the political claim of Ireland. A sincere impression of life became at last impossible, all was apologetics. There was no longer an impartial imagination, delighting in whatever is naturally exciting. Synge was the rushing up of the buried fire, an explosion of all that had been denied or refused, a furious impartiality, an indifferent turbulent sorrow.[15]

Yeats's verbal portrait of Synge was painted again and again in prefaces and essays, letters and poems. In *A Vision*, Synge joins Rembrandt as an example of "The Receptive Man" in Phase Twenty-three: "violent, anarchic . . . at a phase of revolt from every intellectual summary, from all intellectual abstraction."[16] Such a man will to others "seem to care for the immoral and inhuman only, for he will be hostile, or indifferent to moral as to intellectual summaries."[17] His Creative Mind represents "Creation through pity",[18] or, as the text elaborates, a progression from personal melancholy and self-pity through wisdom "ennobled to a pity for all that lived."[19] Synge "had to undergo an aesthetic transformation, analogous to religious conversion, before he became the audacious, joyous, ironical man we know."[20]

The moral and intellectual "summaries" which Synge confronted were represented by various religious and nationalistic groups, contemptuously dismissed by Yeats as "the clubs". In a letter of January 1906 Yeats had written to A.E.:

> . . . I know quite well—I knew when Synge wrote his first play—I will never have the support of the clubs. I am trying for the general public —the only question with me (and it is one I have argued with Synge and Lady Gregory) is whether I should attack the clubs openly.[21]

Thus it was that by January 1907 battle lines were clearly drawn. Since the first opening of the Irish theatre in May 1899 the organization had been plagued with difficulties, not only by public outcries but by dissensions within. Here again is a tale which has never been told fully. Apparently Lady Gregory and Yeats had misgivings regarding *The Playboy* when the first two acts had been read to them two months before, and it is all the more surprising that neither of them had planned to attend the first night. Only by accident was Lady Gregory in Dublin, having been asked by Yeats, who was in Scotland, to see Synge regarding a new director. More than usual secrecy was preserved during rehearsals. Even the Abbey Theatre's familiar, the indefatigable theatre buff and diarist, Joseph Holloway, had been excluded. Undaunted, he sought out one of the actors, Harry Young, at intermission, during which he "pumped him on the subject". When Holloway heard the plot, he jumped to the conclusion that it was "A play in praise of murder." The actor "said he did not think so, but then he could not rightly tell me what it was all about, though taking part in it." Young "added that he heard there is an organized opposition present to hiss

Synge's play." Holloway "pooh-poohed the idea and said it is all rot to think so", but the actor proved to be more nearly right in his prediction, if not on the first night at least during the ensuing week.[22]

The audience at the Saturday night opening remained quiet during the first two acts, and Lady Gregory dispatched a telegram to Yeats, "Play great success."[23] But when in the third act the hero—perhaps, come to think of it, one of the first anti-heroes—voiced his poetically extravagant praise of Pegeen, the theatre was filled with boos and cat-calls. Christy Mahon's metaphor, so offensive to middle-class propriety, touched off the latent hostility of the crowd: "It's Pegeen I'm seeking only, and what'd I care if you brought me a drift of chosen females, standing in their shifts itself maybe, from this place to the Eastern World."[24] The remainder of the play was unheard. A second telegram was dispatched: "Audience broke up in disorder at the word shift."[25]

Contemporary newspaper accounts evoke the heated atmosphere of the bitter week-long conflict, which aroused passions that continued to rankle for decades. The protest marked the defeat of Yeats's noble dream of an Ireland spiritually united by an inherited nobility of outlook and richness of imagination. He would continue fighting, after Synge's death and later in championing O'Casey's early plays, but the cause was lost.

A preliminary announcement in *The Freeman's Journal*, published on the opening day (26 January), was undoubtedly supplied by the management for the purpose of allaying antagonisms. Entitled "Mr. Synge's New Play", it describes the comedy as "a peasant play pure and simple." Several passages of the article were underscored by the compiler of a contemporary scrap-book in my possession:

> No one is better qualified than Mr. Synge to portray truthfully the Irish peasant living away in Western Ireland. He has lived with them for months at a stretch, in the Arran [sic] Islands and Mayo. He has noted their speech, their humours, their vices, and virtues. He is one of the best Irish speakers in the country, and is thus brought into the closest contact with the people. 'The Playboy' is founded on an incident that actually occurred.
> The full strength of the Abbey Theatre Company will be engaged in the piece. Before "The Playboy" Mr. Synge's beautiful little tragedy will be given [i.e., Riders to the Sea].[26]

A marginal comment—"compare p. 5!"—was written by the compiler opposite the bracketed underscorings; page five containing the same newspaper's review of the first performance. Marginal scorings here emphasize the reviewer's statement:

> A strong protest must, however, be entered against this unmitigated, protracted libel upon Irish peasant men and, worse still, upon Irish peasant girlhood. The blood boils with indignation as one recalls the

incidents, expressions, ideas of this squalid, offensive production, incongruously styled a comedy in three acts.[27]

The programme note written by Synge is a brief first draft of what became the well-known preface to the printed play. It records his indebtedness to peasant, fisherman, and beggar for words and phrases: "I am glad to acknowledge how much I owe, directly and indirectly, to the folk-imagination of these people."[28] In an attempt to forestall criticism of his characters, he reprints the concluding paragraph of "The Vagrants of Wicklow," an essay published in *The Shanachie* in 1906. Synge had written that "this tramp life" has "a certain wildness that gives it romance and a peculiar value for those who look at Ireland with an eye that is aware of the arts also."[29] He then made a distinction between an art which is healthy, "founded on the variations which are a condition and effect of all vigorous life", and an art of decadence, "founded on the freak of nature, in itself a mere sign of atavism or disease."[30] To be specific:

> ... the tramp in real life, Hamlet and Faust in the arts are variations; but the maniac in real life, and Des Esseintes and all his ugly crew in the arts are freaks only.[31]

The contrast was to be elaborated in the famous passage of the later preface which points up the dichotomy between the extremes of naturalism and symbolism in the current literary scene, a passage which provided the starting point for Harry Levin's brilliant pioneer study of James Joyce: "One has, on one side, Mallarmé and Huysmans producing this literature" of artificial richness, "and on the other, Ibsen and Zola dealing with the reality of life in joyless and pallid words."[32]

Literary history, like other branches of history, is always tempted to simplify issues. James Joyce was not the only one who failed to sign a student protest against *The Countess Cathleen* in May 1899, though he himself gave this impression, nor were all the first reviews of *The Playboy* unfavourable. The reporter for the *Irish Times* found "much to commend," in that "the atmosphere of 'the West' is all around, and the dialogue full and free." But, bearing in mind the fact that "The majority of theatre-goers are not accustomed to 'remorseless truth' in characterisation", it is to be expected that such plays as this will strengthen "their preference for the conventional form of stage representation." Hence, "it is open to serious question whether he has been well advised in regard to some of the dialogue", for "A large section of Saturday night's audience very properly resented these indiscretions on the part of the author, and brought what, in other respects, was a brilliant success to an inglorious conclusion."[33]

The *Evening Mail* reviewer, one H.S.D., gave an interesting impression of his first visit to the Irish National Theatre:

I went there having heard that wonderful things were being enacted in
that little theatre modestly hidden away behind the shipping offices on
the quay; and prepared to believe that much of this enthusiasm was due
to that familiar habit of mind which extols native products because they
are native, and for that reason chiefly if not only.[34]

Although he considered such an attitude "tiresome", "A few minutes
in the Abbey Theatre on Saturday night convinced me that the Irish
National Theatre had reached the standard of the mere theatre of
commerce." He found the play "a remarkable achievement, a comedy
brilliantly written and brilliantly acted," though the plot seemed
unconvincing. The dialogue was "racy of the soil", the characters "all
conversationalists of abounding imagination and riotously opulent in
flashing phrases." The reviewer pictured the Abbey school of acting,
now only vaguely suggested in quaint photographs. Foregoing the
"cheap artifices" of the commercial theatre, such as the heavy coat,
apple, and pipe of G. P. Huntley, the Irish theatre has "no properties
to speak of, the action all takes place in one room, and you could buy all
the equipment, costumes included, for A Five-Pound Note." After
complimenting the Fay brothers and Miss Allgood on their "wholly
admirable" interpretations, the reviewer regrets "that such fine acting
and such smart dialogue should be wasted on so grotesque a play",
marred by "coarse or blasphemous language."[35]

Disturbances continued throughout the next week. On Monday night
the police were called in, rather ineffectively because, as the *Irish Times*
explained, audience disturbances "can only be stopped on a complaint
either of the members of the audience who desire to hear the play or
of the manager of the theatre."[36] Injudicious as well, for the police had
long symbolized alien oppression. Nor were the statements by Lady
Gregory and by Synge designed to calm an aroused public. Lady
Gregory was quoted as saying that people "are quite at liberty to stay
away, but if they come they must take what is provided for them."[37]
Synge, described by the *Evening Mail* reporter as "excited and restless,"
said, when at last cornered, "I don't care a rap" about the disapproval.[38]
Even worse from the point of view of public relations but refreshing to
those of us who remain in the ranks of genteel conformity was the utterance, more lecture than interview, given by Yeats on his return from
Scotland on Tuesday. Yeats took an even more condescending attitude
toward the opposition, which "had no books in their houses" and merely
echoed dictates of "societies, clubs and leagues."[39] In contrast to earlier
days, when the Irish followed leaders such as Parnell, Stephens, or
Butt, "we must obey the demands of commonplace and ignorant people,
who try to take on an appearance of strength by imposing some crude
shibboleth."[40]

No more tactful was his announcement of a debate to be held next

Monday: "I shall lecture on the freedom of the theatre, and invite our opponents to speak on its slavery to the mob if they have a mind to."[41] An advertisement appeared in the newspapers:

SUPPORT
ABBEY THEATRE
AGAINST
ORGANISED OPPOSITION
———
HE WHO STRIKES AT
FREEDOM OF JUDGMENT
STRIKES
AT THE SOUL OF THE NATION[42]

A claque of students was recruited from Trinity College on Tuesday evening, adding a rendition of "God Save the King" to the pandemonium.[43] Arrests were made, notably of the father of Padraic Colum, and Piaras Beaslai, later a nationalist writer and biographer of Michael Collins. Each was fined 40 shillings.[44] It is interesting to note that the elder Colum was defended by George Lidwell, a crony of Joyce's father who appears in the "Sirens" episode of *Ulysses*.

Remaining performances during the week were more quiet, and, as might be expected in Ireland, humour, both kindly and bitter, emerged. *The Saturday Evening Herald* carried a dialogue of "Rafferty" and "Casey". Rafferty, lucky to be near enough to hear the bad language, thought the play too long, beginning as it did on the Abbey stage and ending in Police Court. It seemed to him that modern writing was far from real life: "Misther Yates shows us what we used to be like, an' Misther Synge shows us what we are not." But Rafferty is tolerant and hopeful as the dialogue ends:

'. . . there ye are, Casey. We're all full of the best intentions, but I'm afraid we go the wrong way about it.'
'They're drawing good crowds, anyway,' said Mr. Casey, 'it might do yet.'
'There's no knowin',' assented Mr. Rafferty. 'Which characters took best the night you were there?' asked Mr. Casey.
'The police,' said Mr. Rafferty.[45]

A street ballad of the "come-all-ye" tradition appeared in the *Evening Telegraph*. It begins:

"THE PLAYBOY"
Air—"Moriaritee"
Come all ye bogus Irishmen, and hear my Synge-y song;
In Abbey Street my form you'll meet, 'mid peelers hundreds strong;
'Tis I'm the "Man for Galway," boys, so raise a joyful shout;
I'm the rattling lad that killed his dad—I'm the dirty stuttering lout.[46]

Six stanzas and a chorus continue the tale, with the lilting inner rhyme of Irish verse. "I understand the Western land", the speaker claims, as "Here girls galore my face adore", while "Trinity boys, with 'booze' and noise, we brought to fill the stalls."[47] Yeats and Lady Gregory express surprise:

> Says Willie B. to Lady G., 'The audience must be mad;
> 'Tis Art, pure Art, why should they start; their lack of taste is sad.'[48]

A caricature of Yeats was more cruel, since the profile showed an unmistakable resemblance to Oscar Wilde.[49] A letter, signed "Connaught Ranger", suggested that at the forthcoming debate alternate seats be assigned to Trinity boys or to the police, "thus ensuring free speech."[50] Meanwhile the press was carrying on a discussion every bit as lively, if less noisy, than that in the theatre. Only a representative selection of the many letters can be recounted here, but a surprising number of correspondents sided with Synge and the Abbey management. A prominent political figure, T. W. Russell, told a reporter that Synge's work was "the only play performed at the Irish National Theatre which he had been able to sit out with complete satisfaction", though when questioned on the topic of "lionizing a parricide", he "dismissed that with a smile, which I was unable to interpret."[51] Someone signing herself "A Much Interested Foreigner" applauded the author's portrayal of his characters as "a strong, untamed, ferocious people, fearless and undaunted" and wished that "they may long retain these characteristics in a time when our nerves are getting the better of us, when we start at shadows, and tremble at the figments of our imaginations."[52] A similar note was sounded by Ellen Duncan in a letter to the *Irish Times* the same day. She thought the characters "at least as convincing as the blameless and attenuated specimens of humanity that we are so familiar with" in current literature: "The banner of 'Erin and Virtue' has been worn a little threadbare of late."[53] She joined with one "Crito" in finding the audience rather than the characters true examples of stage Irishmen, the latter writer noting "The total lack of self-control, the gross ignorance, and childish stupidity" of the crowd, which might lead the English to regard such behaviour "a true exampler [sic] of Irish culture and Irish manners."[54] An anonymous letter denounced the insensitivity of the purportedly patriotic faction:

> The party with the selfish and anti-Christian name and aim of 'Sinn Fein' has not an artist within its narrow ranks, nor with its distorted outlook is it likely to produce one; but I am sure that a peasant painted to its specification would be an idyllic thing, à la Watteau, rather than a rugged actuality in the manner of say, Van Ostade.[55]

Synge excused himself in a letter to the *Irish Times*, explaining that

"The interview took place in conditions that made it nearly impossible for me—in spite of the patience and courtesy of the interviewer—to give a clear account of my views about the play, and the lines I followed in writing it." Though "not a play with 'a purpose' in the modern sense of the word", and despite parts which "are, or are meant to be, extravagant comedy," it, like most comedy, has other sides: "a great deal that is in it, and a great deal more that is behind it, is perfectly serious, when looked at in a certain light." He commends "Pat" (of whom more later) for having seen some of the aspects "in his own way", and concludes that "There may be still others if anyone cares to look for them."[56]

"Pat" (P. D. Kenny), who was to chair the debate on the Monday following, wrote a defence of "That Dreadful Play."[57] Though seemingly repellent, the work was inherently "a highly moral play," "and I cannot but admire the moral courage of the man who has shot his dreadful searchlight into our cherished accumulation of social skeletons."[58] Pegeen's intended, without "enough intelligence to love", hasn't "enough character to have a single vice in him." But Pegeen never thinks of love, nor of his unfitness:

> 'God made him; therefore let him pass for a man,' and in all his unfitness, he is the fittest available! Why? Because the fit ones have fled. He remains because of his cowardice and his idiotcy [sic] in a region where fear is the first of the virtues, and where the survival of the unfittest is the established law of life.[59]

In contrast, Christy "is a real, live man", even though presumed a murderer.[60]

The withdrawal by William Boyle of his popular plays from the Abbey stage on 31 January brought new fuel to the controversy. The author and M.P. Stephen Gwynn thought that Boyle's play *The Building Fund* itself "is mordant satire", and that an experienced writer such as Boyle should never have interpreted Synge as "deliberately vilifying his countrymen."[61] Boyle was in turn defended by the Dublin bookman and librarian D. J. O'Donoghue,[62] and Boyle himself answered Gwynn, claiming that if the public had denounced his plays "I should not have allowed the management of the National Theatre to continue to force the presentment of them; nor should I have appealed to party spirit to sustain my art with the aid of police."[63]

Joseph Holloway was enjoying to the full the excitement of the week, dropping in on almost every performance. On opening night he vented his disapproval to Lady Gregory in one word, "Blackguardism!" In his diary he elaborated, "Synge is the evil genius of the Abbey and Yeats his able lieutenant."[64] On Sunday he chanced to meet W. G. Fay, who "excused Synge on the score that he has had no joy in his life" and who attributed his "vigorous speech" to the influence of Elizabethan drama.[65] Holloway described the disturbances of Monday and Tuesday evenings, but found that Wednesday's audience had gathered "to witness a row, and was very disappointed that they did not get value for their money."[66] Though one Mr. Short thought the publicity would help the theatre, "I have my doubts."[67] By Thursday he has found his labels, reporting that "The police-protected drama by the dramatist of the dungheap" had "got a fair hearing", thanks to more than two hundred policemen.[68] After the Saturday matinée Holloway tackled Yeats, and protested the presence of drunken Trinity students. Yeats replied as had Lincoln when advised that General Grant drank heavily: "There were plenty of drunken men in the pit, and I prefer drunken men who applaud on in the right than drunken men who hiss in the wrong."[69] When Holloway tried to corner him on the freedom to protest, "he fled", because "his flowers of speech did not blossom." With a flourish the diarist concludes, "'Humbug', thy name is Yeats."[70]

The Monday night debate was advertised as a "DISCUSSION ON THE FREEDOM OF THE THEATRE AND MR. SYNGE'S PLAY" with Yeats announced as the opening speaker, and "DEBATE INVITED."[71] Receipts from tickets (one shilling reserved, six pence admission) were "to be given to a Public Fund." Yeats said that "He certainly would never like to set plays before a theatrical audience that was not free to approve or disapprove", since "there was no dramatist that did not desire a live audience."[72] His every statement, according to the transcript in *The Freeman's Journal*, was met with groans, cries, hisses, and calls of "What about the Police?" Yeats reminded the crowd that he had been President of the Wolfe Tone Commemoration when his *Countess Cathleen* had been denounced in 1899. Then, using a phrase that was to come to mind thirty years later in the magnificent poem, "The Municipal Gallery Revisited", Yeats contrasted a timid Liverpool priest with the proud integrity of the Abbey management, which "had not such pliant bones, and did not learn in the house that bred them a so suppliant knee."[73] A new generation was "weary of the tyranny of clubs and Leagues (uproar)."[74]

W. J. Lawrence, the Elizabethan scholar, said jestingly that he spoke as "an Irish play boy", not as "a member of any League." In twenty-five years of playgoing he had never seen "a more thoroughly intellectual, representative audience" than on opening night.[75] The young radical Sheehy-Skeffington (Joyce's friend at University College) brought laughter in saying "he was both for and against." He found the play "bad (hear, hear)", but "the organised disturbance was worse", and "the methods employed to quell that disturbance were worst of all (cheers and dissent)."[76] Few of the speakers defended Synge or the theatre management, the usual charges being repeated. In their biography of Synge, Greene and Stephens quote a long letter in which Lady Gregory described the evening to Synge, who was not present. She observed that "No one came to support us", though "A Dr. Ryan supported us fairly well" and "Old Yeats made a very good speech."[77]

It must have been a good speech indeed. Yeats remembered it as one of the "Beautiful, Lofty Things" in his life, as this valedictory poem was entitled:

> My father upon the Abbey stage, before him a roaring crowd:
> 'This Land of Saints,' and then as the applause died out,
> 'Of plaster Saints': his beautiful mischievous head thrown back.[78]

The account in *The Freeman's Journal* corroborates the poet's memory:

> He knew this was the Island of Saints—plaster saints (disorder and groaning). He (Mr. Yeats) was no great believer in saints, but he engaged to think that this was a land of sinners (cries of "Police, police," and laughter).[79]

The elder Yeats testified to the accuracy of Synge's portrayal, and found his peasants superior to those of Carleton. After several other speeches Yeats arose amid the disorder, announcing himself grandiloquently: "The author of 'Cathleen Ni Houlihan' appeals to you (cheers)."[80] Mary Colum, then a young woman, later recalled in *Life and the Dream*, "The audience, remembering that passionately patriotic play, forgot its antagonism for a few minutes, and Yeats got his cheers."[81] No wonder that Lady Gregory had second thoughts about the success of the evening. In her letter to Synge she confessed that "I was sorry while there that we had ever let such a set inside the theatre, but I am glad today, and I think it was spirited and showed we were not repenting or apologizing."[82]

An amusing by-product of the week's disturbances is the skit, *The Abbey Row, Not Edited by W. B. Yeats*, a parody of the theatre journal, *The Arrow*. According to Page L. Dickinson, in *The Dublin of Yesterday*, the pamphlet was the work of Joseph Hone, Frank Sparrow and himself, and was illustrated by Richard and William Orpen. The cover caricatures that of *The Arrow*, the young hero Cuchulain with a wolfhound on a leash. Here we see instead Mrs. Grundy, umbrella under her arm, leading a dog with the melancholy face of Synge.[83]

The account describes the Tuesday night performance, where "Our position was that of a person who has innocently strayed on to a battlefield."[84] After the performance of *Riders to the Sea*, "beautifully staged and acted", there appeared "a herald" who was "Tall, slight and pale", whose "black hair hung gracefully across his brow until it sagged over his right eye."[85] "Not every theatre, we thought, could afford its own poet."[86] There follows a verse interlude, describing the *genus* poet:

A poet loves to meditate
And use long words and rare;
You usually know him by
The way he does his hair . . .[87]

Full page sketches of Synge (entitled "I Don't Care a Rap") and of Yeats on stage with left hand raised, are among the illustrations; others show a consultation, in which Lady Gregory, Yeats, and Hugh Lane can be recognized, and one in which "The Amateur Chucker-Out", a lean and angular Lane, has his outstretched arms laid on two staggering men.

Shortly after the curtain, the din arose. Verses commemorate the inability of the orchestra to quiet the crowd, and a plea from "Pat" to allow him to hear the play. The arrival of the police is described, with Yeats pointing out offenders, and the tale concludes with a visit to the Store Street police station. The twelve-page account ends with several poems, a page of sketches, and some so-called opinions from the principals. Two of the poems deserve partial quotation. The first opens:

A dramatist once wrote a play
About an Irish peasant,
We heard some of the audience say
"The motive is not pleasant."
Our own opinion, we admit,
Is rather—well—uncertain,
Because we couldn't hear one bit
From rise to fall of curtain.[88]

"Oh, No! We Never Mention It!", by the witty Susan Mitchell, plays on the taboo word, "shift".[89] The "(Air: Early Victorian)" suggests the absurd prudery of such an attitude. The poem concludes:

Then by those early memories, hearken to one who prays
The right to mention once again the word of other days,
Without Police Protection once more her voice to lift—
The right to tell (even to herself) that still she wears—a shift![90]

Later disturbances on English and American tours cannot be chronicled here, but it must be noticed that a Dublin audience accepted the play at a revival shortly after Synge's death in 1909. As for the merits of The Playboy itself, "Pat's" letter in the Irish Times proved prophetic: "It is a play on which many articles could be written."[91]

NOTES

1. The Letters of W. B. Yeats, ed. Alan Wade (London, Rupert Hart-Davis, 1954), pp. 447-448.
2. Ibid., p. 447.

3. *Ibid.*
4. *Ibid.*, p. 448.
5. Susan Mitchell, *Aids to the Immortality of Certain Persons in Ireland* (Dublin, Maunsel, 1913), pp. 52-53.
6. Quoted by Greene and Stephens, *Synge*, p. 156.
7. *Ibid.*
8. *Ibid.*
9. *Ibid.*, p. 157.
10. *Ibid.*
11. *Ibid.*
12 *Ibid.*, p 158.
13 *Ibid.*
14. *Autobiographies*, p. 520
15. *Ibid.*
16. W. B. Yeats, *A Vision* (London, Macmillan, 1962), pp. 164-165.
17. *Ibid.*, p. 165.
18. *Ibid.*, p. 163.
19. *Ibid.*, p. 167.
20. *Ibid.*
21. *The Letters of W. B. Yeats*, p. 466.
22. All passages in this paragraph are from *Synge*, pp. 234-235.
23. Lady Gregory, *Our Irish Theatre* (New York and London, G.P. Putnam's Sons, 1914), p. 112.
24. *C.W.*, IV, p. 167.
25. Lady Gregory, p. 112.
26. *Freeman's Journal*, 26 January 1907. Unless otherwise noted the following reviews and notes are taken from a scrap-book of clippings, original ownership unknown, now in the author's possession.
27. *Freeman's Journal*, 28 January 1907.
28. *C.W.*, IV, p. 53.
29. *C.W.*, II, p. 208.
30. *Ibid.*
31. *Ibid.*
32. *C.W.*, IV, p. 53.
33. *Irish Times*, 28 January 1907.
34. *Evening Mail*, 28 January 1907.
35. *Ibid.*
36. *Irish Times*, 29 January 1907.
37. *Ibid.*
38. *Evening Mail*, 29 January 1907.
39. *Freeman's Journal*, 30 January 1907.
40. *Ibid.*
41. *Ibid.*
42. Clipping not identified in scrapbook. A second slightly different notice, also unidentified, has, for its second sentence "UPHOLD THE RIGHT OF EVERY MAN TO HEAR AND JUDGE FOR HIM-SELF". This second notice can be dated, as it announces "MATINEE TODAY, SATURDAY", that is, Saturday, 2 February 1907. The

notice was rejected by Griffith's weekly, *Sinn Fein*, though it was printed in a denunciatory editorial.

43. *Irish Times*, 30 January 1907.
44. *Irish Times*, 31 January 1907.
45. *Evening Herald*, 2 February 1907.
46. *Evening Telegraph*, 2 February 1907.
47. *Ibid.*
48. *Ibid.*
49. *Ibid.*, 30 January 1907.
50. *Ibid.*, 2 February 1907.
51. *Evening Mail*, 29 January 1907.
52. *Freeman's Journal*, 30 January 1907.
53. *Irish Times*, 30 January 1907.
54. *Evening Mail*, 31 January 1907.
55. *Ibid.*, 1 February 1907.
56. *Irish Times*, 30 January 1907.
57. *Ibid.*
58. *Ibid.*
59. *Ibid.*
60. *Ibid.*
61. *Evening Telegraph*, 2 February 1907.
62. *Ibid.*
63. *Freeman's Journal*, 4 February 1907.
64. Robert Hogan and Michael J. O'Neill, *Joseph Holloway's Abbey Theatre* (Carbondale, Southern Illinois University Press, 1967), p. 81.
65. *Ibid.*, p. 82.
66. *Ibid.*, p. 85.
67. *Ibid.*
68. *Ibid.*
69. *Ibid.*, p. 86.
70. *Ibid.*, p. 87.
71. Unidentified.
72. The account of the debate is derived from that in the *Freeman's Journal*, 5 February 1907.
73. *Ibid.*
74. *Ibid.*
75. *Ibid.*
76. *Ibid.*
77. *Synge*, pp. 248-250.
78. W. B. Yeats, *Collected Poems* (London, Macmillan, 1958), p. 300.
79. *Freeman's Journal*, 5 February 1907.
80. *Ibid.*
81. *Life and the Dream* (Garden City, Doubleday, 1947), p. 139.
82. Quoted by Greene and Stephens, *Synge*, p. 249.
83. P. L. Dickinson, *The Dublin of Yesterday* (London, Methuen, 1929), p. 87.
84. *The Abbey Row, NOT Edited by W. B. Yeats* (Dublin, Maunsel, 1970), p. 1.

85. *Ibid.*, p. 3.
86. *Ibid.*
87. *Ibid.*
88. *Ibid.*, p. 10.
89. *Ibid.*, pp. 10-11.
90. *Ibid.*, p. 12.
91. *Irish Times*, 30 January 1907.

SYNGE AND YEATS[1]

Suheil Badi Bushrui

Synge was the rushing up of the buried fire, an explosion of all that had been denied or refused, a furious impartiality, an indifferent turbulent sorrow.

W. B. Yeats, *Autobiographies*, 1a

I

THE name of John Millington Synge is constantly mentioned in Yeats's work; and reminiscences of Synge seem to come back to Yeats at crucial moments of his career. At such moments, whether it is the occasion of a Nobel Prize award[2] or the discovery of a new poetic technique,[3] Yeats acknowledges his indebtedness to the man whose genius he recognized shortly after their first meeting. From the beginning Yeats was so sure of Synge's talent that he did not hesitate to tell George Moore, "I would I were as sure of your future and of my own as I am of Synge's."[4]

Synge's presence is felt everywhere in Yeats. In *Autobiographies* Yeats describes him as "the greatest dramatic genius of Ireland"[5] and praises Synge's "purity of genius."[6] In the *Letters* we find Yeats encouraging Florence Farr to play Synge,[7] describing him as "a great man"[8] and rejoicing at the success Synge had on the continent:

Did I tell you that *The Well of the Saints* has been accepted by a principal theatre in Berlin? It is a great triumph for us here as I foretold European reputation for Synge at the Catholic College and have been mocked for the prophecy . . .[9]

In the essays, now reprinted in *Essays and Introductions* and in *Explorations*, Synge becomes a symbolic figure representing for Yeats the solitary nature of the creative imagination, aloof and indifferent to popular opinion. He is even compared to the greatest figures in world drama:

Mr. Synge has in common with the great theatre of the world, with that of Greece and that of India, with the creator of Falstaff, with Racine, a delight in language, a preoccupation with individual life. He resembles them also by a preoccupation with what is lasting and noble . . .[10]

In *A Vision* Synge takes his place beside Rembrandt as a "typical" figure (The Receptive Man) of the number 23 of the Phases of the Moon, a man, whose "wisdom is that of general humanity experienced as a form of involuntary emotion and involuntary delight in the 'minute particulars' of life."[11]

In the poetry Synge joins Yeats's pantheon of the great:

> There Hyde before he had beaten into prose
> That noble blade the Muses buckled on,
> There one that ruffled in a manly pose
> For all his timid heart, there that slow man,
> That meditative man, John Synge, and those
> Impetuous men, Shawe-Taylor and Hugh Lane,
> Found pride established in humility,
> A scene well set and excellent company.[12]

He comes to share with Yeats, despite the difference between them, the noble endeavour to master "the book of the people":

> We were the last romantics—chose for theme
> Traditional sanctity and loveliness;
> Whatever's written in what poets name
> The book of the people; whatever most can bless
> The mind of man or elevate a rhyme;
> But all is changed, that high horse riderless,
> Though mounted in that saddle Homer rode
> Where the swan drifts upon a darkening flood.[13]

And finally Synge is included in the triumvirate of the truly great:

> John Synge, I and Augusta Gregory, thought
> All that we did, all that we said or sang
> Must come from contact with the soil, from that
> Contact everything Antaeus-like grew strong.
> We three alone in modern times had brought
> Everything down to that sole test again,
> Dream of the noble and the beggar-man.[14]

Synge's personality left an everlasting impression on Yeats's mind which was equalled only by the impression his art left on Yeats's work and style. The arrival of Synge on the scene took place at an important period in Yeats's artistic career, when the latter was about to introduce a drastic change into his work which has come to be known as his "second manner".

This change in Yeats's style and outlook was accompanied by the development of a new artistic formula; a displacement of the earlier languidness by a new awareness of all life's "toil and risk";[15] and an attempt at a reconciliation between poetry and life. As a result of this, we find the Yeats of the "second manner" using "common syntax" and speaking with a stronger voice in simpler diction and with sharper rhythm. We notice also the precise and powerful satirical tone he has acquired, and the detached ironic stance he has assumed. Consequently he exchanges the occult symbolism for the realities of human existence and he draws closer to his Ireland at the simple level of ordinary life, of politics and of social problems.

Synge had a share in all this, enhancing this change through the influence he exerted on Yeats. This aspect of Synge's relationship to Yeats's career has been commented upon by a number of scholars and critics[16] all of whom have, in varying degrees, suggested parallels or common usages and have provided enough evidence to support T. R. Henn's assertion that "Yeats took from Synge more than we commonly realize."[17]

In this paper aspects of this change will be discussed and related to Synge's influence during the early years of the theatre movement — a period described by Yeats as "the most creative years of [his] artistic life."[18]

II

The radical changes in Yeats's poetic philosophy can best be viewed against the background of Synge's attitude towards language and his ideas on literature. Yeats praised the "abundant, resonant, beautiful, laughing, living speech"[19] of Synge's plays. In fact Yeats's new poetic creed could also be drawn complete from Synge's Preface to The Playboy:

All art is a collaboration; and there is little doubt that in the happy ages of literature striking and beautiful phrases were as ready to the story-teller's or the playwright's hand as the rich cloaks and dresses of his time. It is probable that when the Elizabethan dramatist took his ink-horn and sat down to his work he used many phrases that he had just heard, as he sat at dinner, from his mother or his children. In Ireland, those of us who know the people have the same privilege ... in countries where the imagination of the people, and the language they use, is rich and living, it is possible for a writer to be rich and copious in his words, and at the same time to give the reality which is the root of all poetry, in a comprehensive and natural form ...
On the stage one must have reality, and one must have joy, and that is why the intellectual modern drama has failed, and people have grown sick of the false joy of the musical comedy, that has been given them in place of the rich joy found only in what is superb and wild in reality. In a good play every speech should be as fully flavoured as a nut or apple, and such speeches cannot be written by anyone who works among people who have shut their lips on poetry.[20]

So profound was the influence of Synge on Yeats that it must be explored on many levels. But first, looking at the question of language, it is evident that Yeats was delighted to find that Synge's characters used "no phrase they could not use in daily life . . ."[21] He himself enthusiastically cast aside poetic inversions and archaisms, and took up the vital structure of the "common idiom" for his own poetry:

> I believe more strongly every day that the element of strength in poetic language is common idiom, just as the element of strength in poetic construction is common passion.[22]

The model, as far as Yeats was concerned, was clearly set before him:

> The use of dialect for the expression of the most subtle emotion—Synge's translation of Petrarch—verse where the syntax is that of common life, are but the complement of a philosophy spoken in the common idiom escaped from isolating method, gone back somehow from professor and pupil to Blind Tiresias.[23]

As Synge grew in stature as an artist, he clarified for Yeats the principle that the

> . . . English idiom of the Irish-thinking people of the West . . . is the only good English spoken by any large number of Irish people to-day, and we must found good literature on a living speech.[24]

At about the time Yeats came under Synge's influence he was trying to solve the major problem of modern verse-drama — a problem that later faced Eliot and other English and American poets. He was in search of a style in which poetic rhythm, imagery, and idealization could be expressed in the language of the age. He also wished to reconcile his lyrical genius with his dramatic writing. The idiom Synge chose for his medium and the way he employed it helped Yeats in working out his solution to the problem. The salty tang, the richness of flavour, the admirable terseness, the trenchant and epigrammatic quality of the "idiom of the Irish-thinking people of the West" which Synge succeeded in capturing inspired Yeats to evolve a new style which had its roots firmly planted in "powerful and passionate syntax,"[25] in "vividness"[26] and in "passionate, normal speech."[27]

III

It may not seem easy to disentangle Synge's influence on Yeats from that of Lady Gregory, who comes on the scene some two or three years before Synge does, and whose influence on Yeats is clearly detectable from 1902 to 1903. She had also inspired Synge: he told

Yeats of his amazement to find in her *Cuchulain of Muirthemne* the very style of speech he had tried so hard to convert to dramatic form. He wrote to Lady Gregory declaring: "Your *Cuchulain* is a part of my daily bread."[28] However, although she was "the first to use the Irish idiom as it is spoken,"[29] it was Synge, who eventually transformed that idiom into a rich dramatic medium.

The twin influences of Lady Gregory and Synge were at work when Yeats was revising the three verse plays (*The Shadowy Waters*, *On Baile's Strand*, *The King's Threshold*) included in *Poems, 1899–1905*. However, only in matters of style, dramatic structure, and methods of characterization was Yeats affected to a minor degree by Lady Gregory. On the other hand, what Synge did for him was far more profound and enduring; he helped Yeats to remould not only his technique but his whole outlook on life. Yeats's indebtedness to both is acknowledged in his journal for 1909:

> When I was twenty-five or twenty-six I planned a *Légende des Siècles* of Ireland that was to set out with my *Wanderings of Oisin*, and show something of every century. Lionel Johnson's work and, later, Lady Gregory's, carried on the dream in a different form; and I did not see, until Synge began to write, that we must renounce the deliberate creation of a kind of Holy City in the imagination, and express the individual.[30]

Yet this extract indicates very precisely that Synge's influence is the dominant one; through Synge Yeats learned that the artist must "express the individual", his own "personal life," and thus "life itself."

Synge reverberates throughout all that Yeats did between 1903 and 1910. Examples are many; it is enough to cite a few of the most significant. In his Preface to *Poems and Translations* Synge writes:

> The poetry of exaltation will be always the highest, but when men lose their poetic feeling for ordinary life, and cannot write poetry of ordinary things, their exalted poetry is likely to lose its strength of exaltation, in the way men cease to build beautiful churches when they have lost happiness in building shops.[31]

The stress on "ordinary life" with his desire for the "simple and natural" is echoed by Yeats in *Discoveries*:

> If our characters also were not unconsciously refashioned so completely by the unfolding of the logical energies of Art, that even simple things have in the end a new aspect in our eyes, the arts would not be among those things that return for ever . . .
> Civilization, too, will not that also destroy where it has loved, until it shall bring the simple and natural things again, and a new Argo with all the gilding on her bows sail out to find another Fleece?[32]

Further, the following passage from Synge's Preface to *Poems and Translations* emphasizing that poetry should enfold the sum total of life, good and evil, appealed deeply to Yeats:

> In these days poetry is usually a flower of evil or good, but it is the timber of poetry that wears most surely, and there is no timber that has not strong roots among the clay and worms. Even if we grant that exalted poetry can be kept successful by itself, the strong things of life are needed in poetry also, to show that what is exalted, or tender, is not made by feeble blood. It may almost be said that before verse can be human again it must learn to be brutal.[33]

Yeats took this idea to heart, and in his defence of *The Playboy* he wrote:

> We have claimed for our writers the freedom to find in their own land every expression of good and evil necessary to their art, for Irish life contains, like all vigorous life, the seeds of all good and evil, and a writer must be free here as elsewhere to watch where weed or flower ripens. No one who knows the work of our theatre as a whole can say we have neglected the flower; but the moment a writer is forbidden to take pleasure in the weed, his art loses energy and abundance.[34]

Yeats had learned from Synge the meaning of "the clay and the worms" and the "strong things of life"; he could now discover delight in "a severe appropriate beauty";[35] he knew that his poetry for its true fullness would require the evocation of "the wild will that stirs desire."[36] He saw, too, that he needed, like a simple peasant (perceived now with the deeper sympathy that Synge had brought him), to rejoice in "a mind that delights in strong sensations whether of beauty or of ugliness, in bare facts, and is quite without sentimentality."[37]

It is possible that Synge's vision of things brought Yeats to the experience of "delight in setting the hard virtues by the soft, the bitter by the sweet, salt by mercury, the stone by the elixir."[38] He grew to respect and love Synge's "hunger for harsh facts, for ugly surprising things, for all that defies our hope."[39] Indeed, this element in Synge's vision whetted Yeats's hunger for the "savage imagination"[40] which he found and admired in Ben Johnson and Augustus John.

Yeats always had a taste for the furthest-out, starkest kinds of human-beings: the Fool, the Blind Man, Cripples, Beggars, Crazy Jane, Tom the Lunatic, the Saint and the Hunchback. Akin to Synge's tinkers and tramps, these characters were used by Yeats as representatives of that "wildness", energy and recklessness which he always attributed to the poet when freed from the shackles restraining the "capricious imagination."[41] Yeats's predilection for such strange and deformed figures in his poetry and drama and his employment of such archetypes gathers force and significance as his enthusiasm for Synge's work increases:

Mr. Synge, indeed, sets before us ugly, deformed or sinful people but his people, moved by no practical ambition, are driven by a dream of that impossible life.[42]

"Synge's harsh, independent, heroical, clean, windswept view of things,"[43] and men, helped Yeats to accept both "humanity" and "brutality" as grist for his artistic mill: nothing should be barred as commonplace or wretched if it could add power or interest.

To both the function of art was not didactic. Synge's statement that "the drama, like the symphony does not teach or prove anything"[44] is enthusiastically taken up by Yeats and extended to become a general principle of all true art:

> Only that which does not teach, which does not cry out, which does not persuade, which does not condescend, which does not explain, is irresistible. It is made by men who expressed themselves to the full . . .[45]

Both shared the common realization that all true art whatever its label — classical or romantic — interwove delight with instruction, and objectivity with imagination. The following extract from Synge stresses their mutual belief, and also points the way that Yeats was to go at this time:

> For a long time I have felt that Poetry roughly is of two kinds, the poetry of real life—the poetry of Burns and Shakespeare [and] Villon, and the poetry of a land of the fancy—the poetry of Spenser and Keats and Ronsard. That is obvious enough, but what is highest in poetry is always reached where the dreamer is leaning out to reality, or where the man of real life is lifted out of it, and in all the poets the greatest have both these elements, that is they are supremely engrossed with life, and yet with the wildness of their fancy they are always passing out of what is simple and plain.[46]

Yeats returns several times to the differences between the two types of poetry — more accurately, the two types of poetic temperament. For example, in one of his letters he writes:

> Of recent years instead of 'vision', meaning by vision the intense realisation of a state of ecstatic emotion symbolized in a definite imagined region, I have tried for more self portraiture. I have tried to make my work convincing with a speech so natural and dramatic that the hearer would feel the presence of a man thinking and feeling. There are always two types of poetry—Keats the type of vision, Burns a very obvious type of the other, too obvious indeed. It is in dramatic [lyrical] expression that English poetry is most lacking as compared with French poetry. Villon always and Ronsard at times create a marvellous drama out of their own lives.[47]

In Yeats's dramatic theory we find the same distinction; he differentiates between "the poetical" and "the real" — tragedy and comedy — and the point of their melding. This same idea provoked his theory of "character" and "personality"[48] in drama, and influenced his typology of personality in *A Vision*.

Synge's influence has a further impact on Yeats's art — on its humour. In his Preface to *The Tinker's Wedding* Synge writes:

> The drama is made serious ... by the degree in which it gives the nourishment, not very easy to define, on which our imaginations live ...
> The drama, like the symphony, does not teach or prove anything. Analysts with their problems, and teachers with their systems, are soon as old-fashioned as the pharmacopoeia of Galen,—look at Ibsen and the Germans—but the best plays of Ben Jonson and Molière can no more go out of fashion than the blackberries on the hedges.
> Of the things which nourish the imagination humour is one of the most needful, and it is dangerous to limit or destroy it. Baudelaire calls laughter the greatest sign of the Satanic element in man; and where a country loses its humour, as some towns in Ireland are doing, there will be morbidity of mind, as Baudelaire's mind was morbid.[49]

Yeats must have been convinced by this because after 1903 he emphasizes in his articles in *Samhain* the importance of humour in drama and strengthens this element in his drama and in the plays he revised during this period. Synge's stress on "the rich and genial humorous" aspects of life probably contributed to Yeats's dispassionate mocking tone in the treatment of his heroic characters and to his choice of "heroic farce" as his dramatic medium when he began writing the prose work which was eventually to become the verse-play *The Green Helmet* in 1910.

Finally, and above all, Yeats and Synge drew to their closest point in their shared love for "all that has edge, all that is salt in the mouth, all that is rough to the hand, all that heightens the emotions by contest, all that stings into life the sense of tragedy."[50] Their belief is akin to that expressed in an aphorism from the Indian scripture: "The food of the spiritual-minded is sweet ... but passionate minds love bitter food."[51] Yeats had reacted against a cloying quality in his own style moulded "to sweetness and serenity."[52] The reason he wished to reshape it was in order to experience, like Synge, "a strange wildness and coldness, as of a man born in some far-off spacious land and time."[53]

IV

The fullest force of Synge's influence is most clearly seen in *Discoveries*,[54] a set of critical essays published by Yeats in 1907. Here Yeats elaborates Synge's theories and expounds at length his altered view of life and his new philosophy of art and poetry.

Written between September 1906 and the autumn of 1907, these twenty-one essays stand as the credo of Yeats's new literary faith. Many critics have claimed that Yeats's first statement of his new poetics, his love of "life," and his discovery of "self" is contained in *Responsibilities* (1914). However, this statement had already been made in at least two previous works: the prose essays of 1907, *Discoveries*, and his earlier collection of poems *The Green Helmet and Other Poems* (1910).

Discoveries contains two key words, also favourites of Synge, which unify and give emphasis to its purpose: "personality" and "life". Yeats's chief concerns are now the "human personality" and those regions "where there is visible beauty or mirth, where life is exciting, at high tide as it were."[55]

For Yeats, *Discoveries* marks a new frontier. The point where he crossed is fixed clearly in the following passage; it is an extract from an 1899 essay at a time when he was disputing with John Eglinton (W. K. Magee) and others the nature of a National Drama:

> I believe that the renewal of belief, which is the great movement of our time, will more and more liberate the arts from 'their age' and from life, and leave them more and more free to lose themselves in beauty, and to busy themselves, like all the great poetry of the past and like religions of all times, with 'old faiths, myths, dreams', the accumulated beauty of the age. I believe that all men will more and more reject the opinion that poetry is 'a criticism of life' and be more and more convinced that it is a revelation of a hidden life, and that they may even come to think 'painting, poetry, and music,' 'the only means of conversing with eternity left to man on earth.' I believe, too, that though a Homer or a Dante or a Shakespeare may have used all knowledge, whether of life or philosophy or of mythology or of history, he did so, not for the sake of the knowledge, but to shape to a familiar and intelligent body something he had seen or experienced in the exaltation of his senses. I believe, too, that the difference between good and bad poetry is not in its preference of legendary, or of unlegendary subjects, or for a modern or for an archaic treatment, but in the volume and intensity of its passion for beauty, and in the perfection of its workmanship; and that all criticism that forgets these things is mischievous, and doubly mischievous in a country of unsettled opinion.[56]

Many times during his dramatic development Yeats attempted to escape from the dreamy mood of *The Shadowy Waters*, the mood in fact, of his earlier poetry. In his revisions and rewriting of this play — and others — he was striving to create more "life". Even in December 1904, in *Samhain* there is this new stress on "life":

> . . . the subject of art is not law, which is a kind of death, but the praise of life, and it has no commandments that are not positive.[57]

> The arts are at their greatest when they seek for a life growing always more scornful of everything that is not itself . . . We, who are believers, cannot see reality anywhere but in the soul itself, and seeing it there we cannot do other than rejoice in every energy, whether of gesture, or of action, or of speech, coming out of the personality.[58]

Yet, not until *Discoveries* does "life" oust his concept of the freeing of the arts from "their age and from life," something he put forward in 1899:

> If a man is not ready to face toil and risk and in all gaiety of heart, his body will grow unshapely and his heart lack the wild will that stirs desire.[59]

Yeats now sets out enthusiastically to proclaim his new credo. He takes the *Iliad* and the *Odyssey* and their technique of description: "the swift and natural observation of a man as he is shaped by life."[60] He exalts states that are "a conflagration of all the energies of active life."[61] He sympathizes with those poetic heroes who have snatched the "Promethean fire"[62] to ignite the blaze of true and radiant existence. He turns against the inspiration, that "marmorean stillness" of his youth and goes towards the "minute life" of everyday totality:

> One of the means of loftiness, of marmorean stillness, has been the choice of strange and far-away places for the scenery of art, but this choice has grown bitter to me, and there are moments when I cannot believe in the reality of imaginations that are not inset with the minute life of long familiar things and symbols and places.[63]

He claims that "we are only permitted to desire life, and all the rest should be our complaints or our praise of that exacting mistress who can awake our lips into song with her kisses."[64] The poet must not "seek for what is still and fixed, for that has no life for him."[65] Without the search for life "his style would become cold and monotonous, and his sense of beauty faint and sickly."[66] The poet's art "should rise out of life as the blade out of the spear-shaft, a song out of the mood, the fountain from its pool, all art out of the body, laughter from a happy company."[67]

Discoveries therefore provides a fuller statement of Yeats's poetic philosophy than his "Preface to the First Edition of *The Well of The Saints*", which was also inspired by Synge's ideals:

> When the individual life no longer delights in its own energy, when the body is not made strong and beautiful by the activities of daily life, when men have no delight in decorating the body, one may be certain that one lives in a passing order, amid the inventions of a fading vitality.[68]

It is Yeats's desire that his work should "mean something to vigorous and simple men."[69] He wants his audience from places "where there was no one that did not love life and speak of it continually."[70] He now accepts that

> What moves natural men in the arts is what moves them in life, and that is, intensity of personal life, intonations that show them in a book or a play, the strength, the essential moment of a man who would be exciting in the market or at the dispensary door.[71]

A new standard, that of "intensity of personal life" displaces the old standard of 1899 which upheld the principle that a work's value is measured by "the volume and intensity of its passion for beauty, and . . . the perfection of its workmanship."

This does not mean that Yeats now despises "beauty" but that he has broadened his understanding of it. At one time beauty meant only "states of mind, lyrical moments, intellectual essences,"[72] but now it takes in everything, "the whole man — blood, imagination, intellect, running together."[73] The accumulated beauty of the age needs now to encompass the spirit's "thirst for mere force, mere personality, for the tumult of the blood."[74] The "beauty" he searched for in high and "far-away places" is now revealed to be present in ordinary reality as well:

> Art bids us touch and taste and hear and see the world, and shrinks from what Blake calls mathematic form, from every abstract thing, from all that is of the brain only, from all that is not a fountain jetting from the entire hopes, memories, and sensations of the body.[75]

He comes down to earth, literally, to the "market-arts"; he draws more now from physical beauty and basic natural energy. The body now stands beside the spirit — its sensuality and passion is there for the poet, offering "new and vital material for his art":

> An exciting person, whether the hero of a play or the maker of poems, will display the greatest volume of personal energy, and this energy must seem to come out of the body as out of the mind. We must say to ourselves continually when we imagine a character: 'Have I given him the roots, as it were, of all faculties necessary for life?' And only when one is certain of that may one give him the one faculty that fills the imagination with joy. I even doubt if any play had ever a great popularity that did not use, or seem to use, the bodily energies of its principal actor to the full.[76]

More than anything, Yeats longs to experience the "feeling for his own personality, his delight in singing his own life,"[77] something which he had admired in Verlaine and which Synge had fully demonstrated for him:

I had not learned what sweetness, what rhythmic movement, there is in those who have become the joy that is themselves. Without knowing it, I had come to care for nothing but impersonal beauty. I had set out on life with the thought of putting my very self into poetry, and had understood this as a representation of my own visions and an attempt to cut away the non-essential, but as I imagined the visions outside myself my imagination became full of decorative landscape and of still life. I thought of myself as something unmoving and silent living in the middle of my own mind and body . . . Then one day I understood quite suddenly, as the way is, that I was seeking something unchanging and unmixed and always outside myself, a Stone or an Elixir that was always out of reach, and that I myself was the fleeting thing that held out its hand. The more I tried to make my art deliberately beautiful, the more did I follow the opposite of myself, for deliberate beauty is like a woman always desiring man's desire. Presently I found that I entered into myself and pictured myself and not some essence when I was not seeking beauty at all, but merely to lighten the mind of some burden of love or bitterness thrown upon it by the events of life.[78]

V

In discussing Synge's relationship to Yeats's career there is always the danger of exaggerating its importance and of giving the impression that Synge was the only influence during this period of crucial change in Yeats's work. This would be misleading; for there were certainly other factors at work: Nietzsche; the theatre; Lady Gregory and other friends and literary colleagues; Irish politics and nationalism; and above all the whole complex and frustrating love affair with Maud Gonne.

It would be safe, however, to emphasize the fact that Synge entered Yeats's imaginative consciousness and became an integral part of it, representing a dynamic and creative force in Yeats's career; and that Synge's name seemed always to evoke for Yeats certain values and qualities which he himself sought and developed as time passed. Synge was responsible for "the shock of new material"[79] — Synge's phrase which Yeats liked — that accelerated the changes in Yeats's style and thought which had begun during the first decade of the twentieth century.

NOTES

1. Some of the ideas expressed in this paper have been more fully explored in my *Yeats's Verse-Plays: The Revisions, 1900–1910* (Oxford, Clarendon Press, 1965). For permission to use these ideas here grateful acknowledgment is made to the Oxford University Press.

1a. *Op. cit.* p. 520.

2. *Autobiographies*, pp. 559–572.
3. *Ibid.*, pp. 493–494.
4. George Moore, *Hail and Farewell!*, II (New York, D. Appleton and Co., 1925), p. 307.
5. *Autobiographies*, p. 206.
6. *Ibid.*, p. 472.
7. *The Letters of W. B. Yeats*, ed. Allan Wade (London, Rupert Hart-Davis, 1954), p. 468. This admiration for Synge remains with Yeats to the end, in 1935 he writes to Dorothy Wellesley (*Ibid.*, p. 838): "Yes, Synge was a supreme writer."
8. *Ibid.*, p. 463.
9. *Ibid.*
10. *Essays*, p. 303.
11. W. B. Yeats, *A Vision* (London, Macmillan, 1962), p. 166.
12. W. B. Yeats, "Coole Park, 1929," *Collected Poems* (London, Macmillan, 1958), p. 274.
13. W. B. Yeats, "Coole Park and Ballylee, 1931," *Ibid.*, p. 276.
14. W. B. Yeats, "The Municipal Gallery Revisited," *Ibid.*, p. 369.
15. *Essays*, p. 293.
16. For such comments see:
    (i) S. B. Bushrui, *Yeats's Verse-Plays: The Revisions, 1900–1910* (Oxford, Clarendon Press, 1965), pp. 212–225.
    (ii) Donna Gerstenberger, *John Millington Synge* (New York, Twayne, 1964), pp. 129–133; and her essay "Yeats and Synge: 'A Young Man's Ghost'," *W. B. Yeats, 1865–1965: Centenary Essays*, eds. S. B. Bushrui and D. E. S. Maxwell (Ibadan University Press, 1965), pp. 79–87.
    (iii) T. R. Henn, *The Lonely Tower* (London, Methuen, 1965), pp. 72–87; and his edition of *The Plays and Poems of J. M. Synge* (London, Methuen, 1968), pp. 308–311.
    (iv) References in A. N. Jeffares, *W. B. Yeats: Man and Poet* (London Routledge and Kegan Paul 1962) and in his *Commentary on the Collected Poems of W. B. Yeats* (London, Macmillan, 1968).
    (v) A. Price, *Synge and Anglo-Irish Drama* (London, Methuen, 1961), pp. 51–68.
    (vi) R. Skelton, "The Poetry of J. M. Synge," *Poetry of Ireland*, I, Autumn 1962.
17. *The Plays and Poems of J. M. Synge*, p. 309.
18. *Explorations*, p. 300.
19. *Essays*, p. 301.
20. *C. W.*, IV, pp. 53–54.
21. *Essays*, p. 305.
22. *The Letters of W. B. Yeats*, p. 462.
23. *Explorations*, p. 300.
24. *Ibid.*, p. 94.
25. *Essays*, p. 522.
26. *Ibid.*, p. 527.

27. *Ibid.*, p. 521.
28. Lady Gregory, *Our Irish Theatre* (New York and London, G.P. Putman's Sons, 1914), p. 124.
29. *Ibid.*, Cf. Synge's comment in his review of Lady Gregory's *Cuchulain of Muirthemne* in 1902 (*C.W.*, II, p. 367): ". . . Lady Gregory has made a new selection of these stories . . . she has put them into a wonderfully simple and powerful language that resembles a good deal the peasant dialect of the west of Ireland. Considerable praise is due to the way in which she has accomplished this rather delicate task, but it can hardly be claimed for her, as Mr. Yeats seems to do in his preface to this book, that she has 'discovered' the language she uses. Some time ago Dr. Douglas Hyde used a very similar language in his translations of the 'Love Songs of Connacht,' and more recently Mr. Yeats himself has written some of his articles on folklore with this cadence in his mind . . ."
30. *Autobiographies*, pp. 493–494.
31. *C.W.*, I, p. xxxvi.
32. *Essays*, pp. 289–290.
33. *C.W.*, I, p. xxxvi.
34. *Explorations*, p. 225.
35. *Essays*, p. 263.
36. *Ibid.*, p. 293.
37. *Explorations*, p. 187.
38. *Essays*, p. 308.
39. *Ibid.*
40. *The Letters of W. B. Yeats*, p. 497.
41. *Essays*, p. 311.
42. *Ibid.*, p. 304. Yeats's predilection for such characters in his poetry and drama, using these as special types of human personality in his philosophic system, was also partly influenced by the fantastic characters he found in the *Arabian Nights*. For a reference on the influence of the *Arabian Nights* on Yeats see S. B. Bushrui, "Yeats's Arabic Interests", *In Excited Reverie*, eds. A. N. Jeffares and J. G. W. Cross (London, Macmillan, 1965), pp. 280–314.
43. *The Letters of W. B. Yeats*, p. 495.
44. *C. W.*, IV, p. 3.
45. *Essays*, p. 341.
46. *C. W.*, II, p. 347.
47. *The Letters of W. B. Yeats*, p. 583.
48. For an explanation of this theory see S. B. Bushrui, *Yeats's Verse-Plays: The Revisions, 1900–1910* (Oxford, Clarendon Press, 1965), pp. 43–46.
49. *C. W.*, IV, p. 3.
50. *Essays*, pp. 326–327.
51. *Ibid.*, p. 327.
52. *Autobiographies*, p. 482.
53. *Essays*, p. 328.
54. Published at Dundrum by the Dun Emer Press.

55. *Essays*, p. 276.
56. *Literary Ideals in Ireland*, with articles by J. Eglinton, W. B. Yeats, AE, W. Larminie, (London and Dublin, T. Fisher Unwin and 'Daily Express' Office, 1899), pp. 36–37.
57. *Explorations*, p. 155.
58. *Ibid.*, pp. 169–170; see also pp. 140, 147–148, 149–150, 151, 152, 153–154, 155, 157, 162, 163, 167.
59. *Essays*, p. 293.
60. *Ibid.*, p. 277.
61. *Ibid.*
62. *Ibid.*, p. 278.
63. *Ibid.*, p. 296.
64. *Ibid.*, p. 272.
65. *Ibid.*, p. 287.
66. *Ibid.*
67. *Ibid.*, p. 295.
68. *Ibid.*, pp. 302–303.
69. *Ibid.*, p. 265.
70. *Ibid.*, p. 295.
71. *Ibid..* p. 265.
72. *Ibid.*, p. 271.
73. *Ibid.*, p. 266.
74. *Ibid.*, p. 267.
75. *Ibid.*, pp. 292–293.
76. *Ibid.*, p. 266.
77. *Ibid.*, pp. 270–271.
78. *Ibid.*, pp. 271–272.
79. *Autobiographies*, p. 531.

SYNGE AND JONSON
(with a parenthesis on Ronsard)
Douglas Duncan

> *I am he*
> *Have measur'd all the Shires of* England *over:*
> Wales, *and her mountaines, seen those wilder nations,*
> *Of people in the* Peake, *and* Lancashire;
> *Their Pipers, Fidlers, Rushers, Puppet-masters,*
> *Juglers, and Gipseys, all the sorts of Canters,*
> *And Colonies of beggars, Tumblers, Ape-Carriers,*
> *For to these savages I was addicted,*
> *To search their natures, and make odd discoveries!*
> Ben Jonson, *The New Inn,* V, v, 92-100.

I

A GOOD reason why Synge's relationship to Ben Jonson has never been fully examined might be that it is plainly indeterminable. But hints of its significance, more or less casual, are dropped from time to time. A generation of English readers was introduced to Synge in the Preface by Ernest Rhys to his Everyman edition, where an echo of *The Silent Woman* is incongruously heard in *The Shadow of the Glen,* and *Volpone* and *Bartholomew Fair* are cited among the four comedies which "counted" for Synge "in his salad days." More authoritative, to quote only two examples, have been Corkery's statement that Synge had "steeped himself in Ben Jonson",[1] and the portentous utterance of Raymond Williams, writing of *The Playboy of the Western World,* that "the reference back is to Molière, to Cervantes, perhaps to Rabelais. Even more certainly the reference back is to Jonson."[2] This essay aims, not to prove, but simply to explore the nature of that "reference back": to speculate (one hopes not vapidly) on what Jonson may have meant to Synge; to identify a type of literary influence to which Synge was susceptible; and to examine some areas where comparison of the two dramatists may be fruitful.

Jonson's name appears only twice in the Oxford edition of Synge's works. On each occasion it is linked with another in one of those groupings, typical of Synge's criticism, where at first sight the names seem to have been taken out of a hat, with no very precise focusing on their owners' characteristics. But the occasions could hardly be more central. The first is the Preface to *The Playboy* (January 1907), where a superseded draft reads:

> I have no doubt at all that in all the great literary moments the living speech that was in the ears of Cervantes and Ben Jonson teemed with phrases that surpass anything produced by the Goncourts.

That was to become:

> All art is a collaboration; and there is little doubt that in the happy ages of literature striking and beautiful phrases were as ready to the story-teller's or the play-wright's hand as the rich cloaks and dresses of his time.[3]

The other occasion is the Preface to *The Tinker's Wedding* (December 1907):

> The drama is made serious—in the French sense of the word—not by the degree in which it is taken up with problems that are serious in themselves, but by the degree in which it gives the nourishment, not very easy to define, on which our imaginations live . . .
>
> The drama, like the symphony, does not teach or prove anything. Analysts with their problems, and teachers with their systems, are soon as old-fashioned as the pharmacopoeia of Galen—look at Ibsen and the Germans—but the best plays of Ben Jonson and Molière can no more go out of fashion than the blackberries on the hedges.[4]

Although these references are very far from constituting a proof of creative influence, their apparent casualness may be deceptive. Synge's cancellation of the first passage implies, of course, not that he had second thoughts about Cervantes and Jonson, but merely that he wished to universalise his meaning. And the immediately striking point is that Jonson's name has sprung to his mind in support of two central articles of his literary creed: the "collaboration" of people and play-wright in the creation of a rich dramatic speech, and the justification of dramatic seriousness in terms of "nourishing the imagination."

That it did so suggests, in the first place, that Synge's view of Jonson was original and perceptive. It was more conventional in his day to complain that Jonson's dramatic speech was flawed by pedantry and that his imagination was tied down by the satirist's preoccupation with realism. Nineteenth-century comments on his language generally echo Dryden's, "that he weaved it too closely and laboriously", and Swin-burne, though he blandly conceded to *Volpone* "a touch of something like imagination", barred Jonson from the ranks of the great imaginative creators for failing to fall in love with his creatures. Regretting that "scorn and indignation" were too often the motives of his art, Swin-burne implies that the imagination could no more be nourished on such a "sterile and fiery diet" than "we may hope to find life sustained in happiness and health on a diet of aperients and emetics."[5] In the light of such comments, one is tempted to regard Synge's two undeveloped allusions as a further instance of his power to anticipate the direction of later thought. Certainly the most fruitful of subsequent approaches to Jonson have followed where he seems to have been pointing. Eliot's essay of 1920 freed the satirist from the reproach of imaginative poverty by stressing his creativity: "satire like Jonson's is great in the end not by hitting off its object, but by creating it; the satire is merely . . . the impulse which projects a new world into a new orbit."[6] And the best of more recent studies has been an elucidation of that highly-conscious, "collaborative" art by which Jonson moulded spoken idiom into dramatic speech.[7] To the extent that Synge's achievements have conditioned criticism of older comedy, it becomes almost meaningful to talk of his influence on Jonson.

The two allusions serve also to emphasise aspects of Synge's art which are more clearly understood now than they were in his day. Why did he cite Jonson rather than Shakespeare? For three hundred years they had been separated in the critical consciousness, as poets of Art and Nature respectively. The choice of Jonson, therefore, as the example of a dramatist who moulded "living speech" in the "great moments of literature" would seem to underline Synge's awareness of the high degree of deliberate art involved in his own collaboration with nature. No one who has studied his work-sheets can doubt that with regard to composition he felt a greater affinity with Jonson than with the dramatist who "never blotted out line", and it is certain that if Synge had admitted his art more openly—or been less generous in acknowledging his debts to herdsmen, fishermen, beggar-women, ballad-singers and servant-girls—a great deal of angry discussion about the "authenticity" of his language could have been averted. In the other Preface, rather similarly, the reference to Jonson helps to restore perspective where the writer's true position has been obscured by an impulsive over-statement. Reaction against seedy problem plays provokes a dangerously abrupt distinction between imaginative seriousness and didacticism. Taken out of context, the remark that "the drama, like the symphony, does not teach or prove anything" is open to ridicule on the ground that the symphony, while admittedly free of didacticism, is equally innocent of all moral concern. Intricate and sometimes tendentious moral patterning is a mark of all Synge's comedies. Had he gone on at that point to cite Shakespeare as his ideal he would have clarified his meaning less decisively than he did by citing Jonson and Molière, dramatists whose moral impetus and indeed didacticism (in the broader Horatian sense of the term) were if anything over-acknowledged in 1907.

Some points of contact between Synge and Jonson in their handling of moral issues will be touched on later, but meantime one final inference can be drawn from these solitary clues to their relationship. A lover of Jonson and Molière is delighted to find the perennial freshness of their best work likened to the flourishing of blackberries on hedges. The natural image suggests perception that the masters of supposedly "classical" comic art drew strength from the soil. Six days before Synge left France in May, 1901, an article by Gustave Lanson appeared in the *Revue de Paris* which was destined to subvert academic criticism of Molière by pointing to the origins of his art in popular tradition.[8] Lanson began by noting that Molière's farcical pieces were getting a cold reception from the educated public:

> Quelle glace, les mardis, à la Comédie-Française, quand se distribuent sur les visages, les dos et autres parties des Sganarelle et des Géronte, les claques, les bastonnades et les coups de pied . . . quand se débitent des énormités grotesques décorées de locutions grasses qui semblent 'ramassées dans les ruisseaux des Halles'! Quelles mines froides, et quelles moues de dédain, et qu'il faudrait peu pousser notre beau monde pour lui faire dire: 'Décidément, ce Molière est bon pour la foire!'[9]

(Similar disdain had kept *Bartholomew Fair* off the London stage for nearly two hundred years and was to underlie the complex patriotic objections to *The Playboy*). It was wrong, Lanson argued, to follow Boileau in segregating Molière's farces from his more "thoughtful" plays like *Le Misanthrope* and *Le Tartuffe*, since the latter owed their contact with reality—their power of dramatising moral issues in concrete terms, as when the husband under the table hears the hypocrite cajoling his wife—to the techniques of the much-despised farcical tradition:

> L'inconvénient du dégoût de nos gens du monde et des distinctions de nos critiques, c'est de couper les liens qui attachent la comédie de Molière à la réalité, et de la suspendre comme dans le vide, séparée de ses antécédents historiques et privée du support de ce sol populaire où elle plonge par la racine.[10]

Proof of the popular origin of Molière's art was his continued appeal to "the people": "Molière, du premier coup, lui entre dans l'esprit et lui va au coeur."[11] It is interesting to recall that Synge had watched this happening in the cheap seats on Tuesday evenings at the Comédie-Française while Lanson was noting the sour reaction of the *beau monde* below. He had no similar opportunity of testing the durability of Jonson's popular appeal, which he inferred, perhaps over-generously, from his reading. But Volpone shamming sickness on his couch is archetypally farcical in the same way as Orgon under the table—and may indeed have suggested the theatrical possibilities in Pat Dirane's story of the old man who let on to be dead. It is clear that what Synge admired in both dramatists was the strength they drew from popular idioms of speech and apprehension, and he probably associated their success in nourishing the imagination with their capacity to embody "serious" issues in the elemental situations of farce.

II

No essay of this kind can afford to ignore the question of how Synge used the authors he admired. It has long been clear that his plot-sources —whether literary as in *The Well of the Saints* or from folk-tale as in other plays—were quickly forgotten in the process of composition. Bourgeois was correct in saying that "other writers existed for him only as part of his own being—only in so far as they reinforced his personal tendencies, or made clearer the vision wherein he was absorbed"[12]; and criticism has been understandably hesitant to try to isolate the parts they played. Yet the impression remains that Synge's "tenebrous" mind was peopled by the presences of dead authors, and it will be worth digressing at this point to peer through the curtain of his reticence and notice how one of them could affect him at the conscious level. Not surprisingly this occurs in the poetry, and the reference is to Ronsard.

The poem "To Ronsard" was one which Synge did not choose to publish:

> Am I alone in Leinster, Meath and Connaught
> In Ulster and the south,
> To trace your spirit, Ronsard, in each song and sonnet
> Shining with wine or drouth?
>
> How you were happy in your old sweet France
> Beside the Bellerie
> Where you heard nymphs and Naiads wheel and dance
> In moon-light jovially.[13]

The focus of the first stanza is blurred. Synge is not likely to have written a poem to suggest that he was the only person in Ireland capable of tracing Ronsard's spirit in his poetry, even if he had believed it to be true. Presumably the accumulation of place-names in the first two lines is meant to make an analogy between Synge's Ireland and Ronsard's France. As he journeys through the length and breadth of the Irish countryside, the spirit of Ronsard's country-poems comes alive for him; he feels as Ronsard felt about the Vendomois. The poem's metre is Ronsardian—compare "Jeune beauté mais trop outrecuidée/Des presens de Venus"—and its second stanza alludes to the fourth of "A la Fontaine Bellerie":

> Ainsi tousjours la Lune claire
> Voye à mi-nuict au fond d'un val
> Les Nymphes près de ton repaire
> A mille bonds mener le bal . . .[14]

No date for Synge's poem can be determined but we may compare a letter he wrote to Molly Allgood from Kerry on 1st September, 1906:

> Last night when I was coming back from the cliffs, about seven o'clock, I came on the little girls belonging to the house and two or three others and I got them to dance and sing Irish songs to me in the moonlight for nearly an hour.[15]

Ronsard's recurrent *bal des nymphes* was, as Synge well knew, a transfiguration of a similar country scene; he, too, had been the sophisticated poet who could share and be inspired by the spontaneous ecstasy of simpler people. Sometimes he gave the girls more homely names, as in this "let's have a party" poem:

> Fay venir Janne qu'elle apporte
> Son Luth pour dire une chanson:
> Nous ballerons tous trois au son:
> Et dy à Barbe qu'elle vienne
> Les cheveux tors à la façon
> D'une follastre Italienne.[16]

Bring on the dancing-girls.

> Bring Kateen-beug and Maurya Jude
> To dance in Beg-Innish . . .[17]

"Follastre" exactly describes the mood of Synge's poem, and Ronsard's rejection of the "vieux Medecins" in his second stanza is matched by Synge's refusal to invite "priest or peeler". There is no question of imitation here in the classical sense: Synge does not do to Ronsard what Ronsard did to Horace. "Beg-Innish" draws nine-tenths of its inspiration from Synge's experiences on the Great Blasket,[18] and its aim is much more to evoke those experiences than to follow a literary tradition. None the less, the idea of making a poem about them was probably suggested by the echoes of Ronsard Synge carried in his head and the analogy he made between himself and Ronsard *vis-a-vis* the peasantry.

The sense of kinship extended to their view of nature:

> In the old poets—as Ronsard—who give the delicate lyric one feels their delight in their own art first of all and then beyond that a direct delight—not a thinking or a moralizing about it—in the objects of nature with [which] they unwittingly identify themselves.[19]

The landscape of Synge's later poetry is Ronsardian in its emphasis on trees and birds, and the sense of identification mentioned here comes out most strongly in the love-poems, where in almost every case the lovers are a part of the landscape, lying in the bracken, shaded by trees and visited by birds. In one example, however, it is a tree and not Miss Allgood which the poet is embracing:

My arms are round you, and I lean
Against you, while the lark
Sings over us, and golden lights, and green
Shadows are on your bark.[20]

That poem's title, "To the Oaks of Glencree", is a reminder that
Ronsard had written an ode in the same metre "A la forest de Gastine"
which begins

Couché sous tes ombrages vers

and goes on to celebrate the poet's debt "a ta belle verdure"—"ravy
d'esprit"—"lors qu'en toy je me pers bien loin."[21] What Synge did do
to Ronsard can best be seen in that poem and best explained in terms of
his distinction between "the poetry of a land of the fancy" (Spenser,
Keats and Ronsard) and "the poetry of real life": "what is highest in
poetry is always reached where the dreamer is leaning out to reality or
where the man of real life is lifted out of it."[22] He probably regarded "A
la forest de Gastine" as an over-fanciful poem: it ends with a prayer
that the forest may always be the haunt of satyrs and muses and escape
"la flame sacrilege." For that Synge substitutes a grimmer prophesy,
that the timber will one day return to the clay and worms from which
it sprang, taking the poet along with it:

There'll come a season when you'll stretch
Black boards to cover me:
Then in Mount Jerome I will lie, poor wretch,
With worms eternally.[23]

This spicing of Ronsardian fancy with realism similarly underlies the
intensity of local detail in "Beg-Innish"; and in the "Epitaph: After
reading Ronsard's lines from Rabelais" the addition

And in the starlight beer and stout
Kept his waistcoat bulging out[24]

shows the same purpose, even where Ronsard was himself writing in
Rabelaisian vein. But this is not to say that Synge treated Ronsard
mockingly. The poems which appealed to him were the informal
country-pieces which approximated to his own kind of poetry according
to that other distinction he made between "the poetry of ordinary
things" and "the poetry of exaltation."[25] If Synge intended any unity
in the volume of poems he prepared for the Cuala Press it was that of
the *mélange* of informal pieces which the renaissance called *sylvae*: the
Bocages of Ronsard, the *Divers Jeux Rustiques* of Du Bellay and the
Under-Woods of Ben Jonson.

III

It would be disingenuous to use this relationship with Ronsard to postulate something similar with Jonson. Even in Synge's case the *argumentum ex silentio* can hardly be carried so far. The point of digressing on Ronsard has been merely to urge recognition of the fact that Synge's writings could on occasion be influenced by conscious analogy between himself and another author and by conscious modification of another author's practice; with the result that the possibility of a similar process operating in other contexts cannot be ruled out. In the drama, however, it would tend to operate much less directly than in the short lyric: it would be harder to detect and impossible to prove. A more modestly comparative approach seems therefore to be called for, and comparison will be restricted to the two plays by Synge whose prefatory allusions to Jonson have already been examined and one play by Jonson, *Bartholomew Fair*. When Yeats remarked of that play, in a hastily-scribbled postscript, that it "was one of the things that influenced Synge,"[26] he was probably making no more than a retrospective guess, but of all Jonson's comedies it comes nearest to Synge's in the areas under discussion: the creation of colourful dramatic prose out of popular idiom, and the handling of serious issues in a way which Synge would call "imaginative" rather than "didactic".

Jonson and Synge were alike in forming their dramatic ideals partly in reaction against great contemporaries. In proffering

> deedes, and language, such as men doe use:
> And persons, such as *Comoedie* would chuse,
> When she would shew an Image of the times[27]

Jonson opposed himself to the romanticism of Shakespeare's last plays much as Synge was to reject *The Shadowy Waters*:

> . . . no drama can grow out of anything other than the fundamental realities of life which are never fantastic, are neither modern nor unmodern and, as I see them, rarely spring-dayish, or breezy or Cuchulainoid.[28]

Both sought a dramatic idiom that would be colourful and yet real, copious and yet disciplined, avoiding the extremes of poeticising and drabness. Both set themselves, with more than usual deliberateness and subtlety, to mould the accents of authentic speech into rhythmic and vocal patterns. Where they differed was in their underlying purpose. Synge's respect for "realities", his contempt for Cuchulainoid fantasy, was consistent with a potent strain of romanticism and aestheticism. His concept of romance—"what is superb and wild in reality"—was by no means always presented ironically, as Jonson's was, and to think of *Deirdre of the Sorrows* together with *Catiline* is to measure a divergence which ultimately makes comparison absurd. Even where it is pertinent, as in the prose of their comedies, Synge's greater concern for aesthetic appeal is the distinguishing factor. If it is true that his discovery of the dramatic potential in Irish peasant-speech was the first step in his self-discovery as a dramatist, it is also true that his response to it was primarily aesthetic. It was peasant-speech which enabled him to make drama "a beautiful thing."[29] In its blend of the wild and the earthy, the harsh and the sweet—the index of a "popular imagination that is fiery and magnificent and tender"—it constituted an ideal of beauty which it was his constant passion as an artist to recreate. Relatively speaking, the care he devoted to thematic design and character was secondary, a response to the requirements of play-making. Jonson's priorities were just the reverse. Though his aesthetic relishing of language can hardly be doubted, the rhythmic quality and savour of his speeches were precisely and totally subordinated to the expression of character, which in turn was strictly determined by thematic pattern.

Jonson, that is to say, points us back to the old complaints that Synge's language is undramatically lyrical and that his characters are differentiated in spite of their idiom rather than by means of it. The best answer to these charges is Synge's own analogy between his plays and musical compositions, and certainly a dramatist deserves to be judged by the conventions he persuades us to accept. He claimed that he gained as much as he lost by "keeping my characters bound together as far as possible in one mood."[30] For many, the beauty of his language is sufficient justification and it could also be argued that a homogeneous idiom was a requisite for his enclosed peasant communities as a Babel of tongues was appropriate to the Smithfield Fair. But Jonson's play at least points to a kind of success which Synge did not achieve. The characters at the Fair are broadly separable into fair-people, moral censors, simpletons and sophisticated by-standers, and not only each group but each individual within each group speaks a distinct idiom. The distinctions are more radical than those normally found when a shared idiom is modified by the characters of different speakers, because each idiom has been conceived by the author as separately as the character itself.

Thus, among Jonson's censors, the petulant jargon of the tutor, the cant of the puritan and the magistrate's Roman rhetoric have nothing in common except a share in the infinite resources of Jacobean English, and the comedy which arises when they are aligned in the stocks is as much linguistic as situational. Synge's homogeneous idiom, the key or "mood" in which his symphony was set, scarcely permitted adequate speech-differentiation even when his themes required it, between peasant and playboy or tinker and priest, and one doubts if it could ever have accommodated a civil-servant from Dublin, a returned

émigré from New York, or a fisherman from Fécamp ashore for veget-
ables. Even if Synge's language was adequate for the ends assigned to it,
one must recognise that Jonson's ends were larger, more various and
more properly dramatic. Moreover, almost any of the twenty-odd
idioms employed in *Bartholomew Fair* has as much right to be called
"poetic prose" as Synge's, unless we insist on defining that term by
the standard of romantic lyricism.[31]

Synge was powerless to escape the extreme self-consciousness which
has beset all writers since the eighteenth century in their treatment of
the simple life. Jonson had no scruples about being "true to the folk,"
no sense of the mysterious otherness of a peasant community, and his
approach to the fair-people seems happily uninhibited. But the fact
that a seventeenth-century writer worried less about authenticity does
not mean that he aimed to achieve it. He was moved in quite the opposite direction by the concept of pastoral—older than Rousseau,
older than Ronsard—which assumed that the function of the uneducated in literature was to serve as a point of reference for the
educated. In that sense, though he would have expressed it differently,
Synge's peasants are as much a version of pastoral as are Jonson's fair-
people. While both are presented with a down-to-earth crudity which
superficially suggests a bid for social realism, both were created, not
primarily to be themselves, but to serve as figures in the author's fable.
We glimpse another facet of what Synge meant by drama that is made
serious by nourishing the imagination if we think of these plays as
pastoral fables in which a sophisticated author projects his thoughts
about human nature and himself in particular on to a primitive background. Synge saw himself as a sympathetic alien half-in and half-out
of his pastoral world, committing his whole art to its realisation yet
incapable of belonging to it, like the priest who knew little of the sea,
and compelled to move on, like the tramp and the playboy. Jonson
saw himself as a humanist scholar-poet who, having dedicated his art
to reason and morals, took a walk through the fair and observed the
gulf between the humanist goals and the essential concerns of humanity.
His fair-people embody the instinctual and unexamined life—a fore-
taste of Hobbesian pastoral—an appetitive, amoral, cheerful, unquench-
able and fiercely clannish society against which the moralists fulminate
briefly before collapsing in recognition of complicity with its ethos.
Perhaps the deepest resemblance between *Bartholomew Fair* and *The
Playboy* is in the handling of fable. In each case the author's involvement in it is so strong that the play can be read as self-analysis, yet this is
balanced by so much detachment in the telling that the final impression
is of baffling ambiguity.

Thematically, however, a closer parallel to Jonson's play is provided
by *The Tinker's Wedding*. Both juxtapose in a highly schematised

manner the examined and the unexamined life, those who profess morals and those who don't, using the polarity of extremes to indicate humanity at large ("the whole people," Synge says in his Preface, "from the tinkers to the clergy").[32] Both plots focus on the compulsive meddling of the one group with the other. Jonson's moralists visit the fair with impure motives and end in the stocks; his hobby-horse-seller and gingerbread-woman, who have already been paid for their wares, try to sell them again to the puritan and have them trampled underfoot. In Synge's play the motive of the young tinker-woman for meddling with the priest is not mercenary but poetic—her instinctual life is expressed through a springtime fancy to be married—but it comes to no good; and the mercenary motive belongs to the priest who seeks half-a-sovereign and a tin can for his services, not caring where the money comes from, and ends in a sack. The chief spokesman for the instinctual life is in both cases a hard-drinking, pipe-smoking old woman: Jonson's pagan earth-mother, the pigwoman Ursla, and Synge's "old, flagrant heathen",[33] Mary Byrne. In each play the intermeddling of the two groups is marked at first by communion—all three censors compound their hypocrisy by eating or drinking at the fair; priest and tinker share a ritual sup—and latterly by violent disruption. The difference of emphasis in the conclusion of the two plays is perhaps more apparent than real. Mary Byrne, who first proposed community with the priest ("Aren't we all sinners, God help us!"),[34] finally rejects it outright ("it's little need we ever had of the like of you").[35] In her secondary role as an ironic commentator on the action she corresponds not with Ursla but with Quarlous the gamester, who, by contrast, ends Jonson's play by proposing a conciliatory supper in celebration of common human frailty. If we perceive that Jonson takes a profoundly ironic view of our readiness to applaud that conclusion, we may agree that Synge's openly disruptive ending is not necessarily tougher but merely more explicit.

The crudity of Synge's conclusion is seen in perspective when we recall his practice of ending every play with a visual act which epitomises its main concern: the departures of Nora Burke and of the blind beggars, Maurya standing over Bartley's body, Deirdre's choice of the grave. In farce, the trussing of the priest in sackcloth is physically no cruder than the brawling, gagging, burning and biting in *The Playboy*'s last scene, which Synge meditated so carefully and refused to alter. It is dramatically cruder, however, because it merely underscores an opposition which is already clear to the audience, whereas the violence at the end of *The Playboy* shocks the audience into seeing something new. The same kind of challenge is present in the accumulation of farcical incident towards the end of *Bartholomew Fair*. The coarse brawling of the puppets breeds vulgar delight among the spectators on stage, thus sharply testing the ability of the audience to be more discriminating in its appreciation of the play as a whole; and the humiliation of the puritan after his attack on the puppet-show is Jonson's thrust at those who might fail to admit that his own farce could be morally serious. When the magistrate's wife, now drunk and dressed as a prostitute, vomits on the stage within fifty lines of the end of *Bartholomew Fair*, crude farcical incident is no more gratuitous than when Christy's leg is burned with a lighted sod.

Shaw's remark that *The Playboy of the Western World* was about "the habit of admiring bold scoundrels" is a reminder of how closely it encroaches on Jonsonian terrain, but it is so fully and authentically a work of Synge's own imagination that it would be futile to look to any other play for the kind of thematic correspondence traced between *The Tinker's Wedding* and *Bartholomew Fair*. As already indicated, the significant parallel between Jonson's play and Synge's masterpiece lies in their technique of audience-manipulation. Playwrights who plan their work on the clash of opposite rules of life have a tendency, in their most sophisticated plays, to appear to undermine the positions they have themselves taken in earlier work, and to make the audience a victim of their more complex awareness by robbing it of simple solutions. Neither *Bartholomew Fair* nor *The Playboy* contradicts the established attitudes of its author but instead re-states them with teasing obliquity. Jonson so vividly exposes the perilous consequences of man's obligation to exercise judgment that many critics have thought he denied it altogether. Synge turns his whole concept of romance inside out, showing that "what is superb and wild in reality" can barely be distinguished from "savagery and fine words", (thus making his extravagant idiom for once almost fully functional). The audience is given no help—is indeed actively obstructed—in its attempt to locate the author's attitude towards the ringing proposal which ends each play: that of Quarlous for universal indulgence and Christy's to "go romancing through a romping lifetime."[36] "Gamester" and "playboy", one perceives, are similar terms which denote similarly ambivalent heroes.

To say that this process is one of "nourishing the imagination" as opposed to telling the audience what to think is not quite the whole truth. One critic has written of *The Playboy* that "there are not many plays in which the author is so playful with his audience, or juggles with its feelings and adjusts the focus of its imagination so sportively to achieve his ends."[37] In the techniques of audience-bafflement Jonson was the great precursor. It would be ironic if a dramatist who taught Synge how to "collaborate" with the people also taught him that infallible recipe for forfeiting popular trust. But it would not be altogether surprising. Synge's cloak of indifference to his public covered something of Jonson's satiric animus and something of Jonson's contempt.

Although each—like the character quoted in the epigraph to this essay —could see himself as the detached observer, the *clericus vagans* who tramped among the "wilder nations . . . To search their natures, and make odd discoveries", neither was finally content to believe that the artist is a tramp.

NOTES

1. D. Corkery, *Synge and Anglo-Irish Literature* (Cork University Press, 1931), p. 85.
2. *Drama from Ibsen to Eliot* (London, Chatto and Windus, 1952), p. 162.
3. *C.W.*, IV, p. 53.
4. *Ibid.*, p. 3. In the same Preface the "nourishment" metaphor leads Synge to the comparison, often used by Jonson, of the dramatist and the cook. But an earlier draft (*Ibid.*, p.p. 290–291) traces the comparison to "Fielding and others".
5. *A Study of Ben Jonson* (New York, Worthington, 1889), pp. 35, 39.
6. *Selected Essays* (London, Faber, 1951), pp. 158-159.
7. J. A. Barish, *Ben Jonson and the Language of Prose Comedy* (Cambridge, Mass. [Harvard University Press], 1960).
8. "Molière et la Farce", *Revue de Paris*, 1 May 1901, pp. 129-53.
9. *Ibid.*, p. 130.
10. *Ibid.*, pp. 131-132.
11. *Ibid.*, p. 153.
12. M. Bourgeois, *John Millington Synge and the Irish Theatre* (London, Constable, 1913), p. 52.
13. *C.W.*, I, p. 30.
14. Odes, III, viii; references are to *Les Oeuvres de Pierre de Ronsard: texte de* 1587, III, ed. I. Silver (Chicago, Washington University Press, 1966).
15. Quoted by Greene and Stephens, *Synge*, p. 209.
16. *Odes*, II, x, 3-8.
17. "Beg-Innish", *C.W.*, I, p. 37.
18. *C.W.*, II, pp. 246-257. The poem "On an Island", a tribute to Synge's hostess on the Great Blasket, also suggests humorous awareness of a tradition: the sub-literary, mock-panegyric genre which surfaces in, for example, Skelton's "Elinor Rumming", Burns's "Lady Onlie", and the "Jeanne" of Georges Brassens (an artist whom Synge would have greatly enjoyed).
19. Quoted from a notebook by A. Saddlemyer, " 'A Share in the Dignity of the World': J. M. Synge's Aesthetic Theory", *The World of W. B. Yeats*, ed. R. Skelton and A. Saddlemyer (Dublin, Dolmen Press, 1965), p. 246.
20. *C.W.*, I, p. 47.
21. *Odes*, II, xv.
22. Quoted from a Synge notebook by Skelton, "Introduction", *C.W.*, I, pp. xiv-xv.

23. *C.W.*, I, p. 47.
24. *Ibid.*, p. 39.
25. *Ibid.*, p. xxxvi.
26. *The Letters of W. B. Yeats*, ed. A. Wade (London, Rupert Hart-Davis, 1954), p. 671.
27. *Every Man In His Humour* (Folio Version, 1616), Prologue, 21-23.
28. Letter to Stephen MacKenna, quoted by Greene and Stephens, *Synge*, p. 157.
29. *C.W.*, IV, p. 394.
30. Letter to Paterson quoted by Saddlemyer, *C.W.*, IV, p. xxiv.
31. Ironically, the Achilles heel of Jonson's linguistic virtuosity was his stage-Irish (Whit in *Bartholomew Fair*). But note, in compensation, how his English country-idiom occasionally anticipates Synge, *e.g.* Meg in *The Gypsies Metamorphosed*, 856-859: "And I have lost an enchanted nutmeg all gilded over, was enchanted at Oxford for me, to put i' my sweetheart's ale a-mornings, with a row of white pins that prick me to the very heart, the loss of 'em" (*Complete Masques*, ed. S. Orgel, New Haven, Yale University Press, 1969, p. 352).
32. *C.W.*, IV, p. 3.
33. *Ibid.*, p. 21.
34. *Ibid.*, p. 17.
35. *Ibid.*, p. 49.
36. *Ibid.*, p. 173.
37. J. L. Styan, *The Elements of Drama* (Cambridge University Press, 1963), p. 63.

J. M. SYNGE AND THE DRAMA OF THE LATE NINETEENTH CENTURY

John Munro

IT IS A commonplace of literary history that during the greater part of the nineteenth-century English drama was in decline. Although interest in the theatre actually increased during these years, serious drama was all but drowned under a tidal wave of extravaganzas, burlettas and burlesques, pantomimes and musical entertainments. Up until the closing years of the century, when English drama underwent a minor renaissance, virtually the only serious plays to appear on the popular stage were heavily cut versions of Shakespeare and dramatisations of popular novels, most notably those of Charles Dickens. During this time the play was no longer "the thing"; more important was its star, and audiences flocked to see such great actors as Sir Henry Irving, irrespective of the drama in which he was appearing. Audiences were rowdy and less literate than those of the previous century, and at time actors vied with the pit and the gallery in an attempt to find a hearing. As long as the house was full, theatre managers were happy, for the theatre had become a profit-making institution in which artistic excellence was ignored in favour of commercial gain.

Under these circumstances it is not surprising that few serious authors cared to write for the stage. The public preferred to watch tight-rope walkers and performing bears, and if they attended legitimate drama they expected to be pleasurably thrilled by macabre situations, or hugely entertained by slapstick humour. At the very least they demanded lavish spectacle. Typically one of the most successful plays of the latter half of the nineteenth century was an adaptation of Byron's *Mazeppa*, which was admired chiefly on account of the performance of its star, an American actress Ada Isaacs Menken, who, clad only in flesh-coloured tights, cantered around Astley's Amphitheatre, strapped to the back of a horse. Later, in 1909, this form of spectacular entertainment reached something of a climax with Cecil Raleigh's and Henry Hamilton's sporting drama *The Whip*, at Drury Lane, which included both a train smash and a re-creation of the Derby horse race.

Obviously, spectacles of this kind required a large stage, and as new theatres were built stages became increasingly spacious, auditoriums more cavernous. Simultaneously, a new declamatory style of acting developed, for subtleties of gesture and utterance would have been lost on an audience seated at a considerable distance from the stage. Thus Henry Irving was admired less for his skill in portraying a particular person in a particular dramatic situation than for his ability to suggest generalised states of feeling or emotion. As Arthur Symons wrote, Irving's art is "wholly of rhetoric, that is to say wholly external", and his appeal is "to our sense of what is expected, to our accustomed sense of logic, not of life, but of life as we have always seen it on the stage."[1]

Just as Irving's acting seemed "wholly external", so the same may be said of nineteenth-century stage design, which strove to give a "crude illusion of reality".[2] Thus Shakespeare was presented in such a way that the audience's attention was drawn more to the ingenious, naturalistic verisimilitude of the stage setting than to the essential meaning of the play. When Sir Beerbohm Tree produced *As You Like It*, he included among the *dramatis personae* several live rabbits, who gambolled about in the forest of Arden; and in *The Winter's Tale* he introduced a pretty piece of stage business when Perdita, leaving her childhood home, skipped back across a running brook to bring her pet bird along with her. In short, by the end of the nineteenth century stage conditions favoured the presention of spectacles which bore only a superficial resemblance to real life. Not only were dramatists confronted with a theatre-going public who expected to be entertained rather than intellectually stimulated or provoked to introspection; they were also hampered by theatrical conventions hostile to the presentation of drama which dealt with anything other than surface reality.

Considering the theatrical conventions of the time, it is not surprising that there are few nineteenth-century plays of enduring quality. Occasionally, however, there were indications that the drama had not entirely sacrificed seriousness for spectacle. Thomas W. Robertson's *Caste* (1867), for example, though peopled with caricatures, attempted to deal with an important social problem, the difficulty of bridging the gulf between the so-called "upper" and "lower" classes. Later, as the influence of Henrik Ibsen began to be felt in England, other dramatists endeavoured to confront their audiences with something other than mindless entertainment. Arthur Wing Pinero's *The Second Mrs. Tanqueray* (1893), for example, dealt sympathetically with the problem of a woman with "a past", to use the Victorian euphemism, and in 1896 Henry Arthur Jones's *Michael and His Lost Angel*, a drama of conscience involving a puritanical clergyman, suggested that there was something to be said in favour of the relativity of moral judgment. None of these dramatists, however, wrote genuine "problem plays". They exploited their provocative material for melodramatic effect rather than explored it for its social implications. It was left to George Bernard Shaw to bring nineteenth-century British drama to maturity. His

Widowers' Houses (1892) and *Mrs. Warren's Profession* (1893), which dealt with slum landlords and prostitution respectively, set out to awaken the audience's conscience to the existence of these social ills, and, as he expressed it in "The Problem Play—a Symposium" (1895), exert such pressure "that even governments recognize the necessity for moving."[3] Thereafter he cast a cold eye over society, drawing attention to its ills and weaknesses, determined to bring about such social reforms as he believed necessary.

Although at the close of the nineteenth century English drama regained some of the seriousness it had lacked for almost two hundred years, it tended to consider Man from a relatively restricted point of view. Its concern was Man and his relationship with other men, rather than Man and his relationship with God. Or to put it another way, the nineteenth-century dramatist viewed Man as a social rather than as a moral being. In following Ibsen, British dramatists showed a distinct preference for his social, non-political drama, largely ignoring his early and late symbolic drama, drawing their inspiration from *The Pillars of Society* (1877) and *Ghosts* (1881) rather than from *Peer Gynt* (1869) and *The Wild Duck* (1884).

A few nineteenth-century writers, it is true, did attempt to see Man in relation to the total order of things, but they tended to be verse dramatists whose work, though frequently intended for stage-presentation and occasionally produced, belongs less to the theatre than to the study, and is therefore rightly called "closet drama". To this category belong such works as Matthew Arnold's *Merope* (1858) and Tennyson's *Becket* (1884), both of which have some merit as literature but little or none as drama. The characters are frigid and the action is stilted, and while they contrive to set Man in universal perspective, by removing him from the plane of mundane reality, they drain him of his vitality. Consequently both these dramas are bloodless and dull, and in any event should be considered as being outside the main tradition of nineteenth-century drama.

The same may be said of the verse dramas written at the turn of the century, those of Arthur Symons and John Davidson for example. It may equally be said of those of Stephen Phillips, whose verse plays nonetheless enjoyed considerable success. An actor turned dramatist, whose avowed aim was to bring English tragedy back to the severe classicism of the Greeks, purging it of Elizabethan "luxuriance", Phillips at first attracted a considerable following. Unfortunately, though he looked squarely at the classics and succeeded in creating dramas with simple plots, he was unable to prune his somewhat florid diction. *Paolo and Francesca* (1899), *Herod* (1900), *Nero* (1902) and *Ulysses* (1902) were all well received, but it is difficult nowadays to appreciate the high esteem which many reputable critics had for him.

His plots are unimaginative, his characters wooden, and though he sometimes manages an occasional theatrical effect with some skill, his plays tend to be rather stagey pageants where the action moves forward rheumatically to some all too clearly perceptible conclusion.

In retrospect Phillip's verse dramas are less notable for their merit as plays, than as documents which demonstrate the difficulty of writing viable, modern poetic drama. Though unlike Oscar Wilde's *The Duchess of Padua* (1891) and other late nineteenth-century dramas in pseudo-Shakespearian tradition, which make use of blank verse for much the same reason as they call for doublets and hose—to suggest that the action takes place in the past—Phillips's dramas seem equally artificial. Whereas Wilde's play is naturalistic melodrama set in the past and written in blank verse, Phillips's dramas are crude imitations of classical tragedy which depend upon the effects of naturalistic Victorian melodrama to make them stageworthy. The dramas of one are as artificial and remote from reality as those of the other.

In short, whereas late nineteenth-century naturalistic drama may be censured for presenting a restricted view of Man, being bound by the conventions of external, social reality, the closet dramas of Arnold and Tennyson and the more stageworthy verse dramas of Phillips may be criticised for their artificiality and remoteness. What was needed was drama which would faithfully reflect the world as we know it and at the same time transcend that reality, making "our minds expand convulsively or spread out slowly like some moon-brightened image-crowded sea."[4] This was the kind of drama which J. M. Synge set out to write, and did, in fact, achieve.

Synge believed that the "highest in poetry is always reached when the dreamer is leaning out to reality, or when the man of real life is lifted out of it, and in all the poets the greatest have both these elements, that is they are supremely engrossed with life, and yet with the wildness of their fancy they are always passing out of what is simple and plain."[5] At first Synge appears to have cast himself in the role of dreamer, pursuing first a career as a musician, and in Paris, as his notebooks attest, reading extensively, in the writings of Racine and of the French Symbolists, notably Baudelaire, Mallarmé, Huysmans and Maeterlinck.[6] But in December 1896 he met W. B. Yeats, who persuaded him that a more fruitful approach might be to proceed from the position of "the man of real life", and that in the Aran Islands he might learn to "express a life that has never found expression."[7] Accordingly Synge left Paris, and later claimed that he "got more aid than any learning could have given" him by eavesdropping on the servants in the kitchen of the old Wicklow house where he was staying.[8]

It was not only the experience of living as a "man of real life" that provided Synge with imaginative inspiration. The Anglo-Irish dialect used by the people of Wicklow and the Aran Islands, which Synge adapted as a medium of speech for the characters in his plays, also assisted him in his quest to achieve "the highest in poetry." This dialect, a form of English modified by Gaelic habits of thought, speech, imagery and syntax, is both colourful and vigorous.[9] Though firmly rooted in physical actuality, it evokes, nonetheless, a poetic reality beyond the tangible present, as in Christy's brilliantly suggestive lines in *The Playboy of the Western World:*

> . . . he after drinking for weeks, rising up in the red dawn, or before it maybe, and going out into the yard as naked as an ash tree in the moon of May.[10]

The poetic qualities of this Anglo-Irish dialect Synge acknowledged in his preface to *The Playboy of the Western World,* at the same time underlining its suitability as a mode of expression for the "highest poetry" he was endeavouring to achieve:

> . . . in countries where the imagination of the people, and the language they use, is rich and living, it is possible for a writer to be rich and copious in his words, and at the same time to give the reality which is the root of all poetry, in a comprehensive and natural form. In the modern literature of towns, however, richness is found only in sonnets, or prose poems, or in one or two elaborate books that are far away from the profound and common interests of life. One has, on one side, Mallarmé and Huysman producing this literature; and on the other Ibsen and Zola dealing with the reality of life in joyless and pallid words. On the stage one must have reality, and one must have joy, and that is why intellectual modern drama has failed, and people have grown sick of the false joy of the musical comedy, that has been given them in place of the rich joy found only in what is superb and wild in reality.[11]

It was fortunate that Yeats came to share Synge's view of drama, for it is doubtful whether Synge would have been such a notable success if he had not at this stage of his career found someone who so clearly understood and sympathized with him. Yeats also began to assert that the greatest plays were not those which gave "the sensation of an external reality", but those in which "there is the greatest abundance of life itself, or the reality that is our minds."[12] Or, as he expressed it elsewhere: "the greatest art symbolises not those things that we have observed so much as those things we have experienced."[13] Both men believed, in Synge's words, that "the drama, like the symphony, does not teach or prove anything",[14] and that "serious drama" was made serious "not by the degree in which it is taken up with problems that are serious in themselves, but by the degree in which it gives the nourishment, not very easy to define, on which our imaginations live."[15]

Where Yeats and Synge differed, however, was over the way the imagination might be nourished. Yeats wished to make the Irish conscious of their mythic heritage by putting the old stories into verse. On the other hand Synge believed that "of the things which nourish the imagination humour is one of the most needful", and was pleased to find that "in the greater part of Ireland . . . [the people] have still a life, and a view of life, that are rich and genial and humorous", prompting them to laugh at their fellow countrymen "without malice".[16] Both writers were nonetheless "popular" dramatists: Yeats, however, was "popular" in the *Volk* sense, in much the same way as Wagner may be called "popular", on account of the way he utilized mythic material in his operas; Synge was "popular" in the sense that his plays' substance derived from the everyday life of the people. Thus Yeats's appeal to the imagination depended upon his effectiveness in arousing a response in his audience to the legendary tales of Ireland and, as in *Cathleen ni Houlihan*, evoking parallels with the contemporary scene. Synge, on the other hand, made use of the materials of everyday life, evoking a poetic order beyond that of external circumstances. They worked in opposite directions, Yeats "leaning out to reality", Synge being "lifted out of it."

It was fortunate, of course, that both dramatists were writing primarily for Irish audiences, and were therefore free to create plays which conformed neither to the crude expectations of the public theatre nor to the refined, artificial demands of the "closet". Both writers were conscious of the advantage that this gave them over their counterparts in England. As Yeats wrote in his Prospectus of the Irish Literary Theatre in 1898:

> We hope to find, in Ireland, an uncorrupted and imaginative audience trained to listen by its passion for oratory, and believe that our desire to bring upon the stage the deeper thoughts and emotions of Ireland will ensure for us a tolerant welcome, and that freedom to experiment which is not found in theatres of England, and without which no new movement in art or literature can succeed. We will show that Ireland is not the home of buffoonery and of easy sentiment, as it has been represented, but the home of an ancient idealism.[17]

To some extent Yeats's expectations were fulfilled, and in the beginning, the plays presented at the Irish Literary Theatre reflected something of the "ancient idealism" about which Yeats had spoken. This caused Edward Martyn, one of the co-founders of the Irish drama movement, whose ambition was to write naturalistic plays dealing with serious contemporary ideas, to break away in 1901. Earlier, however, he had been encouraged by Yeats, who had said that he hoped good naturalistic plays would emerge in Ireland, "and means to play them as truthful as a play of Hauptmann's or of Ibsen's upon the German or Scandinavian stage."[18] In spite of Martyn's defection, the theatre prospered, and so popular did it become that in April 1902, people had to be turned away from a performance of Yeats's *Cathleen ni Houlihan* and George Russell's *Deirdre* at St. Theresa's Hall, Dublin. Clearly, there was a sympathetic audience for the kind of plays Yeats and Synge were writing.

The circumstances under which Yeats's and Synge's early plays were presented also contributed to their success. Max Beerbohm, describing in April 1904 a performance of Yeats's *The King's Threshold* and Synge's *Riders to the Sea* and *The Shadow of the Glen* as "one of the rare oases that are in the desert of our drama", put his finger on the essential point when he emphasized the "simplicity" of the production: the "simplicity" of the plays' dramatic structure; the "simplicity" of the stage setting; the "artlessness" of the actors involved. That this "simplicity" was as much the product of material circumstance as artistic design Beerbohm recognised, drawing attention to Yeats's programme note which stated that the Prologue to *The King's Threshold* was not "used in Dublin, as, owing to the smallness of the company, nobody could be spared to speak it."[19] In other words, even assuming that Yeats and Synge had been disposed to stage their dramas in an extravagant way, the exigencies of their financial situation and their restricted productional capabilities would have meant that an elaborate presentation was out of the question. What might have been disabling was turned to productive account.

By 1905 the Irish Literary Theatre had found a permanent home at the Abbey, which provided the company with facilities far more sophisticated than those they had been used to before. By now, however, a tradition had been established which was proof against the temptations created by comparative affluence. From the beginning artlessness and simplicity had been the cornerstones of the Irish theatre's policy, and Yeats and his fellow members saw no reason to change. As Yeats had said:

Why should we thrust our works which we have written with imaginative sincerity and filled with spiritual desire, before those excellent people who think that Rossetti's women are 'guys', that Rodin's women are 'ugly', and that Ibsen is 'immoral', and who only want to be left at peace to enjoy the works so many clever young men have made especially to suit them.[20]

What we must do, Yeats continued, is to "make a theatre for ourselves and our friends, and for a few simple people who understand from sheer simplicity what we understand from scholarship and thought."[21] And this, of course, is what Yeats and his company largely achieved.

Everything was kept as simple as possible. The colours of the scenery and the costumes were neutral tones, and the former, especially, simple

in design. Properties were kept to a minimum, and frequently the action
took place in front of a plain curtain. Action, Yeats said, should never
rival utterances; actors should be discouraged from engaging in
elaborate stage business. He had seen a performance of *Phèdre*, starring
Sarah Bernhardt, in which the action had been kept to the barest
minimum, and at one point was able to count the twenty-seven actors
on stage "quite slowly before anybody on a fairly well-filled stage moved,
as it seemed, so much as an eyelash." In an attempt to approximate this
statuesque repose Yeats once went to the extreme of putting his actors
on barrels on which they could barely move, pushing them around
whenever the action required it, an experiment which, perhaps for-
tunately, he never repeated.[22]

Assisted by William Fay, a talented comic, and his brother Frank, a
fine verse-actor, both of whom had joined Yeats during the early years
of the Irish Literary Theatre, and around whom the company was
formed, Yeats encouraged a new histrionic style. When playing heroes
of myth or legend, the actors were taught to move with measured
dignity, to speak the poetry in a kind of chant, and to sing the songs in
the play without any unnatural prolongation of the vowel sounds.
When playing Synge's peasants, to take another example, they were
asked to walk with a clumsiness appropriate to their role, always being
told, however, to use gestures sparingly.[23] On the whole, this style of
acting was successful in interpreting the plays staged by the Irish
National Theatre, though Max Beerbohm did have mixed feelings
about its appropriateness in relation to the dramas of Synge:

> When [the] players, trained to heed Mr. Yeats's poetry, and untrained to
> express anything dramatically, came to interpret Mr. Synge's prose, they
> did seem decidedly amiss. They, with their blank faces and their stiff
> movements, taking up their cues so abruptly, and seeming not to hear
> anything said by their interlocutors, certainly did impede the right effect
> of the play. For all that; I would not they had been otherwise. One could
> not object to them as to the ordinary amateur. They were not floundering
> in the effort to do something beyond their powers. With perfect simplicity,
> perfect dignity and composure, they were just themselves, speaking a
> task that they had well by heart.[24]

As Beerbohm conceded, much of the Irish Theatre's success depended upon its novelty, and one of the significant features of its early
development was its determined insistence on remaining outside the
nineteenth-century English theatrical tradition. It was self-consciously
independent, and the frequent attacks it was called upon to endure only
strengthened its independence. The theatre was sometimes criticised
for impropriety, as for example when Yeats's *The Countess Cathleen*
was condemned by some people for portraying an Irish girl who sold
her soul to the Devil, or more violently, when audiences at the Abbey

rioted in 1907 over the unflattering portrait of the Irish peasantry presented by Synge in *The Playboy of the Western World*, and the supposed indecency of the language, specifically the use of the word "shift". Some even complained of the inappropriateness of calling the theatre "Irish", when the plays it produced were written in English and seemed to avoid contemporary national issues, a criticism which Yeats countered by reminding his critics that English, not Gaelic, was the language actually spoken, and that a "National literature" is not necessarily one which deals with national issues, but is simply that which is moulded by the influences that are moulding the country.[25] Such attacks, however, did nothing to deflect the Irish theatre from its chosen course. As Yeats said: "I would sooner our theatre failed through the indifference or hostility of our audiences, than gained an immense popularity by any loss of freedom."[26]

The Irish theatre was, in short, self-consciously independent, and in many respects its policies were diametrically opposed to those of the English theatre. While the English theatre tended to concentrate on outward forms, the Irish turned its attention to mythic reality, the inner life. The English theatre depended upon the "star system", and was inclined to emphasize the actor's performance at the expense of the play in which he was appearing. On the other hand Yeats believed that "characters" in a drama were relatively unimportant. As he wrote:

> When we go back a few centuries and enter the great period of drama, character grows less and sometimes disappears, and there is much lyric feeling, and at times a lyric measure will be wrought into the dialogue, a flowing measure that had well-befitted music, or that more lumbering one of the sonnet.[27]

Finally, while the English drama was becoming increasingly dependent upon elaborate stage machinery and effects, the Irish was striving for an ever more artless simplicity.

We cannot say, however, that the Irish theatre was an entirely natural growth, springing, as some would have us believe, from the Irish soil, uncontaminated by alien influences. To some extent it was a deliberate rejection of current English practice, sanctioned and supported by Continental precept and example: the Symbolist dramas of Maurice Maeterlinck and the German Expressionists. Perhaps we may best appreciate its place in the history of modern British drama by seeing it as occupying the middle ground between naturalistic drama on the one hand, and "closet drama" on the other, and as such was both practically and symbolically suited to Synge's artistic aims, capabilities, and mode of expression.

The kind of literature Synge aspired to write falls between "life" and "fancy". The plays themselves deal with characters who are driven with impossible dreams; "each", as one critic has admirably expressed it, "with a single-minded, intense, almost child-like longing to become a 'wonder' is continually reaching out for a finer and fuller life. Imagination is creative in each of them, and it gives them a vision of some good beyond the poverty or drabness or terror which surround them; towards that vision, that dream, they strive."[28] The language Synge's characters use is in itself something between English and Gaelic, and they express themselves in an idiom which is neither prose nor poetry, being characterized by "symbolic density and metaphorical interplay of the images and image-kinds."[29]

Indeed, it is difficult to imagine a kind of theatre more appropriate for Synge's needs than the one for which he originally wrote, and it seems evident that the artistic environment in which his plays were written and presented contributed to his success. Synge himself wrote that a great work of art is distinct and inimitable, being "possible to only one man at one period and in one place",[30] and there is no question that he owed much to Yeats for directing him towards an environment which enabled him to realize his genius. It was Yeats who showed him where he might find the kind of material most suitable for his dramatic talents, and it was Yeats who did more than anyone to ensure that Synge had a theatre in which those talents might find their fullest expression. Therefore it is hardly surprising, as Una Ellis Fermor has noted, that "perhaps the most satisfying interpretations of Synge have been made by his own great contemporary and fellow-poet."[31]

It is ironic that as time went on Abbey Theatre policy favoured more and more the presentation of naturalistic drama, while in England T. S. Eliot began to raise his voice on behalf of drama, not necessarily written in verse, which would impose "a credible order" upon an ordinary reality, "evoking" a condition of serenity, stillness and reconciliation,[32] a drama, in short, closely akin to that written by Yeats and Synge. But neither in England nor in Ireland has a dramatist emerged whose plays approximate the achievement of either of these writers, and the reason is not far to see. As Arthur Symons expressed it:

> Life and beauty are the body and soul of great drama. Mix the two as you will, so long as both are there, resolved into a single substance. But let there be in the making two ingredients, and while one is poetry, and comes bringing beauty, the other is a violent thing which has scornfully been called melodrama, and is the emphasis of action. The greatest plays are melodrama by their skeleton, and poetry by the flesh which clothes that skeleton.[33]

Great drama, as both Yeats and Synge well knew, must be firmly rooted in reality. This is not to say that it should exploit "local colour." Rather, it should be the "making articulate of all the dumb classes each

with its own knowledge of the world, its own dignity, but all objective
with the objectivity of the office and the workshop, of the newspaper
and the street, of mechanism and of politics."[34] As a dramatist Synge
was faithfully attentive to the murmured conversations of the Irish
peasants he heard through the chink in the door, and with their words
echoing in his ears he ploughed his way to the stars. Ultimately, as Yeats
recognised, Synge is less a man of the theatre than of the soil, and therein
lies his genius, for it is "from contact with the soil" that everything,
"Antaeus-like", grows strong.[35] By divorcing itself from life, the English
theatre during the greater part of the nineteenth century lost its vitality
and found itself incapable of producing drama relevant to basic human
experience. In Ireland, however, there emerged a poetic drama which,
in the words of Una Ellis Fermor, "brought back to the drama of the
other English-speaking races the habit of high poetry which it had lost
for two hundred years."[36]

NOTES

1. Arthur Symons, *Plays, Acting and Music* (London, Constable, 1903), p. 54.
2. Arthur Symons, *Studies in Seven Arts* (London, Constable, 1906), pp. 351-352.
3. *Shaw on Theatre*, ed. E. J. West (New York, Hill and Wang, 1958), p. 64.
4. *Essays*, p. 245.
5. J. M. Synge, *Plays* (London, Allen and Unwin, 1932), p. vi.
6. *Synge*, p. 126.
7. *Essays*, p. 299.
8. *C.W.*, IV, p. 53.
9. *Explorations*, pp. 93-95.
10. *C.W.*, IV, p. 83.
11. *Ibid.*, pp. 53-54.
12. *Explorations*, p. 167.
13. *Ibid.*, p. 196.
14. *C.W.*, IV, p. 3.
15. *Ibid.*
16. *Ibid.*
17. Quoted by Lady Gregory, *Our Irish Theatre:* (New York and London, G. P. Putnam's Sons, 1914), p. 9.
18. *Explorations*, p. 223.
19. Max Beerbohm, *Around Theatres* (London, Rupert Hart-Davis, 1953), pp. 314-316.
20. *Essays*, p. 166.
21. *Ibid.*
22. *Explorations*, pp. 86-87.
23. *Ibid.*, pp. 86-88.
24. Max Beerbohm, *Around Theatres*, p. 316.

25. *Essays*, p. 156.
26. *Ibid.*, p. 117.
27. *Ibid.*, p. 240.
28. Alan Price, *Synge and Anglo-Irish Drama* (London, Methuen, 1961), p. 216.
29. Ronald Peacock, *The Art of Drama* (London, Routledge and Kegan Paul, 1957), p. 218.
30. Synge quoted by Greene and Stephens, *Synge*, p. 93.
31. Una Ellis Fermor, *The Irish Dramatic Movement* (London, Methuen, 1954), p. 186.
32. T. S. Eliot, *Poetry and Drama* (London, Faber, 1951), p. 35.
33. Arthur Symons, *Plays, Acting and Music*, p. 200.
34. *Explorations*, p. 249.
35. W. B. Yeats, "The Municipal Gallery Revisited", *Collected Poems* (London, Macmillan, 1958), p. 369.
36. Una Ellis-Fermor, p. 1.

THE INFLUENCE OF SYNGE
IN MODERN IRISH DRAMA

Robert Hogan

I

EVERYONE significant in the Irish theatre knows his Synge. Synge is as inescapable a presence as Bernard Shaw is to the modern English drama or Eugene O'Neill to the American. Yet in recent years Synge is probably more of a vague presence in the background rather than an immediate inspiration. He seems, unfortunately, to have congealed into a classic in which one respectfully finds, of course, certain universal values applicable at any time and in any country. However, Synge's world has receded, and so the qualities in his plays that had once a shocking immediacy about them have now dulled with time.

When W. G. Fay first played Christy Mahon, he played him as a wretched, scruffy, insignificant little fellow, and much of the strength of *The Playboy of the Western World* derived from the elevation of this nonentity into heroism. When Conal O'Riordan first revived the play after Synge's death, the role of Christy was taken over by Fred O'Donovan, and Christy became tidier, handsomer, and more personable. In later years Cyril Cusack and then Donal Donnelly managed to infuse their versions of Christy with some of the original spirit, but still this gradual tidying up of Christy increased, and the play came to be produced more for the easy laugh than for the chilling grotesquerie. In the early 1960's, for instance, there was a musical version called *The Heart's a Wonder*, which was solely a blend of charm and stage-Irish buffoonery. The Siobhan McKenna film of the early 1960's blunted the stage-Irish antics, but proceeded even further into blandness with a Christy played by a young actor handsome enough to be a matinée idol. The effective scenes in the film were some romantic ones between Pegeen Mike and Christy, and this was a very far cry indeed from Synge's original conception.

This blandness was also apparent in the most recent revivals of Synge at the Abbey Theatre. In the last two or three years, *The Shadow of the Glen*, *The Well of the Saints*, and *The Playboy* have all received new productions in English, and *Riders to the Sea* has been done in Irish. All of these productions were done carefully and with taste, and each contained some excellences. However, none of them was a particularly thrilling night in the theatre, and probably the best that can be said of all of them was that they were mildly interesting. One could hardly imagine any fledgling playwright in the audience being deeply enough stirred to go and do likewise. Synge has become a part of the revered past. His plays are now historical dramas, because the world that they mirror has largely disappeared.

This is, of course, an enormous loss, for the qualities that electrified the original audiences of his plays, and the qualities that still can move us in the study, are rare and valuable and eminently needed in the contemporary Irish drama, which is in danger of becoming simply a reflection of the currently fashionable trends in London or Paris or New York.

I would have no idea how those qualities could be recaptured in any contemporary production of Synge, without doing a gross disservice to the basic qualities of the plays. The plays are so much of a particular time and a particular place, that it would be sacrilegious and probably impossible to transplant them to the present by imposing a contemporary style upon them. *Deirdre* or *The Playboy* done in the Berliner Ensemble manner would be just a bit too mind-boggling. Nevertheless, Chekhov, who was certainly as deeply rooted in late nineteenth century Russia as Synge was in late nineteenth century Ireland, still holds the boards with undiminished effectiveness. He does so, though, not in productions which attempt to transplant him to the Deep South of America, but in productions which attempt a minute fidelity to the world Chekhov knew. Perhaps what is needed to revivify the Synge plays for a contemporary audience is a similar close and perhaps even naturalistic fidelity, a fidelity which throws into bold relief the sensuality of the plays and their grotesquerie.

II

Determining precise literary influence is at best an imprecise business. In other times when a smaller premium was placed upon originality, it was possible to say with some certainty that Shakespeare borrowed this portion of his plot from Boccaccio, or that Boucicault stole this device from Augustin Daly. Nowadays, when most countries are signatories to the Berne convention, copyright laws prevent the more overt kind of pillaging, and so literary influence is a good deal more difficult to gauge. It is in this sense an intimate part of the creative process, and one can usually say little with certainty, without being a rather intimate friend of the writer involved. Not always even then.

Let me illustrate by a personal instance. The Irish playwright John O'Donovan is a considerable authority on Bernard Shaw. He has written an excellent book about Vandaleur Lee's influence on Shaw, entitled *Shaw and the Charlatan Genius*. He has written a play, produced by the

Abbey Theatre, entitled *The Shaws of Synge Street*, which is an effective dramatization of the lives of Shaw's family and its friends. He has collaborated with me in a dramatization of Shaw's novel *The Irrational Knot*. His personal collection of Shavian materials is better than that of many libraries. He has been, like Shaw, a music critic. He is, as was Shaw, a teetotaller and a vegetarian, and his handwriting even resembles Shaw's. If ever a writer's knowledge of and admiration for another writer should have caused literary influence, it should, I think, be found in O'Donovan's work. Nevertheless, when reading O'Donovan's plays, one is struck much more by the differences from, rather than the resemblances to Shaw; and I would be quite at a loss in trying to isolate any single facet of O'Donovan's work which is indubitably Shavian in its inspiration.

There are, in other words, difficulties in ascertaining what Irish playwrights have been influenced by Synge and how they have been influenced. Perhaps the safest way to proceed would be to list the notable Syngean characteristics and then to point out where similar characteristics occur in the works of later men.

To me, the most prominent qualities of Synge's plays are the nature of his language and the grotesquerie of his most memorable incidents.

The most individual of Irish playwrights—Synge, Yeats, Lady Gregory, George Fitzmaurice, Sean O'Casey, M. J. Molloy, Brendan Behan, Samuel Beckett—have always been recognizable by the inimitable quality of their dialogue. More ink has probably been spilled in analyzing the rich and individual speech of Synge's people, than in evaluating any of his other characteristics. Yet one quality which Synge's dialogue shares with that of Yeats, Lady Gregory and the others is that it is not really useful to another writer.

The reason, I think, is that its finest quality lies in the startling juxtaposition of alien words to produce the most vivid images. This quality arises from Synge's particular genius, his own quite individual way of regarding the world, and it is therefore really impossible to imitate. Take this quality away from the other principal characteristics of Syngean dialogue—the more noticeable turns of speech and quirks of phrase and heavy rhythms—and there remains only the mannerism and not the soul. Of course, mannerism can be put to some limited use by other writers in the form of parody, and Synge's manner has sometimes been so used with good effect. Gerald MacNamara was parodying Synge, among others, in his *The Mist That Does Be on the Bog*. Denis Johnston parodied Synge in portions of *The Old Lady Says "No !"*, O'Casey parodied him in portions of *Purple Dust*, and Maurice Meldon parodied him in some passages of *Aisling*. But parody has a very limited utility, and I think that Synge's language has been most influential not as a specific model, but as a general example of the vividness and richness towards which stage dialogue may aspire.

The original antipathy toward Synge was probably so marked because the extraordinary richness of his language and the violent grotesquerie of his central incidents seemed to intensify his views. As Yeats pointed out, the work of William Boyle was sometimes as caustic in its attitudes, but Boyle's language was much blander and his incidents much less strikingly extravagant.

This extravagant grotesquerie in the situations of *The Shadow of the Glen*, in the last act of *The Well of the Saints*, and throughout *The Playboy* is a trademark of Synge, but it is also apparent in other Irish dramatists who preceded and followed him. In general, I have in mind the lack of reverence for basic social institutions such as the family and the church, and also a rather insouciant view about the value of life. This may sound heretical, but I have in mind specifically several things. There is the real corpse in *Riders to the Sea* and the businesslike way in which it is treated, and there is the pseudo-corpse of Dan Burke in *The Shadow of the Glen* and the casual way in which it is treated. There is Nora's desertion at the end of the same play, a desertion which is more shattering to custom and more final than the desertion of Ibsen's more famous Nora at the end of *A Doll's House*. There are so many obvious and often discussed incidents and attitudes of this nature in *The Playboy*, that perhaps I need mention here only the fact that the voice of convention is given to the gormless and cowardly Shawn Keogh, who is a figure of fun very largely because he does acquiesce to convention.

There is something of this same irreverence about convention and about man himself in quite a few other Irish dramatists, some of whom were very far from being social critics. Dion Boucicault for most of his long and successful career was a crowd-pleasing hack writer who intended to offend no portion of his audience. Nevertheless, the heroes of his three best known Irish plays are disreputable rascals who gaily drink, poach, steal and swagger through their plays, ignoring convention and delighting in their freedom.

But perhaps I might better exemplify the attitude I mean by noting a situation that occurs in the work of several writers. The corpses which appear in Synge pop up, literally and figuratively, elsewhere, and often in a whimsical or farcical context. In Boucicault's *The Shaughraun*, the most drolly effective scene is Conn's wake in which he, the indomitable Shaughraun, unexpectedly revives and wryly surveys his obsequies. In *The Racing Lug* of 1902, James H. Cousins foreshadowed Synge's treatment of a similar situation in *Riders to the Sea* by two years. In addition to several poetic plays on Irish mythology, Cousins also wrote a full length realistic comedy of Ulster life, entitled *Sold*. Although W. B. Yeats used his influence to prevent the Fays from producing *Sold*, it is not quite the terrible play that Yeats thought. It does tail off badly after a good opening act, but in that act a main character pretends to be dead, and this pseudo-death impels the whole plot.

Precisely the same situation appears years later in M. J. Molloy's vehicle for Siobhan McKenna, *Daughter from over the Water*, when again the man of the house plays dead in order to stave off his creditors. In both plays, the pseudo-corpse is quickly forgotten by people eager to woo the "widow", but an even more grotesque situation occurs in Molloy's masterly one-act *The Paddy Pedlar*, in which the Pedlar is carrying the body of his mother around in a sack.

There are enough other such instances, which could be cited, to make one ponder. It is easy to cry Syngean influence, but it is also possible to wonder if this grotesque fun and this casualness about life may have appeared so frequently in Irish literature because of certain centuries-long conditions of Irish life. Oppression, rebellion, grinding poverty, and unimaginable famine made life so cheap that the only way finally to regard it may have been through the joke. And because a vital matter is treated casually, a sober matter flippantly, the effect is extra-ordinarily grotesque. In contrast, sex in Ireland has been dear rather than cheap, and the treatment of sex in Irish literature has until lately been predominantly romantic or tragic. But, at any rate, it is often difficult to say whether this grotesquerie so frequently found in Irish playwrights is a direct influence of Synge or simply an inevitable effect of Irish history.

III

Undoubtedly one can discern some influence of Synge on his friend John Masefield's 1908 play, *The Tragedy of Nan*, and one must surely note Paul Green's 1927 attempt in *The Last of the Lowries* to write an American folk play based on the pattern of *Riders to the Sea*. Beyond this, attribution becomes a bit tenuous.

Nevertheless, it seems plausible to suggest that Synge's first major influence was upon the early work of George Fitzmaurice, the eccentric Kerryman whose plays were shamefully neglected during his lifetime, and whose reputation since his death in 1963 has grown so enormously that it may yet come to rival Synge's own. Still, it is somewhat mis-leading to compare the two writers, for Fitzmaurice's best work usually has a strong element of the fantastic, which is largely lacking in Synge. It would probably be just to say that Fitzmaurice took the folk play, as practiced by Synge, Hyde and Lady Gregory, and so suffused it with myth, legend and his own quaint and satiric fancies, that the final product, in such plays as *The King of the Barna Men* and *The Enchanted*

Land, resembles a Synge play rewritten by Lewis Carroll collaborating with J. R. R. Tolkien.

In Fitzmaurice's simpler and, usually, earlier work, the similarity to Synge's plays is strongest. *The Toothache*, an unproduced one-act play which is probably among the very first that Fitzmaurice wrote, is a folk play whose grotesque antics might have been written by Synge himself. The popular comedy, *The Country Dressmaker*, was never considered by Yeats to approach the quality of Synge's work, but even Yeats realized that the play's sardonic view of the Irish was akin to that of *The Playboy*. Indeed, Yeats even boasted that the *Dressmaker* would bring more policemen into the theatre than had *The Playboy*. *The Pie-Dish* and *The Magic Glasses* were one-acts presented by the Abbey in, respectively, 1908 and 1913; and with another one-act, *The Dandy Dolls*, they form a trilogy of short fantastic masterpieces, full of vitality, drollery, eccentricity and superb speech. As Austin Clarke remarked,

> Following Synge's example of a rich rhythmic speech, Fitzmaurice, as a Kerryman, drew his own from his native county. It has in it the rapid rhythm of Kerry Irish and it seems to catch its pace from those fantastically long place-names which one finds in the 'Kingdom'. Its imagery expresses the blending of reality and legend. Reading *The Dandy Dolls*, I wondered how Lady Gregory and Yeats could have failed to recognise the energy, vehement rhythm and imaginative originality of its two short acts, especially when they had already been pleased by *The Magic Glasses*.[1]

Keerby's magnificent speech which concludes *The Dandy Dolls* is well known, and so to give the flavour of Fitzmaurice's dialogue let me quote from the speeches of Morgan Quille, as he lies on the floor in convulsions in *The Magic Glasses*, reciting the cure for Jaymony Shanahan:

> Jaymony, Jaymony Shanahan! Let Jaymony Shanahan drink one wineglassful of the bottle left on the table by one Morgan Quille of Beenahorna—three times a day let him drink one wineglass, in the morning and coming on the fall of night. And the price of that bottle is four-and-six—[PADDEN *fumbles in pocket, hands money to* MAINEEN, *who slips it into* QUILLE'S *hand*]—and at the dawn of day let Jaymony Shanahan hop on one leg and make a bow East and West and North and South, and let him pick fourteen roses and make a garland with ferny leaves and eglantine, and leave it on the thatch. [*Works again in convulsions*] Jaymony, Jaymony Shanahan! Let Jaymony Shanahan go turn the red earth every day will rise over him seven hours between dawn and the time the sun goes down, and in the dusk he'll ramble to the neighbours' houses and discourse on cattle and on crops and all things on the agricultural way. He'll go to market and to fair—take drink—a little—and ketch a woman if he wants to when he is coming home. On the twenty-first day a farmer's daughter is to be made out for Jaymony Shanahan. . . Who is the woman to be made out for

Jaymony Shanahan? A lovely woman for a man with four cows, no blemish on her beauty, but a slight impediment in her speech. The birthmarks on her are a pimple under her left ear, three black hairs on her buzzom and one brown. In Beenahorna this damsel does dwell, and on the twenty-first day—if Jaymony obey all the instructions given— one Morgan Quille will bring her to Jaymony Shanahan, and on the twenty-second day he'll be cured for ever and live in the grace of God.[2]

Besides the obvious differences between this dialogue and that of Synge, there is also Fitzmaurice's habit of slipping out of tone, usually for satiric purposes. One sees it here in the line about the price of the bottle or in "take drink—a little." This is a quality which I think uncharacteristic of Synge. But also Fitzmaurice's whimsical images and details are usually intended to raise a spurt of laughter rather than a smile of delight, and here he possibly goes back beyond Synge, Hyde and Lady Gregory to Boucicault for his inspiration. Nevertheless, before Synge, Hyde and Lady Gregory, dialogue with all of Fitzmaurice's qualities could hardly have been written. Compare, for instance, the dialogue of Fitzmaurice's early short stories, which were done around the turn of the century, with the dialogue of the post-1906 plays. He was not really a rival to Synge, for their natures were in too many ways different, but Yeats apparently thought that he was, and so the theatre lost for many years one of its greatest writers.

Other than Fitzmaurice, the Irish theatre up to the emergence of Sean O'Casey showed little obvious influence of Synge. There were some faintly macabre touches in the minor work of Lennox Robinson and in some plays by John Guinan and Winifred Letts, but generally this period was dominated by realistic comedy and tragedy, chiefly from Robinson, T. C. Murray, Rutherford Mayne and St. John Ervine. In the 1920s, the example of Sean O'Casey imposed a pattern of heightened realism upon the Irish drama. Later, O'Casey himself was to develop this pattern into a unique kind of pastoral fantasy, but the influential O'Casey remained the one who had written *Juno and the Paycock*. For years this heightened realism held joint sway on the boards with the more prosaic older realism, now best exemplified by the plays of George Shiels, and the mainstream of the Irish drama seemed very far distant indeed from the impulse of Synge.[3]

Most of the post-war drama written in Ireland shows even less overt influence of Synge. Partly, the reason is that Synge's plays were about an unspoiled rural Ireland which has been quickly dying. Of the writers who still live in the country, who have strong roots there, and whose important work reflects the life there, the best are probably Bryan MacMahon, Michael J. Molloy and John B. Keane.

MacMahon, who has been a life-long schoolmaster in Listowel, County Kerry, has one of the most impressive theatrical talents of his generation, although he has not utilized it much. He was born in 1909, and his early work, poems and stories and essays, appeared in Sean O'Faolain's memorable magazine, *The Bell*. MacMahon made his reputation first as a writer of short stories, and his principal creative energies have always been directed to fiction. Of his three long plays, the first, *Bugle in the Blood*, is the least important. Although it has its grotesqueries and its melodramatic fight, it is primarily reminiscent of the O'Casey of *Juno and the Paycock*. MacMahon's major plays are *Song of the Anvil* and *The Honey Spike*. The first is set in an isolated valley in Kerry where the old ways and traditions linger on, and the play shows how the old ways collide disastrously with the modern world. The story teller, Ulick Madigan, whose tales bring colour and vitality, as well as the interest of the outside world, into the valley, explains the problem well to a reporter from the city:

> To you this place is picturesque. To me it's daft and desolate. And it's dying fast. Once, out of the struggle for the land, came the storytellers, dancers, poets, men who made fiddle-music fit to stir the stars. But they are all dead—all dead, I tell you, man. The young people—they have all gone across the sea. We were alone and moving toward our end. And then, when all seemed lost, one winter's night, we held a trial all night long until the crack of dawn to find who'd tell a flamin' variegated lie . . . I won! And do you know what 'twas like? 'Twas like as if the Voice of God was roaring from my blood.[4]

MacMahon in this play attempts to suggest that the spirit of the Gaelic past may be combined with a Catholic tradition and even with the spirit of the modern world, but although he has written a moving and magnificently theatrical play slashed through with humour and fantasy and romance and extravagance, he has not, I think, found either an aesthetic formula or a social formula to blend the old with the new. This is a play that for the most part gets its strength from the past. Despite its young American heroine and despite the reporter, the modern world remains pretty much offstage. The play is something of a fantasy, something of a wish-fulfilment more than an actuality. It is a superb wish-fulfilment, of course, and much of its comedy, melodrama and what, for lack of a better term, we might call its national colour have a Syngean flavour. In the ferocious ending, for instance, the villagers tie Ulick up and attempt to brand him, as, indeed, Pegeen and the villagers of *The Playboy* had attempted to do with Christy Mahon. There is a further reminiscence in the vitality and sense of aliveness that the old life brings to MacMahon's people, and it comes from the same source that turned Christy into a playboy.

The Honey Spike is the best play to have been written about the travelling people since Synge's *The Tinker's Wedding*. Like Maurice Walsh, MacMahon knows his tinkers intimately; he is mentioned, for instance, in Muriel Rukeyser's rather poor book about Puck Fair, *The Orgy*. MacMahon's play, which he later turned into a novel, is a much more ambitious work than Synge's, for it is not only a re-creation of the tinker life, but it is also an odyssey through the length of Ireland. As young Martin Claffey rushes his wife Breda from the Giant's Causeway to the Honey Spike, the hospital in Kerry, where she wants to have her baby, we are really seeing again the clash of the old Ireland with the new. In their travels with pony and cart, the Claffeys meet a cross-section of modern Ireland, and this world is contrasted with the richness of an older Ireland. The play contains a Syngean abundance of riddles and ballads and fights and violence, and also a death scene of great poignance. I have quoted Martin Claffey's speech on Breda's death elsewhere, but it seems appropriate to do it here again, in this context where we are stressing speech that is "as fully flavoured as a nut or apple":

Breda! Breda Claffey! Breda, you lovely bitch that I love as man has never loved a woman before. Breda! Come out and walk with me again. Come out and swing your arms around my neck. You've made no complaint of me. I raced you from the Causeway in the Six. We made the bed of honour 30, 40, 60 times, we did. Come out, let you! For you I raced my cob. Through guns and hurleys lifted above my head I brought you to your honey spike. Come out, I tell you now. Come out! The two of us were grand. Only come out, let you, and then the pony-bells will ring for us again. Hey! Breda Claffey, listen now! Listen, I tell you! The world is thronged with things is lovely at the break o' day. Come out, you stubborn heedless strap! Come out, or else I'll drag you by your hair. I tell you that I'll drag you by your . . . lovely shining rippling hair.[5]

Michael J. Molloy was born in 1917 in Co. Galway where his father was a shopkeeper and his mother a national schoolteacher, and where he now owns a farm. His plays tend to be either historical dramas, like his masterly *The King of Friday's Men*, or comic dramas of the present day which depict the depopulation of the West. Yet "comic dramas" is a most misleading term for plays like *The Visiting House*, *The Wood of the Whispering*, and *Old Road*. They contain elements of comedy and deeply felt seriousness as well as much farce and melodrama and romance, but the unifying quality of the best of them, and the quality that remains most in the memory, is a pervasive and brooding melancholy over the passing of a civilisation that until recently had remained unchanged in its essentials for centuries.

Molloy is steeped in the traditions, the history, the myths and the folklore of the West. What Synge acquired by persistent inquiry, Molloy obtained by simply living in a certain place for all of his life. It is, then, difficult to say what precisely Molloy owes to Synge and what he owes merely to treating a similar subject-matter. Certainly the resemblances

between their work, and even the manner of their work, are striking.
Molloy, as was Synge, is a slow writer and a meticulous reviser. Much
that goes into his plays is built up of incidents and anecdotes and turns
of speech, remembered and jotted down from first-hand observation.
Much of this has an authentic and arresting piquancy about it. In some
ways, Molloy seems a more authentic Synge, a Synge who was sitting
on a settle in the kitchen rather than listening through a chink in the
bedroom floor. I intend no pejorative comment by the word "authentic".
I mean in part only that Molloy's dialogue, to take but one instance,
is probably closer to the way people talked, while Synge's dialogue
seems to me an embroidery, a dramatization, a heightening. Elsewhere
I have suggested that Molloy's dialogue lies about midway between the
dialogue of George Shiels, which represents a thinning of the language,
and that of Synge, which represents a thickening of it. Each has its
excellences and drawbacks. Synge's dialogue has much of the evocative
power of poetry, while Shiels' has practically none; Synge's dialogue
offers distinct problems as stage speech, while Shiels' has an easy
fluency and force as stage speech. Molloy's dialogue is a kind of compromise which poses few difficulties as stage speech, and which yet
retains a good deal of evocative power. There are rhythms in Molloy's
long speeches which amplify their emotional power, but the rhythms are
much less obtrusive than Syngean rhythms. There is also a much less
imaginative use of metaphor and figure in Molloy than in Synge,
although there is some; the principal evocative power of Molloy's
dialogue comes, I think, from his diction which is, for most of us,
unfamiliar without being baffling, and fresh enough to be engaging.
Some of Molloy's best effects come from a quiet mournfulness, such as
the beautiful speech of the old man, Mickle Conlon, which concludes
The Visiting House, or several speeches of Sanbatch Daly to Sadie the
mute in *The Wood of the Whispering.* Mickle's speech is very long, and
yet this ambling monologue, delivered by the old man after everyone,
unbeknownst to him, has left the stage, is such an exquisite dying fall,
and such a perfect parallel to the gentle fading away of Mickle's world,
that I cannot resist giving it in full:

> And now, Corry, wance you behaved such a decent man, I'll give you
> good advices that'll stand to you well when you're going dying, the same
> as me now. Your first plan, then, asthore, 'll be to coax the Mother of
> God, for she has a great hand with Our Saviour, and anything she wants
> she has only to ask Him. Wan single falling out!—that was all they had
> in all their time together on earth, and there wasn't much to that; there
> was not, asthore. They were going the road this day, asthore, and they
> seen a fellow that was someway crippled, and out of his proper shape.
> "Son," she sez, "you made a poor job of that wan"—she didn't think
> of herself; she did not, asthore. Our Saviour said no word till duskus,

then, "Mother," he said, "in place of you and Me stopping in the wan lodging house tonight, I'll stop in the first house on the right, and you in the first house on the left." So they did, asthore, and she went in, and found a corpse laid overboard on the kitchen table, and snuff and tobaccy, and a gross of pipes and all ready for the wake, asthore. So, the same as everywan had to do before your time, she took a pipe and said, "The Lord have mercy on the dead!" and she smoked away there in honour of the dead; but not a single person come in to the wake, asthore, and she was by herself with the corpse till the morning. That was the penance Our Saviour put on her, so He must be middling vexed to her that day, all right. But that finished that, and 'twas the only falling out they had ever, asthore. Anything she wants she has only to ask Him, so keep her on your side, and when your tenure of time is up 'tis she'll have your bed dressed in Heaven and the finest of welcomes before you. [*Wandering.*] That's sure, asthore, that's sure, asthore . . . [*Suddenly and sternly.*] Corry, did you let that advice to you ? [*Thundering.*] Corry, answer up and don't be disorderly. Corry! [*Finally he pokes out his stick, finds the form empty, and smiles.*] He's at large; he is, asthore. [*Turns back to fire cheerfully.*] No matter; now you'll have two half barrels, and the finest wake since the time of the gentlemen; now you can die away for yourself, asthore . . . [*Gravely.*] For the first while right enough you'll be lonesome for the village; and lonesome for the Visiting House, too. [*Nodding.*] You will, in throth, asthore . . . But wance you have the lonesomeness and your Purgatory over, you'll be all right; [*In great humour.*] you'll be as snug as a lamb in a shed; you will, asthore . . . asthore . . .⁶

This is a quite characteristic passage of Molloy, deep in feeling and melancholy in tone. Its resemblances to and its differences from Synge are probably apparent without comment. What is curious, though, is that Molloy can counterpoint such passages with ones of vigour and violence. And it is violence not only of language, but of action. Like Synge and Fitzmaurice, Molloy is fond of the stage fight, and there are finely melodramatic ones in *Old Road*, in *The King of Friday's Men*, and in that macabre little masterpiece, *The Paddy Pedlar*. "Hullabaloo! Hullabaloo!" cries Molloy's pedlar:

[*Twice he leaps into the air with that hiss of savage joy; drawing back the knife each time as if about to charge at Ooshla. But instead he leaps again, and cries aloud in triumph.*] Now, Mamma! Timmy has his knife! Timmy has his knife! Timmy has his knife! No one'll dare harm you no more!⁷

But perhaps the greatest similarity between Molloy and Synge is that their worlds are both peopled by outcasts and eccentrics. Molloy's is a world of sad, lonely people, pushed into weirdness or quaintness or wildness or madness. His Bully Men and Bards and Mutes and Pedlars are as outcast as Synge's Tramps and Tinkers and Playboys and Blind Men. The one great difference between Molloy's characters and Synge's is that Synge's usually triumph over their circumstances, while Molloy's are defeated by theirs. Molloy is a muted Synge, more sad than bitter, more musing than lyrical, and that perhaps is appropriate because the world they both wrote of is fading.

John B. Keane is probably the most recent writer whose work seems to reflect a Syngean influence. He has been a prolific playwright, and would be mentioned with Hugh Leonard and Brian Friel as one of the important Irish playwrights to emerge since Brendan Behan. As with Molloy, whose influence he admits, Keane has never really left Ireland. In his youth he was, like many other young Irishmen, forced to emigrate to England, but this short exile he resented bitterly, and his one play about the subject, *Hut 42*, is a poignant lament of the exile for his homeland. Most of Keane's plays reflect the life he intimately knows in the Southwest of Ireland. I have elsewhere argued that this was a kind of Hidden Ireland, with a life richer and larger and more basically Irish than life in the modern Dublin of television antennas, exhaust fumes and rectangular office slabs of concrete and glass. Yet this is probably only half-true now. Tourism has become a highly organized and profitable business, and the Irish Tourist Board is industriously tempting hordes of Americans and English to explore the remarkable beauties of the Irish countryside. This influx of people and money has combined with the impact of the modern world as seen through television, to effect considerable change in the West and the South. So while the earlier Keane plays resembled Syngean folk plays about the traditional past, his more recent work—such as *The Field* and *Big Maggie*—reflect a clash of an older way of life with a new.

The plays of Keane which are most Syngean are his first three—*Sive, Sharon's Grave,* and *The Highest House on the Mountain.* In these folk plays, the most prominent reminiscences of Synge are a sardonic grotesquerie of characterization and action and a flowing eloquence in the language. Characters such as the matchmaker and the travelling tinkers in *Sive,* such as Dinzie Conlee, the savage sex-crazed hunchback, in *Sharon's Grave* came down from the mountains out of the same mist and rain as did Michael Casey and Old Mahon fifty years earlier.

One finds also in these early plays much of the Syngean violence. As Martin Doul strikes the can of holy water from the hand of the Saint, as the Caseys truss up the priest and throw him into the ditch, as Christy cleaves his father's head with the loy, and Pegeen Mike burns Christy's leg with the burning turf, so also is Keane's world a violent one. In particular, there is that harrowing scene at the conclusion of *Sharon's Grave,* which begins when Dinzie Conlee cries, "I'll lob this knife between the breasts of her and stick her like a pig",[8] and then crawls across the floor after his cousin Trassie; and which concludes when Neelus, the simpleton, races out with the hunchback on his back to plunge over the cliff into the sea.

Keane's dialogue has sometimes been admired for its force, but in these early folk plays it also has a richness, which is less embroidered than Synge's, but nevertheless reminiscent of it. Here, for instance, is Tomasheen Sean Rua in *Sive* speaking to Mike Glavin and his wife Mena:

> Will you listen to him! You're like the priest in the pulpit! Will you think of the days of your life you spent slavin' for nothin'. You needn't rise off your bottom to earn two hundred sovereigns, and you sit there giving sermons! And you talk about love! In the name of God, what do the likes of us know about love? Did you ever hear the word of love on his lips? Ah, you did not, girl! Did he ever give you a little rub behind the ear or run his fingers through your hair and tell you he would swim the Shannon for you? Did he ever sing the love-songs for you in the far-out part of the night when ye do be alone? He would sooner to stick his snout in a plate of mate and cabbage, or to rub the back of a fattening pig than whisper a bot of his fondness for you. Do he run to you when he come in from the bog and put his arms around you and give you a big smohawnach of a kiss and tell you that the length of the day was like the length of a million years while he was separated from you?[9]

This dialogue lacks the more obvious Syngean characteristics of lengthy sentences and thickly rhythmical speech, but there is something of the same quality in the diction and in the nature of the imagery and certainly in the vitality that pervades it.

In the Preface to *The Playboy*, Synge wrote of "countries where the imagination of the people, and the language they use, is rich and living." He spoke of "the wildest sayings and ideas", of "the rich joy found only in what is superb and wild in reality", of speech that is "fully flavoured as a nut or apple."[10] To us who have come with delight upon these rare qualities in the plays of John Synge, it must seem an appalling loss that the world from which these qualities rose, the world of which Synge was one of the last interpreters, is passing. The playwrights I have mentioned all live in a world which Synge never dreamed of, and their plays either transmute that old Ireland into fantasy or show it grappling, sometimes successfully but more often not, with the modern world. I think that the playwrights to come will not for much longer be able to write plays like Molloy's or MacMahon's or the early ones of Keane —and yet it is possible that the qualities which Synge most valued in his country, joy and richness, may take some new form which is both modern and Irish. In the 1920's, Sean O'Casey found joy and richness in the world of the Dublin slums, and in the 1940's and 1950's he had found another new way to write with joy and richness of the modern world. In the 1950's Brendan Behan found a way. So perhaps it does not matter if Synge's manner be lost; those who were most influenced by him never attempted to imitate it, but only to emulate it, to sieve its spirit through their own individualities. A James Douglas, a Brian Friel, a Tom Coffey may find a new way for a new time. It is only the richness and joy that matter, and in those qualities Synge has given his real legacy to the men who came after.

NOTES

1. Austin Clarke, "Introduction", *The Plays of George Fitzmaurice*, I (Dublin, The Dolmen Press, 1967), p. viii.
2. George Fitzmaurice, "The Dandy Dolls", *Ibid.*, pp. 13-14.
3. This is, of course an over-simplification which takes little account of some remarkable plays by Denis Johnston, Lord Longford, Austin Clarke and others. However, regardless of their often extraordinary merits, such plays cannot be said to have exerted much significant influence. They formed few imitators, and they founded no schools.
4. Bryan MacMahon, "Song of the Anvil", in *Seven Irish Plays, 1946-1964*, ed. Robert Hogan (Minneapolis, University of Minnesota Press, 1967), p. 223.
5. This speech is quoted from the unpublished MS. of the play. Slightly altered, however, the speech may be found in the published novel version of the story. See Bryan MacMahon, *The Honey Spike* (London, The Bodley Head, 1967), p. 245.
6. Michael Molloy, "The Visiting House", in *Seven Irish Plays, 1946-1964*, p. 95.
7. Michael Molloy, *The Paddy Pedlar* (Dublin, James Duffy, 1954), p. 25.
8. John B. Keane, "Sharon's Grave", in *Seven Irish Plays, 1946-1964*, p. 363.
9. John B. Keane, *Sive* (Dublin, Progress House, 1959), pp. 41-42.
10. *C.W.*, IV, pp. 53-54.

SYNGE IN THE ARAB WORLD

Ghassan Maleh

In the Arab World of today there is an active dramatic movement; a movement that goes East and West for new methods and techniques and that delves into the Arab character and heritage in search of themes.

The movement is in a sense a revival of something that started several decades ago. Little experienced in the art of drama, the Arabs came to know of it and to practise it in Syria, Egypt, and Lebanon late in the nineteenth century. The beginnings of drama in Arabic were marked by a translation movement that brought a number of French and English classics within easy reach of the Arab public. Perhaps "translations" may not be the best word to describe a turn-of-the-century *Romeo and Juliet* or *Macbeth* in Arabic; for foreign works were usually "improved", or rather adapted, to suit local tastes and requirements. For example, where the star actor was a singer, as he often was, songs were inserted for his benefit as well as for the benefit of the *operetta*-loving public. This however happened mostly in the Egypt of the turn of the century; in Syria and Lebanon, meanwhile, drama enjoyed a certain measure of academic respectability though very little public favour. There is the case of Abu Khalil Kabbani who had to flee from Damascus to Cairo under pressure from puritans and fanatics. In fact until the nineteen fifties in Egypt and the sixties in Lebanon and Syria, drama remained either academic—in foreign missionary schools—or primitive on the occasionally-rented stages of cinema houses or open-air lots.

With a few exceptions, in Egypt especially, drama, until the late fifties, had played very little part in the cultural life of the Arab world. Indeed, but for a few European classics, usually adapted, the Arab stage had very little to offer; little variety either in theme or technique. But whereas in the late fifties one could count the number of Arab playwrights on the fingers of one hand, today one is hard put to it to remember the many, often very original, authors who are writing for the Arab stage.

The late nineteenth-century translation movement that first introduced the Arabs to the art of drama is paralleled by a much greater translation movement in the late fifties and sixties. This has consolidated the genre in Arab culture, created many Arab playwrights, and established the theatre as one of the central institutions of the nation. John Millington Synge belongs to the second phase in the development of Arab drama; more specifically he belongs to the sixties.

Convinced that drama is an essential means of developing the intellectual and cultural life of the nation and that the theatre is as effective a weapon as armed struggle, Arab thinkers have turned to other nations for guidance. They have found that many countries can provide examples to follow and great works to translate. But nowhere have they found a pattern so similar to their own situation as the Irish one. Here in the Arab World they were engaged in a struggle for freedom, unity and national identity. With parts of the Arab nation occupied by alien powers, others nominally independent, the Arabs felt that, like the Irish, their literary and dramatic movement could only be an offshoot of their political struggle for freedom and independence. In the Ireland of Synge and Yeats they found their example. Anxious to establish a theatre with "a base of reality and apex of beauty", rooted in the tradition and life of the people, the Arabs turned to the experiment of the Irish Dramatic Movement for guidance and inspiration. What helped in the process was that most Arab universities had already come to teach Synge, Yeats, and O'Casey in courses on the Irish Dramatic Movement—there is hardly a university in the Arab world today that does not teach works by Yeats and Synge in English literature courses.

The author of the present essay, writing in a special Drama issue of the Damascus monthly *Al Ma'arifa* in 1964, noted the similarity between the Irish and Arab situations and implied that much could be learnt from the Irish experiment.[1] Quoting extensively from the writings of the founder-leaders of the Irish Dramatic Movement, the author reminded his Arab readers, all eager to found a people's theatre, that Yeats was able to declare as early as 1919:

> We have been the first to create a true 'People's Theatre', and we have succeeded because it is not an exploitation of local colour, or of a limited form of drama possessing a temporary novelty, but the first doing of something for which the world is ripe, something that will be done all over the world and done more and more perfectly: the making articulate of all the dumb classes each with its own knowledge of the world . . .[2]

Yeats's "return to the people", long advocated by ministries of culture and adopted as declared policies of national theatre companies which are usually attached to such ministries in both socialist Egypt and Syria, appealed to those working in the field of drama and directed attention to the works of Yeats and Lady Gregory, and particularly Synge and O'Casey. It was no mere coincidence, therefore, that the first translation of a Synge play should appear in 1960 in socialist Egypt. This was *The Shadow of the Glen*[3] ("في ظلال الوادي") followed four months later by an Arabic rendering of *Riders to the Sea*[4] ("الى البحر"). *Deirdre of the Sorrows*[5] ("ديدري فتـاة الاحزان") ("الراكبون") was

(``فى الغرب المدلل'') translated in 1964, *The Playboy of the Western World*[6]
in 1965, and *The Well of Saints*[7] (``نبع الحقيقــة'') in 1969.

In translation, these works leave much to be desired. The Arabs, whose language has not been contaminated, still possess that quality of speaking in images and uttering poetry. But naturally the imagery they use is different from that of the Irish, and certain Anglo-Irish similes are bound to fall flat on Arab ears. Moreover, the vigour and immediacy of Synge's language derives from its being based on that of the Anglo-Irish speaking peasants of Western Ireland. The language is alive, conversational, and consistently reminiscent of the speaking voice.

In contrast, however hard the Arab translator has tried, he has come out with occasional drabness and staleness where, in the original, we have striking novelty and immediacy. In fact, the general impression of the various translations of Synge's plays into Arabic is one of bookishness. Except for occasional happy renderings by Unsi El Haj, one is constantly left with the feeling that the translations have done little more than transpose the Anglo-Irish words into Arabic, often overlooking the fact that they are Anglo-Irish with connotations frequently different from those which the same words have in standard English. The very title of *The Playboy of the Western World* is mistranslated, for instance, as ``فى الغرب المدلل'' (The Spoilt Youth of the West); the translator understanding the word "playboy" in its popular sense. The Arabic word chosen means a rich and spoilt young man.

Besides the inadequate rendering of the title and the omission of Synge's very important Preface, Hamdi Ahmad Rajab's translation of *The Playboy of the Western World* misses many points. For example, "awkwardly" in the stage direction introducing Shawn Keogh for the first time is translated as "indignantly", and Michael's

> . . . and what would the polis want spying on me, and not a decent house within four miles, the way every living Christian is a bona fide saving one widow alone ?[8]

is rendered as:

. . . and what would the polis want spying on me, and not a decent house within four miles, except for one owned by a widow, the way every Christian is a bona fide.[9]	واي شيء آخر يريد رجال البوليس ان يعرفوه عني ؟ انه لا يوجد فى مدى اربعة اميال نزل آخر محترم ، يقصده كل مسيحي فى اطمئنان، اللهم الا نزل واحد تديره ارملة ؟

Rajab translates literally and unimaginatively. The Arabs, for example, never "hit a box on the ear"; they slap one on the face. To translate, as Rajab does, "box on the ear" literally is to be ludicrous. Equally uninspired and unimaginative is the translator's rendering of Christy's final words:

Ten thousand blessings upon all that's here, for you've turned me a likely gaffer in the end of all, the way I'll go romancing through a romping lifetime from this hour to the dawning of the judgment day.[10]

Important as this declaration is in the development of Christy's character in particular and the whole play in general, the Arabic rendering of it is so drab, erroneous[5] and unimaginative as to strip it of all significance, immediacy, and vigour. It reads as follows:

Thousands of blessings on all of you for having given to me a reliable farmer; and I shall live from this moment until the judgment day in a world of dream, beauty and adventure.[11]

فلتحـــل الآن البركات عليكم جميعاً
فقد منحتموني فلاحاً يعتمد عليه ؛ وسأحيا
من هذه اللحظة ؛ حتى يأتي يوم الحساب
في عالم من الخيال والجمال والمغامرة .

The lack of vigour and immediacy is equally characteristic of the Arabic versions of *Riders to the Sea*, *The Shadow of the Glen*, and *Deirdre of the Sorrows*, although all three read much better than *The Playboy*. Unidiomatic expressions abound and, at best, the text reads as though it were intended for the printed page rather than the stage.

At the heart of the relative inadequacy of translating Synge is the gap between written and spoken Arabic. With each part of the Arab World speaking its own dialect, the use of spoken Arabic in drama tends to confine a play to a single region, and to establish the dialect of this region as a means of dramatic expression. Arab nationalists, and most Arab intellectuals, disapprove of the use of spoken Arabic on these very grounds, advocating the use of that form of written Arabic that is used from Morocco in the west to the Arabian Gulf in the east. This language is certainly capable of expressing all modes, feelings and emotions no matter how intense or prosaic they may be. Yet, this type of Arabic cannot adequately reflect the human voice, its rhythms and cadences. Hence, Synge suffers when translated into the written form of Arabic; the living imagination of the peasant is translated into either heightened poetic prose, highly literary and related to neither soil nor people; or into ordinary prose in which the living image becomes a decorative device in otherwise drab prose.

In fact, the story of modern drama in Arabic is one of constant search for a suitable language, and Unsi El Haj's unpublished translation of *The Well of the Saints* is one effort in this direction. He takes a little further something that we detect in the earlier translation of *The Shadow of the Glen* and one of the two translations of *Riders to the Sea*: the attempt to reproduce the human voice, the rhythm of the spoken word. Though unidiomatic and somewhat bookish at times, Unsi El Haj, a well-known poet in Arabic, gives a racy quality to the

Arabic version of *The Well of the Saints* by using the uninflected structure of spoken Arabic.

An experiment that has not been attempted with Synge yet is to translate his plays into the spoken Arabic of say Egypt or Syria and give them a local setting and flavour. There is no reason why *The Playboy* could not succeed in Arab dress. After all, theme, characters, and situation are as relevant to the Arab World today as they were to the Irish early this century. Besides, adaptation would remove from Synge's plays those many references to local markets and places which mean nothing to an Arab audience (and for that matter to any non-Irish audience), and, at the same time, by making characters speak the language of Arab peasants, the language problem would be partly solved.

Translating the plays of J. M. Synge into Arabic has served not only to introduce this great Irish dramatist to Arab readers and audiences, but has at the same time provided the occasion for studies of Synge and the Irish Dramatic Movement which have usually appeared as introductions to the translations.

Rajab's translation of the *The Playboy of the Western World* is introduced by an eighteen-page study of Synge and the play by Ali al-Ra'i. The introduction opens with an account of the rioting that accompanied the early performances of *The Playboy* and quotes extensively from the reviews which appeared in the Dublin press at the time. It also reviews the various opinions expressed and stands taken by such people as Yeats, Lady Gregory, Stephen Mackenna, George Moore, and William Boyle. The introduction contains moreover, an analysis of the play viewing it as a condemnation of a society with all its double standards, cowardice, hypocrisy, and oppression. It concludes with a rejection of the view that Christy is another Peer Gynt or Don Quixote. These two, writes Ali al-Ra'i, "make us laugh and feel sorry for them, but we are constantly moved on discovering our personal links with them. In our inner depths, there is invariably a Peer Gynt or a Don Quixote. Christy is different; we laugh at him, or even sympathize with him; but we are never moved by him, not deeply enough at least."[12]

Equally informative is 'Abdulla 'Abdulhafez Mitwalli's twenty-five page introduction to Ali Jamal-u-din 'Ezzat's translation of *Deirdre of the Sorrows*. The introduction traces Synge's literary career, discusses the role of nature in his plays in general and particularly in *Deirdre;* and follows all this with an interesting analysis of the play and an account of the Deirdre story for the benefit of the Arab reader. The greatness of *Deirdre of the Sorrows*, Mitwalli writes,

> . . . lies not so much in the feelings and thoughts it arouses, but rather in the colours and images that give lustre to the familiar . . . The dialogue, the events, that beautiful integration between the dramatic and the

poetic, and that interaction between the characters and Irish nature on Aran Islands leave us moved beyond description.[18]

The link between the Irish Dramatic Movement and the Irish nationalist movement, important for Arabs passing through a similar stage of development, is touched upon in Rashad Rushdi's introduction to *Selections of Short Plays*[14] containing a translation of *Riders to the Sea*. The importance of a return to the people for inspiration is stressed in the brief Preface to Fawzi Sama'an's translation of *The Shadow of the Glen*.

With five out of his six plays translated into Arabic and with several studies appearing as introductions to the translations, one may argue that this is not a bad record for a dramatist about whom the Arab world heard for the first time in the early sixties. Yet, Synge has not fared so well on the Arab stage. Out of his six plays only two have been performed; *Riders to the Sea* in 1963 and *The Well of the Saints* in 1969.

The Arabic version of *Riders to the Sea* was produced by Syrian Arab Television in July 1963. It could not have been presented at a better time. It was shown around July 20th, a few days after the failing of an armed attempt to take over the government. Shortly after the break-up of the Union between Egypt and Syria late in 1961, there followed a period of political instability in Syria that ended with the March 1963 Baathist revolution. In July, the revolution was busy consolidating its position when other political forces made their bid for power and launched their armed attack on the radio station, army headquarters, and other key establishments in the Syrian capital. The attempted *coup d'etat* crushed, curfew was imposed and tanks patrolled the streets. Meanwhile, Syrian viewers sat at home watching *Riders to the Sea* on their television sets. It was only natural for them to identify the sea that devours Maurya's sons with the just-ended political strife as well as with the forces that contended for power. The sea became a symbol of those powers that controlled man leaving him helpless and impotent.

Rafik Sabban, a well-known director and drama critic, reviewing the play in a Damascus daily, welcomed the choice of *Riders to the Sea* for presentation on Syrian Arab Television:

This is a happy choice. For we today stand to benefit greatly from further knowledge of Irish drama, revolutionary and simple.[15]

Sabban admired the television production and the technical skill with which it was executed. He thought the set created for it most admirable but unnecessary and favoured a simpler presentation that would give the poetry in the drama freer play. Sabban's review appeared side by side with an obituary notice of Salim Kataya, the young man who had directed the television production of *Riders to the Sea*. He had died of a heart attack a day after the showing of his play on Syrian television. His success in directing *Riders to the Sea* made his loss more widely felt. Today, no mention of Kataya is made without reference to his talented production of Synge's play. Since July 1963, *Riders to the Sea* has been shown on Syrian Arab Television on more than one occasion.

Synge had to wait six years before any of his plays was given a public performance in the Arab World, this time in Lebanon. On August 21st, 1969, *The Well of the Saints* was performed at the Beit Meri Roman Temple by the Baalbeck International Festival's Modern Drama Company. Using Unsi El Haj's translation entitled *The Well of Truth* ("نبع الحقيقة") Director Munir Abu Dibs, gave a melancholy interpretation of the play that linked it in the minds of most reviewers with his earlier densely dark dramatic productions.

Using the beautiful and majestic open-air temple of Beit Meri as setting, Abu Dibs chose set and costumes in such a way as to give action and characters a universal timeless quality. He was helped in this by El Haj's translation which left out of the text several references to purely local places. The director moved his anguished tortured characters superbly well, never relaxing the sombre and melancholy atmosphere enveloping the whole action from beginning to end. The villagers were made into a chorus whose studied movements nevertheless were not lacking in spontaneity. In the conflict between dream and actuality, it was the chorus who were represented as the truly blind. The couple, who stumbled when they regained their eyesight, were shown to be superior to the Saint, and to the villagers who knew neither dream nor actuality. Nowhere in the play did the action or the movement of the principal characters and chorus obscure the poetry in the speech of the men and women, a point that hardly a reviewer failed to make.

The Well of Truth was generally well-received; and although some reviewers objected to the melancholy vision (which they attributed to director rather than playwright), they were all unanimous in welcoming a serious work, seriously executed. All in all, the play enjoyed considerable success; after Beit Meri, it went to Tripoli for five performances at the Crusader Castle overlooking the coastal city. Early in October, the Baalbeck International Festival Committee decided to open its first season at its newly-completed Beirut home with a run of *The Well of Truth*. The play again enjoyed success although many lamented the loss of the Beit Meri and Tripoli settings.

Synge is no longer a new discovery in the Arab World. He has been with us for a decade. Interest in his works is growing, thanks to drama companies and universities as well as to the efforts of those who believe that Synge has something to say to the Arabs, not because they are Arabs but because they belong to humanity.

NOTES

1. Ghassan Maleh, "The Irish Dramatic Movement", *al-Ma'arifa*, XXXIV, 1964, pp. 376-384.
2. *Explorations*, p. 249.
3. Translated by Fawzi Sama'an as *Fi Thelal al-Wadi* and published in *al-Majala*, January 1960, pp. 99-108.
4. Translated by Na'im Attiya as *al-Rakibun ila al-Bahr* and published in *al-Majala*, May 1960, pp. 107-114. About the same time another— but much inferior—translation of *Riders to the Sea* was made by Huda Hbeishe. This appeared in the "Thousand Books" series: *Selections of Short Plays*, introduced by Rashad Rushdi (Cairo, Misr Library, n.d.).
5. Translated by 'Ali Jamal-u-din 'Ezzat as *Deirdre Fatat al-Ahzan*, introduced by 'Abdullah 'Abdulhafez Mitwalli (Cairo, al-Dar al-Misrya li-Ata'lif wal-Tarjmah).
6. Translated by Hamdi Ahmad Rajab as *Fata al-Gharb al-Mudalal*, introduced by 'Ali al-Ra'i (Cairo, al-Dar al-Misrya li-Ata'lif wal-Tarjmah).
7. Translated by Unsi El-Haj as *Nab'u al-Haqiqu* (*The Well of Truth*) and still unpublished.
8. *C.W.*, IV, p. 67.
9. *Fata al-Gharab al-Mudalal* (*The Playboy of the Western World*), p. 39.
10. *C.W.*, IV, p. 173.
11. *Fata al-Gharab al-Mudalal* (*The Playboy of the Western World*), p. 156.
12. 'Ali Ra'i, "Introduction", *Fata al-Gharb al-Mudalal* (*The Playboy of the Western World*), p. 20.
13. 'Abdullah 'Abdulhafez Mitwalli, "Introduction", *Deirdre Fatat al-Ahzan* (*Deirdre of the Sorrows*), p. 27.
14. See note 4 above.
15. *al-Ba'ath*, 24 July 1963.
16. See, for example, *Huna Dimashq* (*Damascus Radio Magazine*), August 1963, p. 17.

SYNGE IN JAPAN

Shotaro Oshima

SEVERAL Irish dramatists have been translated and produced in Japan in the past fifty years: T. C. Murray's *Birthright* was translated as *Kyodai*[1] (Brothers) by Kaoru Osanai (1881-1928) in 1914, Lennox Robinson's *The Harvest* was adapted as *Cha o tsukuru ie*[2] (The House Where They Grow Tea) by Sho'o Matsui (1870-1933) and was performed in 1913, and *The Clancy Name* by the same author was also adapted by Sho'o Matsui[3] and was performed on the stage in Tokyo. But few have exerted as great an influence on the theatrical movement in Japan as John Millington Synge. While other Irish dramatists have also presented the dramatic ideals of the Irish stage, none has been so remarkable for strict adherence to realism as J. M. Synge, especially in his plays *Riders to the Sea, The Well of the Saints* and *The Playboy of the Western World*.

In his prefatory note to *Reigen* (A Miracle), Shoyo Tsubouchi (1859-1935) tells us that the play has its origin in "another language, that of a European dramatist."[4] *Reigen* was published in September 1914, in book form. It had been written as an adaptation of *The Well of the Saints* for performance by the Mumeikai Players (The Association of the Anonymous). Tsubouchi had established Bungeikyokai (The Literary Association) in 1906, and started his literary career as a pioneer in the theatrical reform movement in Japan. Under the influence of modern Western drama, he believed that the younger dramatists must have a feeling for the tradition of their native land and that they should also endeavour to write plays of life and manners imbued with the realistic spirit. Tsubouchi's conviction that in the new dramatic movement there ought to be a vivid presentation of life can be seen in his choice of the dramatists whose plays he produced: Shaw, Ibsen, Sudermann. At the same time he was writing original plays of his own for the Bungeikyokai Players. He also staged *Hamlet* and *Julius Caesar*, with such fresh artistic interpretations that they stimulated a new interest in dramatic circles in Japan. Bungeikyokai continued to give performances for 13 years, playing to packed audiences as it could rely on popular support for the artistic ideals of Shoyo Tsubouchi. Synge was the first of the modern dramatists writing in English to be adapted by Tsubouchi for the Japanese stage.

In the preface to *Reigen*, Tsubouchi says that any Japanese playwright will easily identify the author of this play; that the original author is "an Irish dramatist, who is well known at the present day"; and adds that the main interest of *Reigen* lies in its folk-drama flavour. Tsubouchi found a medium of expression for his adaptation in the country dialect of the later period of the Ashikaga era (the 16th century), paralleling Synge's setting his play a hundred years or more in the past. He compares *Reigen* with *Tsubosaka Reigen-ki*[5] (The Tale of a Kwannon [the Goddess of Mercy] at Tsubosaka), a Japanese traditional Kabuki drama written by an anonymous author and first produced in 1879 in Osaka. The story of the drama is as follows:

There once lived a blind man, named Sawaichi, at Tsubosaka in Osaka. Though he had looked upon the world with a jaundiced eye and doubted his wife's fidelity, he was at last won over by his wife Osato's affection for him and her faith in the Kwannon. He, himself, therefore prayed together with her to the Kwannon; however, unable to believe that his blindness would be cured by a miracle, he committed suicide, throwing himself off a precipice while she was away. His wife then did the same. The Kwannon suddenly appeared before them and restored them to life as a reward for Osato's faith and cured Sawaichi of his blindness.

Tsubosaka Reigen-ki pleases Japanese audiences with its tenderness, pathos and edification. In contrast to this we find in Synge's play realism and irony. For example, in the third act of *The Well of the Saints*, when the Saint says to the beggar couple that he will cure them when they have become "dark" again, Martin, the husband, strikes "the can" [of holy water] from the Saint's hand with a sudden movement, and walks away towards the south with his wife. Again in the scene where the "dark" Martin lashes the Saint with his tongue we see a conflict between illusion and reality over which there hangs the kind of inevitable irony more often associated with tragedy.

At the end of January 1914, this play, together with *Othello*, was staged for six days as the first performance of the Mumeikai Players at the Imperial Theatre, Tokyo. The Mumeikai Players (The Association of the Anonymous) was founded in 1913 with Shinsho Doi (1869-1914) and Tetteki Togi (1869-1925) as its leading members and was dissolved in May 1917. During its active life it gave twenty-one performances of the play in Japan. This fact provides evidence enough of how much the Japanese public appreciated it. Tetteki Togi in the role of Matasa (or Martin Doul in Synge's play) excelled himself by the realism of his acting, which was quite novel to the Japanese theatre. Both Tetteki Togi and Shinsho Doi gained real prominence because of the enthusiasm of their audiences for this new dramatic movement.

Reigen was also produced at the Tokyo Theatre in June 1934, by Nippon Haiyu Gakko Gekidan (Company of the Japan Actors' Training School). Thereafter it was staged by the Sinpageki (New Drama Players) and other companies, and was always favourably received, because there was nothing that smacked of translation or adaptation in this tragi-comedy. In it the audience saw unfolded, as it were, a picture scroll of the Japanese manners and customs of old times. Shoyo Tsubouchi, the adapter of Synge's play, is chiefly famous in Japan as the author of *A Complete Japanese Translation of Shakespeare*[6] (1907-1928). In adapting Synge's play he displayed the same intrinsic qualities of a dramatist which he showed in his Shakespeare translations, capturing the savour, mood and genius of the original. The new play was a great success, and Masao Oda, in the role of Matasa, gave a brilliant performance.

Though Shoyo Tsubouchi and Kan Kikuchi[7] (1888-1948) wrote adaptations of Synge's plays, both had such an appreciation of the traditions of their native countryside that they came nearer to a perfect interpretation of Synge than any other translators of his dramas. Kan Kikuchi, a noteworthy playwright who followed Shoyo Tsubouchi, first presented *Riders to the Sea* on the stage in Japan in 1935. Previous to that, Kan Kikuchi had written a play, *Umi no yusha*[8] (Hero of the Sea) in 1916, which had been adapted from *Riders to the Sea*. Having studied Irish dramas, he wrote such remarkable plays as *Chichi kaeru*[9] (The Father Returns) in 1917 and *Okujo no kyojin*[10] (The Madman on the Roof) in 1919. The first performance of *Chichi kaeru* in 1920 was a great success and was followed by *Okujo no kyojin* in 1921 and *Umi no yusha* in 1922, the leading performers being Kanya Morita (1885-1932) and Ennosuke Ichikawa (1888-1963), two experienced and vigorous Kabuki actors.

Kan Kikuchi published *Umi no yusha* in the *Shin-shicho* (a literary magazine) in July 1916, while he was absorbed in the study of Irish literature. In *Umi no yusha* the scene is transferred from the Ireland of the original play (*Riders to the Sea*) to the seashore near the headland of Sata, Tosa, in Japan, creating for the adapted play a local colour which is purely Japanese.

Two famous actors, Kikugoro Onoe and Takeo Kawai, played in this adaptation at the Ichimuraza Theatre, in April 1922. It was also filmed by the Shochiku Cinema Studio in 1928. Kan Kikuchi was the first dramatist in Japan to deal with contemporary social problems in a realistic manner. At that time the London *Morning Post*,[11] considered Kan Kikuchi to be one of the most famous writers in Japan, and said that he was a dramatist who called out to the public with a furious fighting spirit in which the old social customs are contrasted with the new; and remarked that there was much in his plays that Europeans could learn from. However, Kichizo Nakamura, then a drama critic, contended that Kan Kikuchi had made this adaptation from his own moralistic standpoint and that he focused attention only on the life of the poor rather than on the tragedy of life itself.

In August 1916, Kan Kikuchi rebutted the criticism of his *Umi no yusha* in *Shin-shicho*, saying,

> ... there are two kinds of comments about my piece; one is that the play is more exciting than the original and the other is that it is flat and dull. I willingly accept every criticism about my dramatic art in the play, but I believe I have given my full attention to the dramatic situation in which the characters are presented. I cannot but say that the remarks that my play is commonplace and monotonous are irrelevant. There are some who criticize this play saying it is dull. But I would say that those who say so, don't know what a drama is. Though my piece may be inferior to the original in respect of perfection, yet it never falls behind the original in its dramatic treatment of the situation.[12]

In *Umi no yusha* Kan Kikuchi did not write a tragedy of a hero who faced death, but described the impulsive courage of Suejiro, who dies instead of the drowning man whom he is trying to rescue. In *Riders to the Sea*, in which Bartley is the central figure, the passionate horror of death is described with spiritualized realism. In *Umi no yusha*, on the other hand, Kan Kikuchi does not allow the old woman to grieve; she becomes frantic only on account of her love for Suejiro calling out her son's name in the heavy wind. In *Riders to the Sea* Maurya is presented as one who has the stature of an archetype protesting in vain against fate, like a character in a Greek tragedy. In Kan Kikuchi's play the setting and situation are too naturalistic.

In 1917 Kan Kikuchi contributed a treatise, "An Approach to Synge's Dramas", to the *Teikoku Bungaku*. This was the first important critical work on Synge in Japan. In it he says:

> [*Riders to the Sea*] is the most read of Synge's plays in Japan, but it is not his best one; for it lacks the humour which is the strongest characteristic of his plays. Maurya, after her sons have died one by one, says, unlike ordinary Japanese mothers who will cry with lamentation in such cases, 'They're all gone now, and there isn't anything more the sea can do to me ...' But these words of resignation do not reduce at all the sympathy of the Japanese for the heroine. These words sweep the end of the tragedy to the acme of artistic expression.[13]

He regards this play as a tragedy showing us the irresistible force of fate that overtakes man.

Following *Reigen*, *Riders to the Sea* was produced by the players of the Jiyu Butai (Freedom Stage) in July 1935. It was translated and directed by Kihachi Kitamura with Chieko Higashiyama and presented at the Jinju Hall, Tokyo. Since then it has often been staged by smaller companies—for example by the Budo no Kai (Grape Players) in June 1956. In this translation Junji Kinoshita rendered the Irish dialects born of the soil of Ireland into subtle and musical Japanese dialects.

During the same year, *The Shadow of the Glen*, which was thought to be representative of Synge's comic and satirical vein, was staged by the Budo No Kai. Tomoyuki Inoue, as Dan Burke, succeeded, at the fall of the curtain, in capturing that ironical humour so characteristic of Synge.

The oldest and most important translation of J. M. Synge in Japan is *Itazura-Mono* (*The Playboy of the Western World*) by Mineko Matsumura, published by Okada Misuzu in 1917. In 1922 Mineko Matsumura also translated Synge's five other plays: *The Shadow of the Glen, Riders to the Sea, The Tinker's Wedding, The Well of the Saints, Deirdre of the Sorrows*. These were included in *Shingu Gikyoku Zenshu* (Synge's Collected Plays), which was published by *Shincho-Sha* in 1923.[14] Translations by other Japanese writers are as follows:

Title	Translator	Publisher	Date
The Shadow of the Glen	Kohyo Hosoda	Keibundo	1914
	Watari Heimin	Nippon Hyoronsha Shuppan-bu	1921
	Masaru Fujie	Shueikaku	1923
	Shuji Yamamoto	Iwanami	1939
	Junji Kinoshita	Shingeki-sha	1957
Riders to the Sea	Kohyo Hosoda	Keibundo	1914
	Masao Kusuyama	Shincho-sha	1920
	Masaru Fujie	Shueikaku	1923
	Kihachi Kitamura	Shincho-sha	1938
	Shuji Yamamoto	Iwanami	1938
The Tinker's Wedding	Masaru Fujie	Shueikaku	1923
	Shuji Yamamoto	Iwanami	1939
The Well of the Saints	Masaru Fujie	Shueikaku	1923
The Playboy of the Western World	Masaru Fujie	Shueikaku	1923
	Shuji Yamamoto	Iwanami	1939
Deirdre of the Sorrows	Masaru Fujie	Shueikaku	1923

*　　*　　*

The Aran Islands	Masami Anezaki	Iwanami	1941

Although Mineko Matsumura's translation may be considered to be the standard one, it still lacks the flavour of the local dialect. Masao Kusuyama and Kihachi Kitamura, on the other hand, in their translations of Synge tried to enhance the audience's understanding of the common people and to encourage translations for the popular theatre.

Junji Kinoshita (1914–   ) has been to the Aran Islands and Galway, and being not only a translator but also a playwright like Kan Kikuchi, appreciates Irish drama more fully than the others. Accordingly, we see in his translation a use of dialect closely resembling Synge's use of Anglo-Irish. Kinoshita remarks on Synge's use of dialect:

> Synge wrote in the Anglo-Irish dialect, and without it, he could not have described the lives of fishermen and farmers in Ireland. Furthermore, Synge's polished use of it gave it a universal appeal. This may be one of the reasons why Synge is the greatest English [sic] playwright since Shakespeare.[16]

Adapting Japanese folk tales, Junji Kinoshita published other plays such as *Uriko-hime to Amanjaku, Hikoichi Banashi, Kaeru Shoten, Yuki Onna.* Like J. M. Synge, he searched for the folk tales and sought in them form and content, purely preserved in secluded places in the mountains and shores of his ancient homeland.

For example, as G. S. Fraser, the English poet and critic, remarked after seeing Kinoshita's *Yuzuru*[16] (1949):

> The material of this play is taken from an old Japanese tale . . . we find in Europe the same pattern of tales. A crane transformed into a woman became the wife of a man and brought him peace and happiness. But finally the woman exhausted her strength weaving cloth and in fact the man broke his promise and peeped into the room to find not his wife but a crane at the loom and was very surprised. The woman flew away in the form of a crane.[17]

In the same way the playwrights of the Irish Dramatic Movement were able to evoke unique moods by their use of old legends and folk visions which had been preserved and transmitted in the Anglo-Irish dialect. We should not fail to observe also the first appearance of idiomatic dialect in the plays of Lady Gregory, Hyde and Yeats.

Shuji Yamamoto (1894–   ), an astute drama critic, keeps his translations, which have been remarkably effective on the stage in Japan, faithful to the original. He is also the author of *Airurando Engeki Kenkyu* (A Study of the Irish Dramatic Movement), in which the plays of Yeats, Synge and Lady Gregory are examined in a fresh light. In this work, which was published by Apollon-sha in 1968, Shuji Yamamoto deals with the ideals and source materials of the individual writers of the Irish Dramatic Movement.

In the farming and fishing districts of Ireland, one comes to discover the literary and musical treasures which reside in the manners, customs and dialects of the rural areas. In such secluded places we find simple, plain, every-day language which is not merely of antiquarian or of narrow domestic interest. It is not the expression of refined urban phrases but rather that of a popular tongue heard from the lips of the peasants. One of the outstanding characteristics of Irish literature is that its legends are related to the essence of the world of art; it is not simply a secular aspect. When I saw *Riders to the Sea* at the Abbey Theatre thirty years ago, I noticed that the greatness and strict form of this one-act tragedy is similar to that of the Japanese Noh play. In 1938 I had the following conversation with Yeats about the performance of this play:

[Yeats said,] 'I would often go for inspiration to the Japanese, who create such great beauty, especially when I was writing Plays for Dancers . . . We must have a national literature. Have you seen Synge's *Riders to the Sea* performed at the Abbey Theatre? It is characteristic of our race.'
'Yes,' I answered, 'and I was much impressed by the rhythmical recitation of poetic words in the play. I'm sure there is nothing like that in English literature. We would have to go to the Noh theatre to find its equal.'
Yeats nodded seriously and said, 'There was much argument about the performance of the play, and opinion was divided especially on its production. But finally it was decided that the play should be produced in the way you have seen. There was good reason for coming to that decision. I hope you found in it the ancient, passionate Ireland. A nation or a race should remember its own heroic tradition.'[18]

From this conversation with Yeats I came to realize that the rhythm of the Gaelic is something like the rhythm with which the actors of *Riders to the Sea* spoke. This was further confirmed when I spent three or four days in the Aran Islands listening to recitations and hearing the music that is found in the ballads of these islands.

The reaction of the poet F. R. Higgins was similar to mine. When, in 1917, Professor Tokutaro Sakakura recited the Noh play *Matsukaze* to him and W. B. Yeats, Higgins remarked on the similarity of its rhythm to that of the Gaelic ballad. After Professor Sakakura's performance Higgins sang a ballad in Gaelic with ancient and poetic majesty. The similarity between the two made a great impression upon Yeats and Lennox Robinson, who was also present. As I now remember the production of *Riders to the Sea*, which was performed at the Abbey Theatre in "a manner very like that of the Noh play", I realize that it was a performance conveying the music of the Gaelic.

In the eyes of a Japanese observer, Synge's works have the merit of depicting the type of irony and boisterous humour seen in the

"Kyogen", a type of farce, in which the Japanese spoken language of the day was used. "Kyogen" was performed during the interlude between the Noh plays, not only to allow the Noh actors time for costume changes, but also to relieve the tension of the audience. The pleasant and ironic impression of *The Tinkers' Wedding*, the sombre and comic spirit of *The Well of the Saints*, the primitive and human cheerfulness of *The Shadow of the Glen*, the naive but keen sense of reality of the *Playboy of the Western World*—all reveal Synge's insight into that fascinating, vigorous world of the Irish peasantry. This mood of Synge's plays is very much like that of a "Kyogen" or a farce of Japan. Words in Synge's plays are, like those in "Kyogen", realistic and full of native directness, musical and at the same time rich in expression. The form is perfectly suited to being played on the stage in Anglo-Irish.

The Playboy of the Western World moves us in Japan through its vigorous and effective atmosphere. It was produced in 1955 by the famous dramatic company, "Gekidan Mingei" (People's Theatre Art Players) in the Hokuriku and Chugoku districts. In June 1956 they performed it in theatres in the Tokyo area, when it was again considered to be Synge's masterpiece on account of its sublime poetic nature, which vividly creates the personality of the characters by skilfully fusing reality and illusion.

Mr. Takashi Sugawara (1903-1970) a well-known playwright and producer said, in preparing *The Playboy of the Western World* for the Gekidan Mingei stage, that the play was a masterpiece of realistic comedy in which the hero and his Irish companions are portrayed with the strictest realism. At the Abbey Theatre in 1968 I observed that Synge's realistic method was preserved on the stage, and that even the row of rugged natural stones was included in the decor of the scene.

The Playboy of the Western World was produced again by Gekidan Mingei during the period between 18 November 1955 and 1 July 1956. It was performed fifty-two times in twenty-eight places throughout Japan: at Toyama, Kanazawa, Fukui, Kobe, Kumamoto, Miyazaki in the south; and Aomori, Hirosaki, Akita and Sendai in the north. In December the actor-producer Jukichi Uno (1914-   ) received the prestigious Arts Festival Award for his performance as Christy Mahon. The success of this play depends on the skill of the actor whose job it is to give individual character to a type: robust, masterful, volubly vital and yet inoffensive. Uno, whose production of the play was remarkable, also managed to project this image in his acting.

Irish drama produced excellent playwrights both in style and content over a half-century beginning with Yeats, Lady Gregory and Synge. They all have the most vigorous realism, and focus with deep insight on the humanity of their characters. The effect of a Synge play is achieved through the dialogue of simple fishermen and farmers and though his plays are not in verse, we find in them poetic rhythm. The basic tone throughout his plays is that of a realistic mind. The early plays of Yeats are written in poetic form; yet they do not lose that keen observation of the real which is characteristic of Irish drama. It was Synge, however, who saw Ireland's countryside through the most sensitive eyes—eyes which are, nevertheless, those of a realist.

O'Casey's play *The Plough and the Stars* was presented on the stage at the Sabo Hall in Tokyo in October 1969. Jukichi Uno played Fluther Good, Hiroshi Iwashita played Clitheroe and Yasuko Kusama, Nora Clitheroe. Commenting on this play, I emphasized the description of the lives of the Irish people in the works of Yeats and Synge by saying:

> The task of the Irish Renaissance was the founding of a Romantic idealism. Underlying this movement was, it can be said, realism.[19]

It is all but impossible, when we speak of the poets and dramatists of Japan, not to mention the lasting impression that the Irish Literary Renaissance left upon their works. We Japanese acknowledge that our dramatists such as Masao Kume, Kan Kikuchi, Yutaka Mafune and Junji Kinoshita, to mention but a few names, have written plays with —what I like to call—"an Irish flavour." Some of the works by these dramatists of modern Japan, cannot be fully understood, I believe, until they are viewed in relation to the literary faith and energy of W. B. Yeats, Lady Gregory and Padraic Colum, the regional, realistic experiments of the younger dramatists of the Movement such as Sean O'Casey and Lennox Robinson, and the impressive and rare verbal dexterity of Douglas Hyde, James Joyce and John Millington Synge.

NOTES

1. I have not been able to trace the printed piece of this translation, but for references to the performance of *Kyodai* see Kameo Chiba, "Irish Literature and the Modern Literary Trend in Our Country", *The Study of English* [Tokyo, Kenkyusha], XX, 4, July 1927, pp. 10–15. The play was performed at Kabukiza (Tokyo) during February 1914, the cast included Sadanji Ichikawa (as Hughie), Enjiro Ichikawa (as Shane) and others. For the influence of this realistic play on Japanese drama see Sho-u Ide, "February in Kobiki Street", *Engeishimpo*, February 1914, pp. 170–172.

2. For references to Sho'o Matsui's adaptation see, Kan Kikuchi and Shuji Yamamoto, *Kindaigeki Seizui* (The Quintessence of Modern English and Irish Drama) Tokyo, Shinchosha, 1925, pp. 180–181; see also Kameo Chiba, "Irish Literature and the Modern Literary Trend in Our Country", *loc. cit.*, pp. 14–15. The Japanese version of *The Harvest* is now included in *Nihon-Kindaigeki-Zenshu* [*A collection*

of modern Japanese dramatic works]: *Later Period Series*, II (Tokyo, Shunyodo, 1930).

3. For Sho'o Matsui's adaptation of *The Clancy Name* (which I have not been able to trace) see Kikuchi and Yamamoto, *op. cit.*, pp. 245-246, and Chiba, "Irish Literature and the Modern Literary Trend in Our Country", *loc. cit.*, p. 14. The play was probably produced at the Nakaza Theatre, Osaka, in 1926.

4. Shoyo Tsubouchi, "Preface", *Reigen* (Tokyo, Kinkodo, 1914), pp. iii-v.

5. A Bunraku play by Dampei Toyozawa and Chika Kako based on "The Tale of the Origin of the Tsubosaka Temple". It was first performed under the title of *Kwan-non Reijoki* (The Tale of the Spiritual Realm of the Merciful Goddess) at the Oebashi Little Theatre, Osaka, in 1879. The English version of this play has been published under the title *The Miracle at Tsubosaka Temple* in *Six Kabuki Plays*, trans. Donald Richie and Miyoko Watanabe (Tokyo, The Hokuseido Press, 1963), pp. 35-47. The Japanese original is now published under the title *Tsubosaka Reigen-ki* in *Meisaku Kabuki Zenshu* (A Series of Famous Kabuki Dramas), VII (Tokyo, Tokyo-Sogensha, 1965).

6. Published in 39 volumes at Tokyo by Waseda Daigaku Shuppanbu (Waseda University Press), 1909-1928.

7. Kan Kikuchi, *Tojuro's Love and Four Other Plays*, trans. G. W. Shaw (Tokyo, The Hokuseido Press, 1925).

8. Published in *Shin-Shicho*, July 1916, pp. 49-58.

9. Published in *Shin-Shicho*, January 1917, pp. 48-61. The English version was published under the title *The Father Returns* in *Tojuro's Love and Four Other Plays*, pp. 99-117.

10. Published in *Shin-Shicho*, May 1919, pp. 1-13. The English version was published under the title *The Madman on the Roof* in *Tojuro's Love and Four Other Plays*, pp. 79-97.

11. The London *Morning Post* said: "Indeed the West might learn something from these wonderful little dramas, loaded as they are with significance, beauty and great art. If there are more Japanese dramatists like Kan Kikuchi, Japan has reason to boast of her modern drama. Nor has she anything to learn from Bernard Shaw and John Galsworthy", quoted in *Hokuseido's Catalogue*, Autumn 1938 (Tokyo, The Hokuseido Press, 1939), p. 15.

12. "Editorial Notes", *Shin-Shicho*, August 1916, pp. 82-84.

13. Kan Kikuchi, "An Approach to Synge's Dramas", *Teikoku Bungaku* (The Empire Literature), XXIII, 5, 1917, pp. 32-48.

14. This edition had a Preface by W. B. Yeats which is given below by kind permission of Mr. M. B. Yeats and Miss Anne Yeats:

"So I am to write "a few words of preface" to introduce the plays of John Synge, who had in his mind so much of all that is most ancient in my country, to your countrymen, whose ancient poetry has come to mean so much to me, now that Mr. Whaley [*sic*] and others have published their translations. When I read the plays and essays of John Synge I go back at moments to our middle ages and even further back, but as I go back, though I find much beauty at the journey's end, I am all the time among poor unlucky people, who live in thatched cottages among stony fields by the side of a bleak ocean, or on the slopes of bare wind swept mountains. In your Noh plays, or in that diary of one of your courtladies of the eleventh century that I was reading yesterday, I find beliefs and attitude of mind not very different but I find them among happy cultivated people. Once or twice when I have read some Japanese poem or play I have wished that Synge were living. How like it is in its story, or emotional quality, to something he has recorded in his book on the Aran Islands, or in his "Well of the Saints" or in his "Riders to the Sea" or that Lady Gregory or I have found in Galway or in Sligo. The story of your Nishikigi for instance exists among us but as a mere anecdote which no poet has changed into great poetry. Shortly before his last illness Synge told me that he meant to write no more peasant-plays and his last play, his unfinished "Deirdre of the Sorrows" is about old Irish kings and queens though written in the peasant dialect; and had he lived I think he would have been helped by your literature as I have been helped by it. He told me once that he got no pleasure from the success of his plays in England, and I think the one or two continental productions of his "Playboy" that took place just before his death meant little to him, but I am certain that the translations of his plays into Japanese would have given him very great pleasure.

W. B. YEATS,
Dec., 1921."

15. Junji Kinoshita, *Yuzuru: A Comprehensive Edition* (Tokyo, Mirai-sha, 1953), p. 382.
16. Translated into English by Takeshi Kurahashi as *Twilight of a Crane* (Tokyo, Mirai-sha, 1952).
17. G. S. Fraser, *Impressions of Japan and Other Essays* (Tokyo and Osaka, Asahi Shinbunsha, 1952), p. 17.
18. S. Oshima, *Yeats and Japan* (Tokyo, The Hokuseido Press, 1965), pp. 103-104.
19. S. Oshima, "O'Casey and the Modern Stage", *Ro-en* (Labourers' Dramatic Association Bulletin), 164, September 1969, p. 7.

SYNGE IN FRANCE

Gerard Leblanc

SYNGE's material ties with France are well-known. Whether his French experience in the cultural and literary fields had any influence on his work has long been a moot question, often obscured by polemical motives which had little to do with literary criticism. One might think, however, that the point is hardly worth discussing at all, when only conjectural coincidences and remote parallels between Synge's plays and little known French works can be established to bear evidence of this influence. All that can be said is that some trends of the French drama of his time, which he could not but know, acted rather as temptations which Synge either thrust aside[1] or qualified by his original treatment of them —for example, the reliance in *Riders to the Sea* on symbolical details to suggest an unseen presence, the tendency to replace conflict by tension and action by intimation of an unutterable experience, might be traced back to Maeterlinck's theory of "théâtre statique".

It is therefore somewhat vain to try and assess the impact of French literature and culture on Synge's work. But a relationship goes two ways and it may be less polemical and less disappointing to appraise the response of France to his plays (*The Aran Islands*[2] is the only non-dramatic work translated into French and had a very limited circulation). A brief survey of Synge's place in France will show once more what adverse reactions, what misinterpretations, and what difficulties his work seems to be forever apt to engender.

Synge had a fair knowledge of French as is shown by his articles in *L'Européen*, and his judgment can be trusted when he notes in a letter written to MacKenna and dated June 1904:

> Madame Esposito has translated *Riders to the Sea* into French . . . it loses a good deal, as she has put it in a standard, healthy style but hasn't managed to give it any atmosphere or charm.[3]

He seemed from this early date to point to the main problem challenging any translator of his work into French, or for that matter into any language: how can one preserve or even suggest the special quality given to the plays by the use of dialect transformed into a powerful and essential dramatic medium?

The problem was not solved in 1913 by Maurice Bourgeois,[4] who— with his almost first-hand knowledge of Synge—had just written a thick doctoral dissertation which is still the only full-length study of the Irish dramatist by a French scholar. Bourgeois translated all the published plays[5] but we shall confine ourselves to his *Baladin du Monde Occidental*,[6] as it is the only one of his translations to have been put to the test of stage-production. Bourgeois somewhat complacently dedicated it to "the anonymous writer who in the *English Review* declared that a translation into French of *The Playboy of the Western World* would be duller and even less intelligible than any French version of *Macbeth*—even Mr. Maeterlinck's."[7] As it turned out, the prediction of the anonymous writer proved almost true. The translation lacks the movement and rhythm of the original, fails to convey the comic vigour of the play, and totally obliterates the cadence of Synge's sentence. Bourgeois thought that by using French country-people's pronunciation and syntax (or rather their stereotyped transcription) he could convey the outlandishness of Synge's language. But the device merely turns the characters into conventional stage rustics in whose speech the imagery and the lyrical passages, literally translated, sound quite out of place. Some Irish readers resented the French title: *Le Baladin du Monde Occidental* for its suggestion of Christy as a third-rate mountebank. But what is a "playboy" after all; and what else could the French equivalent be? The German translation: *Der Held der westlichen Welt*, more suggestive of a Paladin than a Baladin, is even more misleading and equally misses the half-poetical, half humorous implications of the name. And should "the western world", with its primarily geographical meaning, be translated—or mistranslated—by anything less emphatic and high-sounding than "le monde occidental"? Bourgeois' title, attractive, if not literally correct, was kept by all later translators and its grandiloquence is indeed in accord with the general theme of a play on the virtues and limits of "grand talk".

The translation was used for the first performance of the *Playboy* in France on 12 December 1913, at Lugné-Poë's Théâtre de l'Oeuvre. Lugné-Poë had dedicated himself to plays breaking with the conventions of the French stage of his time. He had been the introducer of Ibsen to France in 1893 and had produced with courageous eclecticism Gogol's *Revizor*, John Ford's *'Tis Pity She's a Whore* (prudishly entitled *Anabella*) and Oscar Wilde's *Salomé*, a praiseworthy undertaking when one thinks of the kind of intellectual protectionism which caused the producers and audiences of the time to distrust everything foreign.

On the first night of *The Playboy*, the main reaction of the public seems to have been amazement at the paradox of the opening situation, the unchecked flood of language and most of all, the rough-and-tumble action in the third act which shocked the audience much more than any mention of female underwear, not an infrequent property on the Paris stage of the time. "Audiences either bewildered or bored,"[8] "shocking for French ears used to finer wit,"[9] "clumsiness of the author,"[10] "a bitter unpleasant pessimism,"[11] "how ponderous the irony and how importunate!"[12]: such were the comments in most of the reviews. Critics generally recognised the originality of the opening situation, yet they criticised the play for its excess, its wildness and its violence. One of them wrote, "The play is too primitive, too spontaneous . . . it contains too much natural richness, not enough literary clarity."[13] Such criticism Synge would have taken as an acknowledgement of what he considered the essential element in his work: "the rich joy found only in what is superb and wild in reality."[14] It is ironic that whereas the adverse criticism chiefly attacked the play for being alien to French sensibility, the few favourable reviews stressed the essentially French qualities of liveliness and humour. Cultural chauvinism, indeed, does not pertain exclusively to the Dublin rowdies of January 1907.

As to the issues raised by the play, comments mostly centred on the hackneyed theme of the whimsicality of crowds and the inconsistency of women. A poet, however, had a shrewder understanding: Guillaume Apollinaire in *Soirées de Paris*, a short-lived literary magazine, after claiming that "there has been nothing so realistic and so perfect on the stage since Molière or Gogol," thoughtfully adds:

> . . . in Paris all were indifferent except poets . . . Poets have always more or less tried to murder their fathers, but it is not an easy thing and looking at the house on the first night I thought: too many fathers, too few sons.[15]

The fathers' opinion prevailed as Apollinaire felt it would, and the play ran for only six nights.

Between the two world wars Synge seems to have been forgotten by critics, scholars and producers alike. His work was only superficially dealt with in surveys of the Irish Renaissance.[16] As far as we know the only play produced in those years was *Riders to the Sea* in March 1938 and it passed totally unnoticed.

In 1941 Marcel Herrand gave a new production of *The Playboy*. The public, better prepared than in 1913 by their theatrical experience of "l'entre-deux-guerres" to accept the distortion of special data into exasperated paradox, gave the play a very favourable reception. It ran for over six weeks, yet audiences and reviewers, missing the deeper issues, seem to have regarded the play mainly as a bold challenge brilliantly taken up by Synge and Marcel Herrand.

In 1942 Marcel Herrand also gave the first French production of *Deirdre of the Sorrows* beautifully translated by Marie Amouroux,[17] who succeeded in preserving the poetic tension of the language (an easier task perhaps with *Deirdre* than with *The Playboy*) and powerfully suggesting both the saga-like timeless atmosphere and the stark actuality of Deirdre's tragedy. As for us, we remember attending what we think was the only other French production of *Deirdre des Douleurs* in 1969 at the foot of the ramparts of a small fortified town in Brittany. The allegorical level was perhaps overstressed (Owen was dressed up as an easily-recognizable death-figure and Deirdre's double [her fate as a queen], in regal attire, stood permanently at the back of the stage until Deirdre chose her destiny). Yet the young producer, Michel Hermon, certainly made his (scanty) audience feel the secret palpitation through which the anguish of things and beings soon to die is given expression.

In 1954 Cyril Cusack and the Theatre of Ireland gave three performances of *The Playboy* for the Théâtre des Nations. For the first time on a French stage the actors looked like Irish peasants and Synge's words sounded like poetry. It is amusing to note that some reviewers, probably inspired by Christy's verve, themselves yielded to the temptation of fine words and indulged more than usual in brilliant stylistic play.

The same mimetic reaction occurred again in 1956 for the last Paris production of *The Playboy* in a new translation by Armand Panigel. Panigel renounces the artifice of peasant speech for a slightly over-laboured style which sounds both too mannered and too transparent, thus suppressing the subtle distance that the original convention of Synge's medium establishes between theme and expression. The play is made to sound as if it had been written by Molière; it is too clear, it is too French. Moreover René Dupuy's production tended to emphasize the purely psychological issues and slowed down the movement. Reviewers were enthusiastic about the play if not the production ("de la bière irlandaise au goût français"[18]) or the acting ("why don't the actors go to the Aran Islands for a period of instruction?"[19]). They recognized its vitality and richness and emphasized the basic healthiness of its gaiety—an apt answer to those who in 1907 criticized it for its French-inspired unwholesomeness. For the first time they linked the theme of the play with the reality of Irish life and pointed out the importance of the Irish environment in the making of the Playboy and of his language.

Paris, however, is not the whole of France, though it is very nearly so as far as the theatre is concerned. Provincial touring companies are more and more influential in the shaping of new tendencies in stage-production and acting—a wholesome counterbalance to Paris conventionalism or over-sophisticated experiments. We have already alluded to the performance of *Deirdre* in provincial festivals. *The Playboy* was produced by the Comédie de l'Ouest in 1950 and the Comédie de l'Est in 1962 before large audiences in Brittany and Eastern France.

Nevertheless, one cannot conclude this brief survey without stressing how little Synge is known in France. The few translations of Synge's plays that exist have had insiginificant circulation: Bourgeois' *Théâtre de Synge* was published only once and was never re-issued after 1942. One can only hope that this year of Synge's centenary will tempt some publisher to bring out a new edition of the works. To the best of our knowledge, *Riders to the Sea* and *The Tinker's Wedding* have only been produced once—the latter in 1944 by Marcel Herrand, while *The Shadow of the Glen* and *The Well of the Saints* have never been performed, at least on a professional stage. The two productions of *Deirdre* aroused little notice and only served to confirm in the small audiences that attended them the romantic image of Ireland—a land of myth and legend, of primitive lyricism and idealistic poetry—which we in France are apt to cherish, but which is a dangerous misinterpretation as far as Synge's *Deirdre* is concerned.

As for *The Playboy of the Western World*, it has aroused greater and greater interest as Synge appears more and more as a dramatic and linguistic innovator, discovering and effecting this paroxysm of elemental reality which can develop only in a life re-created every night on the stage and in the magic of a rich and suggestive language. For Christy all the world is literally a stage and demands a continuous literary distortion of reality which many critics have considered as the very essence of poetic drama. Unfortunately an essential element is bound to remain forever untranslatable: the full originality and flavour of Synge's language and perhaps also his closeness to the inner spirit of his countrymen, his constant reference to a universe working under its own laws, free from those of "civilised" man.

NOTES

1. The sententious verbosity of Synge's *When the Moon Has Set* (*C.W.*, III, pp. 153-177) reminds one of de Curel's "théâtre d'idées".
2. Translated by Léon Balzagette, *Les Iles Aran* (Paris, Ed. Rieder, 1921).
3. Unpublished letter.
4. Mention must also be made of Louis Pennequin's translations of *The Shadow of the Glen* and *Riders to the Sea* in 1913 published under the title *La Brume du Vallon, La Chevauchée vers la Mer* (Paris, Ed. Figuière)—neither of these translations was ever staged.
5. *L'Ombre de la Ravine* (*The Shadow of the Glen*). *A Cheval vers la Mer* (*Riders to the Sea*), *La Fontaine aux Saints* (*The Well of the Saints*), *Les Noces du Rétameur* (*The Tinker's Wedding*), *Le Baladin du Monde Occidental* (*The Playboy of the Western World*), *Deirdre des Douleurs* (*Deirdre of the Sorrows*)—all, except Deirdre, appeared in one volume under the title *Théâtre de Synge* (Paris, Gallimard, 1942).
6. Also published separately in 1920 (Paris, Ed. de la Sirène).
7. *Grande Revue*, 25 November 1913.
8. *Le Figaro*, 14 December 1913.

9. *Ibid.*
10. *Comoedia*, 13 December 1913.
11. *Le Temps*, 15 December 1913.
12. *Ibid.*
13. *Comoedia*, 13 December 1913.
14. *C.W.*, IV, p. 54.
15. *Soirées de Paris*, 15 January 1914.
16. Such as Simon Tery's *L'Ile des Bardes* (Paris, Flammarion, 1925) and A. Rivoallan's *La Littérature Irlandaise Contemporaine* (Paris, Flammarion, 1932).
17. Published twice in 1921 (Paris, Ed. Figuière) and in 1946 (Paris, Ed. Lientier).
18. *Le Monde*, 11 February 1956.
19. *Les Lettres Françaises*, 16 February 1956.

SYNGE IN GERMANY

Johannes Kleinstück

SYNGE's name was first heard in Germany a ta very early date. In 1906, only one year after its first performance in Dublin, *The Well of the Saints* appeared on the stage of Max Reinhardt's famous *Deutsches Theater* in Berlin.[1] The choice of this particular play seems odd. It may be explained, however, by the then prevailing fashion of neo-romanticism (sometimes also called neo-classicism). People, those people at any rate who moved with the times, had become tired of naturalism, of social problems and of social criticism, of prose and of what had been accepted as "reality", and there arose a new desire for poetry, for myth and legend—a desire not unlike that which had led to the foundation of the Abbey Theatre.

In 1897 Gerhart Hauptmann, up to then the prominent master of naturalist drama, published his *Versunkene Glocke*, a dramatic *Märchen* written in luscious blank verse and set in the wild scenery of his beloved Silesian mountains. In the same decade the young Viennese Hugo von Hofmannsthal delighted a growing circle of admirers with the beauty of his lyrics and highly stylized verse-plays both of which somehow recall the early Yeats; and it may even be said of Hofmannsthal that, like Yeats, Lady Gregory and Synge, he tried to put the clock back and "bring again the theatre of Shakespeare or rather perhaps of Sophocles,"[2] for he made various attempts at great tragedy. Incidentally, his *Oedipus und die Sphinx* was also produced at Reinhardt's theatre in 1906. Thus the two similar dramatic movements rubbed shoulders, but they did not take much notice of each other.

Synge's play met with only moderate applause. The critic Siegfried Jacobsohn decided that it lacked tension, and blamed its all too quietistic philosophy, although he appreciated its humour and naive piety.[3] Another critic, Heinrich Stumcke, who on the whole was of a similar opinion, admitted that the play definitely announced a re-birth of English (*sic.*) drama[4]—a compliment which might not have entirely pleased its author.

The Playboy of the Western World, Synge's acknowledged masterpiece, was produced eighteen years later, again in Berlin. The producer, Heinz Hilpert, apparently overemphasized its burlesque aspects and turned it into a roaring comedy[5]—a danger to which the play is easily exposed when stripped of its native language. Yet even The Dublin Festival Company, which visited both Berlin (West) and Frankfurt in

1960, did not, according to critics, do full justice to its poetic qualities. The audiences, however, were well amused and Siobhan McKenna (as Pegeen Mike) and Donal Donelly (as Christy Mahon) received high praise.[6]

By that time Synge was no longer a stranger in Germany. In the years that followed the second war audiences liked to welcome writers from abroad; they wanted to be modern and up-to-date, and they wanted to know what had been going on in other parts of the world. It was probably on the wave of this post-war fashion that Synge was introduced. With the exception of *Deirdre of the Sorrows* all of his plays have now been performed before German (or German-speaking) audiences.

The following list (which may be incomplete) is based on the newspaper cuttings collected in the Hamburg *Theater-Archiv: The Playboy of the Western World* was performed in Vienna 1954, in East Berlin 1956, in Stuttgart 1959, in Cologne 1960, in Basle 1960, in Darmstadt 1961, in Munich 1962, in Ulm 1962, in Hamburg 1968, in Vienna (again) in 1968.

Riders to the Sea was performed in Freiburg i. Br. 1960. *The Well of the Saints* was performed in Münster 1962. *The Shadow of the Glen* and *The Tinker's Wedding* were performed in Heidelberg 1963.

From this list, it can be seen—and this is hardly surprising—that *The Playboy* has proved to be the champion in the German World also. It has been translated five times; two of these translations have appeared in print: Annemarie and Heinrich Böll's *Ein Wahrer Held*[7] (A True Hero) and Peter Hacks's *Der Held der westlichen Welt*[8] (The Hero of the Western World).

Although the list of performances and translations is quite impressive, it would be wrong to say that Synge occupies an important place in German-speaking countries today. His reputation is slight when compared to the reputation of such writers as Sartre, Camus, or T. S. Eliot. There are, however, obvious reasons for this. Although Synge is usually well reviewed in the press, critics are often at a loss as to what to make of him. Is he a popular playwright, producing the kind of *Bauernkomödien* (peasant comedies) which we see in Bavaria?[9] Or is he, perhaps, a social critic who wanted to castigate his fellow countrymen's passion for "tall" stories?[10] One critic is surprised that the Irish were shocked by the *Playboy* and thinks that we are used to stronger stuff now;[11] while another can only feel disgust for the play.[12]

It can be seen from this that Irish subjects and problems are not easily understood: the main obstacle, however, to a proper reception of Synge is the difficulty, if not the impossibility, of translating him.[13] I have known Germans who loved and admired Synge passionately, but these were students of English with a special interest in Irish literature, and they had been to Ireland and had read, seen and heard his works in the original (Anglo-Irish) idiom. I suppose that anybody who knows Synge will admit that he can be fully appreciated only in the original. He transformed what he gathered on the road and in villages into a poetry quite unmistakably his own; his very characters live in the words which he gives them, and they tend to become flat when they have to speak another language. A German translator could follow Synge's example and set out to find an unbookish idiom. This he could easily find in the peasant language of the North and of Bavaria. However, he would not find the appropriate atmosphere: the peasants and fishermen of the North are Protestants who do not utter "Glory be to God!", or pray to the "Holy Immaculate Mother" to intercede for the souls of the dead; and Bavarian peasants, although Roman Catholics like the Irish and great experts in swearing too, know nothing about the sea. German translations therefore cannot help being inadequate; neither Böll nor Hacks have taken the trouble of studying a spoken idiom and moulding it into dramatic form. Böll uses a literary style mixed with colloquialisms, very near to the style of his novels; Hacks employs ungrammatical constructions, wrong articles and pronouns and thus gains an effect of clownish rusticity—which, however, is by no means the effect aimed at by Synge.[14]

The difficulty of translating Synge becomes evident as soon as one tries to find an equivalent for the very title *The Playboy of the Western World*. Five suggestions have been made: (1) *Der Held von Westerland* by Sil Vara, (2) *Der Wunderheld aus dem Westerland* by Werner Wolff, (3) *Der Gaukler von Mayo* by Katrin Janecke and Günter Blöcker, (4) *Ein wahrer Held* by Annemarie and Heinrich Böll, (5) *Der Held der westlichen Welt* by Peter Hacks.[15] The first may be dismissed as particularly unfortunate, as Westerland is an actual seaside resort on the German island of Sylt, while the second is hardly an improvement. What about the *Gaukler* (juggler) and the *wahrer Held* (true hero)? Both titles contain an interpretation of the play, the first by open statement, the second by ironical implication, and both mean the same thing: they maintain that Christy is just the opposite of what he seems, that he is nothing but a windbag or a sham, and not the daredevil he pretends to be. Surely this misses the main issue. Christy is indeed a playboy, who plays the part which has been thrust upon him, but he plays it so well that eventually he becomes what he pretends to be: appearance and reality merge into each other, very much as in Yeats's *The Player Queen*. Is it possible that the translators have failed to realize this point?

The title re-occurs in Pegeen's final exclamation:

Oh my grief, I've lost him surely. I've lost the only Playboy of the Western World.[16]

As she could not mourn for the loss of a hero who is in reality a sham, Böll makes her cry:

> Oh, ich hab ihn verloren, ich Arme, ich hab ihn verloren. Den einzigen richtigen Kerl in unserer Welt.[17]

That again misses, or at least blurs, the point. A "richtiger Kerl" might be what the English call "a real lad", or the Americans" a tough guy"; it might also be "a dashing fellow" or even "a he-man", none of which corresponds to Synge's playboy.

Peter Hacks's *Der Held der westlichen Welt* sounds fairly adequate—but there is an intention lurking behind it which becomes clear when we realize that Hacks lives in East Berlin, is a communist and a pupil of Brecht's. He wants to convey the idea that only in the West, in that part of the world which still sighs under the yoke of capitalism, are people admired and lionized for killing their fellow human beings. By contrast, in the socialist East, only workers are revered as heroes. This intention was made plain in the production of 1956 in which the audience were told in the programme that Christy Mahon belonged to a series of killers stretching from Ernst Jünger to Micky Spillane, and in which Brecht-like songs from Hacks's own pen were interspersed to enlighten the public.[18]

Seen in this context, Pegeen's final words acquire a subtlety of meaning hitherto unthought of:

> O Jammer, ich hab ihn verloren, den letzten Helden des Abendlands.[19]

"Abendland" is the "West": we are given to understand that Christy Mahon is the *last* Western hero to be glorified, and that the time of universal peace and brotherhood is near at hand.

There is no disputing about tastes, and there is only a limited amount of disputing about interpretations. If one shares Hacks's creed, one may think that he succeeded in bringing out the hidden meaning of the play; but if not, one might say that he is trying to be humorous.

German theatres, on the whole, prefer Böll's version which is, after all, closer to the original as understood by people uninitiated into Marxist dialectics. Yet, as a new brand of Marxism is very much *en vogue* now among West German intellectuals, Hacks has found partisans. One of them, the dramatic and literary critic Klaus Völker, goes as far as to declare that Synge himself was a politically engaged writer who—like Parnell—was a rebel against his own class and took sides with the Irish poor. He therefore showed, according to Völker, that dignified humour (würdiger Humor), solidarity and patriotism thrive among the suppressed; but he also showed that their patriotism may sometimes harden into nationalism and even into downright fascism—as is proved by the example of Christy Mahon, who was worshipped as a hero by a bunch of downtrodden Irish villagers.[20]

I need not point out that Völker's view lacks any textual basis, or that it is inconsistent with everything we know about Synge, who was unpolitical, not interested in national and social questions and who certainly did not write in order to teach or to prove anything. It was precisely because he was neither political nor a nationalist nor a teacher that he was at first violently disliked by those compatriots of his who wanted propaganda instead of art. In the Germany of today, however, the wheel has come full circle: progressive intellectuals have accepted him because of his alleged political engagement and they have transformed him into a militant anti-fascist. It was Hacks's master, Brecht, who demonstrated how such a transformation can be effected. His short play *Die Gewehre der Frau Carrar* (Mrs. Carrar's Guns) was, as acknowledged by a note, written *Unter Benutzung einer Idee von J. M. Synge*—an idea of Synge's was used.[21] Properly understood, this could mean either that Brecht executed something of which Synge had jotted down a first draught—or that he based his own play on an actual play of Synge's. As a matter of fact, *Die Gewehre* does bear a vague resemblance to *Riders to the Sea*, in particular the incident where the body of Bartley is carried in is copied. The rest is as different from anything Synge could have thought or written as one might expect.

As Brecht's play is not widely known, it might be appropriate to give a brief account of its plot. The scene is laid in a small Andalusian house near the sea; the time is 1937, during the Spanish Civil War. Mrs. Carrar, whose husband has died for the people's cause, possesses a few guns which are urgently needed as Franco's soldiers are approaching: however, she will not allow them to be used, nor will she allow either of her two sons to join the battle. The elder, Juan, is out fishing, the younger is indoors. Mrs. Carrar believes in remaining neutral; her brother, a member of the working class, explains that passive neutrality will not save her from the generals, who are determined to kill all the poor in the country. He is soon proved right: Juan is wilfully shot down by a detachment of Francoites (for wearing a shabby cap such as no gentleman would wear). Mrs. Carrar, quickly convinced and quickly resolved, hands the guns over to her brother and snatches one herself—she has decided to fight in place of her murdered son.

The play is obviously a propaganda piece, its over-simplification verges on the ludicrous. We are invited to believe that all generals are wicked and bloodthirsty, and that they delight in slaughter for slaughter's sake. Incidentally, what about socialist generals? Or do socialist armies refrain from employing generals? Brecht, furthermore, teaches us, as he usually does, that the poor are wise and virtuous, sometimes a little obstinate, maybe, but sound at heart. Finally, he tries to persuade us that a good cause is always worth fighting for, even if the odds are overwhelmingly against it; for there is no doubt that the last battle will be won by the "right" people. So far, so good—but what has Synge to do with all this?

The mere fact that the scene is set near the sea, and that Juan's body is carried in by two fishermen, surrounded by a group of wailing and praying women, does not prove that there is any significant link between the two works. In fact the evidence points the other way: Bartley's mother submits to fate, or the will of God, in quiet resignation; Mrs. Carrar is roused to action. Brecht writes in order to change and influence the march of contemporary events; Synge shows a situation where no change is possible.

Perhaps one could argue that Brecht meant to improve on Synge's play, to demonstrate what Synge ought to have written or might have written if he had been a communist or a social reformer. It is well known that he was neither the one nor the other. However, Brecht does not hesitate to violate the truth when it appears recalcitrant to his purposes and beliefs, and his faithful disciples and admirers are always ready to applaud him.

Brecht's assertion that *Die Gewehre der Frau Carrar* was based on an idea of Synge's has never before been challenged. A fact that only goes to show how little Synge is known in Germany—a fate which he hardly deserves.

NOTES

1. cf. Klaus Völker, *Irisches Theater I: Yeats und Synge*, (Friedrichs Dramatiker des Welttheaters, Vol. 29, Velber/b. Hannover, Friedrich, 1967), p. 103.
2. cf. *Explorations*, p. 252.
3. cf. *Die Schaubühne* (Berlin-Charlottenburg, Verlag Die Weltbühne), 3, 1906, p. 70.
4. cf. *Bühne und Welt* (Berlin, Elsner), VIII, 1905-1906, pp. 386 ff..
5. cf. Völker, p. 99.
6. cf. Walther Korsch, *Der Tagesspiegel*, 28 October 1960.
7. Published in the first volume of *Theatrum Mundi* (Frankfurt/M., S. Fischer, 1961), a series of volumes containing (relatively) modern plays. This first volume also includes: Yeats's *The Player Queen*, Christopher Fry's *The Dark is Light Enough*, John Whiting's *A Penny for a Song*, and other works.
8. Published in a small volume in 1967 (Frankfurt/M., Suhrkamp). Suhrkamp is a "progressive" and leftist publisher, his choice of Hack's translation is therefore not surprising. The volume also contains *Reiter ans Meer* (*Riders to the Sea*) translated by Norbert Miller and *Kesselflickers Hochzeit* (*The Tinker's Wedding*) translated by Erich Fried.
9. cf. e.g. Günter Schab, *Hamburger Echo*, 25 March 1960.

10. cf. e.g. Rolf Michaelis, *Stuttgarter Zeitung*, 17 September 1959.

11. cf. Friedrich Luft, *Die Welt*, 29 September 1960.

12. cf. *Die Zeit*, 27 July 1962.

13. This fact is properly recognised by Hildegard Weber, cf. *Frankfurter Allgemeine Zeitung*, 7 July 1960.

14. The shortcomings of Hack's (very Brechtian) version were noticed by Christian Ferber, cf. *Die Welt*, 3 October 1968.

15. Titles given by Völker, p. 107.

16. *C.W.*, IV, p. 17.

17. Böll, *Ein Wahrer Held*, *loc. cit.*, p. 53 (see note 7 above).

18. Hacks's intention is explained (and endorsed) by Völker, pp. 100 ff. Völker calls Hacks's songs "wunderbar"; Ferber (cf. n. 14) is much less enthusiastic.

19. Hacks, *Der Held der westlichen Welt*, *loc. cit.*, p. 127 (see note 8 above).

20. Völker, pp. 29, 71, 101. Völker does not seem to accept what Yeats says about Synge—that "he was the only man I have ever known incapable of a political thought or of a humanitarian purpose" (*Aut.*, p. 567).

21. I quote from Bertolt Brecht, *Gesammelte Werke* (werkausgabe edition suhrkamp), Frankfurt/M., 1967, Stücke, vol. 3, pp. 1195 ff.. It may be mentioned that this play, as well as Brecht's other plays dealing with fascism, betrays an astonishing lack of comprehension of the issues at stake. He suffered from the delusion that fascism was nothing but a conspiracy of the "rich" (or, in the present case, of the "generals") against the "poor", or the "people". Cf. Martin Esslin, *Brecht, das Paradox des politischen Dichters* (Frankfurt/M., Athenäum, 1962), p. 106: "Brechts kommunistische Überzeugung half ihm nicht, das wahre Wesen des Nationalsozialismus zu erkennen, sondern hinderte ihn im Gegenteil daran".

IN MEMORIAM

While this work was being prepared for the press the sudden death of Alan Price occurred. As the author of *J. M. Synge and Anglo-Irish Drama* (London, Methuen, 1961) and the editor of the second volume of *J. M. Synge: The Collected Works* (London, Oxford University Press, 1966), Alan Price will remain an inspiration and a guide to all Synge scholars who follow him.

His last major work before his death was his contribution to the present volume.

A SURVEY OF RECENT WORK ON J. M. SYNGE*

Alan Price

DURING the past ten years much important work has been done on
J. M. Synge. There have appeared the official biography, a four-volume
definitive edition of Synge's works including a lot of previously unpublished material and sundry drafts and worksheets revealing his
methods of composition, several books of literary criticism about his
work as a whole, numerous articles, some of them quite specialized, and
various discussions of Synge in books dealing with drama. In addition,
editions of plays and a selection from his prose for use in schools and
colleges have been issued as he has appeared on syllabuses for examinations such as the G.C.E., the number of academic theses has increased
markedly, radio and television presentations of his plays have been
provided occasionally and an admirable colour film of *The Playboy* has
been showing for over eight years in different parts of the world.

Before 1959 there had been various studies of Synge. Most notable
were those by people who knew Synge personally, Lady Gregory, John
Masefield, Padraic Colum, W. B. Yeats (whose utterances remain of
unique value) and by scholars and critics of the standing of Una
Ellis-Fermor and Raymond Williams. Reviewers also and important
poets and critics (V. S. Pritchett, T. S. Eliot and W. Empson) were
referring appreciatively to Synge to develop or illustrate arguments,
the assumption being that he was becoming established as one whose
writings could be cited as valid pieces of evidence in the structure of
literary criticism.

But none of these sought to supply a comprehensive examination and
assessment of Synge. The books that existed were surveys of Synge's
life and writings and their background; those by F. Bickley, P. P.
Howe and M. Bourgeois were sensible and perceptive, and informative,
especially that by the remarkably diligent Bourgeois, a prime source of
facts. The one by D. Corkery was provokingly uneven and biased; it
increased in an unusual way one's appreciation of Synge's achievement
and of his relationships with the people and land of Ireland but it was
distorted by Corkery's fervent nationalism and his habit of praising
Synge where he fitted in with Corkery's ideal of a Catholic Irish peasant
and of condemning him when (as happened more frequently) he did

---

*As this essay is a survey of modern criticism, discussing recent contributions
in the text, it was felt advisable to leave the references as written by the
author.

not fit in. It is unfortuante that Corkery's has been the book on Synge most widely studied in Ireland and it has contributed to the gross underrating of Synge in his native land.

In my *Synge and Anglo-Irish Drama* (Methuen, London, 1961), I said that by about 1916 the first phase of literary criticism of Synge was complete. Almost entirely favourable to him, it was mainly concerned to describe his writings, to provide information about the circumstances of his life and work, and to relate these to the times and, in particular, to the literary revival. While some of his characteristic features were indicated and a place in world literature claimed for him, the most important aim was to vindicate Synge against his accusers by establishing that he was genuinely Irish and that his writings were a valid expression of peasant life. Later surveying the bulk of literary criticism of Synge from the beginning to 1959, I said:

> It is obvious that much good work has been done on Synge. Background and biographical information, histories of Irish drama and of related social and political trends and pressures, accounts of the Abbey and its personalities, of methods of play-making, production and acting, studies of Synge's relation to these and of aspects of his writings have now been sufficiently supplied. What is still required is literary criticism which will use and synthesize this material . . . The existing comment on Synge, worthy as much of it is, suffers, as a whole, from two shortcomings. First, it is partisan and parochial. Commentators have tended to be unduly concerned with politics and religion; and consequently discussion has ranged around matters irrelevant to the understanding of Synge as an artist. Furthermore, no sustained attempt has been made to see Synge apart from his place in the Abbey Theatre and to approach him as one might approach the dramatists of other nations. Second, critics have applied to Synge the assumptions of early twentieth-century naturalism, and criticism has been mainly an examination of characters as 'real human beings' and of points of stage technique.

The requirements, the gaps in our understanding, the shortcomings, referred to above have been dealt with to a large extent by the work on Synge in the nineteen-sixties. At the same time much fresh biographical and textual knowledge has been made available. All these developments providing finer insights and more exact evaluations, are of considerable significance now and will be, perhaps even more so, in the future.

The work on which much of the progress of the past ten years has depended is the official biography: *J. M. Synge, 1871-1909* by David H. Greene and Edward M. Stephens (Macmillan, New York, 1959). It is based upon the mass of material Synge left—papers, proofs, cuttings, manuscripts of published and unpublished writings, diaries, letters and notebooks—which had been shifting about among the members of Synge's family for years before they were made available to Greene after the death of Stephens in 1955. The biography also draws upon the writings and recollections about Synge that Stephens had assembled and mainly embodied, with amazing industry and regard for the Synge family, in a typescript of nearly a million words. The material Synge left and the Stephens typescript life were supplemented by the information Greene assiduously and tactfully collected in Ireland and elsewhere from records, relatives, acquaintances and friends of Synge. Greene acknowledges his debt to Stephens and others but he makes it clear that the story of Synge's life, the interpretations and conclusions about it, and the actual writing are all his own. His too must be the credit for a job well done.

Compared with the information available about most important twentieth-century writers, that about Synge has been scanty, and tales, some rather fanciful, promoted perhaps by the generous myth-making Yeats, were repeated for lack of anything else. Greene, however, ably sorted out fact and fiction, and provided for the first time a full and well-documented biography. He sensibly allowed the story to tell itself, as far as possible, in the words of the people concerned. Hence, one understands more at first hand about Synge's personal life; the influence of his evangelical mother, his aptitude, despite his reserve, for making friends, his methods of working, his place in the Abbey, his attitudes (quite the reverse of superficial) to politics and social questions, and his relationships with women, especially his fiancée, Molly Allgood. Greene shows uncommon understanding and sympathy not only towards Synge but also towards the Irish people. Where other critics have tended to uphold one at the expense of the other, he maintains a fine and revealing balance. He is very knowledgeable about Irish customs and places, and also about antiquities—he is something of an expert on standing stones and Celtic crosses—and he is in tune with the religious beliefs of the Irish people. The rare quality of his grasp of Synge's and related Anglo-Irish writings is also clear. Yet coming from a much wider, cosmopolitan environment, he is able to place Synge in a larger context and to make necessary and noteworthy connections and contrasts hardly possible for anyone whose existence has been mainly confined to Ireland. Justifiably his biography quite supersedes all previous accounts and will stand for some time as a prime source for the study of Synge.

A volume which perhaps performs a similar function and provides maybe insights not much less notably fresh and comprehensive (though in the area of literary criticism and not biography) is my *Synge and Anglo-Irish Drama*. Applying to Synge for the first time some of the methods and assumptions of modern literary criticism, the need for close analysis of texture and the knowledge that the poetic dramatist often operates on more than one level of significance simultaneously and that he uses symbol and allegory in addition to character and situation, *Synge and Anglo-Irish Drama* seeks to relate Synge's writings not only to Irish life and drama but also to that English (and hence European) literature of which they are an established part. The book provides an assessment of criticism of Synge, an account of the links between Synge and Yeats, of the Anglo-Irish idiom and Synge's use of it and of the disturbances in the Irish theatre, and it shows the authenticity of Synge's vision, through an examination of his writings which is centred on the theme predominant in them all—the tension between dream and actuality.

The December 1961 issue of *Modern Drama* was devoted to Synge and O'Casey. There were five articles on Synge. In his "The Rageous Ossean", David Krause outlines the character of Oisin and the various accounts over the ages of Oisin's great struggle against St. Patrick. He sees Oisin as representing a vigorous Irish pagan tradition, often anti-clerical and irreverent, stressing freedom, the enjoyment of the senses, romantic aspirations, comedy and satire. Despite all the efforts of St. Patrick (the Church) to suppress this tradition, it persisted and although by the end of the nineteenth century it had become enfeebled, it was gloriously reinvigorated and celebrated by Synge and O'Casey. Through brief comments on their writings, Krause shows that the tension between these two Irish traditions—Pagan and Catholic—is salient in Synge and O'Casey, and that although they personally did not adhere to the more powerful one—the Catholic—they were in a genuine native tradition. Hence it is just as Irish to have Oisin as a patron-hero as it is to have St. Patrick. This point of Krause's is not altogether new but he makes it vivaciously and touches on fresh evidence, and the article stands as a further refutation of Corkery's false view that because Synge was of the Ascendancy and not of Catholic country stock he could not truly understand or interpret Ireland. The clash between the puritanic and the sensuous elements in Ireland is further exemplified in a poem, "Girls Bathing, Galway 1965", by the fine young poet, Seamus Heaney. He sees the old restrictive modes weakening, and on a beach where bathing had been forbidden before Vatican Two, girls plunge happily and signify Venus's firm and blossoming advance upon St. Patrick:

> Where crests unfurl like creamy beer
> The Queen's clothes melt into the sea
>
> And generations sighing in
> The salt suds where the wave has crashed
> Labour in fear of flesh and sin
> For the time has been accomplished
>
> As through the shallows in swimsuits,
> Bare-legged, smooth-shouldered and long backed
> They wade ashore with skips and shouts.
> So Venus comes, matter-of-fact.

Another indication of Synge's appreciation of the native tradition is given in David H. Greene's article, "Synge and the Celtic Revival." Deftly reiterating or developing points presented in his biography, Greene shows how Synge, against the wishes of his family, devoted himself to understanding Irish culture and the Irish language through his studies at Dublin University and at the Sorbonne (under the great de Jubainville), through Breton writers such as Pierre Loti, Ernest Renan and Anatole Le Braz, through visits to Brittany and through life on the Aran Islands. For Synge, Greene concludes, "the discovery of the native tradition was crucial" and his "reading in Irish literature seems to have been extensive, probably more extensive than any of his contemporaries, except professional Celticists."

Synge's work is related also to other myths (that of Oedipus) and to fairy-tales—those in which a father is killed. Patricia M. Spacks refers to them in her article "The Making of *The Playboy*." She shows that the myth and fairy-tale elements, the sense of necessary ritual killing in Christy's accounts of the slaying of Old Mahon enable the Mayo folk to accept Christy without abhorrence. But when they actually witness violence, present fact not remote fiction, they turn against him. Together with the power of ritual killing goes the power of ritual language. Christy is created as a man both by the successive "murders" of his father and by the increasing force and flexibility of his language developing from tame prose to extravagant poetry. His self-image of an ideal man of action and ideal poet combined enables him to construct himself before our eyes in the manner of a hero in folk tale or myth. This is an important consideration and it is presented convincingly, although this is not the first or fullest treatment of it—for that one must go to *Synge and Anglo-Irish Drama*.

Further resemblances between Synge and other writings and myths, even the scriptures, can be perceived. Howard D. Pearce in his "Synge's *Playboy* as Mock Christ", in *Modern Drama*, December 1965, suggests that Christy parallels Christ in some ways, but in a mock heroic manner. The Mayo folk, lacking a Man, hail Christy as a saviour (the notion of "saving", from disagreeable matters, great and small, pervades the play). But though Christy comes as Christ (humbly at first as on Palm Sunday) he "licks", defeats, them and wins all for himself. Then, when his father appears, they try to make Christy the scape-goat for their failings. He, however, will not sacrificially succumb to their destroying him, and he is transfigured. But only partially. His "romanticism is strained and ridiculous" and "far from arriving at some deeper truth, he gains a superficial self-assurance." This is cleverly done by Pearce and it reveals possibilities but there is something strained and bizarre about it, and the conclusion is incorrect: that there is a discrepancy between the actuality and the dream. It overlooks the evidence which shows them as one in the end. True, throughout the play there is much comic irony in the contrast between the heroic language and the mundane circumstances but this does not alter the fact that in terms of this Irish society Christy does develop from weed to Playboy by the power of the imagination; he *is* a mighty man at the end, and Pegeen's grief is genuine.

Synge's treatment of the Deirdre legend is considered in "Synge's Last Play" by Harold Orel in *Modern Drama*, December 1961. He says the difficulties Synge was experiencing caused loose ends and uncertainties, but *Deirdre of the Sorrows* is a subtle and complex play. It is about transience and it embodies three elements—asceticism, stoicism and ecstasy—which Synge felt should be united. The presence of each of these is indicated by Orel, but he is wrong in supposing that he is the first to notice the basic theme of transience, and he leans heavily on Greene's biography.

Actors were always vital in that collaboration which is Synge's art. Cyril Cusack in "A Player's Reflections on *Playboy*", in *Modern Drama*, December 1961, says that when he joined the Abbey Theatre in 1932 the tradition of acting with stylized speech and gestures, a deliberate distancing from life, was worn-out and stultifying. He brought in a brisk naturalistic vein, with the dialogue rendered as living speech. Then later he went on to rich extravaganza, finding this most successful. But despite much acclaim, he felt something amiss with *The Playboy*. This, he concludes, is because of a weak denouement, an anti-climax— "reality disappears in a balloon burst of disillusionment and the person of Christy Mahon suddenly resolves itself into a dew." This is a gross misjudgement, and coming from an actor of Cusack's quality it can hardly be explained except on the grounds that it is almost impossible for Synge's countrymen to admire him wholeheartedly. Given his antecedents, they seem to assume, there must be a flaw somewhere.

J. L. Styan in *The Elements of Drama* (Cambridge University Press, 1960) has no doubt about the quality of Synge whom he discusses along with Shakespeare, Ibsen and Chekhov. He brings out the excellence of Synge's collaboration with his audience. "*The Playboy* has the economy of great writing" yet it evokes responses "subtle and delicate and of considerable complexity." In *Deirdre of the Sorrows* there is a "deft manipulation of impressions leaving in their wake a trail of resounding overtones" and through her death Synge moves the audience "to reject the commonplace and associate with and approve her transfiguration into a sublimity of heroism and love." Thus Styan uses Synge to exemplify the quick and crucial flow of relationships between play and audience, and shows again that Synge's dramatic practice is important evidence for a critic seeking to develop a serious theory of drama. Similarly Synge has a place in Styan's *The Dark*

Comedy (Cambridge University Press, 1962) where Synge's genius for blending different entities—irony and lyricism, tenderness and merciless logic, continental sophistication and native homeliness—is touched on together with his ability to use fantasy to undermine our self-satisfaction, rather like the dramatists of the nineteen-fifties.

This fusing, this characteristic of being firmly in a tradition yet at the same time transcending it, is mentioned in Vivian Mercier's *The Irish Comic Tradition* (New York, Oxford University Press, 1962): *The Playboy* "explores the comic possibilities of parricide with a thoroughness unparalleled elsewhere in literature" and it is "the most striking of recent masterpieces which draw on the old Gaelic feeling for the macabre and the grotesque." Yet in other ways Synge stands almost entirely outside the Gaelic literary tradition, since "unlike the class-conscious Gaelic poets and satirists" (who tended to uphold society, the established norm, and to deride deviations from it) "Synge sympathizes with the underdog and the outcast . . . It is the respectable citizen who is exposed to ridicule."

Traditions other than those of the British Isles are affected by Synge, sufficiently so for the British Council to commission a booklet on *J. M. Synge and Lady Gregory* (London, Longmans, 1962) in their "Writers and Their Work" series, intended mainly for overseas students. The booklet, ably written by Elizabeth Coxhead, provides a lively and balanced account of the writings and backgrounds of the two colleagues (whom Yeats wished to have by him as he received the Nobel Prize), and it stands as a useful introduction to them.

Criticism of any of these three sometimes involves one or both of the others; one could hardly be deeply understood alone. Nobly Yeats concludes in "The Municipal Gallery Revisited":

> Think where man's glory most begins and ends,
> And say my glory was I had such friends.

These three united the aristocrat, the peasant and the writer; they alone in modern times

> . . . had brought
> Everything down to that sole test again,
> Dream of the noble and the beggar-man.

So among the heap of writings about Yeats that appeared in his centenary year, 1965, there were some about Synge.

In his writings Yeats presented not so much the ordinary Synge as an idealization of him, Donna Gerstenberger says in her chapter "Yeats and Synge: 'A Young Man's Ghost'," in *W. B. Yeats, Centenary Essays*, edited by S. B. Bushrui and D. E. S. Maxwell (Ibadan University Press, 1965). To suit his own needs Yeats let his imagination play over recent history, elevating people into heroic mythological figures. Synge was the great artist (just as Parnell was the great statesman and Hugh Lane the great patron) driven towards death by the vicious and mediocre pack (Ireland being, in Joyce's phrase, "the old sow that eats her farrow"). Yeats learned from Synge that the flower of poetry must be strongly rooted among the clay and worms, and leaving behind ethereal charm and langorous romance he dealt with contemporary actualities in an astringent and masculine way; he lay down, as Synge at his most profound implies one should, "where all the ladders start,/In the foul rag-and-bone shop of the heart." Mary Byrne of *The Tinker's Wedding*, Miss Gerstenberger goes on, is the grandam of Crazy Jane, and the conflict between Crazy Jane and the Bishop is similar to the conflict between Oisin and St. Patrick, which is at the centre of Synge's art. As Yeats grew and matured as a man and artist, his vision of Synge changed and developed. Representing qualities that Yeats felt he lacked but much admired, it served as an antithesis to Yeats and thus it nourished his imagination "as a very real and substantial presence for the whole extent of his life."

Synge's aesthetic creed was not influenced by Yeats. It was shaped in essentials long before the famous meeting in 1896 and also before the visits to the Aran Islands which are often regarded as of prime importance for Synge as man and writer. This is the view put forth by Ann Saddlemyer in her chapter on "J. M. Synge's Aesthetic Theory" in *The World of W. B. Yeats* (Dublin, Dolmen Press, 1965). It is not an altogether correct view. (Miss Saddlemyer rather contradicts it in her Introduction to Synge's *Plays*, Book One, p. xiv, where she describes the maturing process of Synge as a dramatist upon which "Yeats's sponsorship seems to have acted as a catalyst, while the life Synge discovered on the Aran Islands served as an example.") Synge says that *The Aran Islands* was his "first serious piece of work" and that in working at it and at some Wicklow essays (written after 1901) he "learned to write the peasant dialect and dialogue" of his plays, on which *The Aran Islands* "throws a good deal of light." Moreover there are review articles (not mentioned by Miss Saddlemyer) written after 1900 which reveal incidentally that his aesthetic was continuously developing—as may be seen from a comparison of the muddied and contorted notions and style of the Maeterlinck review, in *The Daily Express* of 17 December 1898, with the penetration and wit of the review of "The Winged Destiny" in *The Academy and Literature* of 12 November 1904. Many of the items Miss Saddlemyer quotes were written after 1896, and it is clear that Synge's theories about literature developed along with his practice of it. He did not first construct a theory and then illustrate it by his writings. Literary principles are embodied in living instances and lose something when considered in the abstract—as F. R. Leavis shows in his celebrated essay "Literary

Criticism and Philosophy," and as Synge earlier indicated: "Young and therefore fresh and living truths, views, what you will, have a certain diffidence or tenderness that makes it impossible to state them without the accompanying emotional or imaginative life in which they naturally arise . . . All theorizing is bad for the artist, because it makes him live in the intelligence instead of in the half subconscious faculties by which all real creation is performed." (*Collected Works*, I, p. 347.) But theorizing is not necessarily bad for the literary critic, and although no one was "less fond of theories and divisions in the arts" than Synge was, he admitted that "they cannot altogether be gone without." Therefore it is good that Miss Saddlemyer brings together material, some of it previously unpublished, and draws on it skilfully to sketch Synge's ideas about his art. She does this as far as possible in Synge's own words and avoids making any synthesis or final judgement—a restraint in keeping with Synge's distaste for constructing systems of literary criticism, and certainly a wise recognition of the fact that one chapter could not possibly deal with the subject. Still it is a useful essay and it contains pointers towards the comprehensive study of Synge's aesthetic which has yet to be made and published.

More material essential for studies of Synge was made available by Ann Saddlemyer in her "Letters of Synge to McKenna: the Mature Years" in "An Irish Gathering" in *The Massachusetts Review* of Winter 1964. Stephen McKenna was perhaps Synge's closest friend and Synge's letters to him, though a bit mutilated by McKenna, anxious to protect Synge's reputation, provide "a moving experience: Synge's warmth, wit and keen intelligence—a whole period and a real life—come through rarely and beautifully."

The brief pregnant utterances Synge made about art continually stimulate thought. Ronald Gaskell in "The Realism of J. M. Synge" in *Critical Quarterly*, V, 3, Autumn 1963, considers what Synge understands by reality and how far his vision of it is dramatic. He finds that reality consists of a constant presence of the natural world and a vivid awareness by the characters, through their senses, of this world, of their bodies and of their relationships to each other. Energetic physical action and vital sensuous dialogue are the embodiment of this reality. But the life of the passions and the natural world is confronted with change, with time and death. Synge faces this grim reality honestly. His realization that beauty and life are to be destroyed makes them more precious and bestows dignity. The grief of Maurya or Deirdre is the counterpart of the rich joy of the Playboy. Synge's strong awareness of death "has nothing morbid about it. If death is real, so is birth." (The Aran Islander can make a cradle or a coffin.) The integrity of Synge's work, Gaskell summarizes, is not in question. He doubts, however, if Synge's vision is fully dramatic. The structure of the plays, as distinct from their action, contributes little to their impact. And the dialogue is not always dramatic, the phrasing can be unduly picturesque, and sometimes the rhythms are not sufficiently varied to distinguish different characters or they tend to be lyrical or meditative—too musical, too melancholy. Nevertheless, "Synge's writing is something to be grateful for in the theatre," it is strong in its grip on the "reality and energy of the body, on the passions of men and women, on wind and rain and sun." This essay of Gaskell's is intelligent and noteworthy, even though it touches on the lyric, romantic and elegaic qualities of Synge rather than on the ironic and savage, and even though stricter definition of terms in one or two places and further consideration and illustration generally seem desirable.

In 1963 T. R. Henn brought out what is (apart from the Oxford University Press definitive edition) the most useful edition of Synge: *The Plays and Poems of J. M. Synge* (London, Methuen). Henn has lived in Ireland and was Director of the Yeats International Summer School in Sligo for some years. Earlier in his *The Lonely Tower* (London, Methuen, 1950), which included a chapter on the relationship between Yeats and Synge, Henn had shown a knowledgeable zest for Anglo-Irish literature and a lively capacity for illuminating issues by drawing on an understanding of Ireland and its people deeper and more extensive probably than that of any other scholar or critic in this area. These qualities and the insights they provide are evident in his edition, in the full and detailed introduction to the plays, in his critical commentary on them, and in his notes. He answers questions and removes misunderstandings as only an Anglo-Irishman could. The ease with which he makes significant links between folklore, the ordinary life of Ireland, various aspects of Irish literature and European literature is remarkable. And always his enthusiasm is real: he would "go most of the way with Edmund Wilson", who said (in *Axel's Castle*, London, Charles Scribner, 1931, p. 43), "Synge succeeded, during the few years before he died, in creating for the Abbey Theatre perhaps the most authentic examples of poetic drama which the modern stage has seen."

Synge is considered worthy to appear beside masters of the modern stage in F. L. Lucas's *The Drama of Chekhov, Synge, Yeats and Pirandello* (London, Cassell, 1963). No connections (apart from obvious ones between Synge and Yeats) are made between these writers and no reason appears why they should be brought together, unless from a desire to compile a book. If this is the case it is perhaps significant that an experienced essayist with a shrewd sense of the literary market, whose stock is moving up, should have included Synge. Lucas's treatment of Synge is curiously uneven, and the intention is not clear; he fluctuates between several levels without getting anywhere much. Most of the time he assumes that Synge is a new writer in need of introduction; he gives a brisk and adroitly illustrated account of Synge's life (drawing freely on Greene's biography) and sketches the action of the plays and the characters, quoting "with unusual fullness," as if one were unable to read Synge's plays for oneself. On other occasions matters are brought up which involve much literary experience and expertise, and recondite parallels are suggested with other international writers. Coherence and point, then, seem lacking, and although Lucas writes with vigour and knowledge of literature and although his keen appreciation of Synge is unmistakable (in contrast to his obtuseness towards Yeats) he reiterates commonplaces rather than adds anything of moment to our understanding of Synge.

A more pointed indication of Synge's relation to other writers is provided by Ann Saddlemyer in a lecture given at the Yeats Summer School in Sligo and published as *J. M. Synge and Modern Comedy* (Dublin, Dolmen Press, 1968). Miss Saddlemyer recalls that the turn of this century was a time of rebellion and disturbance in the theatre, and that Synge's writings were linked to these new continental movements by the hectic responses to the first productions of his plays. The attempts of Yeats and Synge to defend the plays and to prove Synge's genuine Irishness led to misconceptions. Yeats built up the magnificent image of Synge as one who found artistic fulfilment nowhere but among the Irish folk. This, however, is only part of the truth. Synge was at the same time a dramatist with a European reputation, he had a sensitive and comprehensive grasp of the sweep of European literature and "in all his writings Ireland is set against the background of Europe, the Irish theatre movement viewed in terms of the history of world drama." His work is "not just the efforts of a young dramatist wrestling to clothe the Celtic spirit in a native costume, but the inevitable and natural reflection of the general aesthetic climate of the time." Freed then of the Yeatsian vision, Miss Saddlemyer beckons us to look at reality through Synge's eyes. She points to the eternal conflict between illusion and reality which "Synge saw as basic both to life and to nature." (This conflict is fully revealed and shown to be central in all Synge's work in my *Synge and Anglo-Irish Drama*.) Miss Saddlemyer provides examples of it as represented "in the power of external nature, second in the lives and emotions of his characters, third in the most elaborate effect this conflict had on his people—the creation of the myth." She shows "the romantic note" and "the Rabelaisian note" leading towards an ironical vision of life that "could turn the hero into the anti-hero" and provide scope "not only for the heroic, but for the grotesque and even the burlesque." By the end Synge was "attempting to create a yet more sophisticated comedy by parodying the very acting style his first realistic plays had encouraged." He appears, Miss Saddlemyer concludes, to have been moving "towards the European tradition of the absurd" towards "the black comedy of today" and *Waiting for Godot*.

This process of applying the highest standards to Synge and placing him among established writers is further exemplified in the book by Donna Gerstenberger, *John Millington Synge* (New York, Twayne, 1964), number 12 in Twayne's "English Authors" series. Synge's writings are successively described and assessed with varying degrees of attention and illumination. The Aran Islands are rather underplayed and critics who see Synge's experiences there as being of the highest importance are said to be wrong (though, inconsistently, at the beginning of chapter three it declares: "out of his experiences of the Islands and the creation of a book about them came the sense of peasant life which pervades all the plays and gives to Synge coherent expression of his attitudes toward life.") The pain and desolation of the Arans—and of the Blaskets and West Kerry—are mentioned, but the joy and inspiration, the sense of a wholesome folk culture, are missed. The treatment of the Wicklow essays, and of all the prose generally, is slight. Of the plays, Miss Gerstenberger admires *Riders to the Sea*, *The Playboy* and *Deirdre of the Sorrows*, and she writes well about them. The linking of the three women in *Riders to the Sea* with the three Fates and her comments on colours are ingenious and her comparison with Lorca is revealing. With regard to *The Playboy* matters of motivation and personal alignments and various reactions to violence, real and imagined, are gone over efficiently, and among the symbols and metaphorical patterns touched on, the force of the clothing metaphor is for the first time noted. *Deirdre* is seen as Synge's attempt "to create a new kind of tragedy, one which denies the traditional, unreal material of the past while it affirms Synge's view of the grim nature of reality and of man's lot." The other plays, however, are felt to have weaknesses and flaws. *The Shadow of the Glen* is slight and only partially successful, and its conclusion "comes not out of life but middle-class literature." *The Tinker's Wedding* is "inferior drama," "an inflated incident" not properly motivated. And *The Well of the Saints* is unconvincing "because the material of the play failed wholly to engage the playwright." The poems are treated with skill and sensitivity and the point is rightly made that Yeats gave them "a disproportionately large representation in *The Oxford Book of Modern Verse*." Finally, Miss Gerstenberger in a neat summary affirms that "Synge's vision . . . was one which makes his work particularly congenial to the modern reader." The word "reader" is significant. In general, her book is more penetrating on the psychological factors in Synge's writings than on their qualities as drama. It hardly evokes the singularly animating splendour, comedy, tension and tragedy of the theatre, and it provides no more than a modicum of background information of any sort.

Sensible and controlled, it keeps near to the texts, without, however, making any detailed analysis of the shape and texture of the writing. It presents little that is original or exciting but a good deal that is worth knowing and it confirms Synge's presence in the regular academic course.

Another sign of this presence is Denis Johnston's booklet, *John Millington Synge* (New York and London, Columbia University Press, 1965), number 12 in the "Columbia Essays on Modern Writers" series. It outlines Synge's life and works, making one or two perceptive comments but showing little zest or mastery of the subject as a whole. Considered as the response of a reputable dramatist to a notable predecessor, it is disappointing.

The spread of the study of Synge not only in universities and colleges but also in high schools and secondary schools is shown by the appearance of two or three school editions of plays and by the inclusion of my *Riders to the Sea and The Playboy of the Western World* (Oxford, Blackwell, 1969) in Blackwell's "Notes on English Literature," a series intended to provide a full commentary and study of texts prescribed for examinations. Consideration of Synge's plays soon involves reference to people and places in Ireland described in his prose writings, and commentators invariably draw parallels between them and the plays. Unfortunately these prose writings have not been available in a form and at a price suitable for use by students in schools or colleges. It is this need which my *Emerald Apex* (London and Glasgow, Blackie, 1966) a selection from Synge's prose, with introduction, notes and exercises, is designed to meet.

It is a remarkable and intriguing fact (the reasons for which can hardly be gone into) that during the half century after the death of Synge no full and reliable edition or biography of him was produced, though the relevant materials were there in Dublin, within easy reach of the three Irish universities. It took an American to do the biography and a Canadian woman and two Englishmen to do the edition, though, of course, with indispensable help from local people and from the editor of the Oxford University Press.

The first volume, *J. M. Synge: Collected Works, Poems* (London, Oxford University Press, 1962) was most precisely edited by Robin Skelton, poet and author of the best essay so far on Synge's poetry—in *Poetry Ireland*, Autumn 1962. The Poems volume assembles every mite of Synge's verse, including translations, poems taken out of the prose *Vita Vecchia* and fragments of verse plays, together with drafts and variant readings and prefaces, anything, in fact, of the smallest intrinsic value or significance for the understanding of Synge's methods of work and development. Nevertheless, the volume is slight compared to the rest of Synge's work. There is a vast apparatus, necessary, no doubt, but a mere trickle of poetry. Of the poems published for the first time none is of much worth, and it is clear that only a dozen or so of the 58 poems and 24 translations (counting everything) merit much attention. Synge's ideas about poetry seem more mature than the poems he wrote. What becomes apparent are the different levels of artistic maturity and competence inhabited by Synge at one and the same time. While he was showing mastery, great and varied, in *The Playboy*, he was writing thin and sentimental poems. Similarly, his grasp of human psychology revealed in his letters to Molly Allgood is inferior to that displayed in his plays. These are further indications that he was essentially a dramatist and that his personal experiences found their best artistic form in plays rather than in lyrics. Apart from establishing the text, the most original contribution the *Poems* volume makes is in the presentation of Synge's successive revisions and worksheets. From these one is able to understand how meticulously Synge worked, even over immature stuff, and to follow the processes of creation.

Scope for similar understanding in much more substantial terms is offered in Volume Two of the *Collected Works: Prose* (London, Oxford University Press, 1966). This too includes fresh material—and variant readings but only those that really matter since there was so much else of value to be fitted into a limited space.

Synge's work is remarkably unified. The interaction of its parts and some of the sources of his drama are more clearly displayed than those of most considerable writers. Here his prose is crucial. Synge depended a good deal on the land and people of Ireland and the prose he wrote about them is constantly referred to by commentators. Unfortunately this prose has not all been available, even in library editions. A welcome improvement occurred with the appearance of the paperback *The Aran Islands and Other Writings by John M. Synge*, edited by Robert Tracy (New York, Vintage, 1962). But this, while containing nearly all Synge's prose then believed to be in print, did not contain any copyright material. Now, however, in the *Oxford Prose* are assembled all Synge's prose writings of any merit or interest. Over half of it consists of a reprint of *The Aran Islands* and *In Wicklow, West Kerry and Connemara*, checked against and supplemented from Synge's own manuscripts and proofs. About a quarter consists of articles not previously collected outside America, and the rest is work never published before. Of the previously unpublished material perhaps the most useful or engaging parts are those which correct misunderstandings, those which reveal how deep and personal was Synge's attachment to the West of Ireland and its people, those, in particular, about himself, including an Autobiography constructed from material in varying degrees of coherence or legibility and in several versions. The printing of six of the various photographs Synge took show his skill and taste in this new medium, and the reproduction of 35 drawings by Jack B. Yeats, which supplement and blend in with the text amazingly well, freshly confirm the harmony between these two artists.

At last Synge's non-dramatic writings could be assessed in their own right. My article, "Synge's Prose Writings: A First View of the Whole," in *Modern Drama*, Winter 1969, suggests that Synge's autobiographical studies not only throw singular light on the artist and his work but also provide rare insight into human growth generally. A leading theme of Synge's whole work is also perceived—the attempt of a person who wishes to become or has become creative in an original way to demonstrate his vision and values to an indifferent or hostile audience. The attempt is invariably a failure, until in *The Playboy* the spell is broken and the gifted person realizes himself and becomes strong enough to withstand hostility and to triumph. Also touched on are the autobiographical elements in Synge's writings, the influence of music, his capacity in literary criticism for combining close verbal analysis with a sense of wider issues, and, above all, the importance of Ireland (of Wicklow as much as the Aran Islands). Finally it is claimed that the prose writings (while of special value because of their connections with the plays and poems) being products of imagination possess an intrinsic worth, and merit attention quite irrespective of anything else Synge wrote.

The Oxford University Press edition was completed in 1968 with the publication of *J. M. Synge: Collected Works*, Vols. 3 & 4: *Plays*, edited by Ann Saddlemyer. These *Plays* volumes are a masterpiece of editing. The skill and judgement and, most of all, the energy, patience and care, the sheer dedication, that have gone into them are amazing. No item seems to have been too trifling to record, and with the ample space available the text occupies one side of a page while the multitudinous notes appear on and sometimes cover the opposite page. Here is an extreme abundance; regarding textual matters there is no need ever to look elsewhere. For the five plays published in Synge's lifetime, the text is that authorized by Synge himself, and for *Deirdre of the Sorrows* the text follows his final typescript, with variations from the posthumous Cuala and Maunsel editions. Defining the text of the previously unpublished play, *When the Moon Has Set*, must have been a most difficult and delicate operation, involving the assessment of random passages, some hardly decipherable and some in both autobiographical and dramatic forms, and the decision as to whether the one-act or the two-act version was preferable (for Synge was not satisfied with any version) depended for its adequacy on considerable insight and tact, on an immersion in Synge of a depth that apparently only Miss Saddlemyer has reached. Now for the first time the texts of

the seven plays are definitely established and presented with remarkably scrupulous scholarship, along with a packed and diversified storehouse of material—early drafts, revisions, worksheets, corrected proofs
and variant readings—which enables the growth of each play to be
followed in detail. Synge's creative processes (and by analogy those
of other artists) can now be understood in an unusually comprehensive
way and fresh light may be thrown on his aesthetic theories and practice.
Though evaluations of individual plays and the relationships between
them will hardly be changed significantly by the storehouse of material,
it will tell us more about them, and sensitively used might affect
assessments. In every regard, then, these four *Oxford* volumes are the
starting place for any future study of Synge.

My present survey is not exhaustive—for several reasons; among
them are limitations of space and the impossibility of consulting everything that has been written about Synge; inevitably, no notice could
be taken of articles in languages other than English. Nevertheless, I
believe that little of major importance has been overlooked and that the
body of material touched upon is large and representative enough for
one or two conclusions to be drawn more or less firmly.

The first conclusion confirms what one of the better Irish scholars
and critics, Roger McHugh, said in 1952, that "the best literary criticism of our modern writers in English has been written mainly by
writers outside Ireland." Increasingly the bulk of work on Synge (and
on Shaw, Yeats, Joyce and O'Casey) is being done by Americans. The
English still make their contribution. European and Asiatic scholars add
a fresh and acceptable quota. But from the Irish there is almost nothing.
Bluntly, the reasons for this are political, religious and social, and they
involve the belief that there is some special virtue in the Irish and in
Ireland which cannot be appreciated or set forth in English. It can be
embraced only by those of Irish Catholic stock and fluent and creative
in the Irish language. Hence Shaw, Yeats, Synge, Joyce and O'Casey,
no matter how great their international reputations, have a fatal flaw or
failing. This inhibiting tradition, clutched with passionate intensity,
against which these writers, in their different ways, nobly fought,
remains in Ireland. It is less overbearing than it was and there is much
dissatisfaction with it, but to assail it publicly is to be labelled traitor
by zealots determined that Irish must be kept up whatever the consequences, while the authorities set in their unrealistic veneration of
the language continue to insist on paper qualifications in Irish at all
levels of education and for employment in the public service.

The second conclusion is that during the past decade the quality
and quantity of work on Synge has been greater than that of any other
period. The work is noticeably varied—textual and interpretative, the
close analysis of a minor point or a ranging survey of a combination of

issues; it is cool and objective or personal and impressionistic, and it involves sources, influences, parallels and connections either within an individual piece or in its relation to other writings. And more and more the kind of questions posed, the investigations undertaken, the hunches followed, the comments and insights provided are those which are usual in the study of a writer of more than local or temporary significance.

Now, a hundred years after his birth, Synge is established as a classic. In future he is no more likely to disappear from courses of English Literature or from the World Theatre than are Ben Jonson, R. B. Sheridan or G. B. Shaw, nor should his status be inferior to theirs. He is now not merely of one country or one age, but for all mankind. Such an established position has its dangers—of pedantry, of routine respectable performance, of the predominance of the note-stuffed text-book over the intense and moving individual life of the theatre. But for Synge these dangers are not great at the moment. There is a healthy play of diverse ideas and interpretations about him, and people attend performances of his plays not for academic purposes mainly but to enjoy them as plays—"as we go to a dinner where the food we need is taken with pleasure and excitement." Materials, insights, commentaries about Synge, then, exist in plentiful variety; but they tend to be isolated. They now need to be brought together and synthesized in some comprehensive work. It is improbable that this will lead to any radical shift in evaluation—the body of Synge's finished work is not extensive and it has already been fairly well worked over. But the material unpublished before the Oxford University Press edition contains a play, a few poems, a good deal of autobiographical material, and, especially noteworthy, material about the theory and practice of literature and drama, together with a host of drafts and revisions and worksheets. When all this has been assimilated and related to the rest of Synge's work, wider and deeper understanding of matters (such as his aesthetic) which have received comparatively little attention, and of Synge's achievement as a whole and of the ways of the writer in general, may well emerge. And to this process the present volume will, no doubt, make a useful contribution.

A SYNGE GLOSSARY

Alan Bliss

The purpose of this Glossary is to record all the non-Standard words and phrases and all the non-Standard meanings used by J. M. Synge in his Poems and Plays; that is to say, it aims to record not only the words and phrases which are not used at all in Standard (British) English, but also those words and phrases which are used in Standard English, but with a meaning different from that used by Synge. The selection of these last must be to a certain extent subjective; the connotation of some Standard English words is so wide that a usage which to one reader will seem to call for comment will seem to another merely an obvious and unremarkable extension of a familiar meaning.

The edition of the Poems and Plays used as a basis for the Glossary is the Oxford Edition of the *Collected Works* of Synge. The relevant volumes are Volume I, *Poems*, edited by Robin Skelton (O.U.P., 1962), and Volumes III and IV, *Plays*, edited by Anne Saddlemyer (O.U.P., 1968). The Fragments of Plays included in the critical apparatus of these last two volumes have not been taken into consideration, except for *When the Moon has Set*, which is sufficiently substantial and coherent to be worth attention.

Despite the difficulty of Synge's language, even for those who are familiar with Anglo-Irish usage, little glossarial help has hitherto been available. There is, on p. xxxv-xxxvi of Volume IV of the *Collected Works*, a "Glossary and Guide to Pronunciation"; unfortunately it deals only with the three plays in that volume; even so it is incomplete, provides no references, and is often inaccurate. The Notes in *The Plays and Poems of J. M. Synge*, edited by T. R. Henn (London, 1963) also supply some interpretations, but these too are incomplete and often inaccurate, e.g. egregiously on p. 348, where in the phrase *a great gap between a gallous story and a dirty deed* the word *gallous* is glossed "gallows". Appendix A of the same edition gives "Some Pronunciations", but these are untrustworthy. Synge himself has given some guidance in his correspondence with Max Meyerfeld about the translation into German of *The Well of Saints*; some general extracts are cited in Appendix C of Volume III of the Oxford *Collected Works*, especially on pp. 274-5, and other more detailed comments are cited in the notes to the passages in question. However, Synge's interpretations seem to have been very much *post hoc*, and in some instances are quite incredible: *griseldy*, for instance, is glossed by him as "grisly", though both the context and the formation of the word leave no doubt that the true meaning is "grizzled". None of the commentaries at present available attempts to supply information in a form designed to facilitate the accurate assessment of Synge's artistic purpose in his use of non-Standard words and meanings.

★　　　★　　　★

The non-Standard words and phrases used by Synge can be divided into seven classes:

(1) Words directly adopted from the Irish language. These are relatively few in number, and the following is a complete list: *banbh, boreen, cleeve, curagh, Dun, frish-frash, keen, loy, ohone, poteen, Samhain, shebeen, sluigs, sop, streeleen, streel(er), thraneen.*

(2) Words and phrases literally translated from the Irish; see, for instance, *hag, ill-lucky, playboy, ridge, share, skin.* It is not always easy to determine whether these phrases are genuinely a part of Anglo-Irish usage, or have been translated from the Irish by Synge for his own special purposes. It is, for instance, difficult to believe that *on the ridge of the world* has ever been used in natural speech; however, since Anglo-Irish usage is as yet so ill documented, it is impossible to prove in any individual case that Synge has used an artificial rendering.

(3) Words "mistranslated" from the Irish. The connotations of an Irish word rarely coincide exactly with those of any individual English word, so that the correct rendering into English will depend on the context. It seems, however, that at some stage in their acquisition of the English language Irish speakers learned a "standard" equivalent of each Irish word, which they used irrespective of the context; and this type of "mistranslation" from Irish is a fruitful source of special Anglo-Irish usage. For examples see, for instance, *astray, boast, comrade, itself, let, right, soft.*

(4) Words formerly used in Standard English, but now obsolete. Most of the words in question became obsolete about 1700 (e.g. *airy, hooky, lovely, reckon, stray*), but some were already obsolete by 1600 (e.g. *brassy, kind, weep*), others still in use as late as about 1850 (e.g. *heavy, single, switch, tramper*).

(5) Words in general dialect use in England and Scotland; most of these, but not quite all, were formerly in use in Standard English but are now obsolete. For examples see, for instance, *cranky, dummy, likely, perished, slippy, unbeknownst.*

(6) Words in dialect use in limited areas; the vast majority of these are current in Scotland and northern England. The predominance in the Anglo-Irish vocabulary of Scottish and northern English words has often been remarked. "The Hibernicisms to be considered here, have

never at any time been literary English, but have always been provincialisms. By far the greater part of them are Scotch or Northern English." (J. M. Clark, *The Vocabulary of Anglo-Irish* [St. Gallen, 1917] 43.) "The general Anglo-Irish vocabulary is markedly North-British in character." (J. J. Hogan in *Béaloideas* xiv [1944] 187.) No convincing explanation of this fact has been put forward, but some suggestions are made below. For examples see, for instance, *drive, jobber, knacky, lug, raggy, slough, wattle.*

(7) Words and phrases of which no other instance seems to be recorded, and which may have been invented by Synge: *bias, crossing roads, curiosity man, dreepiness, drunken, hoop, lengthy, louty, over, pitchpike, puzzle-the-world, scorch, scruff, sloppy, straitened waistcoat, string gabble, swiggle, tackle, turn of (the) day.*

There is some overlapping between these classes. In particular, words for which an adequate explanation can be found in terms of the Irish language, and which might therefore be placed in class (3), often turn out to be in use in the dialects of England and Scotland, so that they seem to belong also to class (5) or class (6). There are various possible explanations of this phenomenon. If the dialect usage outside Ireland is limited to Scotland and northern England, it is possible that it has developed independently under the influence of Scots Gaelic, and that it has spread from Scotland into northern England. In other cases it is possible that the Irish analogy has exercised a preservative influence, so that out of a number of rival dialect usages the one has survived which receives most support from Irish idiom. In yet other cases it is possible that the English or Scottish dialect usage has influenced the connotation of the Irish word in recent times, so that the supposed origin in Irish is illusory. Allowance must also be made for the parallel working of general semantic tendencies, and even for mere coincidence. In no individual instance is certainty possible.

★   ★   ★

The Glossary attempts to provide, as succinctly as possible, relevant information not only about Synge's use of non-Standard words and meanings, but also about their origin and distribution. Under each head-word the meaning is given first, followed by references to the occurrence of the word or phrase in the Poems and Plays. The three volumes of the *Collected Works* to which reference is made are separately paginated: numbers not preceded by distinguishing letters refer to the pages of Volume I, *Poems*; references to the pages of Volumes III and IV, *Plays*, are preceded by distinguishing letters indicating the play in which the word or phrase occurs, according to the following code:

RS	*Riders to the Sea*	
SG	*The Shadow of the Glen*	Volume III
WS	*The Well of the Saints*	
MS	*When the Moon has Set*	

TW	*The Tinker's Wedding*	
PW	*The Playboy of the Western World*	Volume IV
DS	*Deirdre of the Sorrows*	

No attempt has been made to compile a complete *index verborum*, and in general only one reference is given for the Poems, and only one for each play; however, in a few cases of special interest more ample references have been supplied.

The references are followed by a summary of information about the origin and distribution of the word or phrase. If the word is of Irish origin the Irish form is given: the spelling used is that of early Modern Irish, rather than the new spelling officially adopted in 1948, so as to facilitate reference to Dinneen's *Irish-English Dictionary* (1927), the most recent Irish-English Dictionary at present available. In the case of direct translations, the Irish word or phrase is cited. If the word represents a "mistranslation" of an Irish word, the Irish word is given with the two relevant meanings separated by the "swung dash" ~; it should not, of course, be assumed that the Irish word has no other meanings than these. If the word was at one time Standard English, the approximate date of its obsolescence is given; if it is in dialect use, there is a brief statement of its present distribution among the dialects. Finally, enclosed within square brackets, there is an indication of works of reference in which further information can usefully be sought. The abbreviations used for the three works of reference cited are as follows:

NED   *A New English Dictionary on Historical Principles* (Oxford, 1884-1933)

EDD   J. Wright, *The English Dialect Dictionary* (Oxford, 1896-1905)

PWJ   P. W. Joyce, *English as we Speak it in Ireland* (London and Dublin, 1910).

It is hoped that the other abbreviations occasionally used, which are all in common use, will be readily intelligible.

*　　*　　*

Of the 282 head-words recorded in the Glossary, no less than 193, or a little more than two-thirds of the total, occur in one source only (in the Poems, or in a single one of the plays). It is of some interest to note the distribution of these "unique" words among the various sources.

Since the sources are of very disparate lengths—a three-act play obviously cannot readily be compared with a one-act play—the actual number of "unique" words occurring in each source is followed by the average number occurring in each ten pages of the Oxford *Complete Works*. Among the Poems, those written in Standard English have, of course, been excluded from the count; *The Moon has Set*, part of the dialogue in which is in Standard English, would offer difficulties, but since this play happens to contain no "unique" words the difficulties are theoretical.

	Total occurrences	Occurrences per ten pages
Poems	24	8.6
RS	2	1.7
SG	8	4.8
WS	22	5.4
MS	0	0.0
TW	11	5.2
PW	102	17.0
DS	24	5.5

It will be observed that there is considerable stability in the occurrence of "unique" words in SG, WS, TW and DS, despite the considerable variation in the length of the plays; all four have about five such words to every ten pages. RS and MS contain a very small number of such words. The Poems contain a substantially higher proportion of "unique" words, and the proporti n in PW is more than three times as high as the highest proportion inoany of the other plays. The detailed interpretation of the literary signi ficance of these statistics must be left for another occasion, but it may be noted here that the high proportion of "unique" words in PW confirms the subjective impression that it is more highly wrought, more poetic, and in a sense more artificial than any of the other plays.

GLOSSARY

A

above "up there" SG 43, WS 111, PW 57, DS 183. Cf. Ir. *thuas* "above ~ up".

abroad "outside" PW 83, DS 185. In general dialect use. [EDD]

afeard "afraid" SG 35, WS 83, MS 171, PW 63. Obsolete c.1700; in general dialect use. [NED, EDD]

ail "be wrong with" RS 19, SG 49, TW 7, PW 61, DS 199. Obsolete c.1700; in general dialect use. [NED, EDD]

airy "lively, fond of pleasure" TW 47, DS 189. Obsolete c.1700. Cf. Ir. *aerach*. [NED] **airily** "gaily" 88.

anyplace "anywhere" 98.

astray "wandering about" 92, PW 149; "wrong, mistaken" DS 201; "mad-looking" PW 143. Cf. Ir. *ar seachrán* "astray ~ mistaken".

away in one's head "mad" DS 199. In Scottish dialect use. [EDD]

B

banbh "pig" PW 85. Ir. *banbh*. [EDD s.v. *bonham, bonuv*, PWJ s.v. *bonnive*]

begob "by God" 58, TW 17. Ireland only. [EDD]

below "down there" RS 9, SG 39, WS 129, MS 161, TW 29, PW 127. Cf. Ir. *thíos* "below ~ down".

beyond "over there" SG 33, MS 159, TW 29, PW 63. Cf. Ir. *thall* "beyond ~ over". Ireland and Yorkshire. [EDD]

bias (of the sacks) TW 49. Apparently not recorded elsewhere; meaning uncertain.

blabbing "gossiping" PW 61. Obsolete c.1600; in general dialect use. [NED, EDD]

black "wretched, miserable" 64, SG 57; "gloomy" WS 113; "utter [fool]" TW 35. Cf. Ir. *dubh* "black ~ sad ~ severe". **black curse** "dire imprecation" SG 35, WS 145. Cf. Ir. *dubh-luighe*. **black knot** "knot that cannot easily be untied" RS 15. Cf. Ir. *dubh-shnaidhm*. **blackness** "wickedness" WS 145; "severity" DS 219. For *black hag* see HAG.

blackthorn "stick made from the blackthorn bush, *Prunus spinosa*" PW 145. [NED]

blather "talk voluble nonsense" SG 43, WS 107. In general dialect use except in southern England. From Old Norse *blaðra*, but cf. Ir. *bladar* "flatter". [NED] **blather** "voluble nonsense" SG 57, WS 81, PW 91. **blathering** SG 57.

blink "ray of light" WS 125. Obsolete; Scotland and northern England. [NED, EDD]

blink "wink" TW 45. Such Ir. verbs as *caochadh*, *sméideadh* mean both "blink" and "wink". Cf. WINK.

boast of a man "fine figure of a man" TW 13. Cf. Ir. *gaisce* "boasting ~ champion".

bog "moor, heath" SG 35, WS 77, MS 159, PW 141, DS 221. [NED] **bog-deal** "wood found buried in a bog" DS 263. **bog-hole** "wet trench left by the cutting of peat" TW 45, DS 223.

bona fide "person living at a distance of more than three miles and therefore entitled under (obsolete) licensing laws to obtain drink as a traveller" PW 67.

boreen "lane, usually unmade and leading to house" 70 PW 131. Ir. *bóithrín*, diminutive of *bóthar* "road". [NED, EDD, PWJ]

brassy "made of brass" PW 57. Obsolete c.1600. [NED]

butt "end" SG 55, WS 135, TW 39, PW 69, DS 201. Ireland, northern and western England. [EDD]

C

cabin "cottage, hovel" DS 205. [NED]

call "need" RS 23, WS 139, MS 171, PW 109, DS 189; "right" WS 111, MS 163, DS 205. In general dialect use; but cf. Ir. *call* "need", *cáll* "right". [EDD, PWJ]

carrageen "a kind of edible moss, *Chondrus crispus*" 36. From *Carrigeen*, the name of a village four miles west of Waterford. [NED, EDD]

cess "luck" PW 63. Ireland, Cheshire, Devonshire. Almost certainly a contraction of *success*; cf. Ir. *droch-rath ort!* "bad cess to you", *rath* "success". [NED, EDD, PWJ]

cholera morbus "infectious cholera" PW 163. [NED]

clack "chatter" WS 71. Obsolete c.1850; in general dialect use. [NED, EDD]

clay "soil, earth" 64, DS 231. Cf. Ir. *cré* "clay ~ earth".

cleeve "basket" PW 113. Ir. *cliabh*. [PWJ]

cnuceen "little hill" PW 97, DS 205. Ir. *cnoc* "hill"+diminutive *-ín*; the form *cnuicín* is not recorded, the normal diminutive being *cnocán*.

coax "flatter" PW 161. Cf. Ir. *bladar* "coax ~ flatter".

cock "stack" 36, RS 9. [NED]

cockshot-man "living Anne Sally in cock-shy" PW 133. [Cf. NED s.v. *cock-shot*]

comrade "wife, husband" PW 89, DS 189. Cf. Ir. *céile* "comrade ~ spouse"; also *fear céile* "husband", *bean chéile* "wife".

conceit "desire" PW 59. In general dialect use except in southern England. [EDD]

contrivance "stratagem" PW 117. Obsolete. [NED]

cranky "ill-tempered" TW 31. In general dialect use. [NED, EDD]

crazy-house "lunatic asylum" PW 143. In general dialect use. [EDD]

creel "large wicker basket" 36, WS 141. Ireland, Scotland, and northern England. Ir. *críol* is apparently from northern English dialects. [NED, EDD, PWJ] **creel cart** "cart with (temporary) wicker sides and back" PW 57.

crossing roads "crossroads" WS 77.

cruel "terribly" TW 17. Obsolete c.1650; Ireland and western England. [NED, EDD]

crusted "encrusted" PW 153. [NED]

crusty "short-tempered" PW 73. [NED]

curagh "coracle, boat covered in skins or tarred canvas" RS 21, WS 91, PW 127, DS 217. Ir. *curach*; Ireland and Scotland. [NED, EDD, PWJ]

curiosity man "human prodigy" PW 87.

cut "slice" PW 99. [NED]

cute "clever" WS 77, TW 43. Obsolete; in general dialect use. [NED, EDD] **cuteness** PW 89. **cute thinking** WS 129.

D

da "father" PW 87. Nursery usage, obsolete c. 1850; Ireland, Scotland and northern England. [NED, EDD]

dark "blind" WS 73. Obsolete c.1850; Ireland and western England. Cf. Ir. *dorcha* "dark ~ blind". [NED, EDD, PWJ] **darkness** "blindness" WS 145.

darlint "darling" PW 145.

destroy "kill" MS 157, PW 163; "half-kill" SG 35. PW 67, WS 87, TW 17, PW 67; "ruin" RS 19, SG 55, TW 7; "injure, do harm to" 57, SG 41, WS 77; "drive mad" WS 71, TW 35, DS 221; "starve" RS 11. Cf. Ir. *milleadh* "destroy ~ damage, injure, etc."

differ "difference" TW 41. Ireland, Scotland and northern England. [NED, EDD]

ditch "bank" SG 39, WS 135, TW 11, PW 65. Obsolete c.1650; Ireland and western England. [NED, EDD, PWJ]

dvil: the divil a work "no work at all" PW 121. In Scottish dialect use. [EDD]

doxy "wench, mistress" 34. In general dialect use. [NED, EDD]

draw "bring in" SG 33. Obsolete c.1800; Ireland, Scotland and western England. Cf. Ir. *tarraingt* "draw ~ bring in". [NED ,EDD]

dreepiness "appearance of having a cold in the head" WS 109.

drift "drove, herd, flock" SG 39, PW 155; applied to "females" PW 167. Obsolete c.1750; Scotland and northern England. [NED EDD]

drive "blow" PW 103. In Scottish dialect use. [EDD]

drouth "thirst" 30, SG 43, TW 15; **drought** PW 133. Ireland, Scotland, northern and western England. [NED s.v. *drought*, EDD] **drouthy** "thirsty" TW 17; **droughty** PW 77.

drunken "make drunk" PW 95. Apparently not recorded elsewhere.

dry "thirsty" SG 43. Scotland, northern and western England. Cf. Ir. *tirim* "dry ~ thirsty". [NED, EDD]

duds "clothes" 8. In general colloquial and dialect use. [NED, EDD]

dummy "dumb person" DS 243. In general dialect use. [NED, EDD]

Dun "hill-fortress, fortified mansion" DS 201. Ir. *dún*. Scotland and northern England. [NED, EDD]

E

eastern world "a mythological land located to the east of Ireland" WS 131, PW 83, PW 167. Cf. Ir. *an domhan t(h)oir*. Cf. WESTERN WORLD.

easy "quiet" SG 51, WS 121, MS 159, TW 9; "comfortable" RS 17, SG 41, WS 131. Apparently Ireland only. [NED] **easy** "quietly" PW 169.

F

famished "dying (of cold)" PW 67. Cf. Ir. *préachta* "famished ~ dying of cold". Cf. PERISHED. [PWJ]

fancier "one having a critical judgment" DS 253. [NED]

fawny "fawn-coloured, the colour of unbleached cloth" 37. [NED]

fear "likelihood, danger" WS 103. [NED, PWJ]

fearful "frightened" TW 33, PW 79. Obsolete c.1800; in general dialect use. [NED, EDD]

felt "field-fare, *Turdus pilaris*" PW 123. In general dialect use in Ireland and England. [NED, EDD]

figure "imagine" DS 247; "draw" DS 191. [NED]

foxy "cunning" 36, PW 75. Obsolete c.1600; in general dialect use. [NED, EDD]

fright "terrible thing" PW 137. Obsolete c.1650. [NED]

fright "frighten" PW 143. Obsolete c.1750; in Scottish and English dialect use. [NED, EDD]

frish-frash "a mixture of various ingredients in cooking" PW 107. Ir. *frois-frais.*

furze "gorse, *Ulex europæus*" 43, SG 51, WS 133, PW 83, DS 185. Ireland and western England. [NED, EDD] **furzy** "overgrown with gorse" PW 61.

G

gaffer "lad" PW 153. The use is recorded by Joyce, but is limited to Ireland, and is difficult to explain in view of the word's derivation from *grandfather.* Possibly the meaning has been influenced by Ir. *scafaire* "spruce fellow". [PWJ]

gallant "fine, generous" PW 151; "respectable" PW 157. These meanings are not recorded elsewhere, and probably show the influence of Ir. *galánta.*

gallous "fine, splendid" 83, PW 153, PW 169, PW 171. In dialect use in western England, but with the meaning "mischievous, impudent". [EDD]

game "fun" PW 131; **make game** "joke" WS 89; "make fun (of)" WS 73, PW 65; "make a fool (of)" TW 43. Ireland and northern England. [NED, EDD] **gamey** "merry" WS 95, PW 101, DS 221. **game** "have fun" PW 149. **gaming** "trickery" PW 145.

gaudy "splendid" PW 83. In Scottish dialect use. Cf. Ir. *gréagach* (lit. "Greek") "gaudy ~ splendid".

Gob "God" 9.

gripe "ditch" PW 65. [NED s.v. *grip, gripe,* PWJ]

griseldy "grizzled" WS 131. For the formation cf. SPAVINDY, WIZENDY. Synge in a letter to Meyerfeld inexplicably gives the gloss "grisly", which does not suit the context.

H

hag: black hag "cormorant" RS 17. Cf. Ir. *cailleach dhubh* "cormorant", lit. "black hag".

haggard "stack-yard" DS 219. Ireland, Scotland, Isle of Man. Ir. *agard* is from English. [NED, EDD]

handy "readily" WS 103. Scotland and northern England. [EDD]

hard set "in a difficult position" RS 9, WS 125, TW 7, PW 95, DS 263. Obsolete c.1750; Scotland and northern England. [NED, EDD]

heavy "sad" DS 225. Obsolete c.1850. Cf. Ir. *trom* "heavy ~ sad". [NED]

hen: the old hen "influenza" PW 163. Cf. Ir. *an tsean-chearc* "influenza", lit. "the old hen"; here *sean* has its common pejorative sense, but *cearc* is translated from *hin-flew-in-the-winda,* a traditional perversion of *influenza.* See Arland Ussher, *Cainnt ant Sean-Shaoghail* (Dublin, 1942) 387.

herself "the woman of the house" PW 133; "one's wife" SG 43.

himself "the man of the house" PW 57; "one's husband" SW 125, PW 89.

hobble "catch" PW 133. In general dialect use. [NED, EDD]

honey: mister honey "my dear man" PW 73. *Honey* is in dialect use in Scotland and northern England, but the combination with *mister* seems not to be recorded elsewhere. [NED, EDD]

hooker "fishing-smack" RS 7, PW 127. Apparently Ireland only. [NED, EDD]

hooky "crooked" WS 131. Obsolete c.1700. [NED]

hoop "become crooked" DS 225. Apparently not recorded elsewhere.

hoosh "lift, remove" TW 41; **hoosh on** "encourage" PW 141. Ireland only. Connection with Ir. *thuas* "up" is improbable on phonological and semantic grounds. [EDD]

Horney "policeman" 8. Ireland only. [EDD s.v. *hornie*]

House "workhouse" 8. In general colloquial use. [EDD]

houseen "little house" PW 89. Eng. *house*+Ir. diminutive *-ín*.

hunkers: on one's hunkers "in a squatting position" 80. Ireland, Scotland, and northern England. [NED, EDD]

I

ill-lucky "unlucky" DS 221. Cf. Ir. *mí-adhmharach* "unlucky", lit. "ill-lucky".

in it "there" 79, RS 9, WS 137, TW 19, PW 63, DS 219. Cf. Ir. *ann* "in it~there".

itself "even" 82, RS 9, WS 71, MS 173, TW 19, PW 69, DS 185; "indeed" RS 7. Cf. Ir. *féin* "self~even".

J

jabs "Jesus" 9.

jack-straw "insignificant straw" PW 149 .[NED]

jobber "broker, middleman, small tradesman" 8, RS 9. Scotland and northern England. [NED, EDD] **jobbing** "occasionally employed" PW 105.

K

keen "lament" transitive RS 17, DS 269; intransitive RS 25, DS 251. Ir. *caoineadh*. [NED]

kelp "(burnt) seaweed for use as fertilizer" 66, RS 9. [NED]

kidnab "kidnap" PW 89. The form is a seventeenth-century variant. [NED s.v. *kidnapper*]

kind "nature" PW 169. Obsolete c.1600. [NED]

knacky "artful, ingenious" DS 253. Scotland and northern England. Cf. Ir. *cleas* "knack", *cleasach* "ingenious". [NED EDD]

L

lady of the house SG 33. Cf. WOMAN OF THE HOUSE, the more common rendering of Ir. *bean an tighe.*

leaguing "banding together, confederating" PW 113. [NED]

lengthy "long" PW 57; "numerous" PW 157. Of U.S. origin; these meanings seem not to be recorded elsewhere. [NED]

lep "leap, jump" 56, WS 77, MS 173, PW 89. Western England. [EDD] **lep** "a jump" SG 35, PW 103. **lepper** "jumper" PW 145. **lepping** "jumping" 58, PW 131.

let "utter": **let a cry** SG 35; **let a shout** MS 167; **let a grunt or groan** PW 73; **let a cough or a sneeze** PW 85; **let a roar** PW 123; **let a gasp** DS 243; the use in **let a wink** (PW 89) is anomalous. Cf. Ir. *leigim* "let~utter".

let build rooms "have rooms built" DS 259. Obsolete c.1600 except in the phrase *let (someone) know.* [NED]

let on "pretend" SG 43, WS 75, TW 47, PW 103; "admit" RS 17, SG 43. Ireland, Scotland and northern England. Cf. Ir. *leigim orm* "I pretend", lit. "I let on me".

liefer "rather, sooner" WS 99, PW 91, DS 193. Obsolete c.1600; in general dialect use. [NED, EDD, PWJ] **liefest** "most willingly" PW 171.

like: the like of "just like" SG 35, TW 23.

likely "promising, likely to do well" PW 143. In general dialect use. [NED, EDD, PWJ]

likeness: his likeness "the like of him" PW 87. Cf. Ir. *a mhacsamhail* "the like of him", lit. 'his likeness'.

limber "supple" PW 81. Obsolete c.1850; in general dialect use. [NED, EDD]

loan "lend" PW 115; "borrow" 36. The first meaning is in U.S. usage; the second is recorded only in Berkshire. [NED, EDD]

lone "alone" TW 25, PW 89. Scotland and northern England. [NED, EDD]

looked "look here!" 8. This common Anglo-Irish interjection, usually spelt *lookit*, is of obscure origin; it might possibly represent the survival of the mediaeval Anglo-Irish imperative plural *lokith*, with characteristic confusion of *th* and *t.*

lose "waste" WS 71; "cause to feel lost" 88.

lot "crowd, rabble" DS 191; (ironical) "fine crowd of people" PW 101. [NED]

louty "loutish, clumsy" PW 153. Apparently not recorded elsewhere.

lovely "beautifully" PW 103. Obsolete c.1700. [NED]

loy "long narrow spade" PW 73. Ir. *láighe.* [NED, EDD, PWJ]

lug "ear" TW 9, PW 143. Scotland and northern England. [NED, EDD]

M

madden "go mad" PW 61. Obsolete c.1850. [NED]

madder "dye produced from the root of *Rubia tinctorum*" DS 257. [NED]

master of the house SG 43, PW 67. A rendering of Ir. *fear an tighe*.

mend: God mend them PW 113; **the devil mend you (her,** etc.) SG 41, WS 125, TW 9. *Mend* "improve" is in dialect use in Scotland and northern England; *the devil mend . . .* seems to be an incomplete transposition of *God mend . . .* [NED, EDD]

Mergency man "bailiff's officer" 58. NED s.v. *emergency* 5 gives "(in Ireland) an occasional bailiff's officer, recruited for special service, esp. in evictions." [NED]

mind "remember" 80, WS 129. Obsolete c.1650; in general dialect use. [NED, EDD]

mind "take care" WS 105; "pay attention" WS 73, PW 65, PW 167; "pay attention to" WS 77, MS 171, TW 25, PW 91, DS 235. Identical in origin with the previous verb. Obsolete c.1850; in general dialect use. [NED, EDD, PWJ]

miss "notice the absence of" SG 47. Obsolete c.1800; in dialectal use. [NED]

mitch off "play truant" PW 111. *Mitch* is in general dialect use, but the combination with *off* seems not to be recorded elsewhere. [NED, EDD, PWJ]

mountainy "living in the mountains" PW 113. Ireland only. [NED, EDD]

muck "mud, mire" WS 105, PW 169. In general dialect use. [EDD]

mug: making mugs "making faces" PW 123. *Mug* is in general dialect and slang use, but this combination is unique and implausible. [NED, EDD]

N

naggin "quarter pint" WS 79. *Noggin* is in general dialect use; for the form cf. Ir. *naigín* beside *noigín*. [NED, EDD, PWJ]

noise "make a noise" PW 109. Ed. cit. prints *nose* without comments, see p. 72, note 47 [NED, EDD]

noising "noise" PW 65. Obsolete c.1600; in dialect use in the Isle of Man. [NED s.v. *noise*, EDD]

nor "than" 8. In general dialect use. [NED, EDD]

O

ohone "alas" 88. Ir. *ochón*. Ireland and Scotland. [NED]

out the way "along the road" 57. In common use in Ireland; EDD records *out the road* for northern Scotland. [EDD]

outlandish "foreign" PW 105. Obsolete c. 1700; Ireland, Scotland, and northern England. [NED, EDD]

over "again and again" RS 11. Apparently not recorded elsewhere, though *over and over* is common enough.

over "get over, survive" PW 89. Ireland, Scotland and northern England. [NED, EDD]

P

pandy "beat" PW 163. Ireland, Scotland and northern England. [NED, EDD]

parlatic "paralytic (with drink)" PW 143. A fourteenth-century variant of *paralytic*. The Anglo-Irish form probably shows the influence of the more common ending *-atic*, as in *rheumatic*. [NED]

peeler "policeman" 37. TW 11, PW 61. Named after Mr. Robert Peel, during whose Secretaryship (1812-18) the Irish constabulary was founded; London's Metropolitan Police was not established until 1829. [NED]

perished "dead of cold" 36; "frozen" MS 173. In general dialect use. Cf. FAMISHED. [NED, EDD]

perry "winkle, *Littorina littorea*" 36. Both *perry* and *winkle* are contractions of *periwinkle*.

piece "small distance" SG 39; "small space of time" DS 213. Northern England. Cf. Ir. *piosa*, used in both these meanings. [NED, EDD]

pike "pitchfork" PW 75. Obsolete c.1600; in dialect use in western England. Cf. Ir. *pice*. [NED, EDD]

pitchpike "pitchfork" PW 75. Not recorded elsewhere; but EDD notes *pitching-pikel* for Shropshire. [EDD]

playboy PW *title* and pp. 125, 139, 161, 163, 173. Noted by EDD for Ireland but not defined. The word is apparently a translation of Ir. *buachaill báire* "trickster"; K. E. Younge in *The Gaelic Churchman* (August-September 1923) 155 gives the tentative definition "a tricky, independable person?" Such connotations are clearly present in Synge's use, but there is also a note of admiration which may be ironic.

polis "police" PW 67. The spelling is designed to indicate stress on the first syllable, with a long *o*; this pronunciation is noted by NED for Ireland and Scotland. Cf. Ir. *póilín* "policeman", obscurely derived from *polis*. [NED]

poteen "illicit whiskey" RS 13, WS 129, PW 75. Ireland only. Ir. *poitín*, lit. "little pot", i.e. "illicit still". [NED, EDD, PWJ]

power "large number, great quantity" RS 23, SG 49, WS 73, TW 21, PW 81, DS 235. In general dialect use. [NED, EDD, PWJ]

press "cupboard" DS 183. Ireland, Scotland, northern England. [NED, EDD]

pride "most renowned" TW 33. Cf. Ir. *glóir* "pride ~ renown".

priesteen "little priest" PW 87. Eng. *priest* + Ir. diminutive *-ín*.

pull up on "catch up with" PW 123.

puzzle-the-world "total enigma" PW 71. Apparently unique, but NED records the somewhat similar combinations *puzzle-brain*, *puzzle-wit*.

Q

quality "gentry" WS 131, PW 79. In general dialect use. [NED, EDD, PWJ]

queer "very, extremely" RS 15, WS 77, PW 123. P. W. Joyce records only the Ulster use of *queer and* in this sense. [PWJ]

quench "put out (lights)" 86, DS 269; "put out (eyes)" 56; "kill" PW 161. [NED]

quit off "go away" PW 63. Apparently U.S. only. [NED]

R

raggy "ragged" WS 89. In Scottish dialect use. [NED, EDD] **raggy-looking** WS 121.

ready "prepare" DS 251. Scotland and northern England. Cf. Ir. *réidh* "ready", *réidheadh* "settle, arrange". [NED, EDD]

reckon "count" SG 47. Obsolete c.1700. [NED]

reek "mountain" WS 115. *Reek*, a variant of *rick*, is from Old Eng. *hréac*, cognate with Ir. *cruach* "rick, symmetrically shaped mountain", a name given to many mountains in Ireland. [PWJ]

renege "go back on one's word" PW 157. Obsolete c.1700; Ireland and western England. [NED, EDD]

retch "vomit" PW 151. This, the normal meaning in Ireland, is not recorded by NED.

ridge "back" PW 73. Cf. Ir. *druim* "ridge ~ back".

ridge: on the ridge of the world "in existence" WS 97, DS 231. Cf. Ir. *ar dhruim an domhain* "in existence", lit. "on the ridge of the world".

right "duty" 70, WS 105, MS 157, TW 13, PW 57, DS 185. Cf. Ir. *ceart* "right ~ duty".

right: not right "uncanny" WS 75. Ir. *ceart* "right" is used in a similar way.

romancing "fine talk" WS 113. Cf. Ir. *ráiméis* "gasconade", derived from *romance*.

roughness "harshness" DS 233.

rouser "vigorous man" 9. [NED]

S

sallow "willow, *Salix*" 71. [NED]

Samhain "All-Hallowtide" 36, RS 25, DS 187. An Irish word.

say out "say aloud" DS 193. [NED]

scald "vex, torment" WS 121. TW 49, PW 111. In Scottish dialect use. Always in phrases like *my heart is scalded*, etc., and based on Ir. *scalladh croidhe* "grief", lit. "scalding of the heart". [EDD] **scalding** "cruel" PW 125.

scald crow "hooded crow, *Corvus cornix*" 74. Ireland only. [NED, EDD]

scorch "blaze" PW 161. Apparently not recorded elsewhere.

scribe "long narrow strip (of land)" PW 81. In rare dialect use in England. [EDD]

scruff "back" PW 59. Perhaps *at the scruff (of)* is a fanciful rendering of Ir. *faoi chúl, ar chúl* "at the back (of)"; the most common meaning of *cúl* is "the hair at the back of the head".

seamed "crumpled" DS 243; "wrinkled" DS 245. [NED]

seemly "good-looking" PW 85. Obsolete c.1600; Scotland and northern England. [NED, EDD]

selvage "edge" WS 87. In Scottish dialect use. [NED, EDD]

shake "shaking" SG 51.

share "fate, lot" DS 261. In **my share of sins** (79), **his share of gold** (TW 11), the word *share* translates Ir. *cuid* in such phrases as *a chuid airgid* "his money", lit. "his share of money".

shebeen "low wayside public house" PW 57. More commonly "unlicensed public house"; Ireland, Scotland, Isle of Man. The origin of Ir. *síbín* has been much discussed: see T. F. O'Rahilly, "Miscellanea", *Ériu* ix (1921-3) 12-26; P. S. Dinneen, *Irish-English Dictionary* (1927) s.v. *séibín*; T. S. Ó Máille, "Focla NuaGhaeilge agus a bhFréamh", *Éigse* xi (1964-6) 85-99; T. S. Ó Máille, " 'Sheebeen' and 'Shebang'," *American Speech* xli (1966) 127-131 [NED, EDD, PWJ]

shift "undergarment" TW 23, PW 105. Northern England. [NED, EDD]

show "dreadful sight" WS 101. Current c.1700-1750. Ir. *seó* is no doubt from Eng. [NED]

shut of "rid of" 56, SG 55, TW 43, PW 109. EDD records only the nominal use *good shut of bad rubbish* for the midland counties of England. However, the phrase, though now wholly colloquial, is of long standing in English; cf. Eric Partridge, *A Dictionary of Slang and Unconventional English* (1961) s.v.

sight "great deal" WS 119, TW 15. In general dialect use. [NED, EDD, PWJ]

single "alone" TW 39, PW 153. Obsolete c.1850. [NED]

sink "lower" PW 151. Cf. Ir. *ísliughadh* "sink ~ lower".

skelp "beat" PW 137. In general dialect use except in southern England. Ir. *scealp, sceilp* "a blow" is no doubt from Eng. [NED, EDD, PWJ]

skillet "stew-pan" DS 187. Obsolete c.1800; in general dialect use. Ir. *scilléad* is from Eng. [NED, EDD]

skin: in one's skin "naked" SG 55, WS 105, DS 201. Cf. Ir. *ina chroiceann* "naked", lit. "in his skin".

slate "beat" PW 161. EDD records the word in Northumberland only, but NED shows that it originated in Ireland. [NED, EDD]

slippy "slippery" WS 105, TW 47. In general dialect use. [NED, EDD]

sloppy "tear-stained" DS 243. Apparently unique; the closest recorded meaning is "splashed or soiled with liquid". [NED]

slough "muddy place" WS 133. In Scottish dialect use. [NED, EDD]

sluigs "pits, hollows" SG 41. Ir. *slog*, plural *sluig*.

smart "strong (alcohol)" TW 17, PW 153. Obsolete c.1800. [NED]

so "in that case" PW 71. [PWJ]

sod "piece of peat" PW 111. In Scottish dialect use. [NED]

soft "fair, mild" 70. Ireland, Scotland and northern England. Cf. Ir. *bog* "soft~fair, mild". [EDD]

sop "wisp" PW 89; "sheaf" WS 113. Ir. *sop*.

spancel "fetter together" DS 223. Ireland only. [NED, EDD]

spavindy "spavined, affected with a tumour at the hock" PW 127. for the formation cf. GRISELDY, WIZENDY.

speckled "freckled" TW 35. [NED]

spuds "potatoes" PW 99. In general dialect use. [NED, EDD, PWJ]

stare "starling" 48. Obsolete c.1750; Ireland and western England. [NED, EDD, PWJ]

stiff "difficult, hard" 9. The usage is apparently without precise parallel.

stir "commotion" WS 133, MS 173, DS 199. Obsolete c.1700; in general dialect use. [NED, EDD]

stook "group of sheaves of corn" PW 63. In general dialect use. Ir. *stuaic* in this sense is from Eng. [NED, EDD, PWJ]

straitened waistcoat "strait-jacket" PW 81. Apparently unique.

stray "wander about (a place)" DS 183. Obsolete c.1700. [NED]

streeleen "flow of discourse" PW 81. Apparently Ir. *s(t)raoillín*, but no appropriate meaning seems to be recorded.

streeler "loiterer" PW 119. From Ir. *s(t)raoilleadh* "trail, drag".

stretch "hang" PW 169. Obsolete c.1800. [NED]

string gabble "chatter away" PW 85. Apparently unique.

stuff "whiskey" PW 135. Ireland, Scotland and northern England. [NED, EDD]

sup "small quantity (of liquid)" RS 25, SG 33, WS 77, TW 13, PW 97. In general dialect use except in southern England. [NED, EDD, PWJ]

supeen "little drink" PW 105. Eng. (dialect) *sup*+Ir. diminiutive *-ín*.

swearing out "expelling with an oath" TW 31. [NED]

swiggle PW 109. Apparently a portmanteau word combining *swing* and *wriggle*. EDD records for Ireland *swiggle* "shake liquid in an enclosed vessel", but this can hardly be the same word. [EDD]

switch "flexible shoot cut from a tree" PW 111. Obsolete c.1850 except in the combination *riding switch*. [NED]

T

tackle "tie up" TW 29. Apparently unique.

thraneen "straw, insignificant thing" PW 113. Ir. *tráithnín*; Ireland only. [EDD s.v. *traneen*, PWJ s.v. *traneen*]

tight "capable, vigorous" TW 35. Obsolete c.1750; Scotland and northern England. [NED, EDD]

townland "division of land based on a group of cottages" PW 147. A rendering of Ir. *baile fearainn*. [NED]

tramper "tramp, vagrant" TW 49, PW 119. Obsolete c.1850. [NED]

turbary "right of cutting peat on another person's land" PW 117. [NED, EDD]

turf "peat" 36, RS 7, SG 33, MS 159, PW 63. [NED, EDD] **turf-loft** RS 7.

turn "fit of illness" SG 35. [NED, EDD]

turn of (the) day SG 59, WS 103, TW 31. Apparently not recorded elsewhere. However, EDD records for west Somerset the phrase *turn of the year* "applied indifferently to all seasons, and to be explained by the period at which it is uttered or by the context". The contexts in which *turn of (the) day* appears suggest the meaning "noon", but it is difficult to be confident.

U

unbeknownst "secretly" PW 153. In general dialect use. [NED, EDD, PWJ]

Union "workhouse" SG 55, PW 143. [NED]

unkindly "unkind" PW 71. Current c.1800-50; in dialect use in western England. [NED, EDD]

V

verge "edge" DS 209. [NED]

W

wake "the watching of the dead from death to burial, usually accompanied by drinking and festivities" SG 37, PW 57. Scotland and northern England. [NED, EDD]

walking "living, not imaginary" PW 101.

want "need" SG 41, MS 157, TW 21, PW 103. Rare outside Ireland. [NED] **wanting** "needed, wanted" RS 9, DS 241; "wanted (by police)" PW 69.

want: its want "the lack of it" DS 191. In Yorkshire dialect use. Cf. Ir. *a cheal* "the lack of it", lit. "its want". [EDD]

warrant: a great warrant to tell stories "a great one for telling stories" PW 59. Recorded only by PWJ, but still in common use.

wary "careful" TW 9, PW 91. [NED]

wattle "stick" PW 111. Scotland and northern England. [NED, EDD]

weep "weeping, lamentation" 101. Obsolete c.1550. [NED]

welt "blow" WS 121. Scotland and northern England. [NED, EDD] **welted** "scarred" WS 149. [NED]

western world "a mythological land located to the west of Ireland" WS 87, PW 105, PW 143, Cf. Ir. *an domhan t(h)iar*. Cf. EASTERN WORLD. In **sailing from Mayo to the Western World** (PW 117) the meaning seems to be "America". In **playboy of the western world** (PW *title* and pp. 125, 139, 173) the meaning would seem to be "western Ireland", but this would not be at all in accordance with Irish usage. Some such meaning as "western Europe" is perhaps possible; no doubt Synge intended a play on words.

whack "slash with sharp instrument" WS 103. [EDD]

while "short time" MS 157; "long time" DS 227. [NED]

whisht "be silent" WS 99, PW 61. Ireland, Scotland and northern England. [NED, EDD, PWJ] **whisht!** SG 45, WS 83, TW 11, PW 61, DS 185. **whisht your talking!** PW 107.

whisht: hold your whisht! "be silent!" 8. Ireland, Scotland and northern England. [NED, EDD, PWJ]

whity "whitish" PW 97. [NED]

widow woman "widow" PW 89. In general dialect use; but cf. Ir. *baintreabhach mná* "widow", lit. "widow of a woman". [EDD, PWJ]

wink "blink" PW 165. Cf. BLINK. [NED]

winkered "wearing blinkers" PW 139. [NED s.v. *winker*]

wizendy "wizened" WS 99. Eng. *wizened* was originally a dialect word from Scotland and northern England. For the formation cf. GRISELDY, SPAVINDY.

woman of the house PW 67. Cf. Ir. *bean an tighe*; cf. LADY OF THE HOUSE.

A SELECT BIBLIOGRAPHY

As the title indicates, this bibliography is not exhaustive although it lists most of the significant, and most of the recent work on J. M. Synge. It is, however, representative of the many critical approaches to Synge—various points of view, at various dates, and in various parts of the world.

The following notes concern form and method of bibliography.

(1) Names of authors are those under which they wrote.
(2) In general, entries for periodical articles follow this form: author, title of article, name of periodical, volume and number, date, and page.
(3) Entries for books follow the generally accepted standard form. In the section entitled "Books Devoting Some Attention to Synge's Work or Life" no reference is made to chapters or section titles or page numbers.
(4) In a few instances periodical articles and books which the editor was unable to examine are listed, and in some of these instances one or more of the items in (2) are missing.
(5) Names of publishers are shortened.

A. Works by John Millington Synge

1. First Editions in Book Form:

In the Shadow of the Glen, New York, John Quinn, 1904.
The Shadow of the Glen and *Riders to the Sea*, London, Elkin Mathews, 1905.
The Well of the Saints, London, A. H. Bullen, 1905.
The Aran Islands, London, Elkin Mathews; Dublin, Maunsel, 1907. Illustrated by Jack B. Yeats. A large-paper edition was issued simultaneously.
The Playboy of the Western World, Dublin, Maunsel, 1907.
The Tinker's Wedding, Dublin, Maunsel, 1908.
Poems and Translations, Dublin, Cuala Press, 1909.
Deirdre of the Sorrows, Dublin, Cuala Press, 1910.
The Works of John Millington Synge, Dublin, Maunsel, 1910.

Volume I: *In the Shadow of the Glen, Riders to the Sea, The Tinker's Wedding, The Well of the Saints.*
Volume II: *The Playboy of the Western World, Deirdre of the Sorrows, Poems, Translations from Petrarch, Translations from Villon and Others.*
Volume III: *The Aran Islands.*

Volume IV: *In Wicklow* (The Vagrants of Wicklow, The Oppression
of the Hills, On the Road, The People of the Glens. At
a Wicklow Fair, A Landlord's Garden in County
Wicklow, Glencree), *In West Kerry, In the Congested
Districts, Under Ether.*

2. Standard Editions:

Collected Plays, Harmondsworth, Middlesex, Penguin Books, 1952.
J. M. Synge: Collected Works, general ed. R. Skelton, London, Oxford
University Press, 1962-1968.
Volume I: Poems, ed. R. Skelton, 1962.
Volume II: Prose, ed. A. Price, 1966.
Volumes III, IV: Plays, ed. A. Saddlemyer, 1968.
J. M. Synge's Plays, Poems, and Prose, in the Everyman's Library
edition, with an introduction by M. MacLiammoir, London, J. M.
Dent and Sons, 1961.
Plays and Poems of J. M. Synge, edited by T. R. Henn, London,
Methuen, 1963.

3. Contributions to Periodicals:

"A Celtic Theatre," *Freeman's Journal*, March 22, 1900, 4.
"A Dream on Inishmaan," *Green Sheaf*, 2, 1903, 8-9.
"A Landlord's Garden in County Wicklow," *Manchester Guardian*, July
1, 1907, 12.
"A Story from Inishmaan," *New Ireland Review*, X, November, 1898,
153-156.
"A Translation of Irish Romance," *Manchester Guardian*, March 6,
1906, 5.
"Anatole Le Braz: A Breton Writer," *Daily Express*, January 28, 1899, 3.
"An Autumn Night in the Hills," *The Gael*, April 1903, 117.
"An Epic of Ulster," *Speaker*, June 7, 1902, 284-285.
"An Impression of Aran," *Manchester Guardian*, January 24, 1905,
12.
"An Irish Historian," *Speaker*, September 6, 1902, 605-606.
"At a Wicklow Fair: The Place and the People," *Manchester Guardian*,
May 9, 1907, 12.
"Celtic Mythology," *Speaker*, April 2, 1904, 17-18.
"Glen Cullen," [a Sonnet], *Kottabos*, Hilary Term, 1893, 103.
"Good Pictures in Dublin: The New Municipal Gallery," *Manchester
Guardian*, January 24, 1908, 12.
"In the Congested Districts," a series of twelve articles, illustrated by
Jack Yeats, describing the living conditions of Irish peasants in the
impoverished districts of County Galway and County Mayo; it appeared
in the *Manchester Guardian* as follows:
"From Galway to Gorumna," *Manchester Guardian*, June 10, 1905.
"Between the Bays of Carraroe," *Manchester Guardian*, June 14, 1905.

"Among the Relief Workers," *Manchester Guardian*, June 17, 1905.
"The Ferryman of Dinish Island," *Manchester Guardian*, June 21, 1905.
"The Kelp Makers," *Manchester Guardian*, June 24, 1905.
"The Boat Builders," *Manchester Guardian*, June 28, 1905.
"The Homes of the Harvestmen," *Manchester Guardian*, July 1, 1905.
"The Smaller Peasant Proprietors," *Manchester Guardian*, July 5, 1905.
"Erris," *Manchester Guardian*, July 8, 1905.
"The Inner Lands of Mayo," *Manchester Guardian*, July 19, 1905.
"The Small Town," *Manchester Guardian*, July 22, 1905.
"Possible Remedies," *Manchester Guardian*, July 26, 1905.
"In West Kerry," *Shanachie*, 4, Summer, 1907, 61-70.
"In West Kerry: The Blasket Islands," *Shanachie*, 5, Autumn, 1907, 138-150.
"In West Kerry: To Puck Fair," *Shanachie*, 6, Winter, 1907, 233-243.
"In Wicklow: On the Road," *Manchester Guardian*, December 10, 1908, 14.
"Irish Fairy Stories," *Speaker*, June 21, 1902, 340.
"La Sagesse et la Destinée, " *Daily Express*, December 17, 1898, 3.
"La Vieille Littérature Irlandaise," *L'Européen*, March 15, 1902, 11.
"Le Mouvement Intellectuel Irlandais," *L'Européen*, May 31, 1902, 12.
"Loti and Huysmans," *Speaker*, April 18, 1903, 57-58.
"The Fair Hills of Ireland," *Manchester Guardian*, November 16, 1906, 5.
"The Last Fortress of the Celt," *Gael* [N.Y.], April 1901, 109.
"The Old and New in Ireland," *Academy and Literature*, September 6, 1902, 238-239.
"The Oppression of the Hills," *Manchester Guardian*, February 15, 1905, 12.
"The People of the Glens," *Shanachie*, 3, Spring, 1907, 39-47.
"The Poems of Geoffrey Keating," *Speaker*, December 8, 1900, 245.
"The Vagrants of Wicklow," *Shanachie*, 2, Autumn 1906, 93-98.
"The Winged Destiny," *Academy and Literature*, November 12, 1904, 455.

4. Letters:*
"Letters of John Millington Synge", *Yale Review*, XIII, July 1924, 690-709.
Some Unpublished Letters and Documents by J. M. Synge Formerly in the Possession of Mr. Lawrence Wilson of Montreal, and now for the First Time Published for Him, Montreal, Redpath Press, 1959.
"Synge to MacKenna: The Mature Years," edited by Anne Saddlemyer, *Irish Renaissance: A Gathering of Essays, Memoirs, Letters and*

*Extracts of numerous letters are quoted by D. H. Greene and E. M. Stephens in *J. M. Synge, 1871-1909*, New York, Macmillan, 1959.

Dramatic Poetry from the Massachusetts Review, eds. Robin Skelton and David R. Clark, Dublin, Dolmen Press, 1965, 65-79.

Some Letters of John M. Synge to Lady Gregory and W. B. Yeats, Selected by Ann Saddlemyer, Dublin, Cuala Press, 1971.

Letters to Molly: John M. Synge to Maire O'Neill, edited by Ann Saddlemyer, Harvard University Press, 1971.

B. *Bibliographies, Catalogues and Press-Cuttings*
1. Wholly devoted to Synge:

Dysinger, R. E. (Compiler) — "The John Millington Synge Collection at Colby College," a check list compiled by Dysinger, *Colby Library Quarterly*, series IV, 9, February 1957, 166-172.

Dysinger, R. E. — "Additions to the John Millington Synge Collection: A Supplementary Check List." *Colby Library Quarterly*, series IV, February 1957, 192-194.

MacManus, M. J. — "Bibliographies of Irish Authors—4: John Millington Synge," *Dublin Magazine*, V, 4, October-December 1930, 47-51.

MacPhail, I. — "John Millington Synge: Some Bibliographical Notes," *Irish Book* (Bibliographical Society of Ireland), I, 1960, 3-10.

O'Hegarty, P. S. — "Some Notes on the Bibliography of J. M. Sygne, Supplemental to Bourgeois and Mac-Manus," *Dublin Magazine*, XVII, 1, January-March 1942, 56-58.

Pollard, M. and MacPhail, I. — *John Millington Synge (1871-1909): A Catalogue of an Exhibition Held at Trinity College Library, on the Occasion of the Fiftieth Anniversary of His Death*. For the Friends of the Library of Trinity College (Dublin), Dublin, Dolmen Press, 1959.

2. Devoting Some Attention to Synge:

Henderson, W. A. (Compiler) — *The Irish National Theatre Movement. The Irish Literary Theatre up to the Opening of the Abbey Theatre* [1904], told in press-cuttings collected by W. A. Henderson—National Library, Dublin.

Henderson, W. A. (Compiler) — 1904-1907. *The Irish National Theatre Movement. Three Years Work at the Abbey Theatre*, told in press-cuttings collected by W. A. Henderson, I, IV, X, XIII, XV.

Henderson, W. A. (Compiler) — 1908. *The Irish National Theatre Movement. A Year's Work at the Abbey Theatre*, told in press-cuttings collected by W. A. Henderson, II.

Henderson, W. A. (Compiler) — 1909. *The Irish National Theatre Movement. A Year's Work at the Abbey Theatre*, told in press-cuttings collected by W. A. Henderson, III.

Henderson, W. A. (Compiler)	1910. *The Irish National Theatre Movement. A Year's Work at the Abbey Theatre*, told in press-cuttings collected by W. A. Henderson.
Henderson, W. A. (Compiler)	1911. *The Irish National Theatre Movement. A Year's Work at the Abbey Theatre*, told in press-cuttings collected by W. A. Henderson.
Henderson, W. A. (Compiler)	*The Playboy of the Western World by J. M. Synge. A Play that Shocked! A Compendium of Comments, Criticism, Calumnies, Carpings, Caricatures, Cavillings, Clamours, Congratulations*—National Library, Dublin.
Macnamara, Brinsley [John Weldon]	*Abbey Plays*, 1899-1949, Dublin, Sign of the Three Candles, 1949.

C. *Criticism and Biography*

1. Books Wholly Devoted to Synge:

Bickley, F. L.	*J. M. Synge and the Irish Dramatic Movement*, London, Constable, Boston and New York, Houghton Mifflin, 1912.
Bourgeois, M.	*John Millington Synge and the Irish Theatre*, London, Constable, 1913.
Corkery, D.	*Synge and Anglo-Irish Literature*, Dublin and Cork, Cork University Press, 1931.
Estill, A. D.	*The Sources of Synge* (Privately printed). Pennsylvania, University of Pennsylvania, 1937.
Frenzel, H.	*J. M. Synge's Work as a Contribution to Irish Folklore and to the Psychology of Primitive Tribes*, Düren-Rhld., 1932.
Gerstenberger, D.	*John Millington Synge* [Twayne's English Authors Series, 12], New York, Twayne, 1964.
Greene, D. H. and Stephens, E. M.	*J. M. Synge*, 1871-1909, New York, Macmillan, 1959.
Harmon, M. (Editor)	*Synge Centenary Papers*, Dublin, Dolmen Press, 1971.
Howe, P. P.	*J. M. Synge: A Critical Study*, London, Secker, 1912.
Johnston, D.	*John Millington Synge*, [Columbia Essays on Modern Writers, 12], New York, Columbia University Press, 1965.
Masefield, J.	*John M. Synge: A Few Personal Recollections with Biographical Notes*, Churchtown, Dundrum, Cuala Press, 1915.
Page, C.	*Drama: Synge's Riders to the Sea*, Boston, Ginn, 1966.
Price, A.	*Synge and Anglo-Irish Drama*, London, Methuen, 1961.

Saddlemyer, A.   *J. M. Synge and Modern Comedy*, Dublin, Dolmen Press, 1968.

Setterquist, J.,   *Ibsen and the Beginning of Anglo-Irish Drama. I. John Millington Synge,* [Upsala Irish Studies,2], Upsala, Upsala University, 1951.

Skelton, Robin   *J. M. Synge & his World*, London, Thames & Hudson, 1971.

Skelton, Robin   *The Writings of J. M. Synge*, London, Thames & Hudson, 1971.

Solomont, S.   *The Comic Effect of "Playboy of the Western World,"* Bangor, Signalman Press, 1962.

Strong, L. A. G.   *John Millington Synge*, London, G. Allen and Unwin, 1941.

Synge, Samuel   *Letters to my Daughter: Memories of John Millington Synge*, Dublin and Cork, Talbot Press, 1931.

2. Books Devoting Some Attention to Synge's Work or Life:

Archer, W.   *Playmaking: A Manual of Craftsmanship*, London, Chapman and Hall, 1912.

Bithell, J.   *W. B. Yeats*, translated by F. Hellens, Paris, Editions du Masque; Brussels, H. Lamertin, 1913.

Blythe, E.   *The Abbey Theatre*, Dublin, National Theatre Society, 1963.

Borsa, M.   *The English Stage of To-Day*, translated by S. Brinton, London, The Bodley Head; New York, J. Lane, 1908.

Boyd, E. A.   *Ireland's Literary Renaissance*, Dublin and London, Maunsel, 1916.

Boyd, E. A.   *The Contemporary Drama of Ireland*, Dublin, Talbot Press; London, T. Fisher Unwin, 1918.

Bryant, S.   *The Genius of the Gael. A Study in Celtic Psychology and Its Manifestations*, London, Fisher Unwin, 1913.

Bushrui, S. B.   *Yeats's Verse-Plays: The Revisions, 1900-1910*, Oxford, Clarendon Press, 1965.

Bushrui, S. B. and   *W. B. Yeats, 1865-1965: Centenary Essays on the*
Maxwell, D. E. S.,   *Art of W. B. Yeats*, Ibadan, Ibadan University
(Editors)   Press, 1965.

Byrne, D.   *The Story of Ireland's National Theatre: The Abbey Theatre, Dublin.* Dublin, Talbot Press, 1929.

Colum, M.   *Life and the Dream*, Dublin, Dolmen Press, 1966 (revised edition).

Colum, P.   *The Road Round Ireland*, New York, Macmillan, 1930.

Coxhead, E.   *Daughters of Erin*, London, Secker, 1965.

Coxhead, E.   *Lady Gregory: A Literary Portrait*, London, Macmillan, 1961.

Coxhead, E.   *J. M. Synge and Lady Gregory*, [Writers and Their Work Series, 149], London, published for the British Council and the National Book League by Longmans, 1962.

[Dickson, P. L. and Hone, J. M.]   *The Abbey Row, Not Edited by W. B. Yeats*, [Dublin, Maunsel, 1904].

Dodds, E. R. (Editor)   *Journal and Letters of Stephen MacKenna*, London, Constable, 1936.

Ellis-Fermor, U.   *The Irish Dramatic Movement*, London, Methuen, 1939.

Elton, O.   *Modern Studies*, London, E. Arnold, 1907.

Fay, G.   *The Abbey Theatre: Cradle of Genius*, Dublin, Clonmore and Reynolds, 1958.

Fay, W. G., and Carswell, C.   *The Fays of the Abbey Theatre: An Autobiographical Record*, London, Rich and Cowan, 1935.

Figgis, D.   *Studies and Appreciations*, London, Dent, 1912.

Flannery, James W.   *Miss Annie F. Horniman and the Abbey Theatre* Dublin, Dolmen Press, 1970.

Gassner, J.   *Masters of the Drama*, New York, Random House, 1940.

Gassner, J.   *The Theatre in Our Times: A Survey of the Men, Materials, and Movements in the Modern Theatre*, New York, Crown, 1954.

Gilbert, S. (Editor)   *Letters of James Joyce*, Vol. I, New York, Vicking Press, 1957.

Gregory, Lady   *Our Irish Theatre, a Chapter of Autobiography*, New York and London, G. P. Putnam's Sons, 1913.

Gwynn, S.   *Irish Literature and Drama in the English Language: A Short History*, London, Nelson, 1936.

Harmon, M. (Editor)   *The Celtic Master, Being Contributions to the First James Joyce Symposium in Dublin*, Dublin, Dolmen Press, 1969.

Henn, T. R.   *The Lonely Tower, Studies in the Poetry of W. B. Yeats*, London, Methuen, 1950.

Hoare, D. M.   *The Works of Morris and of Yeats in Relation to Early Saga Literature*, Cambridge, University Press, 1937.

Hogan, R. and O'Neill, M. J. (Editors)	*Joseph Holloway's Abbey Theatre*, Carbondale, Illinois, University Press, 1967.
Howarth, H.	*The Irish Writers, 1880-1940: Literature under Parnell's Star*, London, Rockliff, 1958.
Jackson, H.	*All Manner of Folk: Interpretations and Studies*, London, Grant Richard, 1912.
Jameson, S.	*Modern Drama in Europe*, London, Collins, 1920.
Kavanagh, P.	*The Story of the Abbey Theatre from Its Origins in 1899 to the Present*, New York, Devin-Adair, 1950.
Kavanagh. P.	*The Irish Theatre, Being a History of the Drama in Ireland from the Earliest Period up to the Present Day*, Tralee, Kerryman, 1946.
Kenny, E.	*The Splendid Years: Recollections of Marie Nic Shiubhlaigh; as Told to Edward Kenny*, Dublin, J. Duffy, 1955.
Kilroy, James	*The 'Playboy' Riots*, Dublin, Dolmen Press, 1971.
Krutch, J. W.	*"Modernism" in Modern Drama, a Definition and an Estimate*, New York, Cornell University Press, 1953.
Lamm, M.	*Modern Drama*, translated by Karin Elliott, Oxford, Blackwell, 1952.
Law, H. A.	*Anglo-Irish Literature*, Dublin, Talbot Press, 1926.
Lucas, F. L.	*The Drama of Chekhov, Synge, Yeats and Pirandello*, London, Cassell, 1963.
Lynd, R.	*Home Life in Ireland*, London, Mills and Boon, 1909.
Lynd, R.	*Old and New Masters*, London, Fisher Unwin, 1919.
MacLiammoir, M.	*Theatre in Ireland*, Dublin, Colm O Lochlainn, 1950.
Malone, A. E.	*The Irish Drama*, London, Constable, 1929.
Mayne, R.	*The Drone and Other Plays*, Dublin, Maunsel, 1912.
Mercier, V.	*The Irish Comic Tradition*, New York, Oxford University Press, 1962.
Metwally, A. A.	*Studies in Modern Drama*, Beirut, Beirut Arab University, 1971.
Monahan, M.	*Nova Hibernia*, New York, Kennerly, 1914.
Montague, C. E.	*Dramatic Values*, Garden City [N.Y.], Doubleday, Page and Co., 1925.

Montague, C. E. *Essays and Studies by Members of the English Association*, Vol. II, collected by H. C. Beeching, Oxford, Clarendon Press, 1911.

Moore, G. *Hail and Farewell!*, Vol. III, London, Heinemann, 1920.

Morgan, A. E. *Tendencies of Modern English Drama*, London, Constable, 1924.

Nicoll, A. *World Drama from Aeschylus to Anouilh*, London, Harrap, 1949.

O'Brien, C. C. *Writers and Politics*, London, Chatto and Windus, 1965.

O Síocháin, P. A. *Aran: Islands of Legend*, Dublin, Foilsiúcháin Éireann, 1962.

Peacock, R. *The Poet in the Theatre*, London, Routledge, 1946.

Pritchett, V. S. *In My Good Books*, London, Chatto and Windus, 1942.

Reid, F. *W. B. Yeats: A Critical Study*, London, Secker, 1915.

Robinson, L. (Editor) *The Irish Theatre: Lectures Delivered During the Abbey Theatre Festival Held in Dublin in August, 1938*, London, Macmillan, 1939.

Robinson, L. (Compiler) *Ireland's Abbey Theatre: A History, 1899-1951*, London, Sidgwick and Jackson, 1951.

Roosevelt, T. and Shaw, G. B. *A Note on the Irish Theatre by T. Roosevelt and an "Interview" on the Irish Players in America by G. B. Shaw*, New York, Kennerley, 1912.

Ryan, W. P. *The Poet's Green Ireland*, London, J. Nisbet, 1912.

Saddlemyer, A. and Skelton, R. *The World of W. B. Yeats: Essays in Perspective*, Dublin, Dolmen Press, 1965.

Saul, G. B. (Editor) *Age of Yeats: The Golden Age of Irish Literature*, New York, Dell Publishing Co., 1964.

Shaw, G. B. *Plays and Players. Essays on the Theatre*, Oxford, University Press, 1952 [World's Classics, 585].

Stamm, R. *Three Anglo-Irish Plays*, Vol. V. of Bibliotheca Anglicana (Texts and Studies), Bern, Francke, 1943.

Strong, L. A. G. *Personal Remarks*, New York, Liveright; London, Peter Nevill, 1953.

Styan, J. L. *The Dark Comedy: The Development of Modern Comic Tragedy*, Cambridge, University Press, 1962.

| Styan, J. L. | *The Elements of Drama*, Cambridge University Press, 1960. |

Taylor, E. R. — *The Modern Irish Writers: Cross Currents of Criticism*, Lawrence, University of Kansas Press, 1954.

Walbrook, H. M. — *Nights at the Play*, London, Hamsmith, 1911.

Walkley, A. B. — *Drama and Life*, London, Methuen, 1907.

Weygandt, C. — *Irish Plays and Playwrights*, London, Constable; New York, Houghton Mifflin, 1913.

Williams, H. — *Modern English Writers: Being a Study of Imaginative Literature*, 1890-1914, London, Sidgwick and Jackson, 1918.

Williams, R. — *Drama from Ibsen to Brecht*, London, Chatto and Windus, 1968.

Yeats, W. B. — *Autobiographies*, London, Macmillan, 1965.

Yeats, W. B. — *Essays and Introductions*, London, Macmillan, 1961.

Yeats, W. B. — *Explorations* (selected by Mrs. W. B. Yeats), London, Macmillan, 1962.

Yeats, W. B. — *The Letters*, ed. Alan Wade, London, Rupert Hart-Davis, 1954.

3a. Essays, Articles, etc.:

Adams, J. D. — "The Irish Dramatic Movement," *Harvard Monthly*, November 1911, 44.

"A Lover of the West" — "*The Well of the Saints*," *Dana: A Magazine of Independent Thought*, April 12, 1905, 364-368.

Alspach, R. K. — "Synge's *Well of the Saints*," [*London*] *Times Literary Supplement*, December 28, 1935, 899.

Archer, W. — "Three Poets Departed," *Morning Leader*, May 15, 1909.

Archer, W. — "The Art of the Artless," *Nation* [London], June 4, 1910.

Arnold, S. — "The Abbey Theatre," *Arts and Philosophy*, Summer 1905, 25-30.

Ayling, R. — "Synge's First Love: Some South African Aspects," *English Studies in Africa* [Johannesburg], VI, 1963, 173-185.

Barnes, T. R. — "Yeats, Synge, Ibsen and Strindberg," *Scrutiny*, V, 3, December 1936, 257-262.

Barnett, P. — "The Nature of Synge's Dialogue," *English Literature in Transition*, X, 3, 1967, 119-129.

Bauman, R. — "John Millington Synge and Irish Folklore," *Southern Folklore Quarterly*, XXVII, December 1963, 267-279.

Beerbohm, M.	"Irish Players," *Saturday Review*, July 12, 1909.
Bennett, C. A.	"The Plays of John Millington Synge," *Yale Review*, I, 2, January 1912, 192-205.
Bessai, D. E.	"Little Hound in Mayo: Synge's *Playboy* and the Comic Tradition in Irish Literature," *Dalhousie Review*, XLVIII, 1968, 372-383.
Bewley, C.	"The Irish National Theatre," *Dublin Review*, CLII, 304, January 1913, 132-144.
Bickley, F.	"*Deirdre*," *Irish Review*, II, 17, July 1912, 252-254.
Bickley, F.	"Earth to Earth," *Bookman*, XXXVI, 215, August 1909, 224.
Bickley, F.	"Synge and the Drama," *New Quarterly*, February 1910, 73.
Bickley, F.	"The Widow in the Bye Street," *Bookman*, XLII, 251, August 1912, 211.
Birmingham, G. A.	"The Literary Movement in Ireland," *Fortnightly Review*, LXXXII, 492, December 1907, 947-957.
Blake, W. B.	"An Irish Playwright," *Independent*, April 13, 1911, 792-793.
Blake, W. B.	"John Synge and His Plays," *Dial*, January 16, 1911, 37.
Blake, W. B.	"Synge," *Theatre*, June 1911, 204.
Bourgeois, M.	"Synge and Loti," *Westminster Review*, May 1913.
Boyd, E. A.	"The Abbey Theatre," *Irish Review*, II, 24, February 1913, 628-634.
Boyd, E. A.	"The Irish National Theatre," *Irish Times*, December 27, 1912.
Brooks, S.	"The Irish Peasant as a Dramatic Issue," *Harper's Weekly*, March 9, 1907, 344.
Brophy, G. M.	"J. M. Synge and the Revival of the Irish Drama," *Everyman*, I, 1, October 18, 1912, 8.
Canby, H. S.	"Works of Synge," *Yale Review*, II, July 1913, 767-772.
Casey, H.	"Synge's Use of the Anglo-Irish Idiom," *English Journal*, College ed., XXVII, 773-776.
C.H.H.	"John Synge as I Knew Him," *Irish Statesman*, July 5, 1924, 534.
Clarke, A.	"John Synge Comes Next," *Irish Times*, November 9, 1969.
Collins, R. L.	"The Distinction of *Riders to the Sea*," *University of Kansas City Review*, XIII, 1947, 278-284.

Combs, W. W.   "J. M. Synge's *Riders to the Sea*: A Reading and Some Generalizations," *Papers of the Michigan Academy of Science, Arts and Letters*, L, 1965, 559-607.

Connell, F. N.   "John Millington Synge," *English Review*, II, June 1909, 609-613.

Cooper, B.   "The Drama in Ireland," *Irish Review*, III, 27, May 1913, 140-143.

C.P.   "The Irish Players in Philadelphia," *New Drama*, 1, April 1912, 15-16.

Currie, R. H. and Bryan, M.   "*Riders to the Sea*: Reappraised," *Texas Quarterly*, XI, Winter 1968, 139-146.

Cusack, C.   "A Player's Reflections on *Playboy*," *Modern Drama*, IV, December 1961, 300-305.

Davie, D.   "The Poetic Diction of Synge," *Dublin Magazine*, XXVII, n.s., January-March, 1952, 32-38.

Day-Lewis, S.   "Synge's Song," *Drama*, CXC, Autumn 1968, 35-38.

Donoghue, D.   "Flowers and Timber: A Note on Synge's Poems," *Threshold*, I, 3, 1957, 41-47.

Donoghue, D.   "Synge: *Riders to the Sea*; a Study," *University Review*, I, 5, Summer 1955, 52-58.

Donoghue, D.   "Too Immoral for Dublin: Synge's *The Tinker's Wedding*," *Irish Writing*, 30, March 1955, 56-62.

Lord Dunsany   "The Irish Players in *Deirdre of the Sorrows*," *Saturday Review*, June 4, 1910.

Lord Dunsany   "Romance and the Modern Stage," *National Review*, LVII, 341, July 1911, 827-835.

E.K.D.   "The Irish Theatre Society," *Dial*, I, 1, July 1—December 16, 1911, 521.

Ernright, D. J.   "A Note on Irish Literature and the Irish Tradition," *Scrutiny*, X, January 1942, 252-254.

Fackler, H. V.   "J. M. Synge's *Deirdre of the Sorrows*: Beauty only," *Modern Drama*, XI, February 1969, 404-409.

Fausset, H.   "Synge and Tragedy," *Fortnightly Review*, CXV, 686, February 1924, 258-273.

Figgis, D.   "The Art of J. M. Synge," *Fortnightly Review*, XC, 539, December 1911, 1056-1068.

Figgis, D.   "The Art of J. M. Synge," *Forum* [N.Y.], XLVII, 1, January 1912, 55-70.

Fraser, R. A.   "Ireland Made Him," *Nation Review*, CXC, February 20, 1960, 171-173.

Galsworthy, J.   "New Spirit in the Drama," *Hibbert Journal*, XI, 3, April 1913, 508-520.

Galsworthy, J.   "Meditation on Finality," *English Review*, XI, July 1912, 537-541.

Ganz, A.   "J. M. Synge and the Drama of Art," *Modern Drama*, X, May 1967, 57-68.

Gaskell, R.   "The Realism of J. M. Synge," *Critical Quarterly*, V, Autumn 1963, 242-248.

Gill, M. J.   "Neo-Paganism and the Stage," *New Ireland Review*, XXVIII, 3, May 1907, 179-187.

Gosse, E.   "The Playwright of the Western World," *Morning Post*, January 26, 1911.

Gorki, M.   "Observations on the Theatre," *English Review*, XXXVIII, April 1924, 494-498.

Greene, D. H.   "An Adequate Text of J. M. Synge," *Modern Language Notes*, LXI, 7, November 1946, 466-467.

Greene, D. H.   "Synge and the Celtic Revival," *Modern Drama*, IV, December 1961, 292-299.

Greene, D. H.   "Synge and the Irish," *Colby Literary Quarterly*, Series IV, 9, February 1957, 158-166.

Greene, D. H.   "Synge's Unfinished *Deirdre*," *PMLA*, LXIII, 4, December 1948, 1314-1321.

Greene, D. H.   "*The Playboy* and Irish Nationalism," *Journal of English and Germanic Philology*, XLVI, April 1947, 199-204.

Greene, D. H.   "*The Shadow of the Glen* and *The Widow of Ephesus*," *PMLA*, LXII, March 1947, 233-238.

Greene, D. H.   "*The Tinker's Wedding*, a Revaluation," *PMLA*, LXII, September 1947, 824-827.

Gregory, Lady   "Synge," *English Review*, XIII, March 1913, 556-566.

Gregory, Lady   "The Irish Theatre and the People," *Yale Review*, I, 2, January 1912, 188-191.

Grigson, G.   "Synge," *New Statesman*, LXIV, October 19, 1962, 528-529.

Gunning, G. H.   "The Decline of the Abbey Theatre Drama," *Irish Review*, I, 12, February 1912, 606-609.

Hamilton, C.   [Review of *The Playboy*], *Bookman*, October 1910, 145.

Harding, D. W.   "A Note on Nostalgia," *Scrutiny*, I, May 1932, 9-10.

Harrison, A.   "Strindberg's Plays," *English Review*, XIII, December 1912, 80-97.

Henry, P. L.   *"The Playboy of the Western World,"* Philologia
                      Pragensia, VIII, 1965, 189-204.

Hoare, J. E.   "Ireland's National Drama," *North American
                      Review*, CXCIV, 671, October 1911, 566-575.

Hoare, J. E.   "Synge," *University Magazine*, February 1911,
                      91-109.

Hodgson, G. E.   "Some Irish Poetry," *Contemporary Review*,
                      XCVIII, September 1910, 323-340.

Holloway, J.   *"The Playboy* and its Reception in Montreal,"
                      Evening Herald, February 14, 1913.

Howe, P. P.   *"The Playboy* in the Theatre," *Oxford and
                      Cambridge Review* (now: *British Review*), July
                      1912.

Inkster, L.   "The Irish Players," *Saturday Review*, June 17,
                      1911, 746.

Jacobs, W. D.   "Silent Sinner," *American Mercury*, LXXXI,
                      August 1955, 159-160.

Johnson, W. H.   "The Pagan Setting of Synge's *Playboy,"*
                      Renascence, XIX, 1967, 119-121, 150.

Kain, R. M.   "A Scrapbook of the *Playboy* Riots," *Emory
                      University Quarterly*, XXII, 1966, 5-17.

Kaul, R. K.   "Synge as a Dramatist: An Evaluation," *English
                      Miscellany*, III, 1965, 37-51.

Kenny, F. M.   "The Play of the Irish Players," *America*,
                      November 4, 1911, 78-79.

Kilroy, J. F.   "The *Playboy* as Poet," *PMLA*, LXXXIII, 2,
                      May 1968, 439-442.

Koehler, T.   "The Irish National Theatre," *Dana: A Maga-
                      zine of Independent Thought*, 11, March 1905,
                      351-352.

Krause, D.   " 'The Rageous Ossean': Patron-Hero of Synge
                      and O'Casey," *Modern Drama*, IV, December
                      1961, 268-291.

Leyburn, E. D.   "The Theme of Loneliness in the Plays of
                      Synge," *Modern Drama*, I, September 1958, 84-90.

Lowther, G.   "J. M. Synge and the Irish Revival," *Oxford and
                      Cambridge Review* (now: *British Review*), Nov-
                      ember 1912.

MacHugh, R.   "Yeats, Synge and the Abbey Theatre," *Studies*,
                      XLI, 1952.

MacLean, H. N.   "The Hero as Playboy," *University of Kansas
                      City Review*, XXI, Fall 1954, 9-19.

Maguire, M. C.   "John Synge," *Irish Review*, March 1911, 39-43.

Mantle, B.	"An Irish Fantasy. A New Comedy Farce," *Chicago Daily Tribune*, November 1, 1910.
Masefield, J.	"John M. Synge," *Contemporary Review*, April 1911, 470-478.
Masefield, J.	"The Irish National Theatre," *Manchester Guardian*, January 2, 1905.
Mennloch, W.	"Dramatic Values," *Irish Times*, I, 7, September 1911, 325-329.
Mercer, C. G.	"Stephen Dedalus's Vision and Synge's Peasant Girls," *Notes and Queries*, VII, December 1960, 473-474.
Mercier, V.	"Irish Comedy: The Probable and the Wonderful," *University Review* [Dublin], I, 8, Spring 1956, 45-53.
Mikhail, E. H.	"Sixty Years of Synge Criticism, 1907-1967: A Selective Bibliography," *Bulletin of Bibliography & Magazine Notes*, XXVII, 1, January-March 1970, 11-13, and XXVII, 2, April-June 1970, 53-56.
Montague, C. E.	"The Workmanship of Synge," *Manchester Guardian*, June 24, 1912.
Montgomery, K. L.	"Some Writers of the Celtic Renaissance," *Fortnightly Review*, XC, 537, September 1911, 545-561.
Moore, G.	"Yeats, Lady Gregory and Synge," *English Review*, XVI, January 1914, 167-180.
Morris, L. R.	"Four Irish Poets," *Columbia University Quarterly*, XVIII, September 1916, 332-344.
Moses, M. J.	"Dramatists without a Country," *Book-News Monthly*, February 1912, 409.
Murphy, D. J.	"The Reception of Synge's *Playboy* in Ireland and America: 1907-1912," *Bulletin of the New York Public Library*, LXIV, 10, October 1960, 515-533.
O'Connor, A. C.	"Synge and National Drama," *UNITAS*, 1954.
O'Connor, F.	"All the Olympians," *Saturday Review*, XLIX, December 10, 1966, 30-32.
O'Donoghue, D. J.	"John M. Synge," *Irish Book-Lover*, III, 2, September 1911, 31.
O'Donoghue, D. J.	"John M. Synge, a Personal Appreciation," *Irish Independent*, March 26, 1909.
O'Donoghue, D. J.	"The Synge Boom. Foreign Influence," *Irish Independent*, August 21, 1911.

O'Hegarty, P. S.	"Synge and Irish Literature," *Dublin Magazine*, January-March 1932, 51-56.
O'Neill, F. G.	"Irish Drama and Irish Views," *American Catholic Quarterly*, July 1912.
O'Neill, M. J.	"Holloway on Synge's Last Days," *Modern Drama*, VI, September 1963, 126-130.
Orel, H.	"Synge's Last Play: *And a Story Will Be Told Forever*," *Modern Drama*, IV, December 1961, 306-313.
O'Riordan, C.	"The Cult of the Playboy," Letter to the *Eye-Witness* (now: *New Witness*), February 1, 1912.
O'Riordan, C.	"Synge in Dutch," *Irish Review*, December 1912, 557.
Palmer, J.	"The Acting of the Irish Players," *Saturday Review*, June 24, 1911, 770.
Palmer, J.	"The Extra-Occidental Theatre," *Saturday Review*, February 25, 1911.
Palmer, J.	"The Irish Players," *Saturday Review*, June 10, 1911, 705.
Pearce, H. D.	"Synge's Playboy as Mock-Christ," *Modern Drama*, VIII, December 1965, 303-310.
Pittock, M.	"*Riders to the Sea*," *English Studies*, XLIX, October 1968, 445-449.
Pittwood, E. H.	"John Millington Synge," *Holborn Review*, July 1913.
Podhoretz, N.	"Synge's *Playboy*: Morality and the Hero," *Essays in Criticism*, III, 3, July 1953, 337-344.
Powell, Y.	"Irish Influence on English Literature," *Freeman's Journal*, April 8, 1902.
Price, A. F.	"A Consideration of Synge's *The Shadow of the Glen*," *Dublin Magazine*, XXVI, October—December 1951, 15-24.
Price, A. F.	"Synge's Prose Writings: A First View of the Whole," *Modern Drama*, XI, December 1968, 221-226.
Pritchard, E. W.	"The Theatre. Some Plays Worthwhile," *American Magazine*, February 1912, 491.
Pritchard, E. W.	"The Theatre. The Literary Drama," *American Magazine*, March 1912, 625.
Pritchel, V. S.	"Synge and Joyce," *New Statesman and Nation*, XXI, April 19, 1941, 413.
Quinn, O.	"No Garland for John Synge," *Envoy*, III, 11, October 1950, 44-51.

Roberts, G.   "A National Dramatist," *Shanachie*, II, March 1907, 57-60.

Rollins, R. G.   "Huckleberry Finn and Christy Mahon: *The Playboy of the Western World*," *Mark Twain Journal*, XIII, 2, 1966, 16-19.

Rollins, R. G.   "O'Casey and Synge: The Irish Hero as Playboy and Gunman," *Arizona Quarterly*, 1966.

Ryan, F.   "The Abbey Theatre. The Playboy of the West and the Abbey Peasant," *Evening Telegraph*, May 13, 1911.

Ryan, W. P.   "A Singer o' the Green," *Daily Chronicle*, February 4, 1911, 6.

Saddlemyer, A.   "Rabelais versus A Kempis: The Art of J. M. Synge," *Kosmos*, 1, 1967, 85-96.

Saddlemyer, A., ed. "Synge to MacKenna: The Mature Years," *Massachusetts Review* (University of Mass.), V, Winter 1964, 279-296.

Saddlemyer, A.   "J. M. Synge—Poet and Playwright," *Ireland of the Welcomes*, XIX, 6, March-April 1971, 6.

Saddlemyer, A.   "Infinite Riches in a little Room—The Manuscripts of John Millington Synge," *Long Room* [TCD] I, 3, Spring 1971, 23.

Sanderlin, R. R.   "Synge's *Playboy* and the Ironic Hero," *Southern Quarterly*, VI, 1968, 289-301.

Scott-James, R. A.   "The Dramatist of Ireland," *Daily News* [London and Manchester] (now: *Daily News and Leader*), February 1, 1911, 3.

Scudder, V. D.   "The Irish Literary Drama," *Poet-Lore*, XVI, 1905, 40.

Sherman, S. P.   "John Synge," *Nation* [N.Y.], December 26, 1902, 608.

Sherman, S. P.   "John Synge," *Evening Post*, January 11, 1913, 6.

Sherwin, L.   "*The Playboy of the Western World* is Delightful Comedy," *Globe and Commercial Advertiser* [N.Y.], November 28, 1911.

Sidnell, M. J.   "Synge's *Playboy* and the Champion of Ulster," *Dalhousie Review*, XLV, 1965, 51-59.

Skelton, R.   "The Poetry of J. M. Synge," *Poetry Ireland*, I, Autumn 1962, 32-44.

Spacks, P. M.   "The Making of the *Playboy*," *Modern Drama*, IV, 1961, 134-323.

Stephens, E. M.   "Synge's Last Play," *Contemporary Review*, CLXXXVI, November 1954, 288-293.

Strong, L. A. G.   "John Millington Synge," *Living Age*, CCCXIV, September 9, 1922, 656-660.

Strong, L. A. G.   "John Millington Synge," *Bookman*, LXXIII, April 1931, 125-136.

Strong, L. A. G.   "John Millington Synge," *Dublin Magazine*, VII, 2, April—June 1932, 12-32.

Sullivan, M. R.   "Synge, Sophocles, and the Un-Making of Myth," *Modern Drama*, XII, December 1969, 242-253.

Sultan, S.   "The Gospel According to Synge," *Papers of Language and Literature*, IV, 4, Fall 1968, 428-441.

Suss, I. D.   "The *Playboy* Riots," *Irish Writing*, 18, March 1952, 39-42.

Sutton, G.   "John Millington Synge," *Portrait Bookman*, LXIX, March 1926, 299-301.

Synge, L.   "Uncle John," *Ireland of the Welcomes*, XIX, 6, March-April 1971, 13.

Tennyson, C.   "Irish Plays and Playwrights," *Quarterly Review*, July 1911, 219-243.

Tennyson, C.   "The Rise of the Irish Theatre," *Contemporary Review*, August 1911, 240-247.

Towse,   "Music and Drama. The Irish Players," *Evening Post*, November 24, 1911.

Trewin, J. C.   "The Heart's a Wonder," *London News*, CCXXXIII, October 4, 1958, 578.

Triesch, M.   "Some Unpublished J. M. Synge Papers," *English Language Notes* [University of Texas], IV, 1966, 49-51.

Turner, W. J.   "*The Playboy of the Western World;* Criticism," *London Mercury*, IV, September 1921, 537-539.

Untermeyer, L.   "J. M. Synge and *The Playboy of the Western World*," *Poet Lore*, XIX, September 1908, 364-367.

Van Hamel, A. G.   "On Anglo-Irish Syntax," *Englische Studien*, XLV, 1912, 272-292.

Van Laan, T. F.   "Form as Agent in Synge's *Riders to the Sea*," *Dramatic Survey* [Minneapolis], III, 1964, 352-366.

Watkins, A.   "The Irish Players in America: Their Purpose and Their Art," *Craftsman*, January 1912, 352.

Weygandt, C.   "The Art of the Irish Players and a Comment on Their Plays," *Book-News Monthly*, February 1912, 379.

Weygandt, C. "The Irish Literary Revival," *Sewanee Review*, XII, October 1904, 420-431.

White, H. O. "John Millington Synge," *Irish Writings*, 9, October 1949, 57-61.

Woods, A. S. "Synge Stayed at Home by the Fireside," *Catholic World*, CXLI, April 1935, 46-52.

Yeats, Jack B. "Memories of Synge," *Irish Nation*, August 14, 1909.

Yeats, John B. "Synge and the Irish. Random Reflections on a Much-Discussed Dramatist from the Standpoint of a Fellow-Countryman," *Harper's Weekly*, November 25, 1911, 17.

3b. Anonymous Articles:

"A New Thing in the Theatre. Some Impressions of the Much-Discussed Irish Players," *Harper's Weekly*, December 9, 1911, 19.

"A Note on J. M. Synge," *Broadside*, March 1911.

"Art of Collaboration," *Times Literary Supplement*, MMMCLXV, October 26, 1962, 824.

"Ireland's Greatest Dramatist," *Literary Digest*, April 17, 1909.

"Irish Players Appear in a 'Court Comedy'. No Decision. Answer Charge of 'Immorality' Brought by a Liquor Dealer. 'Playboy' Defended and Attacked by Witnesses," *North American*, January 20, 1912.

"Irish Theatre Society at the Court," *Illustrated London News*, June 12, 1909, 870.

"Irish Tragedy and Comedy," *Athenaeum*, 4419, July 6, 1912, 24.

"Irishmen Will Stamp out *The Playboy*," *Gaelic American*, October 14, 1911.

[On Shakespeare and Synge at Stratford-on-Avon], *Saturday Review*, May 6, 1911, 540.

"Poetry and the Peasant," *New Witness*, February 20, 1913, 504.

[Production of *Deirdre of the Sorrows* at the Court Theatre], *Illustrated London News*, June 4, 1910, 854.

[Prohibition of Representation of *Playboy* in Chicago—Violent Reactions], *Chicago Daily Tribune*, January 30, 1913.

[Reaction of the American Public to *The Playboy*], *New York Times*, November 28, 1911.

[Reference to Synge, his life, works and personality], *Irish Book-Lover*, III, 8, March 1912, 182-183.

"Representative Boston Men Criticize *The Playboy of the Western World*," *Boston Globe*, October 17, 1911, 9.

[Second Production of *The Playboy* at the Adelphi Theatre—Disapproval of Philadelphia Audience], *North American*, January 17, 1912.

"Synge and His Critics," *New Witness*, January 2, 1913, 282-283.

"Synge and the Theatre," *Athenaeum*, 4418, June 29, 1912, 726.

"J. Synge's Future Fame," *Irish Book-Lover*, I, 3, October 1909, 33-34.

"The Court Theatre; the Irish Players," *Academy and Literature*, June 1911, 723.

"The Irish Drama," *Athenaeum*, 4418, June 29, 1912, 741.

"The Irish National Theatre," *Bookman* [N.Y.], January 1912.

"The Irish Players Make Their First Appearance in New York," *Evening Sun*, November 21, 1911.

"The Matter with the *Playboy*," *Papyrus*, February 1912, 18, 30.

[*The Playboy of the Western World* at the Court Theatre], *Athenaeum*, 4415, June 8, 1912, 663.

"The Players," *Everybody's Magazine*, February 1912, 231.

"The Stormy Debut of the Irish Players," *Current Literature*, December 1911, 675.

"*The Well of the Saints* at the Court Theatre," *Athenaeum*, 4417, June 22, 1912, 715.

"*The Well of the Saints:* Criticism," *New Yorker Review*, XXXV, April 18, 1959, 82-83.

[Violent Reaction to Prohibition of *Playboy* in Chicago], *Chicago Record-Herald*, February 1, 1912.

"What the Irish County Associations of Boston Said of Bernard Shaw," *Gaelic American*, January 13, 1912.

"Yeats, Synge and the *Playboy*," *Irish Book-Lover*, IV, 1, August 1912, 7-8.

D. Books and Articles, in Whole or in Part, on Synge, in Languages other than English

In Arabic:

Bushrui, S. B.	"Min Nathr Yeats," *Aswat*, 5, 1962, 99-103.
Bushrui, S. B.	"[The Poetry of] W. B. Yeats," *Aswat*, 8, 1962, 6-27.
Bushrui, S. B.	"*Shi'un Min Yeats: Shi'r, Nathr, Masrah*," Beirut, Department of English of the American University of Beirut, 1969.
Bushrui, S. B.	"*Shi'un Min Synge*," Beirut, Rihani, 1971.
Bushrui, S. B.	"Yeats wa Tajdid Uslub al-Shi'r," *Shi'r*, X, 40, Autumn 1968, 47-60.
Farag, G.	"Masrah Yeats: Thawra 'ala al-Adab al-Waq'i," *Hiwar*, II, 8, January—February 1964, 72-81.
Maleh, G.	"Al-Haraka al-Masrahiya al-Irlandiya," *al-Ma'arifa*, XXXIV, December 1964, 376-384.

In Danish:

Thorning, J. *"John Millington Synge. En Moderne Irsk Dramatiker,"* [Studier fra sprog-og old-tids forskning, udgivne af det Filologisk-historiske samfund, 121], København, V.Rio, 1921.

In Dutch:

Lokhorst, E. van "Toneelkritieken, teleurstelling en voldoening," *de Gids,* CXIX, 5, 1956, 350-354.

In French:

Borel, J. "Sur le Baladin du Monde Occidentale," *Critique* January 1966.

Capin, J. and Alcalay, E. "Ce Théâtre au Milieu d'un Peuple," *Cahiers Renaud-Barrault,* 37, February 1962, 42-51.

Cazamian, M. "Le Théâtre de John Millington Synge," *Revue du Mois,* October 10, 1911, 456.

Cousteau, J. "Synge, Vagabond Solitaire et Passioné," *Cahiers Renaud-Barrault,* 37, February 1962, 37-41.

Dubois-Paul, L. "Le Théâtre Irlandais," *Revue des Deux Mondes,* XXVII, June 1935, 637-644.

Florence, J. "Le Théâtre Irlandais," *Phalange,* January 20, 1911, 52.

Frechet, R. "Le Thème de la Parole dans le Théâtre de Synge," *Etudes Anglaises,* XXI, 3, July 1968, 243-256.

Gunnell, D. "Le Nouveau Théâtre Irlandais," *Revue,* January 1, 1912, 91.

Habart, M. "Une Mère et Deux Fils," *Cahiers Renaud-Barrault,* 37, February 1962, 17-31.

Ruyssen, H. "Le Théâtre Irlandais," *Revue Germanique,* January—February 1909, 123; January—February 1911.

Trivédic, C. "John Millington Synge devant l'Opinion Irlandaise," *Etudes Anglaises,* VII, April 1954, 185-189.

In German:

Erzgräber, W. "John Millington Synge: *The Playboy of the Western World." Das moderne englische Drama,* hrsg. von H. Oppel, Berlin, E. Schmitt, 1966 (2), 87-108.

Fehr, B. *"Die englische Literatur des 19. und 20. Jahrhunderts,"* Berlin-Neubabelsberg, Athenaion, 1923.

Krieger, H.   "*John Millington Synge, ein Dichter der 'keltischen Renaissance'*," Marburg, Elwertsche Verlagsbuchhandlung, 1916.

Rust, A.   "*Beiträge zu einer Geschichte der neukeltischen Renaissance*," Bückeburg, Grimme, 1922.

Völker, K.   "*Irisches Theater, I: Yeats und Synge*," [Friedrichs Dramatiker des Welttheaters, XXIX], Velber/b. Hannover, Friedrich, 1967.

Wieczorek, H.   "*Irische Lebenshaltung im neuen irischen Drama*," Breslau, Priebatsch, 1937.

In Italian:

Riva, S.   "*La tradizione celtica e la moderna letteratura irlandese. I: J. M. Synge*," Roma, Religio, 1937.

In Japanese:

Chiba, K.   "Irish Literature and the Modern Literary Trend in Our Country," *Study of English* [Tokyo], XX, 4, July 1927, 10-15.

Ide, S.   "February in Koboki Street," *Engeishimpo*, February 1914, 170-172.

Kikuchi, K.   "An Approach to Synge's Dramas," *Teikoku Bungaku* ("The Empire Literature"), XXIII, 5, 1917, 32-48.

In Spanish:

Chica Salas, Susana   "Synge y Garcia Lorca: Aproximación de dos mundos poéticos," *Revista Hispanica Moderna*, XXVII, 1961, 128-137.

NOTES ON THE CONTRIBUTORS

JEAN ALEXANDER is Associate Professor of English at the University of Calgary (Canada) where she teaches modern literature, specializing in the Irish Renaissance and comparative studies of the novel and drama. An American by birth, Professor Alexander obtained her doctorate in Comparative Literature at the University of Washington before moving to Canada. She has published comparative studies of nineteen-century poetry and novels and of Renaissance drama, as well as individual studies of Yeats, Katherine Anne Porter and Virginia Woolf. She is currently working on a book on Virginia Woolf.

ALAN J. BLISS studied English at King's College, London, and Balliol College, Oxford. He has taught English in Oxford, Malta, Turkey and Ireland. Since 1961 he has been teaching in University College, Dublin, where he is at present Associate Professor of English. Professor Bliss is the author of numerous books and articles on Old and Middle English language and literature, and is a Joint General Editor of Methuen's Old English Library. He has also written on the Anglo-Irish dialect, and is the Secretary of the Royal Irish Academy's Committee for Anglo-Irish Language and Literature.

DAVID R. CLARK is Professor of English at the University of Massachusetts, Amherst, Mass. The Dolmen Press, Dublin, has published his *W. B. Yeats and the Theatre of Desolate Reality*, his *Irish Renaissance: A Gathering* . . . from *The Massachusetts Review* (co-edited by Robin Skelton), and his *Dry Tree* (poems), and *A Tower of Polished Black Stones*, being selected manuscripts of W. B. Yeats's *The Shadowy Waters*, (co-edited by George Mayhew). *The Druid Craft:*

The Writing of the Shadowy Waters (co-edited by Michael Sidnell and George Mayhew) is forthcoming from the University of Massachusetts Press, Amherst, as the first in the series *Manuscripts of W. B. Yeats*, of which Clark is the general editor. He is also co-author of *A Curious Quire* (poems), University of Massachusetts Press, of *Reading Poetry*, New York, Harper and Row, and editor of *Riders to the Sea* in the Charles E. Merrill Company Literary Casebook Series.

ELIZABETH COXHEAD, novelist, biographer and critic, took her degree in French at Somerville College, Oxford. She became interested in the Irish Renaissance through laying a novel in the Ireland of 1909, and in 1961 published her *Lady Gregory: A Literary Portrait*, followed in 1965 by *Daughters of Erin*, studies of five of Lady Gregory's contemporaries (Maud Gonne, Constance Markievicz, Sarah Purser, Sara Allgood, Maire O'Neill). She is also the author of the British Council pamphlet *Synge and Lady Gregory* in the "Writers and Their Work" series.

DOUGLAS DUNCAN teaches English at McMaster University, Hamilton, Ontario. He taught previously at Aberdeen and Southampton and was Professor of English at the University of Ghana from 1964-67. His publications include *Thomas Ruddiman: A Study in Scottish Scholarship of the Early Eighteenth Century; Emily Dickinson* ("Writers and Critics"); and several articles on Ben Jonson.

T. R. HENN, Fellow of St. Catharine's College, Cambridge (1926-1969), was Senior Tutor (1945-1957) and President of the College (1957-1961); he is an Honorary Fellow of Trumbull College, Yale University. He was educated at the University of Cambridge, where he was later Chairman, Faculty Board of Fine Arts (1952-1963) Chairman, Faculty Board of English (1947-1951 and 1961-1965), and Judith E. Wilson Lecturer in Poetry and Drama. He is a member of the Irish Academy of Letters. He served as Brigadier, General Staff, and was awarded C.B.E.(Mil.) and the U.S. Legion of Merit and was twice mentioned in Despatches. He holds two honorary doctorates. He was director of the Yeats International Summer School (1958-1968) and Warton Lecturer, British Academy (1963). His published work includes: *The Lonely Tower* (1950; 1965); *The Apple and the Spectro-scope* (1951; 1963); *Poems* (1953; 1964); *The Harvest of Tragedy* (1956); *The Plays and Poems of John Millington Synge* (1963); *Passages for Divine Reading* (1964); and *The Bible as Literature* (1969).

ROBERT HOGAN is Professor of English at the University of California, Davis. His recent work on Irish literature includes *Dion Boucicault: A Critical Biography;* an edition of Frank Fay's theatre criticism, *Towards a National Theatre,* an edition of George Fitz-maurice's Short Stories, *The Crows of Mephistopheles and Other Stories;* and the Final volume of *Joseph Holloway's Irish Theatre.*

ALEXANDER NORMAN JEFFARES, M.A., Ph.D. (Dublin), M.A., D.Phil.(Oxon.), F.R.S.A., F.R.S.L., Professor of English Literature in the University of Leeds and Honorary Fellow of the Australian Academy of the Humanities. A former Chairman of the Association for Commonwealth Literature and Language Studies, and co-Chairman of the International Association for the Study of Anglo-Irish Literature, he is the author of *W. B. Yeats: Man and Poet; A Commentary on the Collected Poems of W. B. Yeats; The Circus Animals.* He has edited Congreve, Farquhar, Goldsmith and Sheridan and is an authority on Anglo-Irish literature. He edits the Writers and Critics Series, the New Oxford English Series, and the critical quarterly *ARIEL: A Review of International English Literature.* He has taught at the universities of Dublin, Groningen (Holland), Edinburgh, and Adelaide (South Australia).

RICHARD KAIN is Professor of English and former Chairman of the Division of Humanities in the University of Louisville. He has written two books on Joyce and one on Dublin in the age of Yeats and Joyce. He co-edited a volume of documents related to James Joyce's youth. He has lectured at the Yeats International Summer School in Sligo and at many American universities and has been a Fulbright Lecturer at Venice and Rome.

JOHANNES KLEINSTÜCK is Professor of English at the University of Hamburg. He was born in Dresden, 1920, and studied English, Greek and Latin at the University of Leipzig where he took his Ph.D. with a thesis on Euripides' *Orestes* in 1945. He has taught German literature at the University of Lisbon from 1962 to 1964, and at the University of Algiers in 1968. Apart from various articles in periodicals he has so far published four books: *Chaucers Stellung in der mitte-lalterlichen Literatur* (1956), *W. B. Yeats oder der Dichter in der modernen Welt* (1963), *Mythos und Symbol in englisher Dichtung* (1964), *T. S. Eliot* (1966).

GERARD LEBLANC, who is "agrégé d'anglaise", is a graduate of Poitiers and Sorbonne Universities and teaches at Nantes University. He has been working on a doctoral dissertation on Synge since 1967 and is now preparing a bilingual edition of the *Playboy*, which he hopes to publish during the Synge Centenary.

GHASSAN MALEH is Associate Professor of English at Damascus University and Visiting Professor of English at the Lebanese University, Beirut. He received his B.A. from the University of Leeds in 1959 and his Ph.D. from the University of Birmingham in 1961. He is the author of *Introduction to Prose Fiction* (1968) and the editor of *Studies in the Novel* (1970). He has also written several articles for Arabic journals and magazines.

AUGUSTINE MARTIN is a graduate of University College, Dublin, where he now lectures in English and Anglo-Irish literature. He has published reviews and articles in *The Chicago Review, Studies, The Colby Library Quarterly, The University Review, Threshold, The Critic*. He is editor of the yearly series *Winter's Tales From Ireland* published by Gill and Macmillan. He is a founder editor of the magazine *Atlantis*. He has edited the first volumes of the series *Exploring English* for schools and colleges for Gill and Browne and Nolan, and also *Soundings* for the same publishers. He was a visiting lecturer to the 1969 Yeats International Summer School in Sligo where he lectured on Yeats's *Mythologies*. He has broadcast frequently on literary subjects on Irish radio and television. At the moment he is working on a critical history of the Irish short story and writes essays for such books as *Ireland in the War Years*, Gill and Macmillan, Dublin, 1970, and *Irish Anglicanism* 1869-1969, Allen Figgis, Dublin, 1970.

VIVIAN MERCIER, born in Dublin, 1919, attended Portora Royal School and Trinity College, Dublin (B.A. 1940, Ph.D. 1945). He emigrated to the U.S. in 1946 and has taught at Bennington College, the City College of C.U.N.Y., and the University of California, Berkeley. He is now Professor of English and Comparative Literature at the University of Colorado, Boulder. He has written on Irish, English and

French literature for a wide variety of periodicals and is the author of *The Irish Comic Tradition* (1962) and *The New Novel: From Queueau to Pinget* (1971). The present volume is the twelfth critical symposium to which he has contributed an essay. The other essays dealt with Joyce (5), Swift (2), Landor, Drama of Ideas, Pornography, and the Irish Short Story.

JOHN REES MOORE, Professor of English at Hollins College, was recently in Beirut to take part in the Kahlil Gibran Festival. He is a co-editor of *The Hollins Critic* and a contributor to the forthcoming volume of essays to be published by the University of Georgia Press, *The Sounder Few*, a selection of work from the *Critic*. Long a student of Yeats, on whom he has contributed articles to a number of magazines, Professor Moore is the author of *Masks of Love and Death*, a study of Yeats the dramatist, published in May 1971 by the Cornell University Press.

JOHN M. MUNRO received his B.A. from Durham University (England) and his Ph.D. from Washington University (U.S.A.). He has taught at the Universities of North Carolina, Toronto and London, and is now Professor of English and Associate Dean of the Faculty of Arts and Sciences at the American University of Beirut, Lebanon. A specialist in late nineteen and twentieth-century literature, he is the author and co-author of *The Worlds of Fiction* (1964), *English Poetry in Transition* (1968), *Arthur Symons* (1969), *Images and Memories: A Pictorial Record of the Life and Work of W. B. Yeats* (1970), *The Decadent Poetry of the Eighteen-Nineties* (1970) and *The Royal Aquarium: Failure of a Victorian Compromise* (1971). His critical study, *James Elroy Flecker* is scheduled for publication next year, and *The Collected Letters of Arthur Symons*, on which he has collaborated with Professor Karl Beckson of Brooklyn College, New York, will appear soon.

ROBERT O'DRISCOLL, Chairman of the Canadian Irish Studies Committee and Associate Professor of English at St. Michael's College, is co-editor of *Yeats Studies: An International Journal* and editor of *Theatre and Nationalism in Twentieth-Century Ireland* (University of Toronto Press, 1971). He has written poems and critical articles on Yeats, Lady Gregory, Joyce, Beckett and other Anglo-Irish writers.

SHOTARO OSHIMA, a native of the northern "Twilight" region of Japan, is Professor of English Literature at Waseda University. His interest in W. B. Yeats began in 1917 and later led him to the study of both Celtic myths and legends and modern Irish literature. After graduating from Waseda University in 1923, he devoted himself to further studies, and later travelled in England and Ireland, enjoying intimate association with W. B. Yeats, Douglas Hyde and other prominent figures. In England he spent three years (1936-1939) at Merton College, Oxford, where he made the acquaintance of Edmund Blunden, J. A. W. Bennett, Lascelles Abercrombie, Helen Darbishire, H. C. Wyld and others. He is President of the Yeats Society in Japan, Director of the Japan Poets' Club, and President of the Japan-Ireland Friendship Society. Shotaro Oshima's published works include: *W. B. Yeats: A Study* (1927), *William Blake and Celtic Literature* (1933), *W. B. Yeats: A Critical Biography* (1934), *Studies in English Prose and Verse* (1935), *Poems: Among Shapes and Shadows* (1939), *Poetic Imagination in English Literature: the Development of the Celtic Temperament* (1953), *Studies in Modern Irish Literature* (1956), *Yeats, the Man and the Poet* (1961), *W. B. Yeats and Japan* (1965), *Appreciation of New English Poetry* (1969). *The Collected Poems of W. B. Yeats* (1958), the definitive Japanese translation, is a result of his long endeavour to interpret Yeats's poems with Japanese sensibility.

ALAN PRICE, a graduate of Liverpool and Belfast Universities, was a Senior Lecturer in Queen's University, Belfast. He was born in Chester. He taught in schools and colleges in the United Kingdom, and as Visiting Professor of English in three universities in the U.S.A. He lectured for the British Council in Germany, Roumania and Egypt. Among his various publications are collections of poetry and plays for use in schools, four books on J. M. Synge and one on Graham Greene. He edited the *Prose* volume in the Oxford University Press definitive edition of Synge's *Collected Works*. He died in 1970.

ANN SADDLEMYER, a Canadian by birth, is currently Professor of English at Victoria College, University of Toronto. She received her B.A. from the University of Saskatchewan, her M.A. from Queen's University, Kingston, Ontario, and her Ph.D. from Bedford College, University of London. She has received Fellowships from the Canada Council and the Guggenheim Foundation, and has lectured at the Yeats Summer School in Sligo, the Yeats Centenary Celebrations at Thoor Ballylee, the University of Toronto Irish Studies Seminar, at various universities, and for the Canadian Broadcasting Corporation. She was Professor of English at the University of Victoria, Victoria, British Columbia until mid 1971.

Among her publications are *In Defence of Lady Gregory, Playwright; J. M. Synge*, Volumes III and IV of the definitive Oxford Synge edition; *The Plays of Lady Gregory*, Volumes V, VI, VII, and VIII of the Coole edition. She is currently working on an extended study of the aesthetic and comic theory of W. B. Yeats and J. M. Synge.

MICHAEL SIDNELL is a graduate of King's College, London, of which he is a Ph.D. In 1958 he went to Canada, where he has been lecturing in English for the last twelve years. At present he is Associate Professor of English, Trinity College, University of Toronto. He is author, with D. R. Clark and G. P. Mayhew, of *Druid Craft: The writing of "The Shadowy Waters"* (Amherst, Mass. 1971), the first volume in the series *Manuscripts of W. B. Yeats,* and of a number of articles on Synge, Yeats and other subjects for the most part having to do with Irish writers and the theatre.

MARCUS SMITH, a Texan by birth, has travelled a great deal and has lived for over six years in the Middle East. He is Associate Professor of English at the American University of Beirut and is currently (1970-71) a Visiting Professor at Loyola University of the South in New Orleans, Louisiana. He has published poems and essays in a number of magazines and journals and is presently studying the theme of empire in American literature.

LANTO MILLINGTON SYNGE was born in Dublin in 1945 and was educated at Campbell College, Belfast, and Trinity College, Cambridge. While at Cambridge he studied under T. R. Henn, who greatly encouraged his work on his great-uncle, J. M. Synge. Though devoted to his native County Wicklow, Lanto Synge has recently joined Malletts, the famous antique shop of Bond Street, London.

FRANCIS WARNER was educated at Christ's Hospital, the London College of Music, and St. Catharine's College, Cambridge, where he also taught from 1959 to 1965. Since then he has been a Fellow and Tutor in English Literature at St. Peter's College, Oxford. He was Assistant Director at the Yeats International Summer School in Sligo from 1961 to 1967. In 1967 he was a director of the first James Joyce Symposium in Dublin, and founded the Samuel Beckett Theatre in Oxford. He is a Director of the James Joyce Foundation, Tulsa, Oklahoma. He is author of five volumes of verse; *Perennia* (1962), *Early Poems* (1964), *Experimental Sonnets* (1965), *Madrigals* (1967), and *The Poetry of Francis Warner* (1970). He has published two plays, *Maquettes* (1970) and *Lying Figures* (1971). His critical essay *The Absence of Nationalism in the Work of Samuel Beckett* was published in 1970.

SUHEIL BADI BUSHRUI, who comes from Jordan, is Chairman of the Department of English at the American University of Beirut and a Ph.D. of Southampton University (England), where he was a British Council Scholar. He has taught at the Universities of Ibadan (Nigeria), Calgary and York (Canada), and has lectured at African, American, English and Continental universities. In 1963 he was awarded the Una Ellis-Fermor Prize for his work on W. B. Yeats, on whom he has published four books: *Yeats's Verse Plays; The Revisions, 1900-1910* (1965); *W. B. Yeats: Centenary Essays* (1965); *Shi'un Min Yeats* (1969), the First book in Arabic on Yeats; and *Images and Memories: A Pictorial Record of the life and works of W. B. Yeats* (1970). He has also written on English, Arabic and African literatures as well as on Anglo-Irish literature, his main interest. Last year he organized the Gibran International Festival (Beirut 23-30 May, 1970) and is the editor of *An Introduction to Kahlil Gibran* (1970) and several other works on Gibran and Ameen Rihani. He is on the Executive Council of the International Association for the Study of Anglo-Irish Literature (IASAIL); a member of the International Advisory Council of *Yeats Studies: An International Journal;* A Life Associate of the International Poetry Institute (U.S.A.); Chairman of the Synge Centenary Committee (Lebanon); and President of the Association of University Teachers of English in the Arab World.

The contents of the Notes have been indexed only where additional comment can be found. It is shown thus: 277n.21 (note 21 on page 277).
Emphasis on a point, or fuller discussion of it, is shown by the use of **bold type** for the pages concerned.